Essential Mathematics for Political and Social Research

More than ever before, modern social scientists require a basic level of mathematical literacy, yet many students receive only limited mathematical training prior to beginning their research careers. This textbook addresses this dilemma by offering a comprehensive, unified introduction to the essential mathematics of social science. Throughout the book the presentation builds from first principles and eschews unnecessary complexity. Most importantly, the discussion is thoroughly and consistently anchored in real social science applications, with more than 80 research-based illustrations woven into the text and featured in end-of-chapter exercises. Students and researchers alike will find this first-of-its-kind volume to be an invaluable resource.

Jeff Gill is Associate Professor of Political Science at the University of California, Davis. His primary research applies Bayesian modeling and data analysis to substantive questions in voting, public policy, budgeting, bureaucracy, and Congress. He is currently working in areas of Markov chain Monte Carlo theory. His work has appeared in journals such as the *Journal of Politics*, *Political Analysis*, *Electoral Studies*, *Statistical Science*, *Sociological Methods and Research*, *Public Administration Review*, and *Political Research Quarterly*. He is the author or coauthor of several books including *Bayesian Methods: A Social and Behavioral Sciences Approach* (2002), *Numerical Issues in Statistical Computing for the Social Scientist* (2003), and *Generalized Linear Models: A Unified Approach* (2000).

Analytical Methods for Social Research

Analytical Methods for Social Research presents texts on empirical and formal methods for the social sciences. Volumes in the series address both the theoretical underpinnings of analytical techniques, as well as their application in social research. Some series volumes are broad in scope, cutting across a number of disciplines. Others focus mainly on methodological applications within specific fields such as political science, sociology, demography, and public health. The series serves a mix of students and researchers in the social sciences and statistics.

Series Editors:

R. Michael Alvarez, *California Institute of Technology*
Nathaniel L. Beck, *New York University*
Lawrence L. Wu, *New York University*

Other Titles in the Series:

Event History Modeling: A Guide for Social Scientists, by Janet M. Box-Steffensmeier and Bradford S. Jones
Ecological Inference: New Methodological Strategies, edited by Gary King, Ori Rosen, and Martin A. Tanner
Spatial Models of Parliamentary Voting, by Keith T. Poole

Essential Mathematics for Political and Social Research

Jeff Gill

University of California, Davis

CAMBRIDGE UNIVERSITY PRESS
Cambridge, New York, Melbourne, Madrid, Cape Town, Singapore, São Paulo

Cambridge University Press
40 West 20th Street, New York, NY 10011-4211, USA

www.cambridge.org
Information on this title: www.cambridge.org/9780521834261

First published 2006

Printed in the United States of America

A catalog record for this publication is available from the British Library.

Library of Congress Cataloging in Publication data
Gill, Jeff.
Essential mathematics for political and social research / Jeff Gill.
p.   cm. – (Analytical methods for social research)
Includes bibliographical references and index.
ISBN 0-521-83426-0 – ISBN 0-521-68403-X (pbk.)
1. Mathematics – Study and teaching (Higher) – United States.   2. Social sciences –
Mathematical models – United States.   I. Title.   II. Series.
QA13.G55   2006
510.71′2–dc22   2005055858

ISBN-13   978-0-521-83426-1 hardback
ISBN-10   0-521-83426-0 hardback

ISBN-13   978-0-521-68403-3 paperback
ISBN-10   0-521-68403-X paperback

Contents

List of Tables

List of Illustrations

List of Examples

Preface

This book is intended to serve several needs. First (and perhaps foremost), it is supposed to be an introduction to mathematical principles for incoming social science graduate students. For this reason, there is a large set of examples (83 of them, at last count) drawn from various literatures including sociology, political science, anthropology, psychology, public policy, communications, and geography. Almost no example is produced from "hypothetical data." This approach is intended not only to motivate specific mathematical principles and practices, but also to introduce the *way* that social science researchers use these tools. With this approach the topics presumably retain needed relevance.

The design of the book is such that this endeavor can be a semester-long adjunct to another topic like data analysis or it can support the prefresher "math-camp" approach that is becoming increasingly popular. Second, this book can also serve as a single reference work where multiple books would ordinarily be needed. To support this function there is extensive indexing and referencing designed to make it easy to find topics. Also in support of this purpose, there are some topics that may not be suitable for course work that are deliberately included for this purpose (i.e., things like calculus on trigonometric functions and advanced linear algebra topics). Third, the format is purposely made conducive to self-study. Many of us missed or have forgotten various mathematical topics and then find we need them later.

The main purpose of the proposed work is to address an educational deficiency in the social and behavioral sciences. The undergraduate curriculum in the social sciences tends to underemphasize mathematical topics that are then required by students at the graduate level. This leads to some discomfort whereby incoming graduate students are often unprepared for and uncomfortable with the necessary mathematical level of research in these fields. As a result, the methodological training of graduate students increasingly often begins with intense "prequel" seminars wherein basic mathematical principles are taught in short (generally week-long) programs just before beginning the regular first-year course work. Usually these courses are taught from the instructor's notes, selected chapters from textbooks, or assembled sets of monographs or books. There is currently no *tailored* book-length work that specifically addresses the mathematical topics of these programs. This work fills this need by providing a comprehensive introduction to the mathematical principles needed by modern research social scientists. The material introduces basic mathematical principles necessary to do analytical work in the social sciences, starting from first principles, but without unnecessary complexity. The core purpose is to present fundamental notions in standard notation and standard language with a clear, unified framework throughout

Although there is an extensive literature on mathematical and statistical methods in the social sciences, there is also a dearth of introduction to the underlying *language* used in these works, exacerbating the fact that many students in social science graduate programs enter with an undergraduate education that contains no regularized exposure to the mathematics they will need to succeed in graduate school.

Actually, the book *is itself* a prerequisite, so for obvious reasons the prerequisites to this prerequisite are minimal. The only required material is knowledge of high school algebra and geometry. Most target students will have had very little mathematical training beyond this modest level. Furthermore, the first chapter is sufficiently basic that readers who are comfortable with only arithmetic operations on symbolic quantities will be able to work through the material. No prior knowledge of statistics, probability, or nonscalar representations will be required. The intended emphasis is on a conceptual understanding of key principles and in their subsequent application through examples and exercises. No proofs or detailed derivations will be provided.

The book has two general divisions reflecting a core component along with associated topics. The first section comprises six chapters and is focused on basic mathematical tools, matrix algebra, and calculus. The topics are all essential, deterministic, mathematical principles. The primary goal of this section is to establish the mathematical language used in formal theory and mathematical analysis, as practiced in the social sciences. The second section, consisting of three chapters, is designed to give the background required to proceed in standard empirical quantitative analysis courses such as social science statistics and mathematical analysis for formal theory.

Although structure differs somewhat by chapter, there is a general format followed within each. There is motivation given for the material, followed by a detailed exposition of the concepts. The concepts are illustrated with examples that social scientists care about and can relate to. This last point is not trivial. A great many books in these areas center on engineering and biology examples, and the result is often reduced reader interest and perceived applicability in the social sciences. Therefore, every example is taken from the social and behavioral sciences. Finally, each chapter has a set of exercises designed to reinforce the primary concepts.

There are different ways to teach from this book. The obvious way is to cover the first six chapters sequentially, although aspects of the first two chapters may be skipped for a suitably prepared audience. Chapter 2 focuses on trigonometry, and this may not be needed for some programs. The topics in Chapters 7, 8, and 9 essentially constitute a "pre-statistics" course for social science graduate students. This may or may not be useful for specific purposes. The last chapter on Markov chains addresses a topic that has become increasingly important. This tool is used extensively in both mathematical modeling and Bayesian statistics. In addition, this chapter is a useful way to practice and reinforce the matrix algebra principles covered in Chapters 3 and 4. This book can also be used in a "just in time" way whereby a course on mathematical modeling or statistics proceeds until certain topics in matrix algebra, calculus, or random variables are needed.

As noted, one intended use of this book is through a "math-camp" approach where incoming graduate students are given a pre-semester intensive introduction to the mathematical methods required for their forthcoming study. This is pretty standard in economics and is increasingly done in political science, sociology, and other fields. For this purpose, I recommend one of two possible abbreviated tracks through the material:

Three-Day Program

- Chapter 1: The Basics.
- Chapter 3: Linear Algebra: Vectors, Matrices, and Operations.
- Chapter 5: Elementary Scalar Calculus.

Five-Day Program

- Chapter 1: The Basics.
- Chapter 3: Linear Algebra: Vectors, Matrices, and Operations.
- Chapter 5: Elementary Scalar Calculus.
- Chapter 7: Probability Theory.
- Chapter 8: Random Variables.

The five-day program focuses on a pre-statistics curriculum after the introductory mathematics. If this is not appropriate or desired, then the continuation chapters on linear algebra and calculus (Chapters 4 and 6) can be substituted for the latter two chapters. Conversely, a lighter pre-statistics approach that does not need to focus on theory involving calculus might look like the following:

Standard Pre-Statistics Program

- Chapter 1: The Basics.
- Chapter 3: Linear Algebra: Vectors, Matrices, and Operations.
- Chapter 7: Probability Theory.
- Chapter 8: Random Variables.

This program omits Chapter 5 from the previous listing but sets students up for such standard regression texts as Hanushek and Jackson (1977), Gujarati (1995), Neter et al. (1996), Fox (1997), or the forthcoming text in this series by Schneider and Jacoby. For an even "lighter" version of this program, parts of Chapter 3 could be omitted.

Each chapter is accompanied by a set of exercises. Some of these are purely mechanical and some are drawn from various social science publications. The latter are designed to provide practice and also to show the relevance of the pertinent material. Instructors will certainly want to tailor assignments rather than require the bulk of these problems. In addition, there is an instructor's manual containing answers to the exercises available from Cambridge University Press.

It is a cliche to say, but this book was not created in a vacuum and numerous people read, perused, commented on, criticized, railed at, and even taught from the manuscript. These include Attic Access, Mike Alvarez, Maggie Bakhos, Ryan Bakker, Neal Beck, Scott Desposato, James Fowler, Jason Gainous, Scott Gartner, Hank Heitowit, Bob Huckfeldt, Bob Jackman, Marion Jagodka, Renee Johnson, Cindy Kam, Paul Kellstedt, Gary King, Jane Li, Michael Martinez, Ryan T. Moore, Will Moore, Elise Oranges, Bill Reed, Marc Rosenblum, Johny Sebastian, Will Terry, Les Thiele, Shawn Treier, Kevin Wagner, Mike Ward, and Guy Whitten. I apologize to anyone inadvertently left off this list. In particular, I thank Ed Parsons for his continued assistance and patience in helping get this project done. I have also enjoyed the continued support of various chairs, deans, and colleagues at the University of California–Davis, the ICPSR Summer Program at the University of Michigan, and at Harvard University. Any errors that may remain, despite this outstanding support network, are entirely the fault of the author. Please feel free to contact me with comments, complaints, omissions, general errata, or even praise (`jgill@ucdavis.edu`).

1

The Basics

1.1 Objectives

This chapter gives a very basic introduction to practical mathematical and arithmetic principles. Some readers who can recall their earlier training in high school and elsewhere may want to skip it or merely skim over the vocabulary. However, many often find that the various other interests in life push out the assorted artifacts of functional expressions, logarithms, and other principles.

Usually what happens is that we vaguely remember the basic ideas without specific properties, in the same way that we might remember that the assigned reading of Steinbeck's *Grapes of Wrath* included poor people traveling West without remembering all of the unfortunate details. To use mathematics effectively in the social sciences, however, it is necessary to have a thorough command over the basic mathematical principles in this chapter.

Why is mathematics important to social scientists? There are two basic reasons, where one is more philosophical than the other. A pragmatic reason is that it simply allows us to communicate with each other in an orderly and systematic way; that is, ideas expressed mathematically can be more carefully defined and more directly communicated than with narrative language, which is more susceptible to vagueness and misinterpretation. The causes of these effects include multiple interpretations of words and phrases, near-synonyms, cultural effects, and even poor writing quality.

The second reason is less obvious, and perhaps more debatable in social science disciplines. Plato said "God ever geometrizes" (by extension, the nineteenth-century French mathematician Carl Jacobi said "God ever arithmetizes"). The meaning is something that humans have appreciated since before the building of the pyramids: *Mathematics is obviously an effective way to describe our world.* What Plato and others noted was that there is no other way to formally organize the phenomena around us. Furthermore, awesome physical forces such as the movements of planets and the workings of atoms behave in ways that are described in rudimentary mathematical notation.

What about social behavior? Such phenomena are equally easy to observe but apparently more difficult to describe in simple mathematical terms. Substantial progress dates back only to the 1870s, starting with economics, and followed closely by psychology. Obviously something makes this more of a challenge. Fortunately, some aspects of human behavior have been found to obey simple mathematical laws: Violence increases in warmer weather, overt competition for hierarchical place increases with group size, increased education reduces support for the death penalty, and so on. These are not immutable, constant forces, rather they reflect underlying phenomena that social scientists have found and subsequently described in simple mathematical form.

1.2 Essential Arithmetic Principles

We often use arithmetic principles on a daily basis without considering that they are based on a formalized set of rules. Even though these rules are elementary, it is worth stating them here.

For starters, it is easy to recall that negative numbers are simply positive numbers multiplied by -1, that fractions represent ratios, and that multiplication can be represented in several ways ($a \times b = (a)(b) = a \cdot b = a * b$). Other rules are more elusive but no less important. For instance, the **order of operations** gives a unique answer for expressions that have multiple arithmetic actions. The order is (1) perform operations on individual values first, (2) evaluate parenthetical operations next, (3) do multiplications and divisions in order from left to right and, finally, (4) do additions and subtractions from left to right. So we would solve the following problem in the specified order:

$$2^3 + 2 \times (2 \times 5 - 4)^2 - 30 = 8 + 2 \times (2 \times 5 - 4)^2 - 30$$
$$= 8 + 2 \times (10 - 4)^2 - 30$$
$$= 8 + 2 \times (6)^2 - 30$$
$$= 8 + 2 \times 36 - 30$$
$$= 8 + 72 - 30$$
$$= 50.$$

In the first step there is only one "atomic" value to worry about, so we take 2 to the third power first. Because there are no more of these, we proceed to evaluating the operations in parentheses using the same rules. Thus $2 \times 5 - 4$ becomes 6 before it is squared. There is one more multiplication to worry about followed by adding and subtracting from left to right. Note that we would have gotten a *different* answer if we had not followed these rules. This is important as there can be only one mathematically correct answer to such questions. Also, when parentheses are nested, then the order (as implied above) is to start in the innermost expression and work outward. For instance, $(((2 + 3) \times 4) + 5) = (((5) \times 4) + 5) = ((20) + 5) = 25$.

Zero represents a special number in mathematics. Multiplying by zero produces zero and adding zero to some value leaves it unchanged. Generally the only thing to worry about with zero is that dividing any number by zero ($x/0$ for any x) is *undefined*. Interestingly, this is true for $x = 0$ as well. The number 1 is another special number in mathematics and the history of mathematics, but it has no associated troublesome characteristic.

Some basic functions and expressions will be used liberally in the text without further explanation. Fractions can be denoted x/y or $\frac{x}{y}$. The **absolute value** of a number is the positive representation of that number. Thus $|x| = x$ if x is positive and $|x|$ is $-x$ if x is negative. The square root of a number is a radical of order two: $\sqrt{x} = \sqrt[2]{x} = x^{\frac{1}{2}}$, and more generally the **principle root** is

$$\sqrt[r]{x} = x^{\frac{1}{r}}$$

for numbers x and r. In this general case x is called the **radican** and r is called the **index**. For example,

$$\sqrt[3]{8} = 8^{\frac{1}{3}} = 2$$

because $2^3 = 8$.

1.3 Notation, Notation, Notation

One of the most daunting tasks for the beginning social scientist is to make sense of the *language* of their discipline. This has two general dimensions: (1) the substantive language in terms of theory, field knowledge, and socialized terms; and (2) the *formal* means by which these ideas are conveyed. In a great many social science disciplines and subdisciplines the latter is the notation of *mathematics*. By notation we do not mean the use of specific terms per se (see Section 1.4 for that discussion); instead we mean the broad use of symbology to represent values or levels of phenomena; interrelations among these, and a logical, consistent manipulation of this symbology.

Why would we use mathematics to express ideas about ideas in anthropology, political science, public policy, sociology, psychology, and related disciplines? Precisely because *mathematics let us exactly convey asserted relationships between quantities of interest.* The key word in that last sentence is *exactly*: We want some way to be precise in claims about how some social phenomenon affects another social phenomenon. Thus the purchase of mathematical rigor provides a careful and exacting way to analyze and discuss *the things we actually care about.*

★ **Example 1.1:   Explaining Why People Vote.** This is a simple example from voting theory. Anthony Downs (1957) claimed that a rational voter (supposedly someone who values her time and resources) would weigh the cost of voting against the gains received from voting. These rewards are asserted to be the value from a preferred candidate winning the election times the probability that her vote will make an actual difference in the election. It is common to "measure" the difference between cost and reward as the **utility** that the person receives from the act. "Utility" is a word borrowed from economists that simply specifies an underlying preference scale that we usually cannot directly see. This is generally not complicated: I will get greater utility from winning the state lottery than I will from winning the office football pool, or I will get greater utility from spending time with my friends than I will from mowing the lawn.

Now we should make this idea more "mathematical" by specifying a relevant relationship. Riker and Ordeshook (1968) codified the Downsian model into mathematical symbology by articulating the following variables for an individual voter given a choice between two candidates:

R = the utility satisfaction of voting

P = the actual probability that the voter will
affect the outcome with her particular vote

B = the perceived difference in benefits between the two
candidates measured in utiles (units of utility): $B1 - B2$

C = the actual cost of voting in utiles (i.e., time, effort, money).

Thus the Downsian model is thus represented as

$$R = PB - C.$$

This is an unbelievably simple yet powerful model of political participation. In fact, we can use this statement to make claims that *would not be as clear or as precise if described in descriptive language alone.* For instance, consider these statements:

- The voter will abstain if $R < 0$.

- The voter may still not vote even if $R > 0$ if there exist other competing activities that produce a higher R.

- If P is very small (i.e., it is a large election with many voters), then it is unlikely that this individual will vote.

The last statement leads to what is called *the paradox of participation*: If nobody's vote is decisive, then why would anyone vote? Yet we can see that many people actually do show up and vote in large general elections. This paradox demonstrates that there is more going on than our simple model above.

The key point from the example above is that the formalism such mathematical representation provides gives us a way to say more exact things about social phenomena. Thus the motivation for introducing mathematics into the study of the social and behavioral sciences is to aid our understanding and improve the way we communicate substantive ideas.

1.4 Basic Terms

Some terms are used ubiquitously in social science work. A **variable** is just a *symbol* that represents a single number or group of numbers. Often variables are used as a substitution for numbers that we do not know or numbers that we will soon observe from some political or social phenomenon. Most frequently these are quantities like X, Y, a, b, and so on. Oddly enough, the modern notion of a variable was not codified until the early nineteenth century by the German mathematician Lejeune Dirichlet. We also routinely talk about **data**: collections of observed phenomenon. Note that *data* is plural; a single point is called a *datum* or a *data point*.

There are some other conventions from mathematics and statistics (as well as some other fields) that are commonly used in social science research as well. Some of these are quite basic, and social scientists speak this technical language fluently. Unless otherwise stated, variables are assumed to be defined on the **Cartesian coordinate system**.† If we are working with two variables x and y, then there is an assumed perpendicular set of axes where the x-axis (always given horizontally) is crossed with the y-axis (usually given vertically), such that the number pair (x, y) defines a **point** on the two-dimensional graph. There is actually no restriction to just two dimensions; for instance a point in 3-space is typically notated (x, y, z).

★ **Example 1.2:** **Graphing Ideal Points in the Senate.** One very active area of empirical research in political science is the estimation and subsequent use of *legislative ideal points* [see Jackman (2001), Londregan (2000), Poole and Rosenthal (1985, 1997)]. The objective is to analyze a member's voting record with the idea that this member's ideal policy position in policy-space can be estimated. This gets really interesting when the entire chamber (House, Senate, Parliament) is estimated accordingly, and various voting outcomes are analyzed or predicted.

Figure 1.1 shows approximate ideal points for Ted Kennedy and Oren Hatch on two proposed projects (it is common to propose Hatch as the foil for Kennedy). Senator Hatch is assumed to have an ideal point in this two-dimensional space at $x = 5, y = 72$, and Ted Kennedy is assumed to have an ideal point at $x = 89, y = 17$. These values are obtained from interest group rankings provided by the League of Conservation voters (2003) and the National Taxpayers Union (2003). We can also estimate the ideal points of other Senators in this way: One would guess that Trent Lott would be closer to Hatch than Kennedy, for instance.

---

† Alternatives exist such as "spherical space," where lines are defined on a generalization of circular space so they cannot be parallel to each other and must return to their point of origin, as well as Lobachevskian geometry and Kleinian geometry. These and other related systems are not generally useful in the social sciences and will therefore not be considered here with the exception of general polar coordinates in Chapter 2.

Fig. 1.1. Two Ideal Points in the Senate

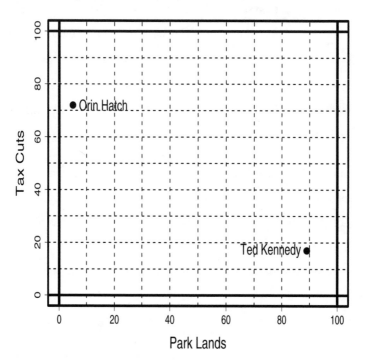

Now consider a hypothetical trade-off between two bills competing for limited federal resources. These are appropriations (funding) for new national park lands, and a tax cut (i.e., national resources protection and development versus reducing taxes and thus taking in less revenue for the federal government). If there is a greater range of possible compromises, then other in-between points are possible. The best way to describe the possible space of solutions here is on a two-dimensional Cartesian coordinate system. Each Senator is assumed to have an *ideal* spending level for the two projects that trades off spending in one dimension against another: the level he or she would pick if they controlled the Senate completely. By convention we bound this in the two dimensions from 0 to 100.

The point of Figure 1.1 is to show how useful the Cartesian coordinate system is at describing positions along political and social variables. It might be more crowded, but it would not be more complicated to map the entire Senate along these two dimensions. In cases where more dimensions are considered, the graphical challenges become greater. There are two choices: show a subset on a two- or three-dimensional plot, or draw combinations of dimensions in a two-dimensional format by pairing two at a time.

Actually, in this Senate example, the use of the Cartesian coordinate system has been made quite restrictive for ease of analysis in this case. In the more typical, and more general, setting both the x-axis and the y-axis span negative infinity to positive infinity (although we obviously cannot *draw* them that way), and the space is labeled $\Re^2$ to denote the crossing of two *real lines*. The **real line** is the line from minus infinity to positive infinity that contains the real numbers: numbers that are expressible in fractional form ($2/5, 1/3$, etc.) as well as those that are not because they have nonrepeating and infinitely continuing decimal values. There are therefore an infinite quantity of real numbers for any interval on the real line because numbers like $\sqrt{2}$ exist without "finishing" or repeating patterns in their list of values to the right of the decimal point ($\sqrt{2} = $ 1.41421356237309504880168872420969807856967187537694807317 . . .).

It is also common to define various sets along the real line. These sets can be convex or nonconvex. A **convex set** has the property that for any two members of the set (numbers) x_1 and x_2, the number $x_3 = \delta x_1 + (1-\delta)x_2$ (for $0 \le \delta \le 1$) is also in the set. For example, if $\delta = \frac{1}{2}$, then x_3 is the average (the mean, see below) of x_1 and x_2.

In the example above we would say that Senators are constrained to express their preferences in the interval $[0:100]$, which is commonly used as a measure of ideology or policy preference by interest groups that rate elected officials [such as the *Americans for Democratic Action* (ADA), and the *American Conservative Union* (ACU)]. **Interval notation** is used frequently in mathematical notation, and there is only one important distinction: Interval ends can be "open" or "closed." An open interval excludes the end-point denoted with parenthetical forms "(" and ")" whereas the closed interval denoted with bracket forms "[" and "]" includes it (the curved forms "{" and "}" are usually reserved for set notation). So, in altering our Senate example, we have the following one-dimensional options for x (also for y):

open on both ends:	$(0{:}100)$,	$0 < x < 100$
closed on both ends:	$[0{:}100]$,	$0 \le x \le 100$
closed left, open right	$[0{:}100)$,	$0 \le x < 100$
open left, closed right	$(0{:}100]$,	$0 < x \le 100$

Thus the restrictions on δ above are that it must lie in $[0{:}1]$. These intervals can also be expressed in *comma notation* instead of *colon notation*: $[0, 100]$.

1.4.1 Indexing and Referencing

Another common notation is the technique of indexing observations on some variable by the use of subscripts. If we are going to list some value like years served in the House of Representatives (as of 2004), we would not want to use some cumbersome notation like

Abercrombie $= 14$	$\vdots$
Acevedo-Vila $= 14$	Wu $= 6$
Ackerman $= 21$	Wynn $= 12$
Aderholt $= 8$	Young $= 34$
$\vdots$	Young $= 32$

which would lead to awkward statements like "Abercrombie's years in office" + "Acevedo-Vila's years in office"...+ "Young's years in office" to express mathematical manipulation (note also the obvious naming problem here as well, i.e., delineating between Representative Young of Florida and Representative Young of Alaska). Instead we could just assign each member ordered alphabetically to an integer 1 through 435 (the number of U.S. House members) and then index them by subscript: $\mathbf{X} = \{X_1, X_2, X_3, \ldots, X_{433}, X_{434}, X_{435}\}$. This is a lot cleaner and more mathematically useful. For instance, if we wanted to calculate the mean (average) time served, we could simply perform:

$$\overline{\mathbf{X}} = \frac{1}{435}(X_1 + X_2 + X_3 + \cdots + X_{433} + X_{434} + X_{435})$$

(the bar over $\mathbf{X}$ denotes that this average is a *mean,* something we will see frequently). Although this is cleaner and easier than spelling names or something like that, there is an even nicer way of indicating a mean calculation that uses the **summation operator**. This is a large version of the Greek letter sigma where the starting and stopping points of the addition process are spelled out over and under the symbol. So the mean House seniority calculation could be specified simply by

$$\bar{\mathbf{X}} = \frac{1}{435}\sum_{i=1}^{435}X_i,$$

where we say that i *indexes* X in the summation. One way to think of this notation is that $\sum$ is just an adding "machine" that instructs us which X to start with and which one to stop with. In fact, if we set $n = 435$, then this becomes the simple (and common) form

$$\bar{\mathbf{X}} = \frac{1}{n}\sum_{i=1}^{n}X_i.$$

More formally,

The Summation Operator

$\longmapsto$ If $X_1, X_2, \ldots, X_n$ are n numerical values,

$\longmapsto$ then their sum can be represented by $\sum_{i=1}^{n} X_i$,

$\longmapsto$ where i is an indexing variable to indicate the starting and
stopping points in the series $X_1, X_2, \ldots, X_n$.

A related notation is the **product operator**. This is a slightly different "machine" denoted by an uppercase Greek pi that tells us to multiply instead of add as we did above:

$$\prod_{i=1}^{n} X_i$$

(i.e., it multiplies the n values together). Here we also use i again as the index, but it is important to note that there is nothing special about the use of i; it is just a very common choice. Frequent index alternatives include j, k, l, and m. As a simple illustration, suppose $p_1 = 0.2$, $p_2 = 0.7$, $p_3 = 0.99$, $p_4 = 0.99$, $p_5 = 0.99$. Then

$$\prod_{j=1}^{5} p_j = p_1 \cdot p_2 \cdot p_3 \cdot p_4 \cdot p_5$$

$$= (0.2)(0.7)(0.99)(0.99)(0.99)$$

$$= 0.1358419.$$

Similarly, the formal definition for this operator is given by

---

The Product Operator

$\rightarrowtail$ If $X_1, X_2, \ldots, X_n$ are n numerical values,

$\rightarrowtail$ then their product can be represented by $\prod_{i=1}^{n} X_i$,

$\rightarrowtail$ where i is an indexing variable to indicate the starting and stopping points in the series $X_1, X_2, \ldots, X_n$.

Subscripts are used because we can immediately see that they are not a mathematical operation on the symbol being modified. Sometimes it is also convenient to index using a superscript. To distinguish between a superscript as an index and an exponent operation, brackets or parentheses are often used. So X^2 is the square of X, but $X^{[2]}$ and $X^{(2)}$ are indexed values.

There is another, sometimes confusing, convention that comes from six decades of computer notation in the social sciences and other fields. Some authors will index values without the subscript, as in $X1, X2, \ldots$, or differing functions (see Section 1.5 for the definition of a function) without subscripting according to $f1, f2, \ldots$. Usually it is clear what is meant, however.

1.4.2 Specific Mathematical Use of Terms

The use of mathematical terms can intimidate readers even when the author does not mean to do so. This is because many of them are based on the Greek alphabet or strange versions of familiar symbols (e.g., $\forall$ versus A). This does not mean that the use of these symbols should be avoided for readability. Quite the opposite; for those familiar with the basic vocabulary of mathematics such symbols provide a more concise and readable story if they can clearly summarize ideas that would be more elaborate in narrative. We will save the complete list

Greek idioms to the appendix and give others here, some of which are critical in forthcoming chapters and some of which are given for completeness.

Some terms are almost universal in their usage and thus are important to recall without hesitation. Certain probability and statistical terms will be given as needed in later chapters. An important group of standard symbols are those that define the set of numbers in use. These are

Symbol	Explanation
$\Re$	the set of real numbers
$\Re^+$	the set of positive real numbers
$\Re^-$	the set of negative real numbers
$\mathcal{I}$	the set of integers
$\mathcal{I}^+$ or $\mathbb{Z}^+$	the set of positive integers
$\mathcal{I}^-$ or $\mathbb{Z}^+$	the set of negative integers
$\mathbf{Q}$	the set of rational numbers
$\mathbf{Q}^+$	the set of positive rational numbers
$\mathbf{Q}^-$	the set of negative rational numbers
$\mathcal{C}$	the set of complex numbers (those based on $\sqrt{-1}$).

Recall that the real numbers take on an infinite number of values: rational (expressible in fraction form) and irrational (not expressible in fraction form with values to the right of the decimal point, nonrepeating, like pi). It is interesting to note that there are an infinite number of irrationals and every irrational falls between two rational numbers. For example, $\sqrt{2}$ is in between $7/5$ and $3/2$. Integers are positive and negative (rational) numbers with no decimal component and sometimes called the "counting numbers." Whole numbers are positive integers along with zero, and natural numbers are positive integers without zero. We will not generally consider here the set of **complex numbers**, but they are those that include the imaginary number: $i = \sqrt{-1}$, as in $\sqrt{-4} = 2\sqrt{-1} = 2i$. In mathematical and statistical modeling it is often important to remember which of these number types above is being considered.

Some terms are general enough that they are frequently used with statements about sets or with standard numerical declarations. Other forms are more obscure but do appear in certain social science literatures. Some reasonably common examples are listed in the next table. Note that all of these are *contextual,* that is, they lack any meaning outside of sentence-like statements with other symbols.

Symbol	Explanation
$\neg$	logical negation statement
$\in$	is an element of, as in $3 \in \mathcal{I}^+$
$\ni$	such that
$\therefore$	therefore
$\because$	because
$\Longrightarrow$	logical "then" statement
$\Longleftrightarrow$	if and only if, also abbreviated "iff"
$\exists$	there exists
$\forall$	for all
$\lozenge$	between
$\parallel$	parallel
$\angle$	angle

Also, many of these symbols can be negated, and negation is expressed in one of two ways. For instance, $\in$ means "is an element of," but both $\notin$ and $\neg \in$ mean "is *not* an element of." Similarly, $\subset$ means "is a subset of," but $\not\subset$ means "is *not* a subset of."

Some of these terms are used in a very linguistic fashion: $3 - 4 \in \mathfrak{R}^- \because 3 < 4$. The "therefore" statement is usually at the end of some logic: $2 \in \mathcal{I}^+ \therefore 2 \in \mathfrak{R}^+$. The last three in this list are most useful in geometric expressions and indicate spatial characteristics. Here is a lengthy mathematical statement using most of these symbols: $\forall x \in \mathcal{I}^+$ and $x \neg$prime, $\exists y \in \mathcal{I}^+ \ni x/y \in \mathcal{I}^+$. So what does this mean? Let's parse it: "For all numbers x such that x is a positive integer and not a prime number, there exists a y that is a positive integer such that x divided by y is also a positive integer." Easy, right? (Yeah, sure.) Can you construct one yourself?

Another "fun" example is $x \in \mathcal{I}$ and $x \neq 0 \implies x \in \mathcal{I}^-$ or $\mathcal{I}^+$. This says that if x is a nonzero integer, it is either a positive integer or a negative integer. Consider this in pieces. The first part, $x \in \mathcal{I}$, stipulates that x is "in" the group of integers and cannot be equal to zero. The right arrow, $\implies$, is a logical consequence statement equivalent to saying "then." The last part gives the result, either x is a negative integer or a positive integer (and nothing else since no alternatives are given).

Another important group of terms are related to the manipulation of **sets** of objects, which is an important use of mathematics in social science work (sets are simply defined groupings of individual objects; see Chapter 7, where sets and operations on sets are defined in detail). The most common are

Symbol	Explanation
$\emptyset$	the empty set
	(sometimes used with the Greek phi: ϕ)
$\cup$	union of sets
$\cap$	intersection of sets
$\backslash$	subtract from set
$\subset$	subset
$\complement$	complement

These allow us to make statements about groups of objects such as $A \subset B$ for $A = \{2, 4\}$, $B = \{2, 4, 7\}$, meaning that the set A is a smaller grouping of the larger set B. We could also observe that the A results from removing seven from B.

Some symbols, however, are "restricted" to comparing or operating on strictly numerical values and are not therefore applied directly to sets or logic expressions. We have already seen the sum and product operators given by the symbols $\sum$ and $\prod$ accordingly. The use of ∞ for infinity is relatively common even outside of mathematics, but the next list also gives two distinct "flavors" of

infinity. Some of the contexts of these symbols we will lea
chapters as they deal with notions like limits and vector quantitie.

Symbol	Explanation
$\propto$	is proportional to
$\doteq$	equal to in the limit (approaches)
$\perp$	perpendicular
∞	infinity
$\infty^+, +\infty$	positive infinity
$\infty^-, -\infty$	negative infinity
$\sum$	summation
$\prod$	product
$\lfloor \rfloor$	floor: round down to nearest integer
$\lceil \rceil$	ceiling: round up to nearest integer
$\vert$	given that: $X\vert Y = 3$

Related to these is a set of functions relating maximum and minimum values. Note the directions of $\vee$ and $\wedge$ in the following table.

Symbol	Explanation
$\vee$	maximum of two values
$\max()$	maximum value from list
$\wedge$	minimum of two values
$\min()$	minimum value from list
$\underset{x}{\operatorname{argmax}} f(x)$	the value of x that maximizes the function $f(x)$
$\underset{x}{\operatorname{argmin}} f(x)$	the value of x that minimizes the function $f(x)$

The latter two are important but less common functions. Functions are formally defined in the next section, but we can just think of them for now as sets of instructions for modifying input values (x^2 is an example function that squares its input). As a simple example of the argmax function, consider

$$\underset{x \in \Re}{\operatorname{argmax}} \; x(1-x),$$

which asks which value on the real number line maximizes $x(1-x)$. The answer is 0.5 which provides the best trade-off between the two parts of the ιunction. The argmin function works accordingly but (obviously) operates on the function minimum instead of the function maximum.

These are not exhaustive lists of symbols, but they are the most fundamental (many of them are used in subsequent chapters). Some literatures develop their own conventions about symbols and their very own symbols, such as ∂ to denote a mathematical representation of a game and $\eqcirc$ to indicate *geometric* equivalence between two objects, but such extensions are rare in the social sciences.

1.5 Functions and Equations

A mathematical equation is a very general idea. Fundamentally, an **equation** "equates" two quantities: They are arithmetically identical. So the expression $R = PB - C$ is an equation because it establishes that R and $PB - C$ are exactly equal to each other. But the idea of a mathematical sentence is more general (less restrictive) than this because we can substitute other relations for equality, such as

Symbol	Meaning
$<$	less than
$\leq$	less than or equal to
$\ll$	much less than
$>$	greater than
$\geq$	greater than or equal to
$\gg$	much greater than
$\approx$	approximately the same
$\cong$	approximately equal to
$\lesssim$	approximately less than (also $\lesssim$)
$\gtrsim$	approximately greater than (also $\gtrsim$)
$\equiv$	equivalent by assumption

So, for example, if we say that $X = 1$, $Y = 1.001$ and $Z = 0.002$, then the following statements are true:

$$X \leq 1 \qquad X \geq 1 \qquad X \ll 1000 \qquad X \gg -1000$$

$$X < 2 \qquad X > 0 \qquad X \cong 0.99. \qquad X \approx 1.0001X$$

$$X \approx Y \qquad Y \lesssim X + Z \qquad X + Z \gtrsim Y$$

$$X + 0.001 \equiv Y \qquad X > Y - Z \qquad X \propto 2Y.$$

The purpose of the equation form is generally to express more than one set of relations. Most of us remember the task of solving "two equations for two unknowns." Such forms enable us to describe how (possibly many) variables are associated to each other and various constants. The formal language of mathematics relies heavily on the idea that equations are the atomic units of relations.

What is a function? A **mathematical function** is a "mapping" (i.e., specific directions), which gives a correspondence from one measure onto exactly one other for that value. That is, in our context it defines a relationship between one variable on the x-axis of a Cartesian coordinate system and an operation on that variable that can produce only one value on the y-axis. So a function is a *mapping* from one defined space to another, such as $f : \Re \to \Re$, in which f maps the real numbers to the real numbers (i.e., $f(x) = 2x$), or $f : \Re \to \mathcal{I}$, in which f maps the real numbers to the integers (i.e., $f(x) = \text{round}(x)$).

This all sounds very technical, but it is not. One way of thinking about functions is that they are a "machine" for transforming values, sort of a box as in the figure to the right.

A Function Represented

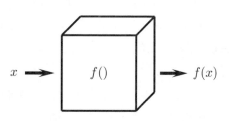

To visualize this we can think about values, x, going in and some modification of these values, $f(x)$, coming out where the instructions for this process are

Table 1.1. TABULARIZING $f(x) = x^2 - 1$

x	$f(x) = x^2 - 1$
1	0
3	8
-1	0
10	99
4	15
$\sqrt{3}$	2

contained in the "recipe" given by $f()$.

Consider the following function operating on the variable x:

$$f(x) = x^2 - 1.$$

This simply means that the mapping from x to $f(x)$ is the process that squares x and subtracts 1. If we list a set of inputs, we can define the corresponding set of outputs, for example, the paired values listed in Table 1.1.

Here we used the $f()$ notation for a function (first codified by Euler in the eighteenth century and still the most common form used today), but other forms are only slightly less common, such as: $g()$, $h()$, $p()$, and $u()$. So we could have just as readily said:

$$g(x) = x^2 - 1.$$

Sometimes the additional notation for a function is essential, such as when more than one function is used in the same expression. For instance, functions can be "nested" with respect to each other (called a composition):

$$f \circ g = f(g(x)),$$

as in $g(x) = 10x$ and $f(x) = x^2$, so $f \circ g = (10x)^2$ (note that this is different than $g \circ f$, which would be $10(x^2)$). Function definitions can also contain wording instead of purely mathematical expressions and may have conditional aspects. Some examples are

$$f(y) = \begin{cases} \frac{1}{y} & \text{if } y \neq 0 \text{ and } y \text{ is rational} \\ 0 & \text{otherwise} \end{cases}$$

$$p(x) = \begin{cases} (6-x)^{-\frac{5}{3}}/200 + 0.1591549 & \text{for } \theta \in [0:6] \\ \frac{1}{2\pi}\dfrac{1}{\left(1+\left(\frac{x-6}{2}\right)^2\right)} & \text{for } \theta \in [6:12]. \end{cases}$$

Note that the first example is necessarily a noncontinuous function whereas the second example is a continuous function (but perhaps not obviously so). Recall that π is notation for $3.1415926535\ldots$, which is often given inaccurately as just 3.14 or even $22/7$. To be more specific about such function characteristics, we now give two important properties of a function.

> ### Properties of Functions, Given for $g(x) = y$
>
> $\rightarrowtail$ A function is **continuous** if it has no "gaps" in its mapping from x to y.
>
> $\rightarrowtail$ A function is **invertible** if its reverse operation exists: $g^{-1}(y) = x$, where $g^{-1}(g(x)) = x$.

It is important to distinguish between a function and a **relation**. A function must have *exactly one value returned by $f(x)$ for each value of x*, whereas a relation does not have this restriction. One way to test whether $f(x)$ is a function or, more generally, a relation is to graph it in the Cartesian coordinate system (x versus y in orthogonal representation) and see if there is a vertical line that can be drawn such that it intersects the function at two values (or more) of y for a single value of x. If this occurs, then it is not a function. There is an important distinction to be made here. The *solution* to a function can possibly have more than one corresponding value of x, but a function cannot have alternate values of y for a ***given*** x. For example, consider the relation $y^2 = 5x$, which is not a function based on this criteria. We can see this algebraically by taking the square root of both sides, $\pm y = \sqrt{5x}$, which shows the non-uniqueness of the y values (as well as the restriction to positive values of x). We can also see this graphically in Figure 1.2, where x values from 0 to 10 each give two y values (a dotted line is given at $(x = 4, y = \pm\sqrt{20})$ as an example).

Fig. 1.2. A RELATION THAT IS NOT A FUNCTION

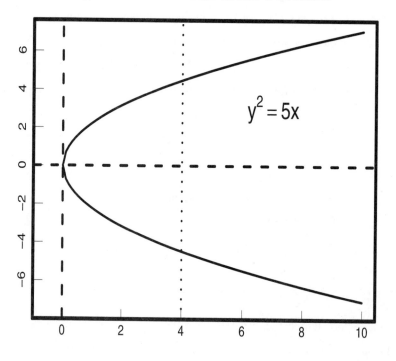

The modern definition of a function is also attributable to Dirichlet: If variables x and y are related such that every acceptable value of x has a corresponding value of y defined by a ***rule***, then y is a function of x. Earlier European period notions of a function (i.e., by Leibniz, Bernoulli , and Euler) were more vague and sometimes tailored only to specific settings.

Fig. 1.3. RELATING x AND $f(x)$

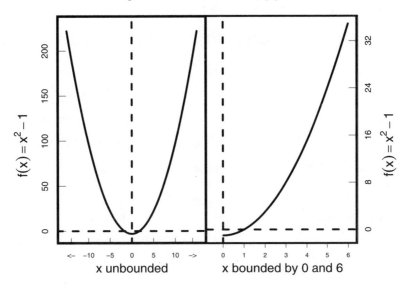

Often a function is explicitly defined as a mapping between elements of an **ordered pair**: (x, y), also called a relation. So we say that the function $f(x) = y$ maps the ordered pair x, y such that for each value of x there is exactly one y (the order of x before y matters). This was exactly what we saw in Table 1.1, except that we did not label the rows as ordered pairs. As a more concrete example, the following set of ordered pairs:

$$\{[1, -2], [3, 6], [7, 46]\}$$

can be mapped by the function: $f(x) = x^2 - 3$. If the set of x values is restricted to some specifically defined set, then obviously so is y. The set of x values is called the **domain** (or support) of the function and the associated set of y values is called the **range** of the function. Sometimes this is highly restrictive (such as to specific integers) and sometimes it is not. Two examples are given in Figure 1.3, which is drawn on the (now) familiar Cartesian coordinate system. Here we see that the range and domain of the function are unbounded in the first panel (although we clearly cannot *draw* it all the way until infinity in both directions), and the domain is bounded by 0 and 6 in the second panel.

A function can also be even or odd, defined by

a function is "odd" if: $f(-x) = -f(x)$

a function is "even" if: $f(-x) = f(x).$

So, for example, the squaring function $f(x) = x^2$ and the absolute value function $f(x) = |x|$ are even because both will always produce a positive answer. On the other hand, $f(x) = x^3$ is odd because the negative sign perseveres for a negative x. Regretfully, functions can also be neither even nor odd without domain restrictions.

One special function is important enough to mention directly here. A **linear function** is one that preserves the algebraic nature of the real numbers such that $f()$ is a linear function if:

$$f(x_1 + x_2) = f(x_1) + f(x_2) \quad \text{and} \quad f(kx_1) = kf(x_1)$$

for two points, x_1 and x_2, in the domain of $f()$ and an arbitrary constant number k. This is often more general in practice with multiple functions and multiple constants, forms such as:

$$F(x_1, x_2, x_3) = kf(x_1) + \ell g(x_2) + mh(x_3)$$

for functions $f(), g(), h()$ and constants k, ℓ, m.

★ **Example 1.3:   The "Cube Rule" in Votes to Seats**. A standard, though somewhat maligned, theory from the study of elections is due to Parker's (1909) empirical research in Britain, which was later popularized in that country by Kendall and Stuart (1950, 1952). He looked at systems with two major parties whereby the largest vote-getter in a district wins regardless of the size of the winning margin (the so-called *first past the post* system used by most English-speaking countries). Suppose that A denotes the proportion of votes for one party and B the proportion of votes for the other. Then, according to this rule, the ratio of seats in Parliament won is approximately the cube of the ratio of votes: A/B in votes implies A^3/B^3 in seats (sometimes ratios are given in the notation $A:B$). The political principle from this theory is that small differences in the vote ratio yield large differences in the seats ratio and thus provide stable parliamentary government.

So how can we express this theory in standard mathematical function notation. Define x as the ratio of votes for the party with proportion A over the party with proportion B. Then expressing the cube law in this notation yields

$$f(x) = x^3$$

for the function determining seats, which of course is very simple. Tufte (1973) reformulated this slightly by noting that in a two-party contest the proportion of votes for the second party can be rewritten as $B = 1 - A$. Furthermore, if we define the proportion of *seats* for the first party as S_A, then similarly the proportion of seats for the second party is $1 - S_A$, and we can reexpress the cube rule in this notation as

$$\frac{S_A}{1 - S_A} = \left[\frac{A}{1 - A}\right]^3.$$

Using this notation we can solve for S_A (see Exercise 1.8), which produces

$$S_A = \frac{A^3}{1 - 3A + 3A^2}.$$

This equation has an interesting shape with a rapid change in the middle of the range of A, clearly showing the nonlinearity in the relationship implied by the cube function. This shape means that the winning party's gains are more pronounced in this area and less dramatic toward the tails. This is shown in Figure 1.4.

Taagepera (1986) looked at this for a number of elections around the world and found some evidence that the rule fits. For instance, U.S. House races for the period 1950 to 1970 with Democrats over Republicans give a value of exactly 2.93, which is not too far off the theoretical value of 3 supplied by Parker.

Fig. 1.4. THE CUBE LAW

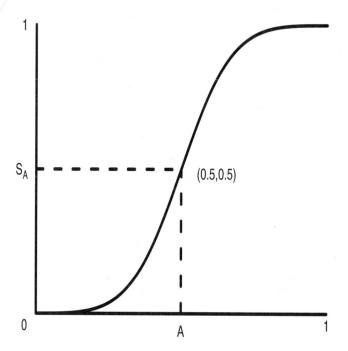

1.5.1 Applying Functions: The Equation of a Line

Recall the familiar expression of a line in Cartesian coordinates usually given as $y = mx + b$, where m is the slope of the line (the change in y for a one-unit change in x) and b is the point where the line intercepts the y-axis. Clearly this is a (linear) function in the sense described above and also clearly we can determine any single value of y for a given value of x, thus producing a matched pair.

A classic problem is to find the slope and equation of a line determined by two points. This is always unique because any two points in a Cartesian coordinate system can be connected by one and only one line. Actually we can generalize this in a three-dimensional system, where three points determine a unique plane, and so on. This is why a three-legged stool never wobbles and a four-legged chair sometimes does (think about it!). Back to our problem... suppose that we want to find the equation of the line that goes through the two points

$\{[2,1],[3,5]\}$. What do we know from this information? We know that for one unit of increasing x we get four units of increasing y. Since slope is "rise over run," then:

$$m = \frac{5-1}{3-2} = 4.$$

Great, now we need to get the intercept. To do this we need only to plug m into the standard line equation, set x and y to one of the known points on the line, and solve (we should pick the easier point to work with, by the way):

$$y = mx + b$$
$$1 = 4(2) + b$$
$$b = 1 - 8 = -7.$$

This is equivalent to starting at some selected point on the line and "walking down" until the point where x is equal to zero.

Fig. 1.5. PARALLEL AND PERPENDICULAR LINES

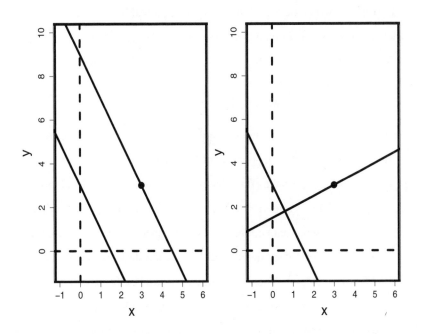

The Greeks and other ancients were fascinated by linear forms, and lines are an interesting mathematical subject unto themselves. For instance, two lines

$$y = m_1 x + b_1$$

$$y = m_2 x + b_2,$$

are parallel *if and only if* (often abbreviated as "iff") $m_1 = m_2$ and perpendicular (also called orthogonal) iff $m_1 = -1/m_2$. For example, suppose we have the line $L_1 : y = -2x + 3$ and are interested in finding the line parallel to L_1 that goes through the point $[3, 3]$. We know that the slope of this new line must be -2, so we now plug this value in along with the only values of x and y that we know are on the line. This allows us to solve for b and plot the parallel line in left panel of Figure 1.5:

$$(3) = -2(3) + b_2, \quad \text{so} \quad b_2 = 9.$$

This means that the parallel line is given by $L_2 : y = -2x + 9$. It is not much more difficult to get the equation of the perpendicular line. We can do the same trick but instead plug in the negative inverse of the slope from L_1:

$$(3) = \frac{1}{2}(3) + b_3, \quad \text{so} \quad b_3 = \frac{3}{2}.$$

This gives us $L_2 \perp L_1$, where $L_2 : y = \frac{1}{2}x + \frac{3}{2}$.

★ **Example 1.4:   Child Poverty and Reading Scores**. Despite overall national wealth, a surprising number of U.S. school children live in poverty. A continuing concern is the effect that this has on educational development and attainment. This is important for normative as well as societal reasons. Consider the following data collected in 1998 by the California Department of Education (CDE) by testing all 2nd–11th grade students in various subjects (the Stanford 9 test). These data are aggregated to the school district level here for two variables: the percentage of students who qualify for reduced or free lunch plans (a common measure of poverty in educational policy studies) and the percent of students scoring over the national median for reading at the 9th grade. The median (average) is the point where one-half of the points are greater and one-half of the points are less.

Because of the effect of limited English proficiency students on district performance, this test was by far the most controversial in California amongst the exam topics. In addition, administrators are sensitive to the aggregated results of reading scores because it is a subject that is at the core of what many consider to be "traditional" children's education.

The relationship is graphed in Figure 1.6 along with a linear trend with a slope of $m = -0.75$ and an intercept at $b = 81$. A very common tool of social scientists is the so-called **linear regression model**. Essentially this is a method of looking at data and figuring out an underlying trend in the form of a straight line. We will not worry about any of the calculation details here, but we can think about the implications. What does this particular line mean? It means that for a 1% positive change (say from 50 to 51) in a district's poverty, they will have an *expected* reduction in the pass rate of three-quarters of a percent. Since this line purports to find the underlying trend across these 303 districts, no district will *exactly* see these results, but we are still claiming that this captures some common underlying socioeconomic phenomena.

1.5.2 The Factorial Function

One function that has special notation is the factorial function. The factorial of x is denoted $x!$ and is defined for positive integers x only:

$$x! = x \times (x - 1) \times (x - 2) \times \ldots 2 \times 1,$$

where the 1 at the end is superfluous. Obviously $1! = 1$, and by convention we assume that $0! = 1$. For example,

$$4! = 4 \times 3 \times 2 \times 1 = 24.$$

Fig. 1.6. Poverty and Reading Test Scores

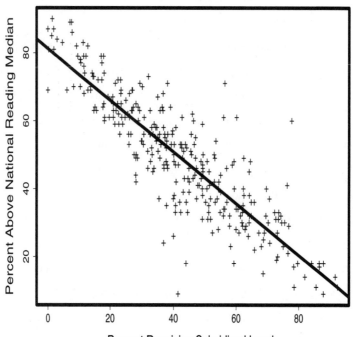

Percent Receiving Subsidized Lunch

It should be clear that this function grows rapidly for increasing values of x, and sometimes the result overwhelms commonly used hand calculators. Try, for instance, to calculate 100! with yours. In some common applications large factorials are given in the context of ratios and a handy cancellation can be used to make the calculation easier. It would be difficult or annoying to calculate 190!/185! by first obtaining the two factorials and then dividing. Fortunately we can use

$$\frac{190!}{185!} = \frac{190 \cdot 189 \cdot 188 \cdot 187 \cdot 186 \cdot 185 \cdot 184 \cdot 183 \cdot \ldots}{185 \cdot 184 \cdot 183 \cdot \ldots}$$

$$= 190 \cdot 189 \cdot 188 \cdot 187 \cdot 186$$

$$= 234,816,064,560$$

(recall that "·" and "×" are equivalent notations for multiplication). It would not initially seem like this calculation produces a value of almost 250 billion, but it does! Because factorials increase so quickly in magnitude, they can sometimes be difficult to calculate directly. Fortunately there is a handy way to get around this problem called **Stirling's Approximation** (curiously named since it is credited to De Moivre's 1720 work on probability):

$$n! \approx (2\pi n)^{\frac{1}{2}} e^{-n} n^n.$$

Here $e \approx 2.71$, which is an important constant defined on page 36. Notice that, as its name implies, this is an approximation. We will return to factorials in Chapter 7 when we analyze various counting rules.

★ **Example 1.5:** **Coalition Cabinet Formation.** Suppose we are trying to form a coalition cabinet with three parties. There are six senior members of the Liberal Party, five senior members of the Christian Democratic Party, and four senior members of the Green Party vying for positions in the cabinet. How many ways could you choose a cabinet composed of three Liberals, two Christian Democrats, and three Greens?

It turns out that the number of possible subsets of y items from a set of n items is given by the "choose notation" formula:

$$\binom{n}{y} = \frac{n!}{y!(n-y)!},$$

which can be thought of as the permutations of n divided by the permutations of y times the permutations of "not y." This is called *unordered without replacement* because it does not matter what order the members are drawn in, and once drawn they are not thrown back into the pool for possible re-selection. There are actually other ways to select samples from populations, and these are given in detail in Chapter 7 (see, for instance, the discussion in Section 7.2).

So now we have to multiply the number of ways to select three Liberals, the two CDPs, and the three Greens to get the *total* number of possible cabinets (we multiply because we want the full number of combinatoric possibilities across the three parties):

$$\binom{6}{3}\binom{5}{2}\binom{4}{3} = \frac{6!}{3!(6-3)!}\frac{5!}{2!(5-2)!}\frac{4!}{3!(4-3)!}$$

$$= \frac{720}{6(6)}\frac{120}{2(6)}\frac{24}{6(1)}$$

$$= 20 \times 10 \times 4$$

$$= 800.$$

This number is relatively large because of the multiplication: For each single choice of members from one party we have to consider *every* possible choice from the others. In a practical scenario we might have many fewer *politically viable* combinations due to overlapping expertise, jealousies, rivalries, and other interesting phenomena.

1.5.3 The Modulo Function

Another function that has special notation is the **modulo function**, which deals with the *remainder* from a division operation. First, let's define a **factor**: y is a factor of x if the result of x/y is an integer (i.e., a prime number has exactly two factors: itself and one). So if we divided x by y and y was *not* a factor of x, then there would necessarily be a noninteger remainder between zero and one. This remainder can be an inconvenience where it is perhaps discarded, or it can be considered important enough to keep as part of the result. Suppose instead that this was the only part of the result from division that we cared about. What symbology could we use to remove the integer component and only keep the remainder?

To divide x by y and keep only the remainder, we use the notation

$$x \pmod{y}.$$

Thus $5 \pmod{2} = 1$, $17 \pmod{5} = 2$, and $10,003 \pmod{4} = 3$, for example. The modulo function is also sometimes written as either

$$x \bmod y \quad \text{or} \quad x \quad \text{mod } y$$

(only the spacing differs).

1.6 Polynomial Functions

Polynomial functions of x are functions that have components that raise x to some power:

$$f(x) = x^2 + x + 1$$
$$g(x) = x^5 - 3^3 - x$$
$$h(x) = x^{100},$$

where these are polynomials in x of power 2, 5, and 100, respectively. We have already seen examples of polynomial functions in this chapter such as $f(x) = x^2$, $f(x) = x(1 - x)$, and $f(x) = x^3$. The convention is that a polynomial degree (power) is designated by its largest exponent with regard to the variable. Thus the polynomials above are of degree 2,5, and 100, respectively.

Often we care about the **roots** of a polynomial function: where the curve of the function crosses the x-axis. This may occur at more than one place and may be difficult to find. Since $y = f(x)$ is zero at the x-axis, root finding means discovering where the right-hand side of the polynomial function equals zero. Consider the function $h(x) = x^{100}$ from above. We do not have to work too hard to find that the only root of this function is at the point $x = 0$.

In many scientific fields it is common to see **quadratic** polynomials, which are just polynomials of degree 2. Sometimes these polynomials have easy-to-determine integer roots (solutions), as in

$$x^2 - 1 = (x - 1)(x + 1) \implies x = \pm 1,$$

and sometimes they do not, requiring the well-known quadratic equation

$$x = \frac{-b \pm \sqrt{b^2 - 4ac}}{2a},$$

where a is the multiplier on the x^2 term, b is the multiplier on the x term, and c is the constant. For example, solving for roots in the equation

$$x^2 - 4x = 5$$

is accomplished by

$$x = \frac{-(-4) \pm \sqrt{(-4)^2 - 4(1)(-5)}}{2(1)} = -1 \text{ or } 5,$$

where $a = 1$, $b = -4$, and $c = -5$ from $f(x) = x^2 - 4x - 5 \equiv 0$.

1.7 Logarithms and Exponents

Exponents and logarithms ("logs" for short) confuse many people. However, they are such an important convenience that they have become critical to quantitative social science work. Furthermore, so many statistical tools use these "natural" expressions that understanding these forms is essential to some work. Basically exponents make convenient the idea of multiplying a number by itself (possibly) many times, and a logarithm is just the opposite operation. We already saw one use of exponents in the discussion of the cube rule relating votes to seats. In that example, we defined a function, $f(x) = x^3$, that used 3 as an exponent. This is only mildly more convenient than $f(x) = x \times x \times x$, but imagine if the exponent was quite large or if it was not a integer. Thus we need some core principles for handling more complex exponent forms.

First let's review the basic rules for exponents. The important ones are as follows.

Key Properties of Powers and Exponents

⟼ Zero Property $x^0 = 1$

⟼ One Property $x^1 = x$

⟼ Power Notation $\text{power}(x, a) = x^a$

⟼ Fraction Property $\left(\dfrac{x}{y}\right)^a = \left(\dfrac{x^a}{y^a}\right) = x^a y^{-a}$

⟼ Nested Exponents $(x^a)^b = x^{ab}$

⟼ Distributive Property $(xy)^a = x^a y^a$

⟼ Product Property $x^a \times x^b = x^{a+b}$

⟼ Ratio Property $x^{\frac{a}{b}} = (x^a)^{\frac{1}{b}} = \left(x^{\frac{1}{b}}\right)^a = \sqrt[b]{x^a}$

The underlying principle that we see from these rules is that multiplication of the base (x here) leads to addition in the exponents (a and b here), but multiplication in the exponents comes from nested exponentiation, for example, $(x^a)^b = x^{ab}$ from above. One point in this list is purely notational: $\text{Power}(x, a)$ comes from the computer expression of mathematical notation.

A **logarithm** of (positive) x, for some **base** b, is the value of the exponent that gets b to x:

$$\log_b(x) = a \implies b^a = x.$$

A frequently used base is $b = 10$, which defines the **common log**. So, for example,

$$\log_{10}(100) = 2 \implies 10^2 = 100$$

$$\log_{10}(0.1) = -1 \implies 10^{-1} = 0.1$$

$$\log_{10}(15) = 1.176091 \implies 10^{1.1760913} = 15.$$

Another common base is $b = 2$:

$$\log_2(8) = 3 \implies 2^3 = 8$$

$$\log_2(1) = 0 \implies 2^0 = 1$$

$$\log_2(15) = 3.906891 \implies 2^{3.906891} = 15.$$

Actually, it is straightforward to change from one logarithmic base to another. Suppose we want to change from base b to a new base a. It turns out that we only need to divide the first expression by the log of the new base *to the old base*:

$$\log_a(x) = \frac{\log_b(x)}{\log_b(a)}.$$

For example, start with $\log_2(64)$ and convert this to $\log_8(64)$. We simply have to divide by $\log_2(8)$:

$$\log_8(64) = \frac{\log_2(64)}{\log_2(8)}$$

$$2 = \frac{6}{3}.$$

We can now state some general properties for logarithms of all bases.

Basic Properties of Logarithms

$\rightarrowtail$ Zero/One $\log_b(1) = 0$

$\rightarrowtail$ Multiplication $\log(x \cdot y) = \log(x) + \log(y)$

$\rightarrowtail$ Division $\log(x/y) = \log(x) - \log(y)$

$\rightarrowtail$ Exponentiation $\log(x^y) = y \log(x)$

$\rightarrowtail$ Basis $\log_b(b^x) = x$, and $b^{\log_b(x)} = x$

A third common base is perhaps the most interesting. The **natural log** is the log with the irrational base: $e = 2.718281828459045235\ldots$. This does not seem like the most logical number to form a useful base, but in fact it turns out to be so. This is an enormously important constant in our numbering system and appears to have been lurking in the history of mathematics for quite some time, however, without substantial recognition. Early work on logarithms in the seventeenth century by Napier, Oughtred, Saint-Vincent, and Huygens hinted at the importance of e, but it was not until Mercator published a table of "natural logarithms" in 1668 that e had an association. Finally, in 1761 e acquired its current name when Euler christened it as such.

Mercator appears not to have realized the theoretical importance of e, but soon thereafter Jacob Bernoulli helped in 1683. He was analyzing the (now-famous) formula for calculating compound interest, where the compounding is done continuously (rather than a set intervals):

$$f(p) = \left(1 + \frac{1}{p}\right)^p.$$

Bernoulli's question was, what happens to this function as p goes to infinity? The answer is not immediately obvious because the fraction inside goes to zero, implying that the component within the parenthesis goes to one and the exponentiation does not matter. But does the fraction go to zero faster than the exponentiation grows ever larger? Bernoulli made the surprising discovery that this function in the limit (i.e., as $p \to \infty$) must be between 2 and 3. Then what others missed Euler made concrete by showing that the limiting value of this function is actually e. In addition, he showed that the answer to Bernoulli's question could also be found by

$$e = 1 + \frac{1}{1!} + \frac{1}{2!} + \frac{1}{3!} + \frac{1}{4!} + \cdots$$

(sometimes given as $e = \frac{1}{1!} + \frac{2}{2!} + \frac{3}{3!} + \frac{4}{4!} + \ldots$). Clearly this (Euler's expansion) is a series that adds declining values because the factorial in the denominator will grow much faster than the series of integers in the numerator.

Euler is also credited with being the first (that we know of) to show that e, like π, is an **irrational number**: There is no end to the series of nonrepeating numbers to the right of the decimal point. Irrational numbers have bothered mankind for much of their recognized existence and have even had negative connotations. One commonly told story holds that the Pythagoreans put one of their members to death after he publicized the existence of irrational numbers. The discovery of negative numbers must have also perturbed the Pythagoreans because they believe in the beauty and primacy of natural numbers (that the diagonal of a square with sides equal to one unit has length $\sqrt{2}$ and that caused them great consternation).

It turns out that nature has an affinity for e since it appears with great regularity among organic and physical phenomena. This makes its use as a base for the log function quite logical and supportable. As an example from biology, the chambered nautilus (*nautilus pompilius*) forms a shell that is characterized as "equiangular" because the angle from the source radiating outward is constant as the animal grows larger. Aristotle (and other ancients) noticed this as well as the fact that the three-dimensional space created by growing new chambers always has the same shape, growing only in magnitude. We can illustrate this with a cross section of the shell created by a growing spiral of consecutive right triangles (the real shell is curved on the outside) according to

$$x = r \times e^{k\theta} \cos(\theta) \qquad y = r \times e^{k\theta} \sin(\theta),$$

where r is the radius at a chosen point, k is a constant, θ is the angle at that point starting at the x-axis proceeding counterclockwise, and sin, cos are functions that operate on angles and are described in the next chapter (see page 56). Notice the centrality of e here, almost implying that these mulluscs sit on the ocean floor pondering the mathematical constant as they produce shell chambers. A two-dimensional cross section is illustrated in Figure 1.7 ($k = 0.2$, going around two rotations), where the characteristic shape is obvious even with the triangular simplification.

Given the central importance of the natural exponent, it is not surprising that

Fig. 1.7. NAUTILUS CHAMBERS

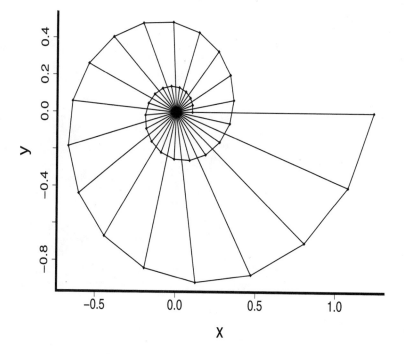

the associated logarithm has its own notation:

$$\log_e(x) = \ln(x) = a \implies e^a = x,$$

and by the definition of e

$$\ln(e^x) = x.$$

This inner function (e^x) has another common notational form, $\exp(x)$, which comes from expressing mathematical notation on a computer. There is another notational convention that causes some confusion. Quite frequently in the statistical literature authors will use the generic form $\log()$ to denote the natural logarithm based on e. Conversely, it is sometimes defaulted to $b = 10$ elsewhere (often engineering and therefore less relevant to the social sciences). Part of the reason for this shorthand for the natural log is the pervasiveness of e in the mathematical forms that statisticians care about, such as the form that defines the *normal* probability distribution.

1.8 New Terminology

Exercises

1.1   Simplify the following expressions as much as possible:

$$(-x^4 y^2)^2 \qquad 9(3^0) \qquad (2a^2)(4a^4)$$

$$\frac{x^4}{x^3} \qquad (-2)^{7-4} \qquad \left(\frac{1}{27b^3}\right)^{1/3}$$

$$y^7 y^6 y^5 y^4 \qquad \frac{2a/7b}{11b/5a} \qquad (z^2)^4$$

1.2   Simplify the following expression:

$$(a+b)^2 + (a-b)^2 + 2(a+b)(a-b) - 3a^2$$

1.3   Solve:

$$\sqrt[3]{2^3} \qquad \sqrt[3]{27} \qquad \sqrt[4]{625}$$

1.4   The relationship between Fahrenheit and Centigrade can be expressed as $5f - 9c = 160$. Show that this is a linear function by putting it in $y = mx + b$ format with $c = y$. Graph the line indicating slope and intercept.

1.5   Another way to describe a line in Cartesian terms is the **point-slope form**: $(y - y') = m(x - x')$, where y' and x' are given values and m is the slope of the line. Show that this is equivalent to the form given by solving for the intercept.

1.6   Solve the following inequalities so that the variable is the only term on the left-hand side:

$$x - 3 < 2x + 15$$

$$11 - \frac{4}{3}t > 3$$

$$\frac{5}{6}y + 3(y-1) \le \frac{11}{6}(1-y) + 2y$$

1.7   A very famous sequence of numbers is called the Fibonacci sequence, which starts with 0 and 1 and continues according to:

$$0, 1, 1, 2, 3, 5, 8, 13, 21, \ldots$$

Figure out the logic behind the sequence and write it as a function using subscripted values like x_j for the jth value in the sequence.

1.8 In the example on page 24, the cube law was algebraically rearranged to solve for S_A. Show these steps.

1.9 Which of the following functions are continuous? If not, where are the discontinuities?

$$f(x) = \frac{9x^3 - x}{(x-1)(x+1)} \qquad g(y,z) = \frac{6y^4z^3 + 3y^2z - 56}{12y^5 - 3zy + 18z}$$

$$f(x) = e^{-x^2} \qquad\qquad f(y) = y^3 - y^2 + 1$$

$$h(x,y) = \frac{xy}{x+y} \qquad\qquad f(x) = \begin{cases} x^3 + 1 & x > 0 \\ \frac{1}{2} & x = 0 \\ -x^2 & x < 0 \end{cases}$$

1.10 Find the equation of the line that goes through the two points $\{[-1,-2],[3/2,5/2]\}$.

1.11 Use the diagram of the square to prove that $(a-b)^2 + 4ab = (a+b)^2$

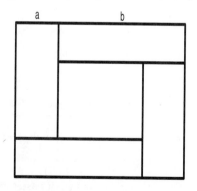

(i.e., demonstrate this equality geo-metrically rather than algebraically with features of the square shown).

1.12 Suppose we are trying to put together a Congressional committee that has representation from four national regions. Potential members are drawn from a pool with 7 from the northeast, 6 from the south, 4 from the Midwest, and 6 from the far west. How many ways can you choose a committee that has 3 members from each region for a total of 12?

1.13   Sørensen's (1977) model of social mobility looks at the process of increasing attainment in the labor market as a function of time, personal qualities, and opportunities. Typical professional career paths follow a logarithmic-like curve with rapid initial advancement and tapering off progress later. Label y_t the attainment level at time period t and y_{t-1} the attainment in the previous period, both of which are defined over $\mathfrak{R}^+$. Sørensen stipulates:

$$y_t = \frac{r}{s}[\exp(st) - 1] + y_{t-1}\exp(st),$$

where $r \in \mathfrak{R}^+$ is the individual's resources and abilities and $s \in \mathfrak{R}^+$ is the structural impact (i.e., a measure of opportunities that become available). What is the domain of s, that is, what restrictions are necessary on what values it can take on in order for this model to make sense in that declining marginal manner?

1.14   The following data are U.S. Census Bureau estimates of population over a 5-year period.

Date	Total U.S. Population
July 1, 2004	293,655,404
July 1, 2003	290,788,976
July 1, 2002	287,941,220
July 1, 2001	285,102,075
July 1, 2000	282,192,162

Characterize the growth in terms of a parametric expression. Graphing may help.

1.15   Using the change of base formula for logarithms, change $\log_6(36)$ to $\log_3(36)$.

1.16   Glottochronology is the anthropological study of language change and evolution. One standard theory (Swadish 1950, 1952) holds that words endure in a language according to a "decay rate" that can be expressed as $y = c^{2t}$, where y is the proportion of words that are retained in a language, t is the time in 1000 years, and $c = 0.805$ is a constant. Reexpress the relation using "e" (i.e., 2.71...), as is done in some settings, according to $y = e^{-t/\tau}$, where τ is a constant you must specify. Van der Merwe (1966) claims that the Romance-Germanic-Slavic language split fits a curve with $\tau = 3.521$. Graph this curve and the curve from τ derived above with an x-axis along 0 to 7. What does this show?

1.17 Sociologists Holland and Leinhardt (1970) developed measures for models of structure in interpersonal relations using ranked clusters. This approach requires extensive use of factorials to express personal choices. The authors defined the notation $x^{(k)} = x(x-1)(x-2)\cdots(x-k+1)$. Show that $x^{(k)}$ is just $x!/(x-k)!$.

1.18 For the equation $y^3 = x^2 + 2$ there is only one solution where x and y are both positive integers. Find this solution. For the equation $y^3 = x^2 + 4$ there are only two solutions where x and y are both positive integers. Find them both.

1.19 Show that in general

$$\sum_{i=1}^{m}\prod_{j=1}^{n} x_i y_j \neq \prod_{j=1}^{n}\sum_{i=1}^{m} x_i y_j$$

and construct a special case where it is actually equal.

1.20 A **perfect number** is one that is the sum of its proper divisors. The first five are

$$6 = 1 + 2 + 3$$
$$28 = 1 + 2 + 4 + 7 + 14$$
$$496 = 1 + 2 + 4 + 8 + 16 + 31 + 62 + 124 + 248.$$

Show that 8128 are 33550336 perfect numbers. The Pythagoreans also defined **abundant numbers**: The number is less than the sum of its divisors, and **deficient numbers**: The number is greater than the sum of its divisors. Any divisor of a deficient number or perfect number turns out to be a deficient number itself. Show that this is true with 496. There is a function that relates perfect numbers to primes that comes from Euclid's **Elements** (around 300 BC). If $f(x) = 2^x - 1$ is a prime number, then $g(x) = 2^{x-1}(2^x - 1)$ is a perfect number. Find an x for the first three perfect numbers above.

1.21   Suppose we had a linear regression line relating the size of state-level unemployment percent on the x-axis and homicides per 100,000 of the state population on the y-axis, with slope $m = 2.41$ and intercept $b = 27$. What would be the expected effect of increasing unemployment by 5%?

1.22   Calculate the following:

$$113 \quad (\mathrm{mod}\ 3)$$
$$256 \quad (\mathrm{mod}\ 17)$$
$$45 \quad (\mathrm{mod}\ 5)$$
$$88 \quad (\mathrm{mod}\ 90).$$

1.23   Use Euler's expansion to calculate e with 10 terms. Compare this result to some definition of e that you find in a mathematics text. How accurate were you?

1.24   Use Stirling's Approximation to obtain 12312!. Show the steps.

1.25   Find the roots (solutions) to the following quadratic equations:

$$4x^2 - 1 = 17$$
$$9x^2 - 3x + 12 = 0$$
$$x^2 - 2x - 16 = 0$$
$$6x^2 - 6x - 6 = 0$$
$$5 + 11x = -3x^2.$$

1.26   The manner by which seats are allocated in the House of Representatives to the 50 states is somewhat more complicated than most people appreciate. The current system (since 1941) is based on the "method of equal proportions" and works as follows:

- Allocate one representative to each state regardless of population.
- Divide each state's population by a series of values given by the formula $\sqrt{i(i-1)}$ starting at $i = 2$, which looks like this for state j with population p_j:

$$\frac{p_j}{\sqrt{2 \times 1}}, \frac{p_j}{\sqrt{3 \times 2}}, \frac{p_j}{\sqrt{4 \times 3}}, \cdots \frac{p_j}{\sqrt{n \times (n-1)}},$$

where n is a large number.

- These values are sorted in descending order for all states and House seats are allocated in this order until 435 are assigned.

(a) The following are estimated state "populations" for the original 13 states in 1780 (Bureau of the Census estimates; the first official U.S. census was performed later in 1790):

Virginia	538,004
Massachusetts	268,627
Pennsylvania	327,305
North Carolina	270,133
New York	210,541
Maryland	245,474
Connecticut	206,701
South Carolina	180,000
New Jersey	139,627
New Hampshire	87,802
Georgia	56,071
Rhode Island	52,946
Delaware	45,385

Calculate under this plan the apportionment for the first House of Representatives that met in 1789, which had 65 members.

(b) The first apportionment plan was authored by Alexander Hamilton and uses only the proportional value and rounds down to get full persons (it ignores the remainders from fractions), and any remaining seats are allocated by the size of the remainders to give $(10, 8, 8, 5, 6, 6, 5, 5, 4, 3, 3, 1, 1)$ in the order above. Relatively speaking, does the Hamilton plan favor or hurt large states? Make a graph of the differences.

(c) Show by way of a graph the increasing proportion of House representation that a single state obtains as it grows from the smallest to the largest in relative population.

1.27   The Nachmias–Rosenbloom Measure of Variation (MV) indicates how many heterogeneous intergroup relationships are evident from the full set of those mathematically possible given the population. Specifically it is described in terms of the "frequency" (their original language) of observed subgroups in the full group of interest. Call f_i the frequency or proportion of the ith subgroup and n the number of these groups. The index is created by

$$MV = \frac{\text{"each frequency} \times \text{all others, summed"}}{\text{"number of combinations"} \times \text{"mean frequency squared"}}$$

$$= \frac{\sum_{i=1}^{n}(f_i \neq f_j)}{\frac{n(n-1)}{2}\bar{f}^2}.$$

Nachmias and Rosenbloom (1973) use this measure to make claims about how integrated U.S. federal agencies are with regard to race. For a population of 24 individuals:

(a) What mixture of two groups (say blacks and whites) gives the maximum possible MV? Calculate this value.

(b) What mixture of two groups (say blacks and whites) gives the minimum possible MV but still has both groups represented? Calculate this value as well.

1.9 Chapter Appendix: It's All Greek to Me

The following table lists the Greek characters encountered in standard mathematical language along with a very short description of the standard way that each is considered in the social sciences (omicron is not used).

Name	Lowercase	Capitalized	Typical Usage
alpha	α	–	general unknown value
beta	β	–	general unknown value
gamma	γ	Γ	small case a general unknown value, capitalized version denotes a special counting function
delta	δ	Δ	often used to denote a difference
epsilon	ϵ	–	usually denotes a very small number or error
zeta	ζ	–	general unknown value
eta	η	–	general unknown value
theta	θ	Θ	general unknown value, often used for radians
iota	ι	–	rarely used
kappa	κ	–	general unknown value
lambda	λ	Λ	general unknown value, used for eigenvalues
mu	μ	–	general unknown value, denotes a mean in statistics

Name	Lowercase	Capitalized	Typical Usage
nu	ν	–	general unknown value
xi	ξ	Ξ	general unknown value
pi	π	Π	small case can be: 3.14159…, general unknown value, a probability function; capitalized version should not be confused with product notation
rho	ρ	–	general unknown value, simple correlation, or autocorrelation in time-series statistics
sigma	σ	Σ	small case can be unknown value or a variance (when squared), capitalized version should not be confused with summation notation
tau	τ	–	general unknown value
upsilon	υ	Υ	general unknown value
phi	ϕ	Φ	general unknown value, sometimes denotes the two expressions of the normal distribution
chi	χ	–	general unknown value, sometimes denotes the chi-square distribution (when squared)
psi	ψ	Ψ	general unknown value
omega	ω	Ω	general unknown value

2

Analytic Geometry

2.1 Objectives (the Width of a Circle)

This chapter introduces the basic principles of analytic geometry and trigonometry specifically. These subjects come up in social science research in seemingly surprising ways. Even if one is not studying some spatial phenomenon, such functions and rules can still be relevant. We will also expand beyond Cartesian coordinates and look at polar coordinate systems. At the end of the day, understanding trigonometric functions comes down to understanding their basis in triangles.

2.2 Radian Measurement and Polar Coordinates

So far we have only used Cartesian coordinates when discussing coordinate systems. There is a second system that can be employed when it is convenient to think in terms of a movement around a circle. **Radian measurement** treats the angular distance around the center of a circle (also called the pole or origin for obvious reasons) in the counterclockwise direction as a proportion of 2π.

Most people are comfortable with another measure of angles, degrees, which are measured from 0 to 360. However, this system is arbitrary (although ancient) whereas radian measurement is based on the formula for the circumference of a circle: $c = 2\pi r$, where r is the radius. If we assume a unit radius ($r = 1$), then the linkage is obvious. That is, from a starting point, moving 2π around the circle (a complete revolution) returns us to the radial point where we began. So 2π is equal to 360° in this context (more specifically for the unit circle described below).

Fig. 2.1. RADIAN MEASUREMENT OF ANGLES

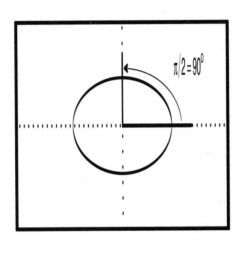

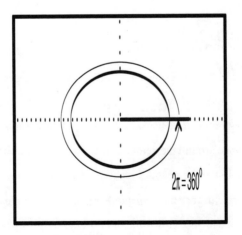

This means that we can immediately translate between radians and degrees for angles simply by multiplying a radian measure by $360/2\pi$ or a degree measure by $2\pi/360$. Figure 2.1 shows examples for angles of size $\theta = \pi/2$ and $\theta = 2\pi$, where $r = 1$ by assumption. Note that the direction is always assumed to be counterclockwise for angles specified in the positive direction.

Negative radian measurement also makes sense because sometimes it will be convenient to move in the negative, that is, clockwise direction. In addition, it is also important to remember that the system also "restarts" at 2π in this direction as well, meaning the function value becomes zero. This means that going in opposite directions has interesting implications. For instance, positive and negative angular distances have interesting equalities, such as $-\frac{3}{2}\pi = \frac{1}{2}\pi$.

The assumption of a unit-radius circle is just a convenience here. It turns out that, simply by standardizing, we can get the same angle measurement for any size circle. Suppose that r is the distance moving away from the origin and θ is the radian measurement. Then for different values of r we have wider circles but same angle, as shown in the top panel of Figure 2.2. Actually this clarification suggests a more broad coordinate definition. **Polar coordinates** are a system in which points on a plane are described by the number pair (θ, r), where θ is the radian measure and r is a distance from the origin. The bottom panel of Figure 2.2 gives some example points.

It is actually quite easy to change between polar and Cartesian coordinates. The following table gives the required transformations.

Polar to Cartesian	Cartesian to Polar
$x = r\cos(\theta)$	$\theta = \arctan(\frac{y}{x})$
$y = r\sin(\theta)$	$r = \sqrt{x^2 + y^2}$

Fig. 2.2. POLAR COORDINATES

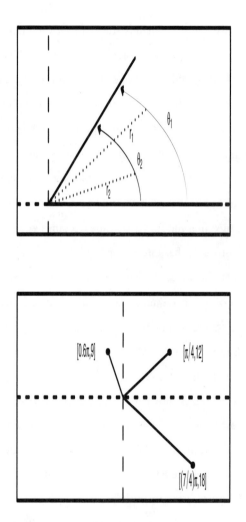

2.3 What Is Trigonometry?

This section provides a short overview of trigonometric (or circular) functions. These ideas are very basic, but sometimes people can get intimidated by the language. Others may have bad memories from high school mathematics classes, which involved for some lots of pointless memorization.

The topic of **trigonometry** started as the study of triangles. Consider the angle θ of a right triangle as shown in the figure at the right. The Greeks were interested in the ratios of the sizes of the sides of this triangle, and they noticed that these could be related to the angle of θ.

Right Triangle

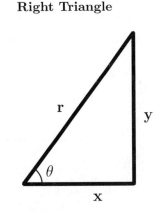

The Greeks were also very interested in the properties of right triangles in particular and considered them to be important cases (they are!). Of course the Pythagorean Theorem (a **theorem** is just a provable mathematical assertion) applies here, but there are additional relations of interest.

The basic relations involve ratios of sides related to the acute angle (i.e., θ less than 90°). There are six core definitions for the even functions cosine and secant, as well as the odd functions sine, cosecant, tangent, and cotangent, given by

$$\sin(\theta) = \frac{y}{r} \qquad\qquad \csc(\theta) = \frac{r}{y}$$

$$\cos(\theta) = \frac{x}{r} \qquad\qquad \sec(\theta) = \frac{r}{x}$$

$$\tan(\theta) = \frac{y}{x} \qquad\qquad \cot(\theta) = \frac{x}{y}.$$

The **sine** (sin), **cosine** (cos), and **tangent** (tan) functions just given are the key foundations for the rest of the trigonometric functions. Note also that these are explicitly functions of θ. That is, changes in the angle θ force changes in the size of the sides of the triangle.

There are also reciprocal relations: $\sin(\theta) = \csc(\theta)^{-1}$, $\cos(\theta) = \sec(\theta)^{-1}$, and $\tan(\theta) = \cot(\theta)^{-1}$. Also from these inverse properties we get $\sin(\theta)\csc(\theta) = 1$, $\cos(\theta)\sec(\theta) = 1$, and $\tan(\theta)\cot(\theta) = 1$. This implies that, of the six basic trigonometric functions, sine, cosine, and tangent are the more fundamental.

Fig. 2.3. A General Trigonometric Setup

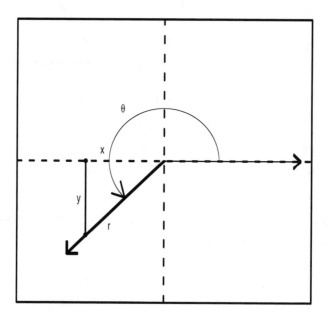

The original definition of the basic trigonometric functions turns out to be too restrictive because defining with a triangle necessarily restricts us to acute angles (we could be slightly more general by using triangles with obtuse angles). To expand the scope to a full $360°$ we need to be broad and use a full Cartesian coordinate system. Figure 2.3 shows the more general setup where the triangle defined by sweeping the angle θ counterclockwise from the positive side of the x-axis along with an r value gives the x and y distances. Now the trigonometric values are defined exactly in the way that they were in the table above except that x and y can now take on negative values.

So we can summarize values of these functions for common angular values (multiples of $45°$) in tabular form to show some repeating patterns. Note the interesting cycling pattern that is similar, yet different, for sine and cosine.

θ^o	0	45	90	135	180	225	270	315	360
$\sin(\theta)$	0	$\sqrt{2}/2$	1	$\sqrt{2}/2$	0	$-\sqrt{2}/2$	-1	$-\sqrt{2}/2$	0
$\csc(\theta)$	–	$\sqrt{2}$	1	$\sqrt{2}$	–	$-\sqrt{2}$	-1	$-\sqrt{2}$	–
$\cos(\theta)$	1	$\sqrt{2}/2$	0	$-\sqrt{2}/2$	-1	$-\sqrt{2}/2$	0	$\sqrt{2}/2$	1
$\sec(\theta)$	1	$\sqrt{2}$	–	$-\sqrt{2}$	-1	$-\sqrt{2}$	–	$\sqrt{2}$	1
$\tan(\theta)$	0	1	–	-1	0	1	–	-1	0
$\cot(\theta)$	–	1	0	-1	–	1	0	-1	–

Here the notation "–" denotes that the value is undefined and comes from a division by zero operation.

The Pythagorean Theorem gives some very useful and well-known relations between the basic trigonometric functions:

$$\sin(\theta)^2 + \cos(\theta)^2 = 1$$

$$\csc(\theta)^2 - \cot(\theta)^2 = 1$$

$$\sec(\theta)^2 - \tan(\theta)^2 = 1.$$

Addition or subtraction of angle values provides the following rules:

$$\sin(a + b) = \sin(a)\cos(b) + \cos(a)\sin(b)$$

$$\sin(a - b) = \sin(a)\cos(b) - \cos(a)\sin(b)$$

$$\cos(a + b) = \cos(a)\cos(b) - \sin(a)\sin(b)$$

$$\cos(a - b) = \cos(a)\cos(b) + \sin(a)\sin(b)$$

$$\tan(a + b) = \frac{\tan(a) + \tan(b)}{1 - \tan(a)\tan(b)}$$

$$\tan(a - b) = \frac{\tan(a) - \tan(b)}{1 + \tan(a)\tan(b)}.$$

Finally, we should mention that there are *reverse* relationships as well:

$$a = \arcsin(b), \quad \text{if } b = \sin(a), \quad \text{provided that} \quad -\frac{\pi}{2} \le a \le \frac{\pi}{2}$$

$$a = \arccos(b), \quad \text{if } b = \cos(a), \quad \text{provided that} \quad 0 \le a \le \pi$$

$$a = \arctan(b), \quad \text{if } b = \tan(a), \quad \text{provided that} \quad -\frac{\pi}{2} \le a \le \frac{\pi}{2}.$$

Confusingly, these also have alternate terminology: $\arcsin(b) = \sin^{-1}(b)$, $\arccos(b) = \cos^{-1}(b)$, and $\arctan(b) = \tan^{-1}(b)$, which can easily be confused with the inverse relationships. Furthermore, some calculators (and computer programming languages) use the equivalent terms asin, acos, and atan. So sometimes the trigonometric functions are difficult in superficial ways even when the basic ideas are simple. We will find that these trigonometric functions are useful in areas of applied calculus and spatial modeling in particular.

Fig. 2.4. BASIC TRIGONOMETRIC FUNCTION IN RADIANS

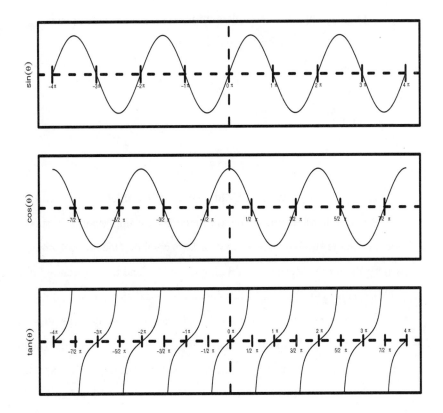

2.3.1 Radian Measures for Trigonometric Functions

Using the trigonometric functions is considerably easier and more intuitive with radians rather than degrees. It may have seemed odd that these functions "reset" at $360°$, but from what we have seen of the circle it makes sense to do this at 2π for sine and cosine or at π for tangent:

$$\sin(\theta + 2\pi) = \sin(\theta) \qquad\qquad \csc(\theta + 2\pi) = \csc(\theta)$$

$$\cos(\theta + 2\pi) = \cos(\theta) \qquad\qquad \sec(\theta + 2\pi) = \sec(\theta)$$

$$\tan(\theta + \pi) = \tan(\theta) \qquad\qquad \cot(\theta + \pi) = \cot(\theta).$$

This property means that these functions "cycle" for increasing theta values. This is illustrated in Figure 2.4.

We say that two angles are **complementary** if they sum to 90°, that is, $\pi/2$. This gives the following interesting relationships:

$$\sin\left(\frac{\pi}{2} - \theta\right) = \cos(\theta) \qquad \cos\left(\frac{\pi}{2} - \theta\right) = \sin(\theta)$$

$$\tan\left(\frac{\pi}{2} - \theta\right) = \cot(\theta) \qquad \cot\left(\frac{\pi}{2} - \theta\right) = \tan(\theta).$$

★ **Example 2.1:   An Expected Utility Model of Conflict Escalation**. One area of research where trigonometric functions are important is in spatial modeling of the utility of increasing state-level conflict. One particular model used by Bueno De Mesquita and Lalman (1986), and more recently Stam (1996), specifies the expected utility for conflict escalation radiating outward from the origin on a two-dimensional polar metric whereby θ specifies an angular direction and r specifies the intensity or stakes of the conflict. The y-axis gives Actor A's utility, where the positive side of the origin gives expected utility increasing outcomes (A continuing to fight) and the negative side of the origin gives expected utility decreasing outcomes (A withdrawing). Likewise, the x-axis gives Actor B's expected utility, where the positive side of the origin gives expected utility increasing outcomes (B continuing to fight) and the negative side of the origin gives utility decreasing outcomes (B withdrawing). Thus the value of θ determines "who wins" and "who loses," where it is possible to have both actors receive positive (or negative) expected utility. The model thus asserts that nations make conflict escalation decisions based on these expected utilities for themselves as well as those assessed for their adversary. This construction is illustrated in the top panel of Figure 2.5.

Even though the circle depiction is a very neat mnemonic about trade-offs, it does not show very well the consequences of θ to an individual actor. Now,

Fig. 2.5. VIEWS OF CONFLICT ESCALATION

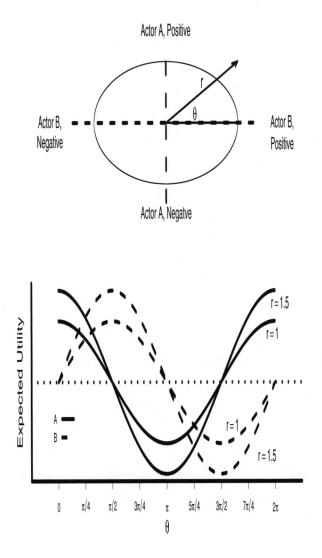

if we transform to Cartesian coordinates (using the formulas above), then we get the illustration in the bottom panel of Figure 2.5. This is helpful because now we can directly see the difference in expected utility between Actor A (solid line) and Actor B (dashed line) at some value of θ by taking the vertical distance between the curves at that x-axis point.

Since r is the parameter that controls the value of the conflict (i.e., what is at stake here may be tiny for Ecuador/Peru but huge for U.S./U.S.S.R.), then the circle in the upper panel of the figure gives the universe of possible outcomes for one scenario. The points where the circle intersects with the axes provide absolute outcomes: Somebody wins or loses completely and somebody has a zero outcome. Perhaps more intuitively, we see in the lower panel that going from $r = 1$ to $r = 1.5$ magnifies the scope of the positive or negative expected utility to A and B. Furthermore, we can now see that increasing r has different effects on the expected utility difference for differing values of θ, something that was not very apparent from the polar depiction because the circle obviously just increased in every direction.

2.3.2 Conic Sections and Some Analytical Geometry

Before we move on to more elaborate forms of analytical geometry, let us start with a reminder of the definition of a circle in analytical geometry terms. Intuitively we know that for a center c and a radius r, a circle is the set of points that are exactly r distance away from c in a two-dimensional Cartesian coordinate system. More formally:

A circle with radius $r > 0$ and center at point $[x_c, y_c]$ is defined by the quadratic, multi-variable expression

$$r^2 = (x - x_c)^2 + (y - y_c)^2.$$

This is "multivalued" because x and y both determine the function value.

The most common form is the **unit circle**, which has radius $r = 1$ and is centered at the origin ($x_c = 0, y_c = 0$). This simplifies the more general form down to merely

$$1 = x^2 + y^2.$$

Suppose we break this quadratic form out and rearrange according to

$$r^2 = (x - x_c)^2 + (y - y_c)^2$$
$$= x^2 - 2x_c x + x_c^2 + y^2 - 2y_c y + y_c^2$$

and then make the variable changes $a = -2x_c$ and $b = -2y_c$. Then

$$= x^2 + ax + \frac{a^2}{4} + y^2 + by + \frac{b^2}{4}$$
$$= x^2 + ax + y^2 + by + c,$$

defining in the last step that $c = \frac{a^2}{4} + \frac{b^2}{4} - r^2$.

Note that r, c, x_c, and y_c are all fixed, known constants. The key part of this is that r can be backed out of c above as $r = \frac{1}{2}\sqrt{a^2 + b^2 - 4c}$. Recall that r is the radius of the circle, so we can look at the size of the radius that results from choices of the constants. First note that if $a^2 + b^2 = 4c$, then the circle has no size and condenses down to a single point. On the other hand, if $a^2 + b^2 < 4c$, then the square root is a complex number (and not defined on the Cartesian system we have been working with), and therefore the shape is undefined. So the only condition that provides a circle is $a^2 + b^2 > 4c$, and thus we have a simple test. The big point here is that the equational form for a circle is always a quadratic in two variables, but this form is not sufficient to guarantee a circle with positive area.

★ **Example 2.2:** **Testing for a Circular Form**. Does this quadratic equation define a circle?

$$x^2 + y^2 - 12x + 12y + 18 = 0$$

Here $a = -12$, $b = 12$, and $c = 18$. So $a^2 + b^2 = 144 + 144 = 288$ is greater than $4c = 4 \cdot 18 = 72$, and this is therefore a circle.

2.3.2.1 The Parabola

The parabola is produced by slicing through a three-dimensional cone with a two-dimensional plane such that the plane goes through the flat bottom of the cone. Of course there is a more *mathematical* definition: A **parabola** in two dimensions is the set of points that are equidistant from a given (fixed) point and a given (fixed) line. The point is called the **focus** of the parabola, and the line is called the **directrix** of the line. Figure 2.6 shows the same parabola in two frames for a focus at $[0, p]$ and a directrix at $y = -p$, for $p = 1$. The first panel shows the points labeled and a single equidistant principle illustrated for a point on the parabola. The second frame shows a series of points on the left-hand side of the access with their corresponding equal line segments to p and d.

Fig. 2.6. CHARACTERISTICS OF A PARABOLA

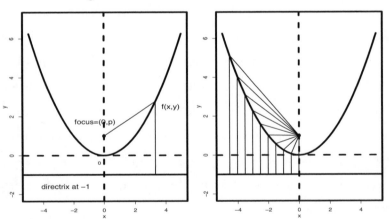

Of course there is a formula that dictates the relationship between the y-axis points and the x-axis points for the parabola:

$$y = \frac{x^2}{4p}.$$

This is a parabola facing upward and continuing toward greater positive values of y for positive values of p. If we make p negative, then the focus will be below the x-axis and the parabola will face downward. In addition, if we swap x and y in the definitional formula, then the parabola will face left or right (depending on the sign of p; see the Exercises). A more general form of a parabola is for the parabola whose focus is not on one of the two axes:

$$(y - y') = \frac{(x - x')^2}{4p},$$

which will have a focus at $[x', p + y']$ and a directrix at $y = y' - p$.

★ **Example 2.3:** **Presidential Support as a Parabola**. It is actually quite common to find parabolic relationships in political science research. Oftentimes the functional form is mentioned in an offhand way to describe a nonlinear relationship, but sometimes exact forms are fit with models. As an example of the latter case, Stimson (1976) found that early post-war presidential support scores fit a parametric curve. Presidents begin their 4 year term with large measures of popularity, which declines and then recovers before the end of their term, all in the characteristic parabolic form. Stimson took Gallup poll ratings of full presidential terms from Truman's first term to Nixon's first term and "fits" (estimates) parabolic forms that best followed the data values. Fortunately, Gallup uses the same question wording for over 30 years, allowing comparison across presidents. Using the general parabolic notation above, the estimated parameters are

	y'	x'	$1/4p$
Truman Term 1	53.37	2.25	8.85
Truman Term 2	32.01	3.13	4.28
Eisenhower Term 1	77.13	1.86	2.47
Eisenhower Term 2	68.52	2.01	1.43
Johnson Term 2	47.90	3.58	2.85
Nixon Term 1	58.26	2.60	4.61

Since y' is the lowest point in the upward facing parabola, we can use these values to readily see low ebbs in a given presidency and compare them as well. Not surprisingly, Eisenhower did the best in this regard. The corresponding parabolas are illustrated in Figure 2.7 by president. It is interesting to note that, while the forms differ considerably, the hypothesized shape bears out (Stimson gave a justification of the underlying statistical work in his article). So, regardless of political party, wartime status, economic conditions, and so on, there was a persistent parabolic phenomenon for approval ratings of presidents across the four years.

Fig. 2.7. Parabolic Presidential Popularity

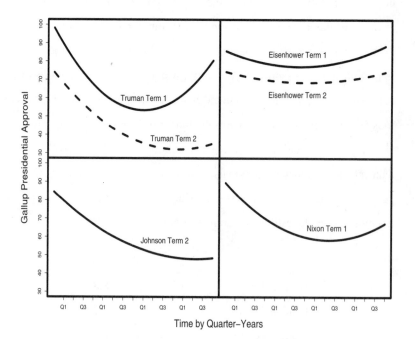

2.3.2.2 The Ellipse

Another fundamental conic section is produced by slicing a two-dimensional plane through a three-dimensional cone such that the plane *does not* cut through the flat base of the cone. More precisely, an **ellipse** in two dimensions is the set of points whose summed distance to two points is a constant: For two **foci** f_1 and f_2, each point p_i on the ellipse has $|p_i - f_1| + |p_i - f_2| = k$ (note the absolute value notation here).

Fig. 2.8. CHARACTERISTICS OF AN ELLIPSE

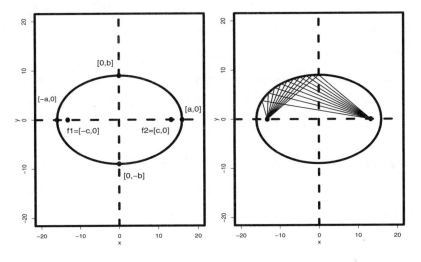

Things are much easier if the ellipse is set up to rest on the axes, but this is not a technical necessity. Suppose that we define the foci as resting on the x-axis at the points $[-c, 0]$ and $[c, 0]$. Then with the assumption $a > b$, we get the **standard form of the ellipse** from

$$\frac{x^2}{a^2} + \frac{y^2}{b^2} = 1, \text{ where } c = \sqrt{a^2 - b^2}.$$

This form is pictured in the two panels of Figure 2.8 for $a = 16, b = 9$. The first panel shows the two foci as well as the four **vertices of the ellipse** where the ellipse reaches its extremum in the two dimensions at $x = \pm 16$ and $y = \pm 9$.

The second panel shows for selected points in the upper left quadrant the line segments to the two foci. For any one of these points along the ellipse where the line segments meet, the designated summed distance of the two segments must be a constant. Can we determine this sum easily? At first this looks like a hard problem, but notice that each of the four vertices must also satisfy this condition. We can now simply use the Pythagorean Theorem and pick one of them:

$$\frac{k}{2} = \sqrt{c^2 + b^2} = \sqrt{(\sqrt{a^2 - b^2})^2 + b^2} = a.$$

Because this hypotenuse is only one-half of the required distance, we know that $k = 2a$, where a is greater than b. This also illustrates an elegant feature of the ellipse: If one picks any of the paired line segments in the second panel of Figure 2.8 and flattens them out down on the x-axis below, they will exactly join the two x-axis vertices. This is called the **major axis of the ellipse**; the other one is called, not surprisingly, the **minor axis of the ellipse**.

★ **Example 2.4:   Elliptical Voting Preferences**. One research area where ellipses are an important modeling construction is describing spatial models of preferences. Often this is done in a legislative setting as a way of quantifying the utility of alternatives for individual lawmakers. Suppose that Congress needs to vote on a budget for research and development spending that divides total possible spending between coal and petroleum. A hypothetical member of Congress is assumed to have an *ideal* spending level for each of the two projects that trades off spending in one dimension against spending in the other. As an example, the highest altitude ideal point, and therefore the mode of the preference structure, is located at $[petroleum = 0.65,\ coal = 0.35]$ on a standardized metric (i.e., dollars removed).

Figure 2.9 shows the example representative's utility preference in two ways: a three-dimensional wire-frame drawing that reveals the dimensionality now present over the petroleum/coal grid (the first panel), and a contour plot that illustrates the declining levels of utility preference, U_1, U_2, U_3 (the second panel). So the further away from $[0.65, \ 0.35]$, the less happy the individual is with any proposed bill: She has a lower returned utility of a spending level at $[0.2, 0.8]$ than at $[0.6, 0.4]$. By this means, any point outside a given contour provides less utility than all the points inside this contour, no matter what direction from the ideal point.

Fig. 2.9. MULTIDIMENSIONAL ISSUE PREFERENCE

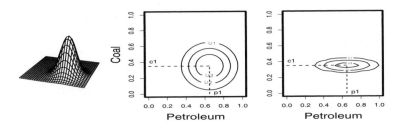

But wait a minute. Is it realistic to assume that utility declines in exactly the same way for the two dimensions? Suppose our example legislator was adamant about her preference on coal and somewhat flexible about petroleum. Then the resulting generalization of circular preferences in two dimensions would be an ellipse (third panel) that is more elongated in the petroleum direction. The fact that the ellipse is a more generalized circle can be seen by comparing the equation of a circle centered at the origin with radius 1 $(1 = x^2 + y^2)$ to the standard form of the ellipses above. If $a = b$, then $c = 0$ and there is only one focus, which would collapse the ellipse to a circle.

2.3.2.3 The Hyperbola

The third fundamental conic section comes from a different visualization. Suppose that instead of one cone we had two that were joined at the tip such that the flat planes at opposite ends were parallel. We could then take this three-dimensional setup of two cones "looking at each other" and slice through it with a plane that cuts equally through each of the flat planes for the two cones. This will produce a **hyperbola,** which is the set of points such that the ***difference*** between two foci f_1 and f_2 is a constant. We saw with the ellipse that $|p_i - f_1| + |p_i - f_2| = 2a$, but now we assert that $|p_i - f_1| - |p_i - f_2| = 2a$ for each point on the hyperbola. If the hyperbola is symmetric around the origin with open ends facing vertically (as in Figure 2.10), then $f_1 c, f_2 = -c$, and the **standard form of the hyperbola** is given by

$$\frac{y^2}{a^2} - \frac{x^2}{b^2} = 1, \text{ where } c = \sqrt{a^2 + b^2}.$$

Notice that this is similar to the equation for the ellipse except that the signs are different.

Fig. 2.10. CHARACTERISTICS OF A HYPERBOLA

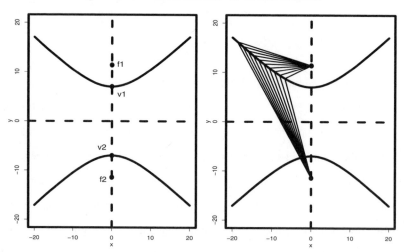

As you can see from Figure 2.10, a hyperbola is actually two separate curves in 2-space, shown here for $a = 9$ and $b = 8$ in the standard form. As with the previous two figures, the first panel shows the individual points of interest, the foci and vertexes, and the second panel shows a subset of the segments that define the hyperbola. Unfortunately these segments are not quite as visually intuitive as they are with the ellipse, because the hyperbola is defined by the difference of the two connected segments rather than the sum.

★ **Example 2.5:** **Hyperbolic Discounting in Evolutionary Psychology and Behavioral Economics**. There is a long literature that seeks to explain why people make decisions about immediate versus deferred rewards [see the review in Frederick et al. (2002)]. The classic definition of this phenomenon is that of Böm-Bawerk (1959): "Present goods have in general greater subjective value than future (and intermediate) goods of equal quantity and quality." While it seems clear that everybody prefers $100 today rather than in one year, it is not completely clear what larger value is required to induce someone to wait a year for the payment. That is, what is an appropriate discounting schedule that reflects general human preferences and perhaps accounts for differing preferences across individuals or groups. This is a question of human and social cognitive and emotional affects on economic decisions.

One way to mathematically model these preferences is with a declining curve that reflects discounted value as time increases. A person might choose to wait one week to get $120 instead of $100 but not make such a choice if the wait was one year. The basic model is attributed to Samuelson (1937), who framed these choices in discounted utility terms by specifying (roughly) a positive constant followed by a positive discount rate declining over time. This can be linear or curvilinear, depending on the theory concerned. The first (and perhaps obvious) mathematical model for such discounted utility is the exponential function

$$\phi(t) = \exp(-\beta t),$$

where t is time and β is a parameter that alters the rate of decay. This is illustrated in Figure 2.11.

Fig. 2.11. Exponential Curves

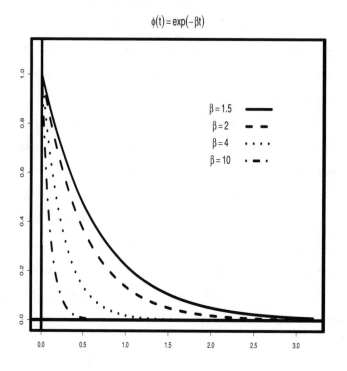

While the exponential function is simple and intuitive, it apparently does not explain discounting empirically because with only one parameter to control the shape it is not flexible enough to model observed human behavior. Recall that the exponentiation here is just raising 2.718282 to the $-\beta t$ power. Because there is nothing special about the constant, why not parameterize this as well? We can also add flexibility to the exponent by moving t down and adding a second parameter to control the power; the result is

$$\phi(t) = \pm(\gamma t)^{-\beta/\gamma}.$$

This is actually a hyperbolic functional form for $t = x$ and $\phi(t) = y$, in a more general form than we saw above. To illustrate this as simply as possible, set $\gamma = 1$, $\beta = 1$, and obtain the plot in Figure 2.12. So this is just

Fig. 2.12. DERIVED HYPERBOLA FORM

$$\phi(t) = +/-(\gamma t)^{(-\beta/\gamma)}$$

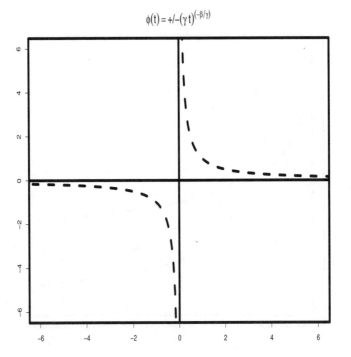

like the hyperbola that we saw before, except that it is aligned with axes such that the two curves are confined to the first and third quadrants. But wait. The phenomenon that we are interested in (discounting) is confined to $\mathfrak{R}^+$, so we only need the form in the upper right quadrant. Also, by additively placing a 1 inside the parentheses we can standardize the expression such that discounting at time zero is 1 (i.e., people do not have a reduction in utility for immediate payoff) for every pair of parameter values. Loewenstein and Prelec (1992) used the constant to make sure that the proposed hyperbolic curves all intersect at the point (0,0.3). The constant is arbitrary, and the change makes it very easy to compare different hyperbolic functions, as in Figure 2.13. Interestingly, as γ gets very small and approaches zero, the hyperbolic function above becomes the previous exponential form.

Fig. 2.13. GENERAL HYPERBOLA FORM FOR DISCOUNTING

$$\phi(t) = (1 + \gamma t)^{(-\beta/\gamma)}$$

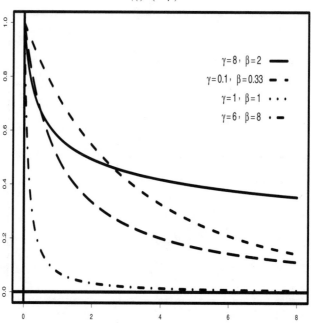

The existing literature on utility discounting over time is quite large and stretches far back in time. There seems to be a majority that have settled on the hyperbolic form as the best alternative given empirical data [see Loewenstein and Prelec (1992), Harvey (1986), and Weitzman (2001), just to name a few recent examples].

2.4 New Terminology

Exercises

2.1   For the following values of θ in radians or degrees (indicated), calculate $\sin(\theta)$, $\cos(\theta)$, and $\tan(\theta)$:

0	$\dfrac{3\pi}{2}$	$\dfrac{11\pi}{4}$	80π
$\dfrac{22}{7}$	150°	$-\dfrac{2\pi}{5}$	390°
$80,000\pi$	-4π	$3\pi + .001$	10°

2.2   Fill in the missing values below:

$$\sin\left(\frac{\pi}{4}\right) = \sin(\quad^{\circ}) = \frac{\text{opposite}}{\text{hypotenuse}} = \frac{1}{\underline{\quad}}$$

$$\cos\left(\frac{\pi}{4}\right) = \frac{\text{hypotenuse}}{\underline{\quad}} = \frac{\underline{\quad}}{\sqrt{\underline{\quad}}}$$

$$\tan\left(\frac{\pi}{4}\right) = \frac{\underline{\quad}}{\text{adjacent}} = \frac{\underline{\quad}}{\underline{\quad}}$$

2.3   Show that $\cos(\theta)\tan(\theta) = \sin(\theta)$.

2.4   Which functions, $\sin$, $\cos()$, $\tan()$, are odd functions and which are even functions?

2.5   Identify and sketch the conic sections:

$$x^2 + y^2 = 2 \qquad\qquad \frac{x^2}{9} - \frac{y^2}{4} = 1$$

$$25a^2 + 100b^2 = 1 \qquad\qquad y = 1 - \frac{z^2}{3}$$

2.6   What is the definitional formula for a parabola facing (open) to the right on a standard Cartesian coordinate system?

2.7   Draw in the same figure an ellipse with $a = 9$, $b = 4$, and a hyperbola with $a = 4$, $b = 1$. Calculate the four points of intersection.

2.8 Transform the following points in Cartesian coordinates to polar coordinates and graph:

$$[2, 0], \quad [5, 3\pi/2], \quad [-4, -\pi/6], \quad [-1, \pi/2], \quad [11, 0].$$

Now transform these points in polar coordinates to Cartesian coordinates and graph:

$$[2, 2], \quad [-3, \sqrt{3}], \quad [7, -2], \quad [0, 2\pi], \quad [-\sqrt{6}, \sqrt{6}].$$

2.9 Data analysts sometimes find it useful to transform variables into more convenient forms. For instance, data that are bounded by $[0:1]$ can sometimes be inconvenient to model due to the bounds. Some transformations that address this (and can be easily undone to revert back to the original form) are

$$\text{inverse logit: } f(x) = \log(x/(1 - x))$$

$$\text{cloglog: } f(x) = \log(-\log(1 - x))$$

$$\text{arc sine: } f(x) = \arcsin(\sqrt{x}).$$

For $x \in [0:1]$, what advantage does the arcsine transformation have? Graph each of these functions over this domain in the same graph. If you were modeling the underlying preference or utility for a dichotomous choice (0 and 1, such as a purchase or a vote), which form would you prefer? Write the inverse function to the arcsine transformation. Note: The arcsine transformation has been useful in analysis of variance (ANOVA) statistical tests when distributional assumptions are violated.

2.10 Lalman (1988) extended the idea using polar coordinates to model the conflict between two nations discussed on page 60 by defining circumstances whereby the actors escalate disputes according to the ordered pair of expected utilities: $s = \{E_i(U_{ij}), E_j(U_{ij})\}$, which define the expected utility of i against j and the expected utility of

j against i. These are plotted in polar coordinates [as in Bueno De Mesquita and Lalman (1986)], where the first utility is given along the x-axis and the second along the y-axis. As an example, Lalman gave the following probabilities of escalation by the two actors:

$$p(Esc_i) = 0.4(r\cos\theta) + 0.5 \qquad p(Esc_j) = 0.4(r\sin\theta) + 0.5,$$

where r is the radius and θ is the angle in polar coordinates. Lalman then gives the following event probabilities based on these:

$$p(\text{War}) = p(Esc_i)p(Esc_j)$$
$$p(\text{Violence}) = 1 - (1 - p(Esc_i))(1 - p(Esc_j))$$
$$p(\text{Intervention}) = (1 - p(Esc_i))p(Esc_j)$$
$$+ p(Esc_i)(1 - p(Esc_j)).$$

Plot these functions in the same graph along the continuum from 0 to 2π with $r = 1$, with Lalman's regions shown below.

Fig. 2.14. CONFLICT PROBABILITIES

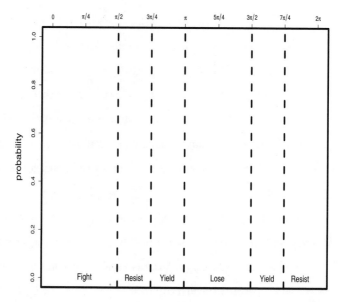

Using your plot, answer the following questions:

(a) How do you interpret his differing substantive regions along the x-axis?

(b) Is there a region where the probability of violence is high but the probability of war is low?

(c) Why is the probability of intervention high in the two regions where the probability of war is low?

(d) What happens when $r < 1$? How do you interpret this substantively in terms of international politics?

2.11   Suppose you had an ellipse enclosed within a circle according to:

$$\text{ellipse:} \quad \frac{x^2}{a^2} + \frac{y^2}{b^2} = 1, \quad a > b$$
$$\text{circle:} \quad x^2 + y^2 = a^2.$$

What is the area of the ellipse?

2.12   Fourier analysis redefines a function in terms of sine and cosine functions by assuming a periodicity in the data. This is a useful tool in time series analysis where reoccuring effects are of interest. The basic Fourier function is given by

$$f(x) = \frac{1}{2}a_0 + \sum_{n=1}^{\infty}(a_n \cos(nx) + b_n \sin(nx)),$$

where the a and b values are provided constants (some of which can be zero). Show that the Fourier series

$$g(x) = \frac{8}{\pi^2}\sin(\pi x) - \frac{8}{3^2\pi^2}\sin(3\pi x)$$
$$+ \frac{8}{5^2\pi^2}\sin(5\pi x) - \frac{8}{7^2\pi^2}\sin(7\pi x) + \frac{8}{9^2\pi^2}\sin(9\pi x)$$
$$- \frac{8}{11^2\pi^2}\sin(11\pi x) + \frac{8}{13^2\pi^2}\sin(13\pi x) - \frac{8}{15^2\pi^2}\sin(15\pi x)$$

is an approximation of the triangular function

$$f(x) = \begin{cases} 2x \\ 2 - 2x. \end{cases}$$

2.13   Yeats, Irons, and Rhoades (1975) found that annual deposit growth for
        48 commercial banks can be modeled by the function:

$$\frac{D_{t+1}}{D_t} = 1.172 - 0.125t^{-1} + 1.135t^{-2},$$

where D is year-end deposits and t is years. Graph this equation for
20 years and identify the form of the curve.

2.14   Southwood (1978) was concerned with the interpretation (and misin-
        terpretation) of interaction effects in sociological models. These are
        models where explanatory factors are assumed to contribute to some
        outcome in a manner beyond additive forms. For example, a family's
        socioeconomic status is often assumed to interact with the child's in-
        telligence to affect occupational or educational attainment in a way
        that is beyond the simple additive contribution of either. In explain-
        ing interaction between two such contributing variables ($X1$ and $X2$
        here), Southwood looked at the relations in Figure 2.15 below.

        It turns out that the value of θ is critical to making statements about
        the interactivity of $X1$ and $X2$. Fill in the missing values from the
        following statements where two capital letters indicates the length of
        the associate segment:

        (a) $OR = QR$___θ.

        (b) $OR = $___$\cot\theta$.

        (c) $QP = OT - OR = X1\cot$_____.

        (d) $SP = X1$___$\theta - X2$___θ.

Fig. 2.15. DERIVATION OF THE DISTANCE

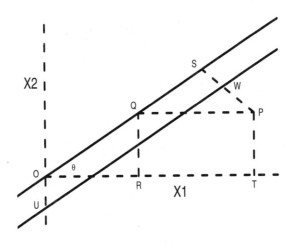

Give the equation for the line along OS, and give the equation for the line along UW in terms of values of $X1$, θ, and SP (i.e., the length of the segment from S to P).

2.15 In studying the labor supply of nurses, Manchester (1976) defined ν as the wage and $H(\nu)$ as the units of work per time period (omitting a constant term, which is unimportant to the argument). He gave two possible explanatory functions: $H(\nu) = a\nu^2 + b\nu$ with constants $a < 0, b >$, and $H(\nu) = a + b/\nu$ with constants a unconstrained, $b < 0$. Which of these is a hyperbolic function? What is the form of the other?

3

Linear Algebra: Vectors, Matrices, and Operations

3.1 Objectives

This chapter covers the *mechanics* of vector and matrix manipulation and the next chapter approaches the topic from a more theoretical and conceptual perspective. The objective for readers of this chapter is not only to learn the mechanics of performing algebraic operations on these mathematical forms but also to start seeing them as organized collections of numerical values where the manner in which they are put together provides additional mathematical information. The best way to do this is to perform the operations oneself. Linear algebra is fun. Really! In general, the mechanical operations are nothing more than simple algebraic steps that anybody can perform: addition, subtraction, multiplication, and division. The only real abstraction required is "seeing" the rectangular nature of the objects in the sense of visualizing operations at a high level rather than getting buried in the algorithmic details.

When one reads high visibility journals in the social sciences, matrix algebra (a near synonym) is ubiquitous. Why is that? Simply because it lets us express extensive models in quite readable notation. Consider the following linear statistical model specification [from real work, Powers and Cox (1997)]. They are relating political blame to various demographic and regional political variables:

for $i = 1$ to n, $(BLAMEFIRST)Y_i =$

$$\beta_0 + \beta_1 CHANGELIV + \beta_2 BLAMECOMM + \beta_3 INCOME$$

$$+ \beta_4 FARMER + \beta_5 OWNER + \beta_6 BLUESTATE$$

$$+ \beta_7 WHITESTATE + \beta_8 FORMMCOMM + \beta_9 AGE$$

$$+ \beta_{10} SQAGE + \beta_{11} SEX + \beta_{12} SIZEPLACE$$

$$+ \beta_{13} EDUC + \beta_{14} FINHS + \beta_{15} ED * HS$$

$$+ \beta_{16} RELIG + \beta_{17} NATION + E_i$$

This expression is way too complicated to be useful! It would be easy for a reader interested in the political argument to get lost in the notation. In matrix algebra form this is simply $\mathbf{Y} = \mathbf{X}\beta + \epsilon$. In fact, even for very large datasets and very large model specifications (many data variables of interest), this form is exactly the same; we simply indicate the size of these objects. This is not just a convenience (although it *really is* convenient). Because we can notate large groups of numbers in an easy-to-read structural form, we can concentrate more on the theoretically interesting properties of the analysis.

While this chapter provides many of the foundations for working with matrices in social sciences, there is one rather technical omission that some readers may want to worry about later. All linear algebra is based on properties that define a **field**. Essentially this means that logical inconsistencies that could have otherwise resulted from routine calculations have been precluded. Interested readers are referred to Billingsley (1995), Chung (2000), or Grimmett and Stirzaker (1992).

3.2 Working with Vectors

Vector. A vector is just a serial listing of numbers where the order matters. So we can store the first four positive integers in a single vector, which can be

a row vector: $\mathbf{v} = [1, 2, 3, 4]$,   or a column vector: $\mathbf{v} = \begin{bmatrix} 1 \\ 2 \\ 3 \\ 4 \end{bmatrix}$,

where $\mathbf{v}$ is the name for this new object. Order matters in the sense that the two vectors above are different, for instance, from

$$\mathbf{v}^* = [4, 3, 2, 1], \qquad \mathbf{v}^* = \begin{bmatrix} 4 \\ 2 \\ 3 \\ 1 \end{bmatrix}.$$

It is a convention that vectors are designated in bold type and individual values, *scalars*, are designated in regular type. Thus $\mathbf{v}$ is a vector with elements v_1, v_2, v_3, v_4, and v would be some *other* scalar quantity. This gets a little confusing where vectors are themselves indexed: $\mathbf{v}_1, \mathbf{v}_2, \mathbf{v}_3, \mathbf{v}_4$ would indicate four *vectors*, not four scalars. Usually, however, authors are quite clear about which form they mean.

Substantively it does not matter whether we consider a vector to be of column or row form, but it does matter when performing some operations. Also, some disciplines (notably economics) tend to default to the column form. In the row form, it is equally common to see spacing used instead of commas as delimiters: $[1\ 2\ 3\ 4]$. Also, the contents of these vectors can be integers, rational or irrational numbers, and even complex numbers; there are no restrictions.

So what kinds of operations can we do with vectors? The basic operands are very straightforward: addition and subtraction of vectors as well as multiplication and division by a scalar. The following examples use the vectors $\mathbf{u} = [3, 3, 3, 3]$ and $\mathbf{v} = [1, 2, 3, 4]$

★ **Example 3.1:   Vector Addition Calculation.**

$$\mathbf{u} + \mathbf{v} = [u_1 + v_1, u_2 + v_2, u_3 + v_3, u_4 + v_4] = [4, 5, 6, 7].$$

★ **Example 3.2:**   **Vector Subtraction Calculation.**

$$\mathbf{u} - \mathbf{v} = [u_1 - v_1, u_2 - v_2, u_3 - v_3, u_4 - v_4] = [2, 1, 0, -1].$$

★ **Example 3.3:**   **Scalar Multiplication Calculation.**

$$3 \times \mathbf{v} = [3 \times v_1, 3 \times v_2, 3 \times v_3, 3 \times v_4] = [3, 6, 9, 12].$$

★ **Example 3.4:**   **Scalar Division Calculation.**

$$\mathbf{v} \div 3 = [v_1/3, v_2/3, v_3/3, v_4/3] = \left[\frac{1}{3}, \frac{2}{3}, 1, \frac{4}{3}\right].$$

So operations with scalars are performed on every vector element in the same way. Conversely, the key issue with addition or subtraction between two vectors is that the operation is applied only to the corresponding vector elements as pairs: the first vector elements together, the second vector elements together, and so on. There is one concern, however. With this scheme, *the vectors have to be exactly the same size* (same number of elements). This is called **conformable** in the sense that the first vector must be of a size that conforms with the second vector; otherwise they are (predictably) called **nonconformable**. In the examples above both $\mathbf{u}$ and $\mathbf{v}$ are 1×4 (row) vectors (alternatively called length $k = 4$ vectors), meaning that they have one row and four columns. Sometimes size is denoted beneath the vectors:

$$\underset{1\times 4}{\mathbf{u}} + \underset{1\times 4}{\mathbf{v}}.$$

It should then be obvious that there is no logical way of adding a 1×4 vector to a 1×5 vector. Note also that this is not a practical consideration with scalar multiplication or division as seen above, because we apply the scalar identically to each element of the vector when multiplying: $s(u_1, u_2, \ldots, u_k) = (su_1, su_2, \ldots, su_k)$.

There are a couple of "special" vectors that are frequently used. These are **1** and **0**, which contain all 1's or 0's, respectively. As well shall soon see, there are a larger number of "special" matrices that have similarly important characteristics.

It is easy to summarize the formal properties of the basic vector operations. Consider the vectors **u**, **v**, **w**, which are identically sized, and the scalars s and t. The following intuitive properties hold.

Elementary Formal Properties of Vector Algebra

$\rightarrowtail$ Commutative Property $\mathbf{u} + \mathbf{v} = (\mathbf{v} + \mathbf{u})$

$\rightarrowtail$ Additive Associative Property $(\mathbf{u} + \mathbf{v}) + \mathbf{w} = \mathbf{u} + (\mathbf{v} + \mathbf{w})$

$\rightarrowtail$ Vector Distributive Property $s(\mathbf{u} + \mathbf{v}) = s\mathbf{u} + s\mathbf{v}$

$\rightarrowtail$ Scalar Distributive Property $(s + t)\mathbf{u} = s\mathbf{u} + t\mathbf{u}$

$\rightarrowtail$ Zero Property $\mathbf{u} + \mathbf{0} = \mathbf{u} \Longleftrightarrow \mathbf{u} - \mathbf{u} = \mathbf{0}$

$\rightarrowtail$ Zero Multiplicative Property $0\mathbf{u} = \mathbf{0}$

$\rightarrowtail$ Unit Rule $1\mathbf{u} = \mathbf{u}$

★ **Example 3.5:   Illustrating Basic Vector Calculations.** Here is a numerical case that shows several of the properties listed above. Define $s = 3$, $t = 1$, $\mathbf{u} = [2, 4, 8]$, and $\mathbf{v} = [9, 7, 5]$. Then:

$(s+t)(\mathbf{v}+\mathbf{u})$	$s\mathbf{v}+t\mathbf{v}+s\mathbf{u}+t\mathbf{u}$
$(3+1)([9,7,5]+[2,4,8])$	$3[9,7,5]+1[9,7,5]+3[2,4,8]+1[2,4,8]$
$4[11,11,13]$	$[27,21,15]+[9,7,5]+[6,12,24]+[2,4,8]$
$[44,44,52]$	$[44,44,52]$

Multiplication of vectors is not quite so straightforward, and there are actually different forms of multiplication to make matters even more confusing. We will start with the two most important and save some of the other forms for the last section of this chapter.

Vector Inner Product. The *inner product*, also called the **dot product**, of two vectors, results in a scalar (and so it is also called the **scalar product**). The inner product of two conformable vectors of arbitrary length k is the sum of the item-by-item products:

$$\mathbf{u} \cdot \mathbf{v} = [u_1v_1 + u_2v_2 + \cdots u_kv_k] = \sum_{i=1}^{k} u_iv_i.$$

It might be somewhat surprising to see the return of the summation notation here (Σ, as described on page 11), but it makes a lot of sense since running through the two vectors is just a mechanical additive process. For this reason, it is relatively common, though possibly confusing, to see vector (and later matrix) operations expressed in summation notation.

★ **Example 3.6:** **Simple Inner Product Calculation**. A numerical example of an inner product multiplication is given by

$$\mathbf{u} \cdot \mathbf{v} = [3,3,3] \cdot [1,2,3] = [3 \cdot 1 + 3 \cdot 2 + 3 \cdot 3] = 18.$$

When the inner product of two vectors is zero, we say that the vectors are **orthogonal**, which means they are at a right angle to each other (we will be more visual about this in Chapter 4). The notation for the orthogonality of two vectors is $\mathbf{u} \perp \mathbf{v}$ iff $\mathbf{u} \cdot \mathbf{v} = 0$. As an example of orthogonality, consider $\mathbf{u} = [1, 2, -3]$, and $\mathbf{v} = [1, 1, 1]$. As with the more basic addition and subtraction or scalar operations, there are formal properties for inner products:

Inner Product Formal Properties of Vector Algebra

⟼ Commutative Property $\mathbf{u} \cdot \mathbf{v} = \mathbf{v} \cdot \mathbf{u}$

⟼ Associative Property $s(\mathbf{u} \cdot \mathbf{v}) = (s\mathbf{u}) \cdot \mathbf{v} = \mathbf{u} \cdot (s\mathbf{v})$

⟼ Distributive Property $(\mathbf{u} + \mathbf{v}) \cdot \mathbf{w} = \mathbf{u} \cdot \mathbf{w} + \mathbf{v} \cdot \mathbf{w}$

⟼ Zero Property $\mathbf{u} \cdot \mathbf{0} = 0$

⟼ Unit Rule $1\mathbf{u} = \mathbf{u}$

★ **Example 3.7:**   **Vector Inner Product Calculations**. This example demonstrates the first three properties above. Define $s = 5$, $\mathbf{u} = [2, 3, 1]$, $\mathbf{v} = [4, 4, 4]$, and $\mathbf{w} = [-1, 3, -4]$. Then:

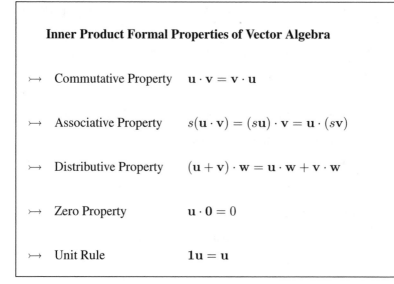

$s(\mathbf{u} + \mathbf{v}) \cdot \mathbf{w}$	$s\mathbf{v} \cdot \mathbf{w} + s\mathbf{u} \cdot \mathbf{w}$
$5([2,3,1] + [4,4,4]) \cdot [-1,3,-4]$	$5[4,4,4] \cdot [-1,3,-4]$
	$+5[2,3,1] \cdot [-1,3,-4]$
$5([6,7,5]) \cdot [-1,3,-4]$	$[20,20,20] \cdot [-1,3,-4]$
	$+[10,15,5] \cdot [-1,3,-4]$
$[30,35,25] \cdot [-1,3,-4]$	$-40 + 15$
-25	-25

Vector Cross Product. The *cross product* of two vectors (sometimes called the **outer product**, although this term is better reserved for a slightly different operation; see the distinction below) is slightly more involved than the inner product, in both calculation and interpretation. This is mostly because the result is a vector instead of a scalar. Mechanically, the cross product of two conformable vectors of length $k = 3$ is

$$\mathbf{u} \times \mathbf{v} = [u_2 v_3 - u_3 v_2, u_3 v_1 - u_1 v_3, u_1 v_2 - u_2 v_1],$$

meaning that the first element is a difference equation that leaves out the first elements of the original two vectors, and the second and third elements proceed accordingly. In the more general sense, we perform a series of "leave one out" operations that is more extensive than above because the suboperations are themselves cross products.

Fig. 3.1. VECTOR CROSS PRODUCT ILLUSTRATION

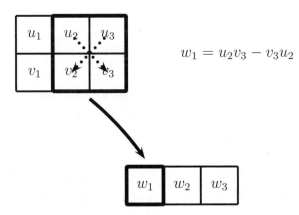

$$w_1 = u_2 v_3 - v_3 u_2$$

Figure 3.1 gives the intuition behind this product. First the $\mathbf{u}$ and $\mathbf{v}$ vectors are stacked on top of each other in the upper part of the illustration. The process of calculating the first vector value of the cross product, which we will call w_1, is done by "crossing" the elements in the solid box: $u_2 v_3$ indicated by the first arrow and $u_3 v_2$ indicated by the second arrow. Thus we see the result for

Fig. 3.2. THE RIGHT-HAND RULE ILLUSTRATED

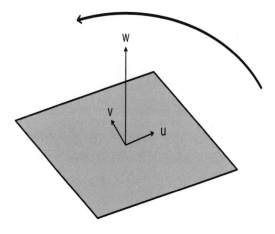

w_1 as a difference between these two individual components. This is actually the ***determinant*** of the 2×2 submatrix, which is an important principle considered in some detail in Chapter 4.

Interestingly, the resulting vector from a cross product is orthogonal to both of the original vectors in the direction of the so-called "right-hand rule." This handy rule says that if you hold your hand as you would when hitchhiking, the curled fingers make up the original vectors and the thumb indicates the direction of the orthogonal vector that results from a cross product. In Figure 3.2 you can imagine your right hand resting on the plane with the fingers curling to the left ($\circlearrowleft$) and the thumb facing upward.

For vectors $\mathbf{u}, \mathbf{v}, \mathbf{w}$, the cross product properties are given by

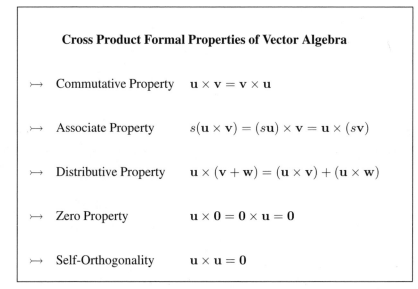

Cross Product Formal Properties of Vector Algebra

$\rightarrowtail$ Commutative Property $\mathbf{u} \times \mathbf{v} = \mathbf{v} \times \mathbf{u}$

$\rightarrowtail$ Associate Property $s(\mathbf{u} \times \mathbf{v}) = (s\mathbf{u}) \times \mathbf{v} = \mathbf{u} \times (s\mathbf{v})$

$\rightarrowtail$ Distributive Property $\mathbf{u} \times (\mathbf{v} + \mathbf{w}) = (\mathbf{u} \times \mathbf{v}) + (\mathbf{u} \times \mathbf{w})$

$\rightarrowtail$ Zero Property $\mathbf{u} \times \mathbf{0} = \mathbf{0} \times \mathbf{u} = \mathbf{0}$

$\rightarrowtail$ Self-Orthogonality $\mathbf{u} \times \mathbf{u} = \mathbf{0}$

★ **Example 3.8:**   **Cross Product Calculation**. Returning to the simple numerical example from before, we now calculate the cross product instead of the inner product:

$$\mathbf{u} \times \mathbf{v} = [3, 3, 3] \times [1, 2, 3]$$
$$= [(3)(3) - (3)(2), (3)(1) - (3)(3), (3)(2) - (3)(1)] = [3, -6, 3].$$

We can then check the orthogonality as well:

$$[3, 3, 3] \cdot [3, -6, 3] = 0 \qquad [1, 2, 3] \cdot [3, -6, 3] = 0.$$

Sometimes the distinction between row vectors and column vectors is important. While it is often glossed over, vector multiplication should be done in a conformable manner with regard to multiplication (as opposed to addition discussed above) where a row vector multiplies a column vector such that their adjacent "sizes" match: a $(1 \times k)$ vector multiplying a $(k \times 1)$ vector for k

elements in each. This operation is now an inner product:

$$
[v_1, v_2, \ldots, v_k] \times \begin{bmatrix} u_1 \\ u_2 \\ \vdots \\ u_k \end{bmatrix}.
$$
$$
\underset{1 \times k}{} \qquad \underset{k \times 1}{}
$$

This adjacency above comes from the k that denotes the columns of **v** and the k that denotes the rows of **u** and manner by which they are next to each other. Thus an inner product multiplication operation is implied here, even if it is not directly stated. An outer product would be implied by this type of adjacency:

$$
\begin{bmatrix} u_1 \\ u_2 \\ \vdots \\ u_k \end{bmatrix} \times [v_1, v_2, \ldots, v_k],
$$
$$
\underset{k \times 1}{} \qquad \underset{1 \times k}{}
$$

where the 1's are next to each other. So the cross product of two vectors is a vector, and the outer product of two conformable vectors is a matrix: a rectangular grouping of numbers that generalizes the vectors we have been working with up until now. This distinction helps us to keep track of the objective. Mechanically, this is usually easy. To be completely explicit about these operations we can also use the **vector transpose**, which simply converts a row vector to a column vector, or vice versa, using the apostrophe notation:

$$
\begin{bmatrix} u_1 \\ u_2 \\ \vdots \\ u_k \end{bmatrix}' = [u_1, u_2, \ldots, u_k], \qquad [u_1, u_2, \ldots, u_k]' = \begin{bmatrix} u_1 \\ u_2 \\ \vdots \\ u_k \end{bmatrix}.
$$

This is essentially book-keeping with vectors and we will not worry about it extensively in this text, but as we will see shortly it is important with matrix operations. Also, note that the order of multiplication now matters.

★ **Example 3.9:** **Outer Product Calculation**. Once again using the simple numerical forms, we now calculate the outer product instead of the cross product:

$$
\mathbf{u} \times \mathbf{v} = \begin{bmatrix} 1 \\ 2 \\ 3 \end{bmatrix} [3, 3, 3] = \begin{bmatrix} 3 & 3 & 3 \\ 6 & 6 & 6 \\ 9 & 9 & 9 \end{bmatrix}.
$$

And to show that order matters, consider:

$$
\mathbf{u} \times \mathbf{v} = \begin{bmatrix} 3 \\ 3 \\ 3 \end{bmatrix} [1, 2, 3] = \begin{bmatrix} 3 & 6 & 9 \\ 3 & 6 & 9 \\ 3 & 6 & 9 \end{bmatrix}.
$$

3.2.1 Vector Norms

Measuring the "length" of vectors is a surprisingly nuanced topic. This is because there are different ways to consider Cartesian length in the dimension implied by the size (number of elements) of the vector. It is obvious, for instance, that $(5, 5, 5)$ should be considered longer than $(1, 1, 1)$, but it is not clear whether $(4, 4, 4)$ is longer than $(3, -6, 3)$. The standard version of the **vector norm** for an n-length vector is given by

$$
\|\mathbf{v}\| = (v_1^2 + v_2^2 + \cdots + v_n^2)^{\frac{1}{2}} = (\mathbf{v}' \cdot \mathbf{v})^{\frac{1}{2}}.
$$

In this way, the vector norm can be thought of as the distance of the vector from the origin. Using the formula for $\|\mathbf{v}\|$ we can now calculate the vector norm for $(4, 4, 4)$ and $(3, -6, 3)$:

$$
\|(4, 4, 4)\| = \sqrt{4^2 + 4^2 + 4^2} = 6.928203
$$
$$
\|(3, -6, 3)\| = \sqrt{3^2 + (-6)^2 + 3^2} = 7.348469.
$$

So the second vector is actually longer by this measure. Consider the following properties of the vector norm (notice the reoccurrence of the dot product in the Multiplication Form):

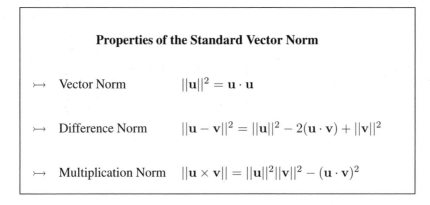

★ **Example 3.10:   Difference Norm Calculation**. As an illustration of the second property above we now include a numerical demonstration. Suppose $\mathbf{u} = [-10, 5]$ and $\mathbf{v} = [3, 3]$. Then:

$||\mathbf{u} - \mathbf{v}||^2$	$||\mathbf{u}||^2 - 2(\mathbf{u} \cdot \mathbf{v}) + ||\mathbf{v}||^2$
$|| [-10, 5] - [3, 3] ||^2$	$|| [-10, 5] ||^2 - 2([-10, 5] \cdot [3, 3]) + || [3, 3] ||^2$
$|| [-13, 2] ||^2$	$(100) + (25) - 2(-30 + 15) + (9) + (9)$
$169 + 4$	$125 + 30 + 18$
173	173

★ **Example 3.11:   Multiplication Norm Calculation**. The third property is also easy to demonstrate numerically. Suppose $\mathbf{u} = [-10, 5, 1]$ and $\mathbf{v} = [3, 3, 3]$. Then:

$\|\mathbf{u} \times \mathbf{v}\|$	$\|\mathbf{u}\|^2\|\mathbf{v}\|^2 - (\mathbf{u} \cdot \mathbf{v})^2$
$\|[-10, 5, 1] \times [3, 3, 3]\|$	$\|[-10, 5, 1]\|^2\|[3, 3, 3]\|^2$
	$-([-10, 5, 1] \cdot [3, 3, 3])^2$
$\|[(15) - (3), (3) - (-30), (-30) - (15)]\|$	$((100 + 25 + 1)(9 + 9 + 9)$
	$-(-30 + 15 + 3)^2$
$(144) + (1089) + (2025)$	$(3402 - 144)$
3258	3258

Interestingly, norming can also be applied to find the n-dimensional distance between the endpoints of two vectors starting at the origin with a variant of the Pythagorean Theorem known as the **law of cosines**:

$$\|\mathbf{v} - \mathbf{w}\|^2 = \|\mathbf{v}\|^2 + \|\mathbf{w}\|^2 - 2\|\mathbf{v}\|\|\mathbf{w}\| \cos\theta,$$

where θ is the angle from the $\mathbf{w}$ vector to the $\mathbf{v}$ vector measured in radians. This is also called the cosine rule and leads to the property that $\cos(\theta) = \frac{\mathbf{vw}}{\|\mathbf{v}\|\|\mathbf{w}\|}$.

★ **Example 3.12:** **Votes in the House of Commons.** Casstevens (1970) looked at legislative cohesion in the British House of Commons. Prime Minister David Lloyd George claimed on April 9, 1918 that the French Army was stronger on January 1, 1918 than on January 1, 1917 (a statement that generated considerable controversy). Subsequently the leader of the Liberal Party moved that a select committee be appointed to investigate claims by the military that George was incorrect. The resulting motion was defeated by the following vote: Liberal Party 98 yes, 71 no; Labour Party 9 yes, 15 no; Conservative Party 1 yes, 206 no; others 0 yes, 3 no. The difficult in analyzing this vote is the fact that 267 Members of Parliament (MPs) did not vote. So do we include them in the denominator when making claims about voting patterns? Casstevens says no because large numbers of abstentions mean that such indicators are misleading. He alternatively looked at party cohesion for the two large parties as vector norms:

$$\|L\| = \|(98, 71)\| = 121.0165$$

$$\|C\| = \|(1, 206)\| = 206.0024.$$

From this we get the obvious conclusion that the Conservatives are more cohesive because their vector has greater magnitude. More interestingly, we can contrast the two parties by calculating the angle between these two vectors (in radians) using the cosine rule:

$$\theta = \arccos\left[\frac{(98, 71) \cdot ((1, 206)}{121.070 \times 206.002}\right] = 0.9389,$$

which is about 54 degrees. Recall that arccos is the inverse function to cos. It is hard to say exactly how dramatic this angle is, but if we were analyzing a series of votes in a legislative body, this type of summary statistic would facilitate comparisons.

Actually, the norm used above is the most commonly used form of a **p-norm**:

$$\|\mathbf{v}\|_p = (|v_1|^p + |v_2|^p + \cdots + |v_n|^p)^{\frac{1}{p}}, \ p \geq 0,$$

where $p = 2$ so far. Other important cases include $p = 1$ and $p = \infty$:

$$\|\mathbf{v}\|_\infty = \max_{1 \leq i \leq n} |x_i|,$$

that is, just the maximum vector value. Whenever a vector has a p-norm of 1, it is called a **unit vector**. In general, if p is left off the norm, then one can safely assume that it is the $p = 2$ form discussed above. Vector p-norms have the following properties:

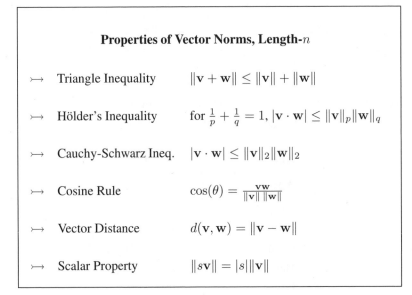

Properties of Vector Norms, Length-n

↦ Triangle Inequality $\quad \|\mathbf{v} + \mathbf{w}\| \leq \|\mathbf{v}\| + \|\mathbf{w}\|$

↦ Hölder's Inequality $\quad$ for $\frac{1}{p} + \frac{1}{q} = 1$, $|\mathbf{v} \cdot \mathbf{w}| \leq \|\mathbf{v}\|_p \|\mathbf{w}\|_q$

↦ Cauchy-Schwarz Ineq. $\quad |\mathbf{v} \cdot \mathbf{w}| \leq \|\mathbf{v}\|_2 \|\mathbf{w}\|_2$

↦ Cosine Rule $\quad \cos(\theta) = \frac{\mathbf{v}\mathbf{w}}{\|\mathbf{v}\|\,\|\mathbf{w}\|}$

↦ Vector Distance $\quad d(\mathbf{v}, \mathbf{w}) = \|\mathbf{v} - \mathbf{w}\|$

↦ Scalar Property $\quad \|s\mathbf{v}\| = |s|\,\|\mathbf{v}\|$

★ **Example 3.13:** **Hölder's Inequality Calculation.** As a revealing mechanical demonstration that Hölders' Inequality holds, set $p = 3$ and $q = 3/2$
for the vectors $\mathbf{v} = [-1, 3]$ and $\mathbf{w} = [2, 2]$, respectively. Hölder's Inequality
uses $|\mathbf{v} \cdot \mathbf{w}|$ to denote the absolute value of the dot product. Then:

$$\|\mathbf{v}\|_3 = (|-1|^3 + |3|^3)^{\frac{1}{3}} = 3.036589$$

$$\|\mathbf{w}\|_3 = (|2|^{\frac{3}{2}} + |2|^{\frac{3}{2}})^{\frac{2}{3}} = 3.174802$$

$$|\mathbf{v} \cdot \mathbf{w}| = |(-1)(2) + (3)(2)| = 4 < (3.036589)(3.174802) = 9.640569.$$

★ **Example 3.14:** **The Political Economy of Taxation.** While taxation is
known to be an effective policy tool for democratic governments, it is also
a very difficult political solution for many politicians because it can be un-
popular and controversial. Swank and Steinmo (2002) looked at factors that
lead to changes in tax policies in "advanced capitalist" democracies with
the idea that factors like internationalization of economies, political pressure

from budgets, and within-country economic factors are influential. They found that governments have a number of constraints on their ability to enact significant changes in tax rates, even when there is pressure to increase economic efficiency.

As part of this study the authors provided a total taxation from labor and consumption as a percentage of GDP in the form of two vectors: one for 1981 and another for 1995. These are reproduced as

Nation	1981	1995
Australia	30	31
Austria	44	42
Belgium	45	46
Canada	35	37
Denmark	45	51
Finland	38	46
France	42	44
Germany	38	39
Ireland	33	34
Italy	31	41
Japan	26	29
Netherlands	44	44
New Zealand	34	38
Norway	49	46
Sweden	50	50
Switzerland	31	34
United Kingdom	36	36
United States	29	28

A natural question to ask is, how much have taxation rates changed over the 14-year period for these countries collectively? The difference in mean averages, 38 versus 40, is not terribly revealing because it "washes out" important differences since some countries increased and other decreased. That is, what does a 5% difference in average change in total taxation over GDP say about how these countries changed as a group when some countries changed very little and some made considerable changes? Furthermore, when changes go in opposite directions it lowers the overall sense of an effect. In other words, summaries like averages are not good measures when we want some sense of net change.

One way of assessing total country change is employing the difference norm to compare aggregate vector difference.

$$\|t_{1995} - t_{1981}\|^2 = t'_{1995} \cdot t_{1995} - 2(t'_{1995} \cdot t_{1981}) + t'_{1981} \cdot t_{1981}$$

$$=
\begin{bmatrix} 30 \\ 44 \\ 45 \\ 35 \\ 45 \\ 38 \\ 42 \\ 38 \\ 33 \\ 31 \\ 26 \\ 44 \\ 34 \\ 49 \\ 50 \\ 31 \\ 36 \\ 29 \end{bmatrix}'
\cdot
\begin{bmatrix} 30 \\ 44 \\ 45 \\ 35 \\ 45 \\ 38 \\ 42 \\ 38 \\ 33 \\ 31 \\ 26 \\ 44 \\ 34 \\ 49 \\ 50 \\ 31 \\ 36 \\ 29 \end{bmatrix}
- 2
\begin{bmatrix} 30 \\ 44 \\ 45 \\ 35 \\ 45 \\ 38 \\ 42 \\ 38 \\ 33 \\ 31 \\ 26 \\ 44 \\ 34 \\ 49 \\ 50 \\ 31 \\ 36 \\ 29 \end{bmatrix}'
\cdot
\begin{bmatrix} 31 \\ 42 \\ 46 \\ 37 \\ 51 \\ 46 \\ 44 \\ 39 \\ 34 \\ 41 \\ 29 \\ 44 \\ 38 \\ 46 \\ 50 \\ 34 \\ 36 \\ 28 \end{bmatrix}
+
\begin{bmatrix} 31 \\ 42 \\ 46 \\ 37 \\ 51 \\ 46 \\ 44 \\ 39 \\ 34 \\ 41 \\ 29 \\ 44 \\ 38 \\ 46 \\ 50 \\ 34 \\ 36 \\ 28 \end{bmatrix}'
\cdot
\begin{bmatrix} 31 \\ 42 \\ 46 \\ 37 \\ 51 \\ 46 \\ 44 \\ 39 \\ 34 \\ 41 \\ 29 \\ 44 \\ 38 \\ 46 \\ 50 \\ 34 \\ 36 \\ 28 \end{bmatrix}$$

$$= 260$$

So what does this mean? For comparison, we can calculate the same vector norm except that instead of using t_{1995}, we will substitute a vector that increases the 1981 uniformly levels by 10% (a hypothetical increase of 10% for every country in the study):

$$\hat{t}_{1981} = 1.1 t_{1981} = [33.0, 48.4, 49.5, 38.5, 49.5, 41.8, 46.2, 41.8, 36.3$$
$$34.1, 28.6, 48.4, 37.4, 53.9, 55.0, 34.1, 39.6, 31.9].$$

This allows us to calculate the following benchmark difference:

$$||\hat{t}_{1981} - t_{1981}||^2 = 265.8.$$

So now it is clear that the observed vector difference for total country change from 1981 to 1995 is actually similar to a 10% across-the-board change rather than a 5% change implied by the vector means. In this sense we get a true multidimensional sense of change.

3.3 So What Is the Matrix?

Matrices are all around us: A **matrix** is nothing more than a rectangular arrangement of numbers. It is a way to individually assign numbers, now called **matrix elements** or **entries**, to specified positions in a single structure, referred to with a single name. Just as we saw that the order in which individual entries appear in the vector matters, the ordering of values within *both* rows and columns now matters. It turns out that this requirement adds a considerable amount of structure to the matrix, some of which is not immediately apparent (as we will see).

Matrices have two definable **dimensions**, the number of rows and the number of columns, whereas vectors only have one, and we denote matrix size by *row* × *column*. Thus a matrix with i rows and j columns is said to be of dimension $i \times j$ (by convention rows comes before columns). For instance, a simple (and rather uncreative) 2×2 matrix named **X** (like vectors, matrix names are bolded) is given by:

$$\underset{2\times 2}{\mathbf{X}} = \begin{bmatrix} 1 & 2 \\ 3 & 4 \end{bmatrix}.$$

Note that matrices can also be explicitly notated with size.

Two things are important here. First, these four numbers are now treated together as a single unit: They are *grouped* together in the two-row by two-column matrix object. Second, the positioning of the numbers is specified.

That is, the matrix $\mathbf{X}$ is different than the following matrices:

$$\mathbf{W} = \begin{bmatrix} 1 & 3 \\ 2 & 4 \end{bmatrix}, \qquad \mathbf{Y} = \begin{bmatrix} 3 & 4 \\ 1 & 2 \end{bmatrix}, \qquad \mathbf{Z} = \begin{bmatrix} 4 & 3 \\ 2 & 1 \end{bmatrix},$$

as well as many others. Like vectors, the elements of a matrix can be integers, real numbers, or complex numbers. It is, however, rare to find applications that call for the use of matrices of complex numbers in the social sciences.

The matrix is a system. We can refer directly to the specific elements of a matrix by using *subscripting* of addresses. So, for instance, the elements of $\mathbf{X}$ are given by $x_{11} = 1$, $x_{12} = 2$, $x_{21} = 3$, and $x_{22} = 4$. Obviously this is much more powerful for larger matrix objects and we can even talk about arbitrary sizes. The element addresses of a $p \times n$ matrix can be described for large values of p and n by

$$\mathbf{X} = \begin{bmatrix} x_{11} & x_{12} & \cdots & \cdots & x_{1(p-1)} & x_{1p} \\ x_{21} & x_{22} & \cdots & \cdots & x_{2(p-1)} & x_{2p} \\ \vdots & \vdots & \ddots & & & \vdots \\ \vdots & \vdots & & \ddots & & \vdots \\ \vdots & \vdots & & & \ddots & \vdots \\ x_{(n-1)1} & x_{(n-1)2} & \cdots & \cdots & x_{(n-1)(p-1)} & x_{(n-1)p} \\ x_{n1} & x_{n2} & \cdots & \cdots & x_{n(p-1)} & x_{np} \end{bmatrix}.$$

Using this notation we can now define **matrix equality**. Matrix $\boldsymbol{A}$ is equal to matrix $\boldsymbol{B}$ if and only if every element of $\mathbf{A}$ is equal to the corresponding element of $\boldsymbol{B}$: $\boldsymbol{A} = \boldsymbol{B} \iff a_{ij} = b_{ij} \ \forall i, j$. Note that "subsumed" in this definition is the requirement that the two matrices be of the same dimension (same number of rows, i, and columns, j).

3.3.1 Some Special Matrices

There are some matrices that are quite routinely used in quantitative social science work. The most basic of these is the **square matrix**, which is, as the name implies, a matrix with the same number of rows and columns. Because one number identifies the complete size of the square matrix, we can say that a $k \times k$ matrix (for arbitrary size k) is a matrix of **order-k**. Square matrices can contain any values and remain square: The square property is independent of the contents. A very general square matrix form is the **symmetric matrix**. This is a matrix that is symmetric across the diagonal from the upper left-hand corner to the lower right-hand corner. More formally, $\mathbf{X}$ is a symmetric matrix iff $a_{ij} = a_{ji}$ $\forall i, j$. Here is an unimaginative example of a symmetric matrix:

$$\mathbf{X} = \begin{bmatrix} 1 & 2 & 3 & 4 \\ 2 & 8 & 5 & 6 \\ 3 & 5 & 1 & 7 \\ 4 & 6 & 7 & 8 \end{bmatrix}.$$

A matrix can also be **skew-symmetric** if it has the property that the rows and column switching operation would provide the same matrix except for the sign. For example,

$$\mathbf{X} = \begin{bmatrix} 0 & -1 & 2 \\ 1 & 0 & -3 \\ -2 & 3 & 0 \end{bmatrix}.$$

By the way, the symmetric property does not hold for the other diagonal, the one from the upper right-hand side to the lower left-hand side.

Just as the symmetric matrix is a special case of the square matrix, the **diagonal matrix** is a special case of the symmetric matrix (and therefore of the square matrix, too). A diagonal matrix is a symmetric matrix with all zeros on the off-diagonals (the values where $i \neq j$). If the (4×4) $\mathbf{X}$ matrix above were a diagonal matrix, it would look like

$$\mathbf{X} = \begin{bmatrix} 1 & 0 & 0 & 0 \\ 0 & 8 & 0 & 0 \\ 0 & 0 & 1 & 0 \\ 0 & 0 & 0 & 8 \end{bmatrix}.$$

We can also define the diagonal matrix more generally with just a vector. A diagonal matrix with elements $[d_1, d_2, \ldots, d_{n-1}, d_n]$ is the matrix

$$
\mathbf{X} = \begin{bmatrix}
d_1 & 0 & 0 & 0 & 0 \\
0 & d_2 & 0 & 0 & 0 \\
0 & 0 & \ddots & 0 & 0 \\
0 & 0 & 0 & d_{n-1} & 0 \\
0 & 0 & 0 & 0 & d_n
\end{bmatrix}.
$$

A diagonal matrix can have any values on the diagonal, but all of the other values must be zero. A very important special case of the diagonal matrix is the **identity matrix**, which has only the value 1 for each diagonal element: $d_i = 1$, $\forall i$. A 4×4 version is

$$
\mathbf{I} = \begin{bmatrix}
1 & 0 & 0 & 0 \\
0 & 1 & 0 & 0 \\
0 & 0 & 1 & 0 \\
0 & 0 & 0 & 1
\end{bmatrix}.
$$

This matrix form is always given the name $\mathbf{I}$, and it is sometimes denoted to give size: $I_{4 \times 4}$ or even just $\mathbf{I}(4)$. A seemingly similar, but actually very different, matrix is the $\mathbf{J}$ matrix, which consists of all 1's:

$$
\mathbf{J} = \begin{bmatrix}
1 & 1 & 1 & 1 \\
1 & 1 & 1 & 1 \\
1 & 1 & 1 & 1 \\
1 & 1 & 1 & 1
\end{bmatrix},
$$

given here in a 4×4 version. As we shall soon see, the identity matrix is very commonly used because it is the matrix equivalent of the scalar number 1, whereas the $\mathbf{J}$ matrix is not (somewhat surprisingly). Analogously, the **zero**

matrix is a matrix of all zeros, the 4×4 case being

$$\mathbf{0} = \begin{bmatrix} 0 & 0 & 0 & 0 \\ 0 & 0 & 0 & 0 \\ 0 & 0 & 0 & 0 \\ 0 & 0 & 0 & 0 \end{bmatrix},$$

also given as a 4×4 matrix. Consider for a moment that the zero matrix and the **J** matrix here are also square, symmetric, diagonal, and particular named cases. Yet neither of these two *must* have these properties as both can be nonsquare as well: $i \neq j$.

This is a good time to also introduce a special nonsymmetric square matrix called the **triangular matrix**. This is a matrix with all zeros above the diagonal, **lower triangular**, or all zeros below the diagonal, **upper triangular**. Two versions based on the first square matrix given above are

$$\mathbf{X}_{LT} = \begin{bmatrix} 1 & 0 & 0 & 0 \\ 2 & 8 & 0 & 0 \\ 3 & 5 & 1 & 0 \\ 4 & 6 & 7 & 8 \end{bmatrix}, \quad \mathbf{X}_{UT} = \begin{bmatrix} 1 & 2 & 3 & 4 \\ 0 & 8 & 5 & 6 \\ 0 & 0 & 1 & 7 \\ 0 & 0 & 0 & 8 \end{bmatrix},$$

where LT designates "lower triangular" and UT designates "upper triangular." This general form plays a special role in **matrix decomposition**: factoring matrices into multiplied components. This is also a common form in more pedestrian circumstances. Map books often tabulate distances between sets of cities in an upper triangular or lower triangular form because the distance from Miami to New York is also the distance from New York to Miami.

★ **Example 3.15:   Marriage Satisfaction**. Sociologists who study marriage often focus on indicators of self-expressed satisfaction. Unfortunately marital satisfaction is sufficiently complex and sufficiently multidimensional that single measurements are often insufficient to get a full picture of underlying attitudes. Consequently, scholars such as Norton (1983) ask multiple questions designed to elicit varied expressions of marital satisfaction and therefore care a lot about the correlation between these. A correlation (described in detail in Chapter 8) shows how "tightly" two measures change with each other over a range from -1 to 1, with 0 being no evidence of moving together. His correlation matrix provides the correlational structure between answers to the following questions according to scales where higher numbers mean that the respondent agrees more (i.e., 1 is strong disagreement with the statement and 7 is strong agreement with the statement). The questions are

Question	Measurement Scale	Valid Cases
We have a good marriage	7-point	428
My relationship with my partner is very stable	7-point	429
Our marriage is strong	7-point	429
My relationship with my partner makes me happy	7-point	429
I really feel like *part of a team* with my partner	7-point	426
The degree of happiness, everything considered	10-point	407

Since the correlation between two variables is symmetric, it does not make sense to give a correlation matrix between these variables across a full matrix because the lower triangle will simply mirror the upper triangle and make the display more congested. Consequently, Norton only needs to show a triangular version of the matrix:

$$
\begin{array}{cccccc}
(1) & (2) & (3) & (4) & (5) & (6) \\
\end{array}
$$

$$
\begin{array}{c}
(1) \\
(2) \\
(3) \\
(4) \\
(5) \\
(6)
\end{array}
\left(
\begin{array}{cccccc}
1.00 & 0.85 & 0.83 & 0.83 & 0.74 & 0.76 \\
     & 1.00 & 0.82 & 0.86 & 0.72 & 0.77 \\
     &   & 1.00 & 0.78 & 0.68 & 0.70 \\
     &   &   & 1.00 & 0.71 & 0.76 \\
     &   &   &   & 1.00 & 0.69 \\
     &   &   &   &   & 1.00
\end{array}
\right).
$$

Interestingly, these analyzed questions all correlate highly (a 1 means a perfectly positive relationship). The question that seems to covary greatly with the others is the first (it is phrased somewhat as a summary, after all). Notice that strength of marriage and part of a team covary less than any others (a suggestive finding). This presentation is a bit different from an upper triangular matrix in the sense discussed above because we have just deliberately omitted redundant information, rather than the rest of matrix actually having zero values.

3.4 Controlling the Matrix

As with vectors we can perform arithmetic and algebraic operations on matrices. In particular addition, subtraction, and scalar operations are quite simple. Matrix addition and subtraction are performed only for two conformable matrices by performing the operation on an element-by-element basis for corresponding elements, so the number of rows and columns must match. Multiplication or division by a scalar proceeds exactly in the way that it did for vectors by affecting each element by the operation.

★ **Example 3.16:** **Matrix Addition.**

$$\mathbf{X} = \begin{bmatrix} 1 & 2 \\ 3 & 4 \end{bmatrix}, \quad \mathbf{Y} = \begin{bmatrix} -2 & 2 \\ 0 & 1 \end{bmatrix}$$

$$\mathbf{X} + \mathbf{Y} = \begin{bmatrix} 1-2 & 2+2 \\ 3+0 & 4+1 \end{bmatrix} = \begin{bmatrix} -1 & 4 \\ 3 & 5 \end{bmatrix}.$$

★ **Example 3.17:** **Matrix Subtraction.**

$$\mathbf{X} = \begin{bmatrix} 1 & 2 \\ 3 & 4 \end{bmatrix}, \quad \mathbf{Y} = \begin{bmatrix} -2 & 2 \\ 0 & 1 \end{bmatrix}$$

$$\mathbf{X} - \mathbf{Y} = \begin{bmatrix} 1-(-2) & 2-2 \\ 3-0 & 4-1 \end{bmatrix} = \begin{bmatrix} 3 & 0 \\ 3 & 3 \end{bmatrix}.$$

★ **Example 3.18:** **Scalar Multiplication.**

$$\mathbf{X} = \begin{bmatrix} 1 & 2 \\ 3 & 4 \end{bmatrix}, \quad s = 5$$

$$s \times \mathbf{X} = \begin{bmatrix} 5 \times 1 & 5 \times 2 \\ 5 \times 3 & 5 \times 4 \end{bmatrix} = \begin{bmatrix} 5 & 10 \\ 15 & 20 \end{bmatrix}.$$

★ **Example 3.19:** **Scalar Division.**

$$\mathbf{X} = \begin{bmatrix} 1 & 2 \\ 3 & 4 \end{bmatrix}, \quad s = 5$$

$$\mathbf{X} \div s = \begin{bmatrix} 1 \div 5 & 2 \div 5 \\ 3 \div 5 & 4 \div 5 \end{bmatrix} = \begin{bmatrix} \frac{1}{5} & \frac{2}{5} \\ \frac{3}{5} & \frac{4}{5} \end{bmatrix}.$$

One special case is worth mentioning. A common implied scalar multiplication is the negative of a matrix, $-\mathbf{X}$. This is a shorthand means for saying that every matrix element in $\mathbf{X}$ is multiplied by -1.

These are the most basic matrix operations and obviously consist of nothing more than being careful about performing each individual elemental operation. As with vectors, we can summarize the arithmetic properties as follows.

Properties of (Conformable) Matrix Manipulation

⟼   Commutative Property $\qquad\qquad \mathbf{X} + \mathbf{Y} = \mathbf{Y} + \mathbf{X}$

⟼   Additive Associative Property $\quad (\mathbf{X} + \mathbf{Y}) + \mathbf{Z} = \mathbf{X} + (\mathbf{Y} + \mathbf{Z})$

⟼   Matrix Distributive Property $\qquad s(\mathbf{X} + \mathbf{Y}) = s\mathbf{X} + s\mathbf{Y}$

⟼   Scalar Distributive Property $\qquad (s + t)\mathbf{X} = s\mathbf{X} + t\mathbf{X}$

⟼   Zero Property $\qquad\qquad\qquad \mathbf{X} + \mathbf{0} = \mathbf{X} \text{ and } \mathbf{X} - \mathbf{X} = \mathbf{0}$

★ **Example 3.20:**   **Matrix Calculations**. This example illustrates several of the properties above where $s = 7$, $t = 2$, $\mathbf{X} = \begin{bmatrix} 2 & 0 \\ 1 & 1 \end{bmatrix}$, and $\mathbf{Y} = \begin{bmatrix} 3 & 4 \\ 0 & -1 \end{bmatrix}$. The left-hand side is

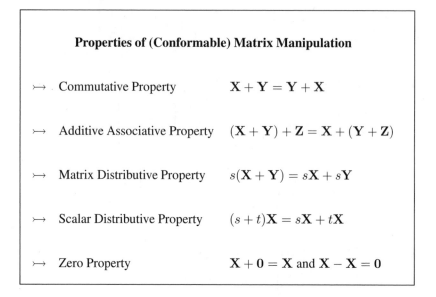

$$(s + t)(\mathbf{X} + \mathbf{Y}) = (7 + 2) \left(\begin{bmatrix} 2 & 0 \\ 1 & 1 \end{bmatrix} + \begin{bmatrix} 3 & 4 \\ 0 & -1 \end{bmatrix} \right)$$

$$= 9 \begin{bmatrix} 5 & 4 \\ 1 & 0 \end{bmatrix} = \begin{bmatrix} 45 & 36 \\ 9 & 0 \end{bmatrix},$$

and the right-hand side is

$$t\mathbf{Y} + s\mathbf{Y} + t\mathbf{X} + s\mathbf{X}$$

$$= 2 \begin{bmatrix} 3 & 4 \\ 0 & -1 \end{bmatrix} + 7 \begin{bmatrix} 3 & 4 \\ 0 & -1 \end{bmatrix} + 2 \begin{bmatrix} 2 & 0 \\ 1 & 1 \end{bmatrix} + 7 \begin{bmatrix} 2 & 0 \\ 1 & 1 \end{bmatrix}$$

$$= \begin{bmatrix} 6 & 8 \\ 0 & -2 \end{bmatrix} + \begin{bmatrix} 21 & 28 \\ 0 & -7 \end{bmatrix} + \begin{bmatrix} 4 & 0 \\ 2 & 2 \end{bmatrix} + \begin{bmatrix} 14 & 0 \\ 7 & 7 \end{bmatrix}$$

$$= \begin{bmatrix} 45 & 36 \\ 9 & 0 \end{bmatrix}.$$

Matrix multiplication is necessarily more complicated than these simple operations. The first issue is conformability. Two matrices are conformable for multiplication if the number of columns in the first matrix match the number of rows in the second matrix. Note that this implies that *the order of multiplication matters with matrices.* This is the first algebraic principle that deviates from the simple scalar world that we all learned early on in life. To be specific, suppose that $\mathbf{X}$ is size $k \times n$ and $\mathbf{Y}$ is size $n \times p$. Then the multiplication operation given by

$$\underset{(k \times n)(n \times p)}{\mathbf{X} \ \mathbf{Y}}$$

is valid because the inner numbers match up, but the multiplication operation given by

$$\underset{(n \times p)(k \times n)}{\mathbf{Y} \ \mathbf{X}}$$

is not unless $p = k$. Furthermore, the inner dimension numbers of the operation determine conformability and the outer dimension numbers determine the size of the resulting matrix. So in the example of $\mathbf{XY}$ above, the resulting matrix would be of size $k \times p$. To maintain awareness of this order of operation distinction, we say that $\mathbf{X}$ **pre-multiplies** $\mathbf{Y}$ or, equivalently, that $\mathbf{Y}$ **post-multiplies** $\mathbf{X}$.

So how is matrix multiplication done? In an attempt to be somewhat intuitive, we can think about the operation in *vector terms*. For $\mathbf{X}_{k \times n}$ and $\mathbf{Y}_{n \times p}$, we take each of the n column vectors in $\mathbf{X}$ and perform a vector inner product with the n row vectors in $\mathbf{Y}$. This operation starts with performing the inner product of the first column in $\mathbf{X}$ with the first row in $\mathbf{Y}$ and the result will be the first element of the product matrix. Consider a simple case of two arbitrary 2×2 matrices:

$$
\mathbf{XY} = \begin{bmatrix} x_{11} & x_{12} \\ x_{21} & x_{22} \end{bmatrix} \begin{bmatrix} y_{11} & y_{12} \\ y_{21} & y_{22} \end{bmatrix}
$$

$$
= \begin{bmatrix} (x_{11}\ x_{12}) \cdot (y_{11}\ y_{21}) & (x_{11}\ x_{12}) \cdot (y_{12}\ y_{22}) \\ (x_{21}\ x_{22}) \cdot (y_{11}\ y_{21}) & (x_{21}\ x_{22}) \cdot (y_{12}\ y_{22}) \end{bmatrix}
$$

$$
= \begin{bmatrix} x_{11}y_{11} + x_{12}y_{21} & x_{11}y_{12} + x_{12}y_{22} \\ x_{21}y_{11} + x_{22}y_{21} & x_{21}y_{12} + x_{22}y_{22} \end{bmatrix} .
$$

Perhaps we can make this more intuitive visually. Suppose that we notate the four values of the final matrix as $\mathbf{XY}[1, 1]$, $\mathbf{XY}[1, 2]$, $\mathbf{XY}[2, 1]$, $\mathbf{XY}[2, 2]$ corresponding to their position in the 2×2 product. Then we can visualize how the rows of the first matrix operate against the columns of the second matrix to produce each value:

$$
\boxed{\begin{array}{cc} x_{11} & x_{12} \end{array}} \boxed{\begin{array}{c} y_{11} \\ y_{21} \end{array}} = \mathbf{XY}[1, 1], \qquad \boxed{\begin{array}{cc} x_{11} & x_{12} \end{array}} \boxed{\begin{array}{c} y_{12} \\ y_{22} \end{array}} = \mathbf{XY}[1, 2],
$$

$$\boxed{x_{21} \quad x_{22}} \begin{array}{c} y_{11} \\ y_{21} \end{array} = \mathbf{XY}[2,1], \qquad \boxed{x_{21} \quad x_{22}} \begin{array}{c} y_{12} \\ y_{22} \end{array} = \mathbf{XY}[2,2].$$

While it helps to visualize the process in this way, we can also express the product in a more general, but perhaps intimidating, scalar notation for an arbitrary-sized operation:

$$\underset{(k\times n)(n\times p)}{\mathbf{X}\ \mathbf{Y}} = \begin{bmatrix} \sum_{i=1}^{n} x_{1i}y_{i1} & \sum_{i=1}^{n} x_{1i}y_{i2} & \cdots & \sum_{i=1}^{n} x_{1i}y_{ip} \\ \sum_{i=1}^{n} x_{2i}y_{i1} & \sum_{i=1}^{n} x_{2i}y_{i2} & \cdots & \sum_{i=1}^{n} x_{2i}y_{ip} \\ \vdots & & \ddots & \vdots \\ \sum_{i=1}^{n} x_{ki}y_{i1} & \cdots & \cdots & \sum_{i=1}^{n} x_{ki}y_{ip} \end{bmatrix}.$$

To further clarify, now perform matrix multiplication with some actual values. Starting with the matrices

$$\mathbf{X} = \begin{bmatrix} 1 & 2 \\ 3 & 4 \end{bmatrix}, \quad \mathbf{Y} = \begin{bmatrix} -2 & 2 \\ 0 & 1 \end{bmatrix},$$

calculate

$$\mathbf{XY} = \begin{bmatrix} (1\ 2)\cdot(-2\ 0) & (1\ 2)\cdot(2\ 1) \\ (3\ 4)\cdot(-2\ 0) & (3\ 4)\cdot(2\ 1) \end{bmatrix}$$

$$= \begin{bmatrix} (1)(-2)+(2)(0) & (1)(2)+(2)(1) \\ (3)(-2)+(4)(0) & (3)(2)+(4)(1) \end{bmatrix}$$

$$= \begin{bmatrix} -2 & 4 \\ -6 & 10 \end{bmatrix}.$$

As before with such topics, we consider the properties of matrix multiplication:

Properties of (Conformable) Matrix Multiplication

↣   Associative Property $(\mathbf{XY})\mathbf{Z} = \mathbf{X}(\mathbf{YZ})$

↣   Additive Distributive Property $(\mathbf{X} + \mathbf{Y})\mathbf{Z} = \mathbf{XZ} + \mathbf{YZ}$

↣   Scalar Distributive Property $s\mathbf{XY} = (\mathbf{X}s)\mathbf{Y}$
$$= \mathbf{X}(s\mathbf{Y}) = \mathbf{XY}s$$

↣   Zero Property $\mathbf{X0} = \mathbf{0}$

★ **Example 3.21:   LU Matrix Decomposition.** Many square matrices can be decomposed as the product of lower and upper triangular matrices. This is a very general finding that we will return to and extend in the next chapter. The principle works like this for the matrix $\mathbf{A}$:

$$\underset{(p\times p)}{\mathbf{A}} = \underset{(p\times p)}{\mathbf{L}}\ \underset{(p\times p)}{\mathbf{U}},$$

where $\mathbf{L}$ is a lower triangular matrix and $\mathbf{U}$ is an upper triangular matrix (sometimes a permutation matrix is also required; see the explanation of permutation matrices below).

Consider the following example matrix decomposition according to this scheme:

$$\begin{bmatrix} 2 & 3 & 3 \\ 1 & 2 & 9 \\ 1 & 1 & 12 \end{bmatrix} = \begin{bmatrix} 1.0 & 0 & 0 \\ 0.5 & 1 & 0 \\ 0.5 & -1 & 1 \end{bmatrix} \begin{bmatrix} 2 & 3.0 & 3.0 \\ 0 & 0.5 & 7.5 \\ 0 & 0.0 & 18.0 \end{bmatrix}.$$

This decomposition is very useful for solving systems of equations because much of the mechanical work is already done by the triangularization.

Now that we have seen how matrix multiplication is performed, we can return to the principle that pre-multiplication is different than post-multiplication. In the case discussed we could perform one of these operations but not the other, so the difference was obvious. What about multiplying two square matrices? Both orders of multiplication are possible, but it turns out that except for special cases the result will differ. In fact, we need only provide one particular case to prove this point. Consider the matrices $\mathbf{X}$ and $\mathbf{Y}$:

$$\mathbf{XY} = \begin{bmatrix} 1 & 2 \\ 3 & 4 \end{bmatrix} \begin{bmatrix} 0 & 1 \\ 1 & 0 \end{bmatrix} = \begin{bmatrix} 2 & 1 \\ 4 & 3 \end{bmatrix}$$

$$\mathbf{YX} = \begin{bmatrix} 0 & 1 \\ 1 & 0 \end{bmatrix} \begin{bmatrix} 1 & 2 \\ 3 & 4 \end{bmatrix} = \begin{bmatrix} 3 & 4 \\ 1 & 2 \end{bmatrix}.$$

This is a very simple example, but the implications are obvious. Even in cases where pre-multiplication and post-multiplication are possible, these are different operations and matrix multiplication is not commutative.

Recall also the claim that the identity matrix $\mathbf{I}$ is operationally equivalent to 1 in matrix terms rather than the seemingly more obvious $\mathbf{J}$ matrix. Let us now test this claim on a simple matrix, first with $\mathbf{I}$:

$$\mathbf{XI} = \begin{bmatrix} 1 & 2 \\ 3 & 4 \end{bmatrix} \begin{bmatrix} 1 & 0 \\ 0 & 1 \end{bmatrix}$$

$$= \begin{bmatrix} (1)(1) + (2)(0) & (1)(0) + (2)(1) \\ (3)(1) + (4)(0) & (3)(0) + (4)(1) \end{bmatrix} = \begin{bmatrix} 1 & 2 \\ 3 & 4 \end{bmatrix},$$

and then with J:

$$\mathbf{XJ_2} = \begin{bmatrix} 1 & 2 \\ 3 & 4 \end{bmatrix} \begin{bmatrix} 1 & 1 \\ 1 & 1 \end{bmatrix}$$

$$= \begin{bmatrix} (1)(1) + (2)(1) & (1)(1) + (2)(1) \\ (3)(1) + (4)(1) & (3)(1) + (4)(1) \end{bmatrix} = \begin{bmatrix} 3 & 3 \\ 7 & 7 \end{bmatrix}.$$

The result here is interesting; post-multiplying by $\mathbf{I}$ returns the $\mathbf{X}$ matrix to its original form, but post-multiplying by $\mathbf{J}$ produces a matrix where values are the sum by row. What about pre-multiplication? Pre-multiplying by $\mathbf{I}$ also returns the original matrix (see the Exercises), but pre-multiplying by $\mathbf{J}$ gives

$$\mathbf{J}_2\mathbf{X} = \begin{bmatrix} 1 & 1 \\ 1 & 1 \end{bmatrix} \begin{bmatrix} 1 & 2 \\ 3 & 4 \end{bmatrix}$$

$$= \begin{bmatrix} (1)(1) + (1)(3) & (1)(2) + (1)(4) \\ (1)(1) + (1)(3) & (1)(2) + (1)(4) \end{bmatrix} = \begin{bmatrix} 4 & 6 \\ 4 & 6 \end{bmatrix},$$

which is now the sum down columns assigned as row values. This means that the $\mathbf{J}$ matrix can be very useful in calculations (including linear regression methods), but it does not work as a "one" in matrix terms. There is also a very interesting multiplicative property of the $\mathbf{J}$ matrix, particularly for nonsquare forms:

$$\underset{(p\times n)}{\mathbf{J}}\;\underset{(n\times k)}{\mathbf{J}} = n\;\underset{(p\times k)}{\mathbf{J}}.$$

Basic manipulations of the identity matrix can provide forms that are enormously useful in matrix multiplication calculations. Suppose we wish to switch two rows of a specific matrix. To accomplish this we can multiply by an identity matrix where the placement of the 1 values is switched:

$$\begin{bmatrix} 1 & 0 & 0 \\ 0 & 0 & 1 \\ 0 & 1 & 0 \end{bmatrix} \begin{bmatrix} x_{11} & x_{12} & x_{13} \\ x_{21} & x_{22} & x_{23} \\ x_{31} & x_{32} & x_{33} \end{bmatrix} = \begin{bmatrix} x_{11} & x_{12} & x_{13} \\ x_{31} & x_{32} & x_{33} \\ x_{21} & x_{22} & x_{23} \end{bmatrix}.$$

This pre-multiplying matrix is called a **permutation matrix** because it permutes the matrix that it operates on. Interestingly, a permutation matrix can be applied to a conformable vector with the obvious results.

The effect of changing a single 1 value to some other scalar is fairly obvious:

$$\begin{bmatrix} 1 & 0 & 0 \\ 0 & 1 & 0 \\ 0 & 0 & s \end{bmatrix} \begin{bmatrix} x_{11} & x_{12} & x_{13} \\ x_{21} & x_{22} & x_{23} \\ x_{31} & x_{32} & x_{33} \end{bmatrix} = \begin{bmatrix} x_{11} & x_{12} & x_{13} \\ x_{21} & x_{22} & x_{23} \\ sx_{31} & sx_{32} & sx_{33} \end{bmatrix},$$

but the effect of changing a single 0 value is not:

$$
\begin{bmatrix} 1 & 0 & s \\ 0 & 1 & 0 \\ 0 & 0 & 1 \end{bmatrix}
\begin{bmatrix} x_{11} & x_{12} & x_{13} \\ x_{21} & x_{22} & x_{23} \\ x_{31} & x_{32} & x_{33} \end{bmatrix}
$$

$$
= \begin{bmatrix} x_{11} + sx_{31} & x_{12} + sx_{32} & x_{13} + sx_{33} \\ x_{21} & x_{22} & x_{23} \\ x_{31} & x_{32} & x_{33} \end{bmatrix}.
$$

★ **Example 3.22:** **Matrix Permutation Calculation.** Consider the following example of permutation with an off-diagonal nonzero value:

$$
\begin{bmatrix} 1 & 0 & 3 \\ 0 & 0 & 1 \\ 0 & 1 & 0 \end{bmatrix}
\begin{bmatrix} 3 & 2 & 3 \\ 7 & 0 & 1 \\ 3 & 3 & 3 \end{bmatrix}
$$

$$
= \begin{bmatrix} (1 \cdot 3 + 0 \cdot 7 + 3 \cdot 3) & (1 \cdot 2 + 0 \cdot 0 + 3 \cdot 3) & (1 \cdot 3 + 0 \cdot 1 + 3 \cdot 3) \\ (0 \cdot 3 + 0 \cdot 7 + 1 \cdot 3) & (0 \cdot 2 + 0 \cdot 0 + 1 \cdot 3) & (0 \cdot 3 + 0 \cdot 1 + 1 \cdot 3) \\ (0 \cdot 3 + 1 \cdot 7 + 0 \cdot 3) & (0 \cdot 2 + 1 \cdot 0 + 0 \cdot 3) & (0 \cdot 3 + 1 \cdot 1 + 0 \cdot 3) \end{bmatrix}
$$

$$
= \begin{bmatrix} 12 & 11 & 12 \\ 3 & 3 & 3 \\ 7 & 0 & 1 \end{bmatrix},
$$

which shows the switching of rows two and three as well as the confinement of multiplication by 3 to the first row.

3.5 Matrix Transposition

Another operation that is commonly performed on a single matrix is **transposition**. We saw this before in the context of vectors: switching between column and row forms. For matrices, this is slightly more involved but straightforward to understand: simply switch rows and columns. The transpose of an $i \times j$

matrix $\mathbf{X}$ is the $j \times i$ matrix $\mathbf{X}'$, usually called "X prime" (sometimes denoted $\mathbf{X}^T$ though). For example,

$$\mathbf{X}' = \begin{bmatrix} 1 & 2 & 3 \\ 4 & 5 & 6 \end{bmatrix}' = \begin{bmatrix} 1 & 4 \\ 2 & 5 \\ 3 & 6 \end{bmatrix}.$$

In this way the inner structure of the matrix is preserved but the shape of the matrix is changed. An interesting consequence is that transposition allows us to calculate the "square" of some arbitrary-sized $i \times j$ matrix: $\mathbf{X}'\mathbf{X}$ is always conformable, as is $\mathbf{X}\mathbf{X}'$, even if $i \neq j$. We can also be more precise about the definition of symmetric and skew-symmetric matrices. Consider now some basic properties of transposition.

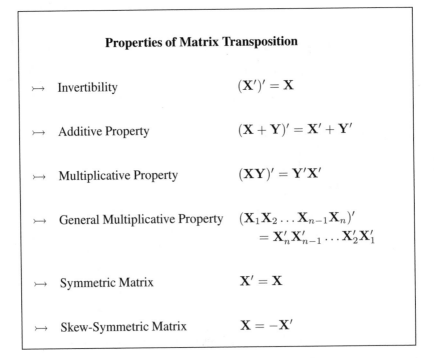

Properties of Matrix Transposition

$\rightarrowtail$	Invertibility	$(\mathbf{X}')' = \mathbf{X}$
$\rightarrowtail$	Additive Property	$(\mathbf{X} + \mathbf{Y})' = \mathbf{X}' + \mathbf{Y}'$
$\rightarrowtail$	Multiplicative Property	$(\mathbf{X}\mathbf{Y})' = \mathbf{Y}'\mathbf{X}'$
$\rightarrowtail$	General Multiplicative Property	$(\mathbf{X}_1\mathbf{X}_2\ldots\mathbf{X}_{n-1}\mathbf{X}_n)'$ $= \mathbf{X}_n'\mathbf{X}_{n-1}'\ldots\mathbf{X}_2'\mathbf{X}_1'$
$\rightarrowtail$	Symmetric Matrix	$\mathbf{X}' = \mathbf{X}$
$\rightarrowtail$	Skew-Symmetric Matrix	$\mathbf{X} = -\mathbf{X}'$

Note, in particular, from this list that the multiplicative property of transposition reverses the order of the matrices.

★ **Example 3.23:** **Calculations with Matrix Transpositions**. Suppose we have the three matrices:

$$\mathbf{X} = \begin{bmatrix} 1 & 0 \\ 3 & 7 \end{bmatrix} \quad \mathbf{Y} = \begin{bmatrix} 2 & 3 \\ 2 & 2 \end{bmatrix} \quad \mathbf{Z} = \begin{bmatrix} -2 & -2 \\ 1 & 0 \end{bmatrix}.$$

Then the following calculation of $(\mathbf{XY'} + \mathbf{Z})' = \mathbf{Z'} + \mathbf{YX'}$ illustrates the invertibility, additive, and multiplicative properties of transposition. The left-hand side is

$$(\mathbf{XY'} + \mathbf{Z})' = \left(\begin{bmatrix} 1 & 0 \\ 3 & 7 \end{bmatrix} \begin{bmatrix} 2 & 3 \\ 2 & 2 \end{bmatrix}' + \begin{bmatrix} -2 & -2 \\ 1 & 0 \end{bmatrix} \right)'$$

$$= \left(\begin{bmatrix} 2 & 2 \\ 27 & 20 \end{bmatrix} + \begin{bmatrix} -2 & -2 \\ 1 & 0 \end{bmatrix} \right)'$$

$$= \left(\begin{bmatrix} 0 & 0 \\ 28 & 20 \end{bmatrix} \right)',$$

and the right-hand side is

$$\mathbf{Z'} + \mathbf{YX'} = \begin{bmatrix} -2 & -2 \\ 1 & 0 \end{bmatrix}' + \begin{bmatrix} 2 & 3 \\ 2 & 2 \end{bmatrix} \begin{bmatrix} 1 & 0 \\ 3 & 7 \end{bmatrix}'$$

$$= \begin{bmatrix} -2 & 1 \\ -2 & 0 \end{bmatrix} + \begin{bmatrix} 2 & 27 \\ 2 & 20 \end{bmatrix}$$

$$= \begin{bmatrix} 0 & 28 \\ 0 & 20 \end{bmatrix}.$$

3.6 Advanced Topics

This section contains a set of topics that are less frequently used in the social sciences but may appear in some literatures. Readers may elect to skip this section or use it for reference only.

3.6.1 Special Matrix Forms

An interesting type of matrix that we did not discuss before is the **idempotent matrix**. This is a matrix that has the multiplication property

$$\mathbf{XX} = \mathbf{X}^2 = \mathbf{X}$$

and therefore the property

$$\mathbf{X}^n = \mathbf{XX}\cdots\mathbf{X} = \mathbf{X}, \quad n \in \mathcal{I}^+$$

(i.e., n is some positive integer). Obviously the identity matrix and the zero matrix are idempotent, but the somewhat weird truth is that there are lots of other idempotent matrices as well. This emphasizes how different matrix algebra can be from scalar algebra. For instance, the following matrix is idempotent, but you probably could not guess so by staring at it:

$$\begin{bmatrix} 2 & -1 & 1 \\ -2 & 3 & -3 \\ -4 & 4 & -3 \end{bmatrix}$$

(try multiplying it). Interestingly, if a matrix is idempotent, then the difference between this matrix and the identity matrix is also idempotent because

$$(\mathbf{I} - \mathbf{X})^2 = \mathbf{I}^2 - 2\mathbf{X} + \mathbf{X}^2 = \mathbf{I} - 2\mathbf{X} + \mathbf{X} = (\mathbf{I} - \mathbf{X}).$$

We can test this with the example matrix above:

$$(\mathbf{I} - \mathbf{X})^2 = \left(\begin{bmatrix} 1 & 0 & 0 \\ 0 & 1 & 0 \\ 0 & 0 & 1 \end{bmatrix} - \begin{bmatrix} 2 & -1 & 1 \\ -2 & 3 & -3 \\ -4 & 4 & -3 \end{bmatrix} \right)^2$$

$$= \begin{bmatrix} -1 & 1 & -1 \\ 2 & -2 & 2 \\ 4 & -4 & 4 \end{bmatrix}^2 = \begin{bmatrix} -1 & 1 & -1 \\ 2 & -2 & 2 \\ 4 & -4 & 4 \end{bmatrix}.$$

Relatedly, a square **nilpotent** matrix is one with the property that $\mathbf{X}^n = \mathbf{0}$, for a positive integer n. Clearly the zero matrix is nilpotent, but others exist as well. A basic 2×2 example is the nilpotent matrix

$$\begin{bmatrix} 1 & 1 \\ -1 & -1 \end{bmatrix}.$$

Another particularistic matrix is a **involutory matrix**, which has the property that when squared it produces an identity matrix. For example,

$$\begin{bmatrix} -1 & 0 \\ 0 & 1 \end{bmatrix}^2 = \mathbf{I},$$

although more creative forms exist.

3.6.2 Vectorization of Matrices

Occasionally it is convenient to rearrange a matrix into vector form. The most common way to do this is to "stack" vectors from the matrix on top of each other, beginning with the first column vector of the matrix, to form one long column vector. Specifically, to **vectorize** an $i \times j$ matrix $\mathbf{X}$, we consecutively stack the j-length column vectors to obtain a single vector of length ij. This is denoted $\text{vec}(\mathbf{X})$ and has some obvious properties, such as $s\text{vec}(\mathbf{X}) = \text{vec}(s\mathbf{X})$ for some vector s and $\text{vec}(\mathbf{X} + \mathbf{Y}) = \text{vec}(\mathbf{X}) + \text{vec}(\mathbf{Y})$ for matrices conformable by addition. Returning to our simple example,

$$\text{vec} \begin{bmatrix} 1 & 2 \\ 3 & 4 \end{bmatrix} = \begin{bmatrix} 1 \\ 3 \\ 2 \\ 4 \end{bmatrix}.$$

Interestingly, it is not true that $\text{vec}(\mathbf{X}) = \text{vec}(\mathbf{X}')$ since the latter would stack rows instead of columns. And vectorization of products is considerably more involved (see the next section).

A final, and sometimes important, type of matrix multiplication is the **Kronecker product** (also called the *tensor product*), which comes up naturally in the statistical analyses of time series data (data recorded on the same measures of interest at different points in time). This is a slightly more abstract process but has the advantage that there is no conformability requirement. For the $i \times j$ matrix $\mathbf{X}$ and $k \times \ell$ matrix $\mathbf{Y}$, a Kronecker product is the $(ik) \times (j\ell)$ matrix

$$
\mathbf{X} \otimes \mathbf{Y} =
\begin{bmatrix}
x_{11}\mathbf{Y} & x_{12}\mathbf{Y} & \cdots & \cdots & x_{1j}\mathbf{Y} \\
x_{21}\mathbf{Y} & x_{22}\mathbf{Y} & \cdots & \cdots & x_{2j}\mathbf{Y} \\
\vdots & \vdots & \ddots & & \vdots \\
\vdots & \vdots & & \ddots & \vdots \\
x_{i1}\mathbf{Y} & x_{i2}\mathbf{Y} & \cdots & \cdots & x_{ij}\mathbf{Y}
\end{bmatrix},
$$

which is different than

$$
\mathbf{Y} \otimes \mathbf{X} =
\begin{bmatrix}
y_{11}\mathbf{X} & y_{12}\mathbf{X} & \cdots & \cdots & y_{1j}\mathbf{X} \\
y_{21}\mathbf{X} & y_{22}\mathbf{X} & \cdots & \cdots & y_{2j}\mathbf{X} \\
\vdots & \vdots & \ddots & & \vdots \\
\vdots & \vdots & & \ddots & \vdots \\
y_{i1}\mathbf{X} & y_{i2}\mathbf{X} & \cdots & \cdots & y_{1j}\mathbf{X}
\end{bmatrix}.
$$

As an example, consider the following numerical case.

★ **Example 3.24:   Kronecker Product**. A numerical example of a Kronecker product follows for a (2×2) by (2×3) case:

$$
\mathbf{X} =
\begin{bmatrix}
1 & 2 \\
3 & 4
\end{bmatrix},
$$

$$\mathbf{Y} = \begin{bmatrix} -2 & 2 & 3 \\ 0 & 1 & 3 \end{bmatrix}$$

$$\mathbf{X} \otimes \mathbf{Y} = \begin{bmatrix} 1\begin{bmatrix} -2 & 2 & 3 \\ 0 & 1 & 3 \end{bmatrix} & 2\begin{bmatrix} -2 & 2 & 3 \\ 0 & 1 & 3 \end{bmatrix} \\ 3\begin{bmatrix} -2 & 2 & 3 \\ 0 & 1 & 3 \end{bmatrix} & 4\begin{bmatrix} -2 & 2 & 3 \\ 0 & 1 & 3 \end{bmatrix} \end{bmatrix}$$

$$= \begin{bmatrix} -2 & 2 & 3 & -4 & 4 & 6 \\ 0 & 1 & 3 & 0 & 2 & 6 \\ -6 & 6 & 9 & -8 & 8 & 12 \\ 0 & 3 & 9 & 0 & 4 & 12 \end{bmatrix},$$

which is clearly different from the operation performed in reverse order:

$$\mathbf{Y} \otimes \mathbf{X} = \begin{bmatrix} -2\begin{bmatrix} 1 & 2 \\ 3 & 4 \end{bmatrix} & 2\begin{bmatrix} 1 & 2 \\ 3 & 4 \end{bmatrix} & 3\begin{bmatrix} 1 & 2 \\ 3 & 4 \end{bmatrix} \\ 0\begin{bmatrix} 1 & 2 \\ 3 & 4 \end{bmatrix} & 1\begin{bmatrix} 1 & 2 \\ 3 & 4 \end{bmatrix} & 3\begin{bmatrix} 1 & 2 \\ 3 & 4 \end{bmatrix} \end{bmatrix}$$

$$= \begin{bmatrix} -2 & -4 & 2 & 4 & 3 & 6 \\ -6 & -8 & 6 & 8 & 9 & 12 \\ 0 & 0 & 1 & 2 & 3 & 6 \\ 0 & 0 & 3 & 4 & 9 & 12 \end{bmatrix},$$

even though the resulting matrices are of the same dimension.

The vectorize function above has a product that involves the Kronecker function. For $i \times j$ matrix $\mathbf{X}$ and $j \times k$ matrix $\mathbf{Y}$, we get $\text{vec}(\mathbf{XY}) = (\mathbf{I} \otimes \mathbf{X})\text{vec}(\mathbf{Y})$, where $\mathbf{I}$ is an identity matrix of order i. For three matrices this is only slightly more complex: $\text{vec}(\mathbf{XYZ}) = (\mathbf{Z}' \otimes \mathbf{X})\text{vec}(\mathbf{Y})$, for $k \times \ell$ matrix $\mathbf{Z}$. Kronecker products have some other interesting properties as well (matrix inversion is discussed in the next chapter):

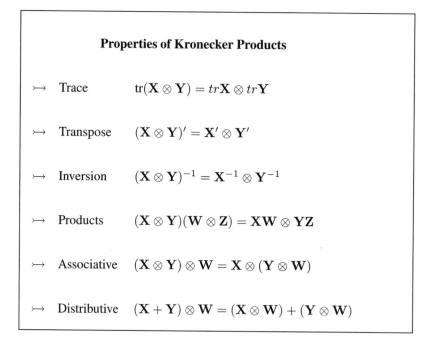

Properties of Kronecker Products

$\longmapsto$ Trace $\text{tr}(\mathbf{X} \otimes \mathbf{Y}) = tr\mathbf{X} \otimes tr\mathbf{Y}$

$\longmapsto$ Transpose $(\mathbf{X} \otimes \mathbf{Y})' = \mathbf{X}' \otimes \mathbf{Y}'$

$\longmapsto$ Inversion $(\mathbf{X} \otimes \mathbf{Y})^{-1} = \mathbf{X}^{-1} \otimes \mathbf{Y}^{-1}$

$\longmapsto$ Products $(\mathbf{X} \otimes \mathbf{Y})(\mathbf{W} \otimes \mathbf{Z}) = \mathbf{XW} \otimes \mathbf{YZ}$

$\longmapsto$ Associative $(\mathbf{X} \otimes \mathbf{Y}) \otimes \mathbf{W} = \mathbf{X} \otimes (\mathbf{Y} \otimes \mathbf{W})$

$\longmapsto$ Distributive $(\mathbf{X} + \mathbf{Y}) \otimes \mathbf{W} = (\mathbf{X} \otimes \mathbf{W}) + (\mathbf{Y} \otimes \mathbf{W})$

Here the notation tr() denotes the "trace," which is just the sum of the diagonal values going from the uppermost left value to the lowermost right value, for square matrices. Thus the trace of an identity matrix would be just its order. This is where we will pick up next in Chapter 4.

★ **Example 3.25:** **Distributive Property of Kronecker Products Calculation.** Given the following matrices:

$$\mathbf{X} = \begin{bmatrix} 1 & 1 \\ 2 & 5 \end{bmatrix} \quad \mathbf{Y} = \begin{bmatrix} -1 & -3 \\ 1 & 1 \end{bmatrix} \quad \mathbf{W} = \begin{bmatrix} 2 & -2 \\ 3 & 0 \end{bmatrix},$$

we demonstrate that $(\mathbf{X} + \mathbf{Y}) \otimes \mathbf{W} = (\mathbf{X} \otimes \mathbf{W}) + (\mathbf{X} \otimes \mathbf{W})$. The left-hand side is

$$(\mathbf{X} + \mathbf{Y}) \otimes \mathbf{W} = \left(\begin{bmatrix} 1 & 1 \\ 2 & 5 \end{bmatrix} + \begin{bmatrix} -1 & -3 \\ 1 & 1 \end{bmatrix} \right) \otimes \begin{bmatrix} 2 & -2 \\ 3 & 0 \end{bmatrix}$$

$$= \begin{bmatrix} 0 & -2 \\ 3 & 6 \end{bmatrix} \otimes \begin{bmatrix} 2 & -2 \\ 3 & 0 \end{bmatrix}$$

$$= \begin{bmatrix} 0 \begin{bmatrix} 2 & -2 \\ 3 & 0 \end{bmatrix} & -2 \begin{bmatrix} 2 & -2 \\ 3 & 0 \end{bmatrix} \\ 3 \begin{bmatrix} 2 & -2 \\ 3 & 0 \end{bmatrix} & 6 \begin{bmatrix} 2 & -2 \\ 3 & 0 \end{bmatrix} \end{bmatrix}$$

$$= \begin{bmatrix} 0 & 0 & -4 & 4 \\ 0 & 0 & -6 & 0 \\ 6 & -6 & 12 & -12 \\ 9 & 0 & 18 & 0 \end{bmatrix},$$

and the right-hand side, $(\mathbf{X} \otimes \mathbf{W}) + (\mathbf{X} \otimes \mathbf{W})$, is

$$
= \left(\begin{bmatrix} 1 & 1 \\ 2 & 5 \end{bmatrix} \otimes \begin{bmatrix} 2 & -2 \\ 3 & 0 \end{bmatrix} \right) + \left(\begin{bmatrix} -1 & -3 \\ 1 & 1 \end{bmatrix} \otimes \begin{bmatrix} 2 & -2 \\ 3 & 0 \end{bmatrix} \right)
$$

$$
= \begin{bmatrix} 1 \begin{bmatrix} 2 & -2 \\ 3 & 0 \end{bmatrix} & 1 \begin{bmatrix} 2 & -2 \\ 3 & 0 \end{bmatrix} \\ 2 \begin{bmatrix} 2 & -2 \\ 3 & 0 \end{bmatrix} & 5 \begin{bmatrix} 2 & -2 \\ 3 & 0 \end{bmatrix} \end{bmatrix}
$$

$$
+ \begin{bmatrix} -1 \begin{bmatrix} 2 & -2 \\ 3 & 0 \end{bmatrix} & -3 \begin{bmatrix} 2 & -2 \\ 3 & 0 \end{bmatrix} \\ 1 \begin{bmatrix} 2 & -2 \\ 3 & 0 \end{bmatrix} & 1 \begin{bmatrix} 2 & -2 \\ 3 & 0 \end{bmatrix} \end{bmatrix},
$$

which simplifies down to

$$
= \begin{bmatrix} 2 & -2 & 2 & -2 \\ 3 & 0 & 3 & 0 \\ 4 & -4 & 10 & -10 \\ 6 & 0 & 15 & 0 \end{bmatrix} + \begin{bmatrix} -2 & 2 & -6 & 6 \\ -3 & 0 & -9 & 0 \\ 2 & -2 & 2 & -2 \\ 3 & 0 & 3 & 0 \end{bmatrix}
$$

$$
= \begin{bmatrix} 0 & 0 & -4 & 4 \\ 0 & 0 & -6 & 0 \\ 6 & -6 & 12 & -12 \\ 9 & 0 & 18 & 0 \end{bmatrix}.
$$

3.7 New Terminology

Exercises

3.1   Perform the following vector multiplication operations:

$$\begin{bmatrix} 1 & 1 & 1 \end{bmatrix} \cdot \begin{bmatrix} a & b & c \end{bmatrix}'$$

$$\begin{bmatrix} 1 & 1 & 1 \end{bmatrix} \times \begin{bmatrix} a & b & c \end{bmatrix}'$$

$$\begin{bmatrix} -1 & 1 & -1 \end{bmatrix} \cdot \begin{bmatrix} 4 & 3 & 12 \end{bmatrix}'$$

$$\begin{bmatrix} -1 & 1 & -1 \end{bmatrix} \times \begin{bmatrix} 4 & 3 & 12 \end{bmatrix}'$$

$$\begin{bmatrix} 0 & 9 & 0 & 11 \end{bmatrix} \cdot \begin{bmatrix} 123.98211 & 6 & -6392.38743 & -5 \end{bmatrix}'$$

$$\begin{bmatrix} 123.98211 & 6 & -6392.38743 & -5 \end{bmatrix} \cdot \begin{bmatrix} 0 & 9 & 0 & 11 \end{bmatrix}'.$$

3.2   Recalculate the two outer product operations in Example 3.2 only by using the vector $(-1) \times [3, 3, 3]$ instead of $[3, 3, 3]$. What is the interpretation of the result with regard to the direction of the resulting row and column vectors compared with those in the example?

3.3   Show that $\|v - w\|^2 = \|v\|^2 + \|w\|^2 - 2\|v\|\|w\| \cos \theta$ implies $\cos(\theta) = \frac{vw}{\|v\| \|w\|}$.

3.4   What happens when you calculate the difference norm ($\|u - v\|^2 = \|u\|^2 - 2(u \cdot v) + \|v\|^2$) for two orthogonal vectors? How is this different from the multiplication norm for two such vectors?

3.5   Explain why the perpendicularity property is a special case of the triangle inequality for vector p-norms.

3.6   For p-norms, explain why the Cauchy-Schwarz inequality is a special case of Hölder's inequality.

3.7   Show that pre-multiplication and post-multiplication with the identity matrix are equivalent.

3.8   Recall that an involutory matrix is one that has the characteristic $X^2 = I$. Can an involutory matrix ever be idempotent?

3.9   For the following matrix, calculate X^n for $n = 2, 3, 4, 5$. Write a rule for calculating higher values of n.

$$\mathbf{X} = \begin{bmatrix} 0 & 0 & 1 \\ 0 & 1 & 0 \\ 1 & 0 & 1 \end{bmatrix}.$$

3.10 Perform the following vector/matrix multiplications:

$$\begin{bmatrix} 1 & \frac{1}{2} & 2 \\ 1 & \frac{1}{3} & 5 \\ 1 & 1 & 2 \end{bmatrix} \begin{bmatrix} 0.1 \\ 0.2 \\ 0.3 \end{bmatrix} \qquad \begin{bmatrix} 0 & 1 & 0 \\ 1 & 0 & 0 \\ 0 & 0 & 1 \end{bmatrix} \begin{bmatrix} 9 \\ 7 \\ 5 \end{bmatrix}$$

$$\begin{bmatrix} 9 & 7 & 5 \end{bmatrix} \begin{bmatrix} 0 & 1 & 0 \\ 1 & 0 & 0 \\ 0 & 0 & 1 \end{bmatrix} \qquad \begin{bmatrix} 3 & 3 & 1 \\ 3 & 1 & 3 \\ 1 & 3 & 3 \end{bmatrix} \begin{bmatrix} \frac{1}{3} \\ \frac{1}{3} \\ \frac{1}{3} \end{bmatrix}.$$

3.11 Perform the following matrix multiplications:

$$\begin{bmatrix} 3 & -3 \\ -3 & 3 \end{bmatrix} \begin{bmatrix} 2 & 1 \\ 0 & 0 \end{bmatrix} \qquad \begin{bmatrix} 0 & 1 & 1 \\ 1 & 0 & 1 \\ 1 & 1 & 0 \end{bmatrix} \begin{bmatrix} 4 & 7 \\ 3 & 0 \\ 1 & 2 \end{bmatrix}$$

$$\begin{bmatrix} 3 & 1 & -2 \\ 6 & 3 & 4 \end{bmatrix} \begin{bmatrix} 4 & 7 \\ 3 & 0 \\ 1 & 2 \end{bmatrix} \qquad \begin{bmatrix} 1 & 0 \\ -3 & 1 \end{bmatrix} \begin{bmatrix} 1 & 0 \\ 3 & 1 \end{bmatrix}$$

$$\begin{bmatrix} -1 & -9 \\ -1 & -4 \\ 1 & 2 \end{bmatrix} \begin{bmatrix} -4 & -4 \\ -1 & 0 \\ -3 & -8 \end{bmatrix}' \qquad \begin{bmatrix} 0 & 0 \\ 0 & \infty \end{bmatrix} \begin{bmatrix} 1 & 1 \\ -1 & -1 \end{bmatrix}.$$

3.12 An **equitable matrix** is a square matrix of order n where all entries are positive and for any three values $i, j, k < n$, $x_{ij}x_{jk} = x_{ik}$. Show that for equitable matrices of order n, $X^2 = nX$. Give an example of an equitable matrix.

3.13   Communication within work groups can sometimes be studied by looking analytically at individual decision processes. Roby and Lanzetta (1956) studied at this process by constructing three matrices: OR, which maps six observations to six possible responses; PO, which indicates which type of person from three is a source of information for each observation; and PR, which maps who is responsible of the three for each of the six responses. They give these matrices (by example) as

$$
OR = \begin{array}{c} \\ O_1 \\ O_2 \\ O_3 \\ O_4 \\ O_5 \\ O_6 \end{array}
\begin{array}{c} \begin{array}{cccccc} R_1 & R_2 & R_3 & R_4 & R_5 & R_6 \end{array} \\
\left(\begin{array}{cccccc}
1 & 1 & 0 & 0 & 0 & 0 \\
0 & 1 & 1 & 0 & 0 & 0 \\
0 & 0 & 1 & 1 & 0 & 0 \\
0 & 0 & 0 & 1 & 1 & 0 \\
0 & 0 & 0 & 0 & 1 & 1 \\
1 & 0 & 0 & 0 & 0 & 1
\end{array} \right) \end{array} .
$$

$$
PO = \begin{array}{c} \\ P_1 \\ P_2 \\ P_3 \end{array}
\begin{array}{c} \begin{array}{cccccc} O_1 & O_2 & O_3 & O_4 & O_5 & O_6 \end{array} \\
\left(\begin{array}{cccccc}
1 & 0 & 1 & 0 & 0 & 0 \\
0 & 1 & 0 & 1 & 0 & 0 \\
0 & 0 & 0 & 0 & 1 & 1
\end{array} \right) \end{array} .
$$

$$
PR = \begin{array}{c} \\ R_1 \\ R_2 \\ R_3 \\ R_4 \\ R_5 \\ R_6 \end{array}
\begin{array}{c} \begin{array}{ccc} P_1 & P_2 & P_3 \end{array} \\
\left(\begin{array}{ccc}
1 & 0 & 0 \\
1 & 0 & 1 \\
0 & 1 & 0 \\
0 & 1 & 0 \\
0 & 0 & 1 \\
0 & 0 & 1
\end{array} \right) \end{array} .
$$

The claim is that multiplying these matrices in the order OR, PO, PR produces a personnel-only matrix (OPR) that reflects "the degree of operator interdependence entailed in a given task and personnel structure" where the total number of entries is proportional to the system complexity, the entries along the main diagonal show how autonomous the relevant agent is, and off-diagonals show sources of information in the organization. Perform matrix multiplication in this order to obtain the OPR matrix using transformations as needed where your final matrix has a zero in the last entry of the first row. Which matrix most affects the diagonal values of OPR when it is manipulated?

3.14 Singer and Spilerman (1973) used matrices to show social mobility between classes. These are stochastic matrices indicating different social class categories where the rows must sum to 1. In this construction a diagonal matrix means that there is no social mobility. Test their claim that the following matrix is the cube root of a stochastic matrix:

$$\mathbf{P}^{\frac{1}{3}} = \begin{pmatrix} \frac{1}{2}(1 - 1/\sqrt[3]{-\frac{1}{3}}) & \frac{1}{2}(1 + 1/\sqrt[3]{-\frac{1}{3}}) \\ \frac{1}{2}(1 + 1/\sqrt[3]{-\frac{1}{3}}) & \frac{1}{2}(1 - 1/\sqrt[3]{-\frac{1}{3}}). \end{pmatrix}$$

3.15 Element-by-element matrix multiplication is a **Hadamard product** (and sometimes called a Schur product), and it is denoted with either "$*$" or "$\odot$" (and occasionally "$\circ$") This element-wise process means that if $\mathbf{X}$ and $\mathbf{Y}$ are arbitrary matrices of identical size, the Hadamard product is $\mathbf{X} \odot \mathbf{Y}$ whose ijth element $(\mathbf{XY}_{ij})$ is $\mathbf{X}_{ij}\mathbf{Y}_{ij}$. It is trivial to see that $\mathbf{X} \odot \mathbf{Y} = \mathbf{Y} \odot \mathbf{X}$ (an interesting exception to general matrix multiplication properties), but show that for two nonzero matrices $\mathrm{tr}(\mathbf{X} \odot \mathbf{Y}) = \mathrm{tr}(\mathbf{X}) \cdot \mathrm{tr}(\mathbf{Y})$. For some nonzero matrix $\mathbf{X}$ what does $\mathbf{I} \odot \mathbf{X}$ do? For an order k $\mathbf{J}$ matrix, is $\mathrm{tr}(\mathbf{J} \odot \mathbf{J})$ different from $\mathrm{tr}(\mathbf{JJ})$? Show why or why not.

3.16   For the following LU matrix decomposition, find the permutation matrix $\mathbf{P}$ that is necessary:

$$
\begin{bmatrix} 1 & 3 & 7 \\ 1 & 1 & 12 \\ 4 & 2 & 9 \end{bmatrix} = \mathbf{P} \begin{bmatrix} 1.00 & 0.0 & 0 \\ 0.25 & 1.0 & 0 \\ 0.25 & 0.2 & 1 \end{bmatrix} \begin{bmatrix} 4 & 2.0 & 9.00 \\ 0 & 2.5 & 4.75 \\ 0 & 0.0 & 8.80 \end{bmatrix}.
$$

3.17   Prove that the product of an idempotent matrix is idempotent.

3.18   In the process of developing multilevel models of sociological data DiPrete and Grusky (1990) and others performed the matrix calculations $\boldsymbol{\Phi} = \mathbf{X}(\mathbf{I} \otimes \boldsymbol{\Delta}_\mu)\mathbf{X}' + \boldsymbol{\Sigma}_\epsilon$, where $\boldsymbol{\Sigma}_\epsilon$ is a $T \times T$ diagonal matrix with values $\sigma_1^2, \sigma_2^2, \ldots, \sigma_T^2$; $\mathbf{X}$ is an arbitrary (here) nonzero $n \times T$ matrix with $n > T$; and $\boldsymbol{\Delta}_\mu$ is a $T \times T$ diagonal matrix with values $\sigma_{\mu_1}^2, \sigma_{\mu_2}^2, \ldots, \sigma_{\mu_T}^2$. Perform this calculation to show that the result is a "block diagonal" matrix and explain this form. Use generic x_{ij} values or some other general form to denote elements of $\mathbf{X}$. Does this say anything about the Kronecker product using an identity matrix?

3.19   Calculate the LU decomposition of the matrix $\left[\begin{smallmatrix} 2 & 3 \\ 4 & 7 \end{smallmatrix}\right]$ using your preferred software such as with the `lu` function of the `Matrix` library in the R environment. Reassemble the matrix by doing the multiplication without using software.

3.20   The **Jordan product** for matrices is defined by

$$
\mathbf{X} * \mathbf{Y} = \frac{1}{2}(\mathbf{XY} + \mathbf{YX}),
$$

and the **Lie product** from group theory is

$$
\mathbf{X}x\mathbf{Y} = \mathbf{XY} - \mathbf{YX}
$$

(both assuming conformable $\mathbf{X}$ and $\mathbf{Y}$). The Lie product is also sometimes denoted with $[\mathbf{X}, \mathbf{Y}]$. Prove the identity relating standard matrix multiplication to the Jordan and Lie forms: $\mathbf{XY} = [\mathbf{X} * \mathbf{Y}] + [\mathbf{X}x\mathbf{Y}/2]$.

3.21   Demonstrate the inversion property for Kronecker products, $(\mathbf{X} \otimes \mathbf{Y})^{-1} = \mathbf{X}^{-1} \otimes \mathbf{Y}^{-1}$, with the following matrices:

$$\mathbf{X} = \begin{bmatrix} 9 & 1 \\ 2 & 8 \end{bmatrix}, \quad \mathbf{Y} = \begin{bmatrix} 2 & -5 & 1 \\ 2 & 1 & 7 \end{bmatrix}.$$

3.22   Vectorize the following matrix and find the vector norm. Can you think of any shortcuts that would make the calculations less repetitious?

$$\tilde{\mathbf{X}} = \begin{bmatrix} 1 & 2 & 1 \\ 2 & 4 & 3 \\ 3 & 1 & 2 \\ 4 & 3 & 6 \\ 5 & 5 & 5 \\ 6 & 7 & 6 \\ 7 & 9 & 9 \\ 8 & 8 & 8 \\ 9 & 8 & 3 \end{bmatrix}.$$

3.23   For two vectors in $\mathfrak{R}^3$ using $1 = \cos^2 \theta + \sin^2 \theta$ and $\|\mathbf{u} \times \mathbf{v}\|^2 = \|\mathbf{u}\|^2 \|\mathbf{v}\|^2 - \mathbf{u}^2 \cdot \mathbf{v}^2$, show that the norm of the cross product between two vectors, $\mathbf{u}$ and $\mathbf{v}$, is: $\|\mathbf{u} \times \mathbf{v}\| = \|\mathbf{u}\| \|\mathbf{v}\| \sin(\theta)$.

4

Linear Algebra Continued: Matrix Structure

4.1 Objectives

This chapter introduces more theoretical and abstract properties of vectors and matrices. We already (by now!) know the mechanics of manipulating these forms, and it is important to carry on to a deeper understanding of the properties asserted by specific row and column formations. The last chapter gave some of the algebraic basics of matrix manipulation, but this is really insufficient for understanding the full scope of linear algebra. Importantly, there are characteristics of a matrix that are not immediately obvious from just looking at its elements and dimension. The structure of a given matrix depends not only on the arrangement of numbers within its rectangular arrangement, but also on the relationship between these elements and the "size" of the matrix. The idea of size is left vague for the moment, but we will shortly see that there are some very specific ways to claim size for matrices, and these have important theoretical properties that define how a matrix works with other structures. This chapter demonstrates some of these properties by providing information about the internal dynamics of matrix structure. Some of these topics are a bit more abstract than those in the last chapter.

4.2 Space and Time

We have already discussed basic Euclidean geometric systems in Chapter 1. Recall that Cartesian coordinate systems define real-measured axes whereby points are uniquely defined in the subsequent space. So in a Cartesian plane defined by $\mathfrak{R}^2$, points define an ordered pair designating a unique position on this 2-space. Similarly, an ordered triple defines a unique point in $\mathfrak{R}^3$ 3-space. Examples of these are given in Figure 4.1.

Fig. 4.1. VISUALIZING SPACE

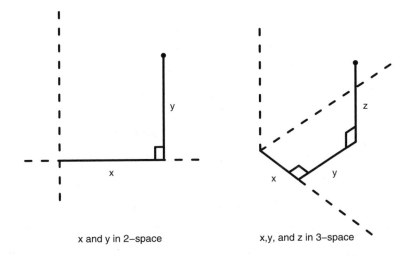

x and y in 2–space   x,y, and z in 3–space

What this figure shows with the lines is that the ordered pair or ordered triple defines a "path" in the associated space that uniquely arrives at a single point. Observe also that in both cases the path illustrated in the figure begins at the origin of the axes. So we are really defining a *vector* from the zero point to the arrival point, as shown in Figure 4.2.

Wait! This looks like a figure for illustrating the Pythagorean Theorem (the little squares are reminders that these angles are right angles). So if we wanted to get the length of the vectors, it would simply be $\sqrt{x^2 + y^2}$ in the first panel and $\sqrt{x^2 + y^2 + z^2}$ in the second panel. This is the intuition behind the basic vector norm in Section 3.2.1 of the last chapter.

Fig. 4.2. VISUALIZING VECTORS IN SPACES

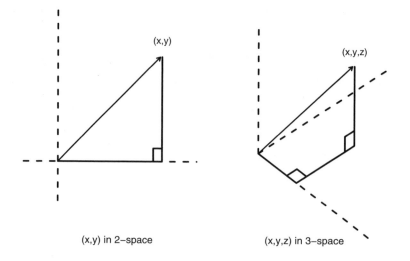

(x,y) in 2–space   (x,y,z) in 3–space

Thinking broadly about the two vectors in Figure 4.2, they take up an amount of "space" in the sense that they define a triangular planar region bounded by the vector itself and its two (left panel) or three (right panel) **projections** against the axes where the angle on the axis from this projection is necessarily a right angle (hence the reason that these are sometimes called **orthogonal projections**). Projections define how far along that axis the vector travels in total. Actually a projection does not have be just along the axes: We can project a vector $\mathbf{v}$ against another vector $\mathbf{u}$ with the following formula:

$$p = \text{ projection of } \mathbf{v} \text{ on to } \mathbf{u} = \left(\frac{\mathbf{u} \cdot \mathbf{v}}{\|\mathbf{u}\|}\right)\left(\frac{\mathbf{u}}{\|\mathbf{u}\|}\right).$$

This is shown in Figure 4.3. We can think of the second fraction on the right-hand side above as the unit vector in the direction of $\mathbf{u}$, so the first fraction is a scalar multiplier giving length. Since the right angle is preserved, we can also think about rotating this arrangement until $\mathbf{v}$ is lying on the x-axis. Then it will be the same type of projection as before. Recall from before that two vectors at right angles, such as Cartesian axes, are called orthogonal. It should be reasonably easy to see now that orthogonal vectors produce zero-length projections.

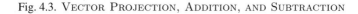

Fig. 4.3. VECTOR PROJECTION, ADDITION, AND SUBTRACTION

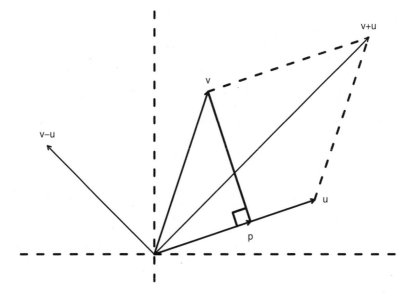

Another interesting case is when one vector is simply a multiple of another, say $(2, 4)$ and $(4, 8)$. The lines are then called **collinear** and the idea of a projection does not make sense. The plot of these vectors would be along the exact same line originating at zero, and we are thus adding no new geometric information. Therefore the vectors still consume the same space.

Also shown in Figure 4.3 are the vectors that result from $\mathbf{v} + \mathbf{u}$ and $\mathbf{v} - \mathbf{u}$ with angle θ between them. The area of the parallelogram defined by the vector $\mathbf{v} + \mathbf{u}$ shown in the figure is equal to the absolute value of the length of the orthogonal vector that results from the cross product: $\mathbf{u} \times \mathbf{v}$. This is related to the projection in the following manner: Call h the length of the line defining the projection in the figure (going from the point p to the point v). Then the parallelogram has size that is height times length: $h\|\mathbf{u}\|$ from basic geometry. Because the triangle created by the projection is a right triangle, from the trigonometry rules in Chapter 2 (page 55) we get $h = \|\mathbf{v}\| \sin\theta$, where θ is the angle between $\mathbf{u}$ and $\mathbf{v}$. Substituting we get $\mathbf{u} \times \mathbf{v} = \|\mathbf{u}\| \|\mathbf{v}\| \sin\theta$ (from an exercise in the last chapter). Therefore the size of the parallelogram is $|\mathbf{v} + \mathbf{u}|$ since the order of the cross product could make this negative. Naturally all these principles apply in higher dimension as well.

These ideas get only slightly more complicated when discussing matrices because we can think of them as collections of vectors rather than as purely rectangular structures. The **column space** of an $i \times j$ matrix $\mathbf{X}$ consists of every possible linear combination of the j columns in $\mathbf{X}$, and the **row space** of the same matrix consists of every possible linear combination of the i rows in $\mathbf{X}$. This can be expressed more formally for the $i \times j$ matrix $\mathbf{X}$ as

- <u>Column Space:</u>

  all column vectors $\mathbf{x}_{.1}, \mathbf{x}_{.2}, \ldots, \mathbf{x}_{.j}$,

  and scalars $s_1, s_2, \ldots, s_j$

  producing vectors $s_1\mathbf{x}_{.1} + s_2\mathbf{x}_{.2} + \cdots + s_j\mathbf{x}_{.j}$

- <u>Row Space:</u>

  all row vectors $\mathbf{x}_{1.}, \mathbf{x}_{2.}, \ldots, \mathbf{x}_{i.}$,

  and scalars $s_1, s_2, \ldots, s_i$

  producing vectors $s_1\mathbf{x}_{1.} + s_2\mathbf{x}_{2.} + \cdots + s_i\mathbf{x}_{i.}$,

where $\mathbf{x}_{.k}$ denotes the kth column vector of $\mathbf{x}$ and $\mathbf{x}_{k.}$ denotes the kth row vector of $\mathbf{x}$. It is now clear that the column space here consists of i-dimensional vectors and the row space consists of j-dimensional vectors. Note that the expression of space exactly fits the definition of a linear function given on page 24 in Chapter 1. This is why the field is called linear algebra. To make this process more practical, we return to our most basic example: The column space of the matrix $\left[\begin{smallmatrix} 1 & 2 \\ 3 & 4 \end{smallmatrix}\right]$ includes (but is not limited to) the following resulting vectors:

$$3\begin{bmatrix} 1 \\ 3 \end{bmatrix} + 1\begin{bmatrix} 2 \\ 4 \end{bmatrix} = \begin{bmatrix} 5 \\ 13 \end{bmatrix}, \quad 5\begin{bmatrix} 1 \\ 3 \end{bmatrix} + 0\begin{bmatrix} 2 \\ 4 \end{bmatrix} = \begin{bmatrix} 5 \\ 15 \end{bmatrix}.$$

★ **Example 4.1:** **Linear Transformation of Voter Assessments**. One difficult problem faced by analysts of survey data is that respondents often answer
ordered questions based on their own interpretation of the scale. This means
that an answer of "strongly agree" may have different meanings across a
survey because individuals anchor against different response points, or they
interpret the spacing between categories differently. Aldrich and McKelvey
(1977) approached this problem by applying a linear transformation to data
on the placement of presidents on a spatial issue dimension (recall the spatial representation in Figure 1.1). The key to their thinking was that while
respondent i places candidate j at X_{ij} on an ordinal scale from the survey
instrument, such as a 7-point "dove" to "hawk" measure, their real view was
Y_{ij} along some smoother underlying metric with finer distinctions. Aldrich
and McKelvey gave this hypothetical example for three voters:

Placement of Candidate Position on the Vietnam War, 1968

	Dove	1	2	3	4	5	6	7	Hawk
Voter 1		H,J,N			W			V	
Voter 2		H	J		N,V			W	
Voter 2		V		H	J,N			W	
Y		‖‖‖‖‖‖‖‖‖‖‖‖‖‖‖‖‖‖‖‖‖‖‖‖‖‖‖‖‖‖‖‖‖‖‖‖‖‖							

H=Humphrey, J=Johnson, N=Nixon, W=Wallace, V=Voter

The graphic for Y above is done to suggest a noncategorical measure such
as along $\Re$. To obtain a picture of this latent variable, Aldrich and McKelvey
suggested a linear transformation for each voter to relate observed categorical
scale to this underlying metric: $c_i + \omega_i X_{ij}$. Thus the perceived candidate

positions for voter i are given by

$$
Y_i =
\begin{bmatrix}
c_i + \omega_i X_{i1} \\
c_i + \omega_i X_{i2} \\
\vdots \\
c_i + \omega_i X_{iJ}
\end{bmatrix},
$$

which gives a better vector of estimates for the placement of all J candidates by respondent i because it accounts for individual-level "anchoring" by each respondent, c_i. Aldrich and McKelvey then estimated each of the values of c and ω. The value of this linear transformation is that it allows the researchers to see beyond the limitations of the categorical survey data.

Now let $x_{.1}, x_{.2}, \ldots, x_{.j}$ be a set of column vectors in $\mathfrak{R}^i$ (i.e., they are all length i). We say that the set of linear combinations of these vectors (in the sense above) is the **span** of that set. Furthermore, any additional vector in $\mathfrak{R}^i$ is spanned by these vectors if and only if it can be expressed as a linear combination of $x_{.1}, x_{.2}, \ldots, x_{.j}$. It should be somewhat intuitive that to span $\mathfrak{R}^i$ here $j \geq i$ must be true. Obviously the minimal condition is $j = i$ for a set of linearly independent vectors, and in this case we then call the set a **basis**.

This brings us to a more general discussion focused on matrices rather than on vectors. A **linear space**, $\mathfrak{X}$, is the nonempty set of matrices such that remain **closed** under linear transformation:

- If $X_1, X_2, \ldots, X_n$ are in $\mathfrak{X}$,
- and $s_1, s_2, \ldots, s_n$ are any scalars,
- then $X_{n+1} = s_1 X_1 + s_2 X_2 + \cdots + s_n X_n$ is in $\mathfrak{X}$.

That is, linear combinations of matrices in the linear space have to remain in this linear space. In addition, we can define **linear subspaces** that represent some enclosed region of the full space. Obviously column and row spaces as discussed above also comprise linear spaces. Except for the pathological case where the linear space consists only of a null matrix, every linear space contains an infinite number of matrices.

Okay, so we still need some more terminology. The span of a finite set of matrices is the set of all matrices that can be achieved by a linear combination of the original matrices. This is confusing because a span is also a linear space. Where it is useful is in determining a minimal set of matrices that span a given linear space. In particular, the finite set of *linearly independent* matrices in a given linear space that span the linear space is called a basis for this linear space (note the word "a" here since it is not unique). That is, it cannot be made a smaller set because it would lose the ability to produce parts of the linear space, and it cannot be made a larger set because it would then no longer be linearly independent.

Let us make this more concrete with an example. A 3×3 identity matrix is clearly a basis for $\Re^3$ (the three-dimensional space of real numbers) because any three-dimensional coordinate, $[r_1, r_2, r_3]$ can be produced by multiplication of $\mathbf{I}$ by three chosen scalars. Yet, the matrices defined by $\begin{bmatrix} 1 & 0 & 0 \\ 0 & 0 & 1 \\ 0 & 0 & 1 \end{bmatrix}$ and $\begin{bmatrix} 1 & 0 & 0 & 0 \\ 0 & 1 & 0 & 0 \\ 0 & 0 & 1 & 1 \end{bmatrix}$ do not qualify as a basis (although the second still *spans* $\Re^3$).

4.3 The Trace and Determinant of a Matrix

We have already noticed that the diagonals of a square matrix have special importance, particularly in the context of matrix multiplication. As mentioned in Chapter 3, a very simple way to summarize the overall magnitude of the diagonals is the **trace**. The trace of a square matrix is simply the sum of the diagonal values $\text{tr}(\mathbf{X}) = \sum_{i=1}^{k} x_{ii}$ and is usually denoted $\text{tr}(\mathbf{X})$ for the trace of square matrix $\mathbf{X}$. The trace can reveal structure in some surprising ways. For instance, an $i \times j$ matrix $\mathbf{X}$ is a zero matrix iff $\text{tr}(A'A) = 0$ (see the Exercises). In terms of calculation, the trace is probably the easiest matrix summary. For example,

$$\text{tr}\begin{pmatrix} 1 & 2 \\ 3 & 4 \end{pmatrix} = 1 + 4 = 5 \qquad \text{tr}\begin{pmatrix} 12 & \frac{1}{2} \\ 9 & \frac{1}{3} \end{pmatrix} = 12 + \frac{1}{3} = \frac{37}{3}.$$

One property of the trace has implications in statistics: $\text{tr}(\mathbf{X}'\mathbf{X})$ is the sum of the square of every value in the matrix $\mathbf{X}$. This is somewhat counterintuitive, so now we will do an illustrative example:

$$\text{tr}\left(\begin{bmatrix} 1 & 2 \\ 1 & 3 \end{bmatrix}' \begin{bmatrix} 1 & 2 \\ 1 & 3 \end{bmatrix}\right) = \text{tr}\left(\begin{array}{cc} 2 & 5 \\ 5 & 13 \end{array}\right) = 15 = 1 + 1 + 4 + 9.$$

In general, though, the matrix trace has predictable properties:

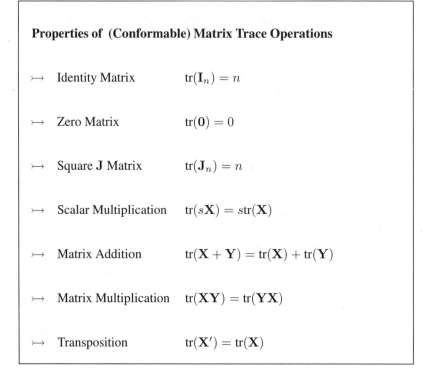

Properties of (Conformable) Matrix Trace Operations

⟼   Identity Matrix $\text{tr}(\mathbf{I}_n) = n$

⟼   Zero Matrix $\text{tr}(\mathbf{0}) = 0$

⟼   Square **J** Matrix $\text{tr}(\mathbf{J}_n) = n$

⟼   Scalar Multiplication $\text{tr}(s\mathbf{X}) = s\text{tr}(\mathbf{X})$

⟼   Matrix Addition $\text{tr}(\mathbf{X} + \mathbf{Y}) = \text{tr}(\mathbf{X}) + \text{tr}(\mathbf{Y})$

⟼   Matrix Multiplication $\text{tr}(\mathbf{XY}) = \text{tr}(\mathbf{YX})$

⟼   Transposition $\text{tr}(\mathbf{X}') = \text{tr}(\mathbf{X})$

Another important, but more difficult to calculate, matrix summary is the **determinant**. The determinant uses all of the values of a square matrix to provide a summary of structure, not just the diagonal like the trace. First let us look at how to calculate the determinant for just 2×2 matrices, which is the difference in diagonal products:

$$\det(\mathbf{X}) = |\mathbf{X}| = \begin{vmatrix} x_{11} & x_{12} \\ x_{21} & x_{22} \end{vmatrix} = x_{11}x_{22} - x_{12}x_{21}.$$

The notation for a determinant is expressed as $\det(\mathbf{X})$ or $|\mathbf{X}|$. Some simple numerical examples are

$$\begin{vmatrix} 1 & 2 \\ 3 & 4 \end{vmatrix} = (1)(4) - (2)(3) = -2$$

$$\begin{vmatrix} 10 & \frac{1}{2} \\ 4 & 1 \end{vmatrix} = (10)(1) - \left(\frac{1}{2}\right)(4) = 8$$

$$\begin{vmatrix} 2 & 3 \\ 6 & 9 \end{vmatrix} = (2)(9) - (3)(6) = 0.$$

The last case, where the determinant is found to be zero, is an important case as we shall see shortly.

Unfortunately, calculating determinants gets much more involved with square matrices larger than 2×2. First we need to define a **submatrix**. The submatrix is simply a form achieved by deleting rows and/or columns of a matrix, leaving the remaining elements in their respective places. So for the matrix $\mathbf{X}$, notice the following submatrices whose deleted rows and columns are denoted by subscripting:

$$\mathbf{X} = \begin{bmatrix} x_{11} & x_{12} & x_{13} & x_{14} \\ x_{21} & x_{22} & x_{23} & x_{24} \\ x_{31} & x_{32} & x_{33} & x_{34} \\ x_{41} & x_{42} & x_{43} & x_{44} \end{bmatrix},$$

$$\mathbf{X}_{[11]} = \begin{bmatrix} x_{22} & x_{23} & x_{24} \\ x_{32} & x_{33} & x_{34} \\ x_{42} & x_{43} & x_{44} \end{bmatrix}, \quad \mathbf{X}_{[24]} = \begin{bmatrix} x_{11} & x_{12} & x_{13} \\ x_{31} & x_{32} & x_{33} \\ x_{41} & x_{42} & x_{43} \end{bmatrix}.$$

To generalize further for $n \times n$ matrices we first need to define the following: The ijth **minor** of $\mathbf{X}$ for x_{ij}, $|\mathbf{X}_{[ij]}|$ is the determinant of the $(n-1) \times (n-1)$ submatrix that results from taking the ith row and jth column out. Continuing, the **cofactor** of $\mathbf{X}$ for x_{ij} is the minor signed in this way: $(-1)^{i+j}|\mathbf{X}_{[ij]}|$. To exhaust the entire matrix we cycle recursively through the columns and take sums with a formula that multiplies the cofactor by the determining value:

$$\det(\mathbf{X}) = \sum_{j=1}^{n} (-1)^{i+j} x_{ij} |\mathbf{X}_{[ij]}|$$

for some constant i. This is not at all intuitive, and in fact there are some subtleties lurking in there (maybe I should have taken the *blue* pill). First, *recursive* means that the algorithm is applied iteratively through progressively smaller submatrices $\mathbf{X}_{[ij]}$. Second, this means that we lop off the top row and multiply the values across the resultant submatrices without the associated column. Actually we can pick any row or column to perform this operation, because the results will be equivalent. Rather than continue to pick apart this formula in detail, just look at the application to a 3×3 matrix:

$$\begin{vmatrix} x_{11} & x_{12} & x_{13} \\ x_{21} & x_{22} & x_{23} \\ x_{31} & x_{32} & x_{33} \end{vmatrix}$$

$$= (+1)x_{11}\begin{vmatrix} x_{22} & x_{23} \\ x_{32} & x_{33} \end{vmatrix} + (-1)x_{12}\begin{vmatrix} x_{11} & x_{13} \\ x_{31} & x_{33} \end{vmatrix} + (+1)x_{13}\begin{vmatrix} x_{11} & x_{12} \\ x_{21} & x_{22} \end{vmatrix}.$$

Now the problem is easy because the subsequent three determinant calculations are on 2×2 matrices. Here we picked the first row as the starting point as per the standard algorithm. In the bad old days before ubiquitous and powerful computers people who performed these calculations by hand first looked to start with rows or columns with lots of zeros because each one would mean that the subsequent contribution was automatically zero and did not need to be calculated. Using this more general process means that one has to be more careful about the alternating signs in the sum since picking the row or column to "pivot" on determines the order. For instance, here are the signs for a 7×7

matrix produced from the sign on the cofactor:

$$\begin{bmatrix} + & - & + & - & + & - & + \\ - & + & - & + & - & + & - \\ + & - & + & - & + & - & + \\ - & + & - & + & - & + & - \\ + & - & + & - & + & - & + \\ - & + & - & + & - & + & - \\ + & - & + & - & + & - & + \end{bmatrix}.$$

★ **Example 4.2: Structural Shortcuts.** There are a number of tricks for calculating the determinants of matrices of this magnitude and greater, but mostly these are relics from slide rule days. Sometimes the shortcuts are revealing about matrix structure. Ishizawa (1991), in looking at the return to scale of public inputs and its effect on the transformation curve of an economy, needed to solve a system of equations by taking the determinant of the matrix

$$\begin{bmatrix} \ell^1 & k^1 & 0 & 0 \\ \ell^2 & k^2 & 0 & 0 \\ L_w^D & L_r^D & \ell^1 & \ell^2 \\ K_w^D & K_r^D & k^1 & k^2 \end{bmatrix},$$

where these are all abbreviations for longer vectors or complex terms. We can start by being very mechanical about this:

$$\det = \ell^1 \begin{bmatrix} k^2 & 0 & 0 \\ L_r^D & \ell^1 & \ell^2 \\ K_r^D & k^1 & k^2 \end{bmatrix} - k^1 \begin{bmatrix} \ell^2 & 0 & 0 \\ L_w^D & \ell^1 & \ell^2 \\ K_w^D & k^1 & k^2 \end{bmatrix}.$$

The big help here was the two zeros on the top row that meant that we could stop our 4×4 calculations after two steps. Fortunately this trick works again because we have the same structure remaining in the 3×3 case. Let us be a bit more strategic though and define the 2×2 lower right matrix as

$\mathbf{D} = \begin{bmatrix} \ell^1 & \ell^2 \\ k^1 & k^2 \end{bmatrix}$, so that we get the neat simplification

$$\det = \ell^1 k^2 |\mathbf{D}| - k^1 \ell^2 |\mathbf{D}| = (\ell^1 k^2 - k^1 \ell^2)|\mathbf{D}| = |\mathbf{D}|^2.$$

Because of the squaring operations here this is guaranteed to be positive, which was substantively important to Ishizawa.

The trace and the determinant have interrelated uses and special properties as well. For instance, Kronecker products on square matrices have the properties $\mathrm{tr}(\mathbf{X} \otimes \mathbf{Y}) = \mathrm{tr}(\mathbf{X})\mathrm{tr}(\mathbf{Y})$, and $|\mathbf{X} \otimes \mathbf{Y}| = |\mathbf{X}|^\ell |\mathbf{Y}|^j$ for the $j \times j$ matrix $\mathbf{X}$ and the $\ell \times \ell$ matrix $\mathbf{Y}$ (note the switching of exponents). There are some general properties of determinants to keep in mind:

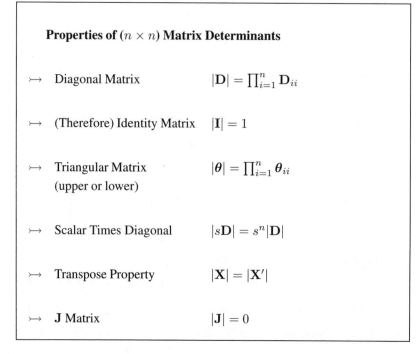

Properties of $(n \times n)$ Matrix Determinants

$\rightarrowtail$ Diagonal Matrix $|\mathbf{D}| = \prod_{i=1}^{n} \mathbf{D}_{ii}$

$\rightarrowtail$ (Therefore) Identity Matrix $|\mathbf{I}| = 1$

$\rightarrowtail$ Triangular Matrix $|\boldsymbol{\theta}| = \prod_{i=1}^{n} \boldsymbol{\theta}_{ii}$
        (upper or lower)

$\rightarrowtail$ Scalar Times Diagonal $|s\mathbf{D}| = s^n |\mathbf{D}|$

$\rightarrowtail$ Transpose Property $|\mathbf{X}| = |\mathbf{X}'|$

$\rightarrowtail$ **J Matrix** $|\mathbf{J}| = 0$

It helps some people to think abstractly about the meaning of a determinant. If the columns of an $n \times n$ matrix $\mathbf{X}$ are treated as vectors, then the area of the parallelogram created by an n-dimensional space of these vectors is the absolute value of the determinant of $\mathbf{X}$, where the vectors originate at zero and the opposite point of the parallelogram is determined by the product of the columns (a cross product of these vectors, as in Section 4.2). Okay, maybe that is a bit *too* abstract! Now view the determinant of the 2×2 matrix $\left[\begin{smallmatrix} 1 & 2 \\ 3 & 4 \end{smallmatrix}\right]$. The resulting parallelogram looks like the figure on the right. This figure indicates that the determinant is somehow a description of the size of a matrix in the geometric sense. Suppose that our example matrix were slightly different, say $\left[\begin{smallmatrix} 1 & 2 \\ 2 & 4 \end{smallmatrix}\right]$.

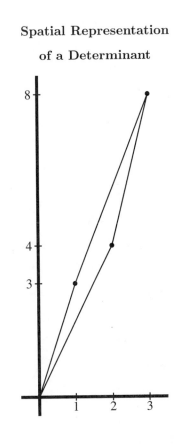

Spatial Representation of a Determinant

This does not seem like a very drastic change, yet it is quite fundamentally different. It is not too hard to see that the size of the resulting parallelogram would be zero since the two column (or row) vectors would be right on top of each other in the figure, that is, collinear. We know this also almost immediately from looking at the calculation of the determinant ($ad - bc$). Here we see that two lines on top of each other produce no area. What does this mean? It means that the column dimension exceeds the offered "information" provided by this matrix form since the columns are simply scalar multiples of each other.

4.4 Matrix Rank

The ideas just described are actually more important than they might appear at first. An important characteristic of any matrix is its **rank**. Rank tells us the "space" in terms of columns or rows that a particular matrix occupies, in other words, how much unique information is held in the rows or columns of a matrix. For example, a matrix that has three columns but only two columns of unique information is given by $\begin{bmatrix} 0 & 1 & 1 \\ 1 & 1 & 1 \\ 1 & 1 & 1 \end{bmatrix}$. This is also true for the matrix $\begin{bmatrix} 0 & 1 & 1 \\ 1 & 1 & 1 \\ 1 & 2 & 2 \end{bmatrix}$, because the third column is just two times the second column and therefore has no new relational information to offer.

More specifically, when any one column of a matrix can be produced by nonzero scalar multiples of other columns added, then we say that the matrix is not **full rank** (sometimes called **short rank**). In this case at least one column is **linearly dependent**. This simply means that we can produce the relative relationships defined by this column from the other columns and it thus adds nothing to our understanding of the relationships defined by the matrix. One way to look at this is to say that the matrix in question does not "deserve" its number of columns.

Conversely, the collection of vectors determined by the columns is said to be **linearly independent** columns if the only set of scalars, $s_1, s_2, \ldots, s_j$, that satisfies $s_1 \mathbf{x}_{.1} + s_2 \mathbf{x}_{.2} + \cdots + s_j \mathbf{x}_{.j} = \mathbf{0}$ is a set of all zero values, $s_1 = s_2 = \ldots = s_j = 0$. This is just another way of looking at the same idea since such a condition means that we *cannot* reproduce one column vector from a linear combination of the others.

Actually this emphasis on columns is somewhat unwarranted because the rank of a matrix is equal to the rank of its transpose. Therefore, everything just said about columns can also be said about rows. To restate, *the row rank of any matrix is also its column rank*. This is a very important result and is proven in virtually every text on linear algebra. What makes this somewhat confusing is additional terminology. An $(i \times j)$ matrix is **full column rank** if its rank equals the number of columns, and it is **full row rank** if its rank equals its number of rows. Thus, if $i > j$, then the matrix can be full column rank but never full row rank. This does not necessarily mean that it *has* to be full column rank just because there are fewer columns than rows.

It should be clear from the example that a (square) matrix is full rank if and only if it has a nonzero determinant. This is the same thing as saying that a matrix is full rank if it is nonsingular or invertible (see Section 4.6 below). This is a handy way to calculate whether a matrix is full rank because the linear dependency within can be subtle (unlike our example above). In the next section we will explore matrix features of this type.

★ **Example 4.3:** **Structural Equation Models**. In their text Hanushek and Jackson (1977, Chapter 9) provided a technical overview of structural equation models where systems of equations are assumed to simultaneously affect each other to reflect endogenous social phenomena. Often these models are described in matrix terms, such as their example (p. 265)

$$
\mathbf{A} = \begin{bmatrix}
\gamma_{24} & 1 & \gamma_{26} & 0 & -1 \\
0 & -1 & \gamma_{56} & 0 & 0 \\
0 & \gamma_{65} & -1 & 0 & 0 \\
\beta_{34} & 0 & \beta_{36} & 0 & \beta_{32} \\
\beta_{44} & 0 & \beta_{46} & 0 & \beta_{42}
\end{bmatrix}.
$$

Without doing any calculations we can see that this matrix is of rank less than 5 because there is a column of all zeros. We can also produce this result by calculating the determinant, but that is too much trouble. Matrix determinants are not changed by multiplying the matrix by an identity in advance, multiplying by a permutation matrix in advance, or by taking transformations.

Therefore we can get a matrix

$$
\mathbf{A}^* =
\begin{bmatrix}
0 & 0 & 0 & 1 & 0 \\
0 & 1 & 0 & 0 & 0 \\
0 & 0 & 1 & 0 & 0 \\
1 & 0 & 0 & 0 & 0 \\
0 & 0 & 0 & 0 & 1
\end{bmatrix}
\begin{bmatrix}
\gamma_{24} & 1 & \gamma_{26} & 0 & -1 \\
0 & -1 & \gamma_{56} & 0 & 0 \\
0 & \gamma_{65} & -1 & 0 & 0 \\
\beta_{34} & 0 & \beta_{36} & 0 & \beta_{32} \\
\beta_{44} & 0 & \beta_{46} & 0 & \beta_{42}
\end{bmatrix}'
$$

$$
=
\begin{bmatrix}
0 & 0 & 0 & 0 & 0 \\
0 & -1 & \gamma_{65} & 0 & 0 \\
\gamma_{26} & \gamma_{56} & -1 & \beta_{36} & \beta_{46} \\
\gamma_{24} & 0 & 0 & \beta_{34} & \beta_{44} \\
-1 & 0 & 0 & \beta_{32} & \beta_{42}
\end{bmatrix}
$$

that is immediately identifiable as having a zero determinant by the general determinant form given on page 142 because each ith minor (the matrix that remains when the ith row and column are removed) is multiplied by the ith value on the first row.

Some rank properties are more specialized. An idempotent matrix has the property that

$$\text{rank}(\mathbf{X}) = \text{tr}(\mathbf{X}),$$

and more generally, for any square matrix with the property that $A^2 = sA$, for some scalar s

$$s\text{rank}(\mathbf{X}) = \text{tr}(\mathbf{X}).$$

To emphasize that matrix rank is a fundamental principle, we now give some standard properties related to other matrix characteristics.

Properties of Matrix Rank

$\rightarrowtail$	Transpose	$\text{rank}(\mathbf{X}) = \text{rank}(\mathbf{X}')$
$\rightarrowtail$	Scalar Multiplication (nonzero scalars)	$\text{rank}(s\mathbf{X}) = \text{rank}(\mathbf{X})$
$\rightarrowtail$	Matrix Addition	$\text{rank}(\mathbf{X} + \mathbf{Y}) \leq \text{rank}(\mathbf{X}) + \text{rank}(\mathbf{Y})$
$\rightarrowtail$	Consecutive Blocks	$\text{rank}[\mathbf{X}\mathbf{Y}] \leq \text{rank}(\mathbf{X}) + \text{rank}(\mathbf{Y})$ $\text{rank}\left[\begin{smallmatrix}\mathbf{X}\\\mathbf{Y}\end{smallmatrix}\right] \leq \text{rank}(\mathbf{X}) + \text{rank}(\mathbf{Y})$
$\rightarrowtail$	Diagonal Blocks	$\text{rank}\left[\begin{smallmatrix}\mathbf{X}&0\\0&\mathbf{Y}\end{smallmatrix}\right] = \text{rank}(\mathbf{X}) + \text{rank}(\mathbf{Y})$
$\rightarrowtail$	Kronecker Product	$\text{rank}(\mathbf{X} \otimes \mathbf{Y}) = \text{rank}(\mathbf{X})\text{rank}(\mathbf{Y})$

4.5 Matrix Norms

Recall that the vectors norm is a measure of length:

$$\|\mathbf{v}\| = (v_1^2 + v_2^2 + \cdots + v_n^2)^{\frac{1}{2}} = (\mathbf{v}'\mathbf{v})^{\frac{1}{2}}.$$

We have seen matrix "size" as described by the trace, determinant, and rank. Additionally, we can describe matrices by norming, but matrix norms are a little bit more involved than the vector norms we saw before. There are two general types, the **trace norm** (sometimes called the Euclidean norm or the Frobenius norm):

$$\|\mathbf{X}\|_F = \left[\sum_i \sum_j |x_{ij}|^2\right]^{\frac{1}{2}}$$

(the square root of the sum of each element squared), and the p-norm:

$$\|\mathbf{X}\|_p = \max_{\|\mathbf{v}\|_p} \|\mathbf{X}\mathbf{v}\|_p,$$

which is defined with regard to the unit vector $\mathbf{v}$ whose length is equal to the number of columns in $\mathbf{X}$. For $p = 1$ and an $I \times J$ matrix, this reduces to summing absolute values down columns and taking the maximum:

$$\|\mathbf{X}\|_1 = \max_J \sum_{i=1}^{I} |x_{ij}|.$$

Conversely, the infinity version of the matrix p-norm sums across rows before taking the maximum:

$$\|\mathbf{X}\|_\infty = \max_I \sum_{j=1}^{J} |x_{ij}|.$$

Like the infinity form of the vector norm, this is somewhat unintuitive because there is no apparent use of a limit. There are some interesting properties of matrix norms:

Properties of Matrix Norms, Size $(i \times j)$

$\longmapsto$ Constant Multiplication $\quad \|k\mathbf{X}\| = |k| \|\mathbf{X}\|$

$\longmapsto$ Addition $\quad \|\mathbf{X} + \mathbf{Y}\| \leq \|\mathbf{X}\| + \|\mathbf{Y}\|$

$\longmapsto$ Vector Multiplication $\quad \|\mathbf{X}\mathbf{v}\|_p \leq \|\mathbf{X}\|_p \|\mathbf{v}\|_p$

$\longmapsto$ Norm Relation $\quad \|\mathbf{X}\|_2 \leq \|\mathbf{X}\|_F \leq \sqrt{j} \|\mathbf{X}\|_2$

$\longmapsto$ Unit Vector Relation $\quad \mathbf{X}'\mathbf{X}\mathbf{v} = (\|\mathbf{X}\|_2)^2 \mathbf{v}$

$\longmapsto$ P-norm Relation $\quad \|\mathbf{X}\|_2 \leq \sqrt{\|\mathbf{X}\|_1 \|\mathbf{X}\|_\infty}$

$\longmapsto$ Schwarz Inequality $\quad |\mathbf{X} \cdot \mathbf{Y}| \leq \|\mathbf{X}\| \|\mathbf{Y}\|,$
$\qquad\qquad\qquad\qquad\qquad$ where $|\mathbf{X} \cdot \mathbf{Y}| = \mathrm{tr}(\mathbf{X}'\mathbf{Y})$

★ **Example 4.4:** **Matrix Norm Sum Inequality**. Given matrices

$$\mathbf{X} = \begin{bmatrix} 3 & 2 \\ 5 & 1 \end{bmatrix} \quad \text{and} \quad \mathbf{Y} = \begin{bmatrix} -1 & -2 \\ 3 & 4 \end{bmatrix},$$

observe that

$\|\mathbf{X} + \mathbf{Y}\|_\infty$	$\|\mathbf{X}\|_\infty + \|\mathbf{Y}\|_\infty$
$\left\| \begin{bmatrix} 2 & 0 \\ 8 & 5 \end{bmatrix} \right\|_\infty$	$\max(5,6) + \max(3,7)$
$\max(2,13)$	$13,$

showing the second property above.

★ **Example 4.5:** **Schwarz Inequality for Matrices**. Using the same $\mathbf{X}$ and $\mathbf{Y}$ matrices and the $p = 1$ norm, observe that

$\|\mathbf{X} \cdot \mathbf{Y}\|$	$\|\mathbf{X}\|_1 \|\mathbf{Y}\|_1$
$(12) + (0)$	$\max(8,3) \cdot \max(4,6)$

showing that the inequality holds: $12 < 48$. This is a neat property because it shows a relationship between the trace and matrix norm.

4.6 Matrix Inversion

Just like scalars have inverses, some *square* matrices have a **matrix inverse**. The inverse of a matrix $\mathbf{X}$ is denoted $\mathbf{X}^{-1}$ and defined by the property

$$\mathbf{X}\mathbf{X}^{-1} = \mathbf{X}^{-1}\mathbf{X} = \mathbf{I}.$$

That is, when a matrix is pre-multiplied or post-multiplied by its inverse the result is an identity matrix of the same size. For example, consider the following matrix and its inverse:

$$\begin{bmatrix} 1 & 2 \\ 3 & 4 \end{bmatrix} \begin{bmatrix} -2.0 & 1.0 \\ 1.5 & -0.5 \end{bmatrix} = \begin{bmatrix} -2.0 & 1.0 \\ 1.5 & -0.5 \end{bmatrix} \begin{bmatrix} 1 & 2 \\ 3 & 4 \end{bmatrix} = \begin{bmatrix} 1 & 0 \\ 0 & 1 \end{bmatrix}$$

Not all square matrices are invertible. A singular matrix cannot be inverted, and often "singular" and "noninvertible" are used as synonyms. Usually matrix inverses are calculated by computer software because it is quite time-consuming with reasonably large matrices. However, there is a very nice trick for immediately inverting 2×2 matrices, which is given by

$$\mathbf{X} = \begin{bmatrix} x_{11} & x_{12} \\ x_{21} & x_{22} \end{bmatrix}$$

$$\mathbf{X}^{-1} = \det(\mathbf{X})^{-1} \begin{bmatrix} x_{22} & -x_{12} \\ -x_{21} & x_{11} \end{bmatrix}.$$

A matrix inverse is unique: There is only one matrix that meets the multiplicative condition above for a nonsingular square matrix.

For inverting larger matrices there is a process based on **Gauss-Jordan elimination** that makes use of linear programming to invert the matrix. Although matrix inversion would normally be done courtesy of software for nearly all problems in the social sciences, the process of Gauss-Jordan elimination is a revealing insight into inversion because it highlights the "inverse" aspect with the role of the identity matrix as the linear algebra equivalent of 1. Start with the matrix of interest partitioned next to the identity matrix and allow the following operations:

- Any row may be multiplied or divided by a scalar.
- Any two rows may be switched.
- Any row may be multiplied or divided by a scalar and then added to another row. Note: This operation does not change the original row; its multiple is used but not saved.

Of course the goal of these operations has not yet been given. We want to iteratively apply these steps until the identity matrix on the right-hand side is on the left-hand side. So the operations are done with the intent of zeroing out the off-diagonals on the left matrix of the partition and then dividing to obtain 1's on the diagonal. During this process we do not care about what results on the right-hand side until the end, when this is known to be the inverse of the original matrix.

Let's perform this process on a 3×3 matrix:

$$\left[\begin{array}{ccc|ccc} 1 & 2 & 3 & 1 & 0 & 0 \\ 4 & 5 & 6 & 0 & 1 & 0 \\ 1 & 8 & 9 & 0 & 0 & 1 \end{array}\right].$$

Now multiply the first row by -4, adding it to the second row, and multiply the first row by -1, adding it to the third row:

$$\left[\begin{array}{ccc|ccc} 1 & 2 & 3 & 1 & 0 & 0 \\ 0 & -3 & -6 & -4 & 1 & 0 \\ 0 & 6 & 6 & -1 & 0 & 1 \end{array}\right].$$

Multiply the second row by $\frac{1}{2}$, adding it to the first row, and simply add this same row to the third row:

$$\left[\begin{array}{ccc|ccc} 1 & \frac{1}{2} & 0 & -1 & \frac{1}{2} & 0 \\ 0 & -3 & -6 & -4 & 1 & 0 \\ 0 & 3 & 0 & -5 & 1 & 1 \end{array}\right].$$

Multiply the third row by $-\frac{1}{6}$, adding it to the first row, and add the third row (un)multiplied to the second row:

$$\left[\begin{array}{ccc|ccc} 1 & 0 & 0 & -\frac{1}{6} & \frac{1}{3} & -\frac{1}{6} \\ 0 & 0 & -6 & -9 & 2 & 1 \\ 0 & 3 & 0 & -5 & 1 & 1 \end{array}\right].$$

Finally, just divide the second row by -6 and the third row by -3, and then switch their places:

$$\left[\begin{array}{ccc|ccc} 1 & 0 & 0 & -\frac{1}{6} & \frac{1}{3} & -\frac{1}{6} \\ 0 & 1 & 0 & -\frac{5}{3} & \frac{1}{3} & \frac{1}{3} \\ 0 & 0 & 1 & \frac{3}{2} & -\frac{1}{3} & -\frac{1}{6} \end{array}\right],$$

thus completing the operation. This process also highlights the fact that matrices are representations of linear equations. The operations we performed are linear transformations, just like those discussed at the beginning of this chapter.

We already know that singular matrices cannot be inverted, but consider the described inversion process applied to an obvious case:

$$\left[\begin{array}{cc|cc} 1 & 0 & 1 & 0 \\ 1 & 0 & 0 & 1 \end{array}\right].$$

It is easy to see that there is nothing that can be done to put a nonzero value in the second column of the matrix to the left of the partition. In this way the Gauss-Jordan process helps to illustrate a theoretical concept.

Most of the properties of matrix inversion are predictable (the last property listed relies on the fact that the product of invertible matrices is always itself invertible):

Properties of $n \times n$ Nonsingular Matrix Inverse

$\rightarrowtail$	Diagonal Matrix	$\mathbf{D}^{-1}$ has diagonal values $1/d_{ii}$ and zeros elsewhere.
$\rightarrowtail$	(Therefore) Identity Matrix	$\mathbf{I}^{-1} = \mathbf{I}$
$\rightarrowtail$	(Non-zero) Scalar Multiplication	$(s\mathbf{X})^{-1} = \frac{1}{s}\mathbf{X}^{-1}$
$\rightarrowtail$	Iterative Inverse	$(\mathbf{X}^{-1})^{-1} = \mathbf{X}$
$\rightarrowtail$	Exponents	$\mathbf{X}^{-n} = (\mathbf{X}^n)^{-1}$
$\rightarrowtail$	Multiplicative Property	$(\mathbf{X}\mathbf{Y})^{-1} = \mathbf{Y}^{-1}\mathbf{X}^{-1}$
$\rightarrowtail$	Transpose Property	$(\mathbf{X}')^{-1} = (\mathbf{X}^{-1})'$
$\rightarrowtail$	Orthogonal Property	If $\mathbf{X}$ is orthogonal, then $\mathbf{X}^{-1} = \mathbf{X}'$
$\rightarrowtail$	Determinant	$|\mathbf{X}^{-1}| = 1/|\mathbf{X}|$

★ **Example 4.6:** **Calculating Regression Parameters**. The classic "ordinary least squares" method for obtaining regression parameters proceeds as follows. Suppose that $\mathbf{y}$ is the outcome variable of interest and $\mathbf{X}$ is a matrix of explanatory variables with a leading column of 1's. What we would like is the vector $\hat{\mathbf{b}}$ that contains the intercept and the regression slope, which is calculated by the equation $\hat{\mathbf{b}} = (\mathbf{X}'\mathbf{X})^{-1}\mathbf{X}'\mathbf{y}$, which might have seemed hard before this point in the chapter. What we need to do then is just a series of multiplications, one inverse, and two transposes.

To make the example more informative, we can look at some actual data with two variables of interest (even though we could just do this in scalar algebra since it is just a bivariate problem). Governments often worry about the economic condition of senior citizens for political and social reasons. Typically in a large industrialized society, a substantial portion of these people obtain the bulk of their income from government pensions. One important question is whether there is enough support through these payments to provide subsistence above the poverty rate. To see if this is a concern, the European Union (EU) looked at this question in 1998 for the (then) 15 member countries with two variables: (1) the median (EU standardized) income of individuals age 65 and older as a percentage of the population age 0–64, and (2) the percentage with income below 60% of the median (EU standardized) income of the national population. The data from the European Household Community Panel Survey are

Nation	Relative Income	Poverty Rate
Netherlands	93.00	7.00
Luxembourg	99.00	8.00
Sweden	83.00	8.00
Germany	97.00	11.00
Italy	96.00	14.00
Spain	91.00	16.00
Finland	78.00	17.00
France	90.00	19.00
United.Kingdom	78.00	21.00
Belgium	76.00	22.00
Austria	84.00	24.00
Denmark	68.00	31.00
Portugal	76.00	33.00
Greece	74.00	33.00
Ireland	69.00	34.00

So the $\mathbf{y}$ vector is the second column of the table and the $\mathbf{X}$ matrix is the first column along with the leading column of 1's added to account for the intercept (also called the constant, which explains the 1's). The first quantity that we want to calculate is

$$\mathbf{X'X} = \begin{bmatrix} 15.00 & 1252 \\ 1252 & 105982 \end{bmatrix},$$

which has the inverse

$$(\mathbf{X'X})^{-1} = \begin{bmatrix} 4.76838 & -0.05633 \\ -0.05633 & 0.00067 \end{bmatrix}.$$

So the final calculation is

$$
\begin{bmatrix} 4.76838 & -0.05633 \\ -0.05633 & 0.00067 \end{bmatrix}
\begin{bmatrix} 1 & 93 \\ 1 & 99 \\ 1 & 83 \\ 1 & 97 \\ 1 & 96 \\ 1 & 91 \\ 1 & 78 \\ 1 & 90 \\ 1 & 78 \\ 1 & 76 \\ 1 & 84 \\ 1 & 68 \\ 1 & 76 \\ 1 & 74 \\ 1 & 69 \end{bmatrix}'
\begin{bmatrix} 7 \\ 8 \\ 8 \\ 11 \\ 14 \\ 16 \\ 17 \\ 19 \\ 21 \\ 22 \\ 24 \\ 31 \\ 33 \\ 33 \\ 34 \end{bmatrix}
=
\begin{bmatrix} 83.69279 \\ -0.76469 \end{bmatrix}
$$

These results are shown in Figure 4.4 for the 15 EU countries of the time, with a line for the estimated underlying trend that has a slope of $m = -0.77$ (rounded) and an intercept at $b = 84$ (also rounded). What does this mean? It means that for a one-unit positive change (say from 92 to 93) in over-65 relative income, there will be an *expected* change in over-65 poverty rate of -0.77 (i.e., a reduction). This is depicted in Figure 4.4.

Once one understands linear regression in matrix notation, it is much easier to see what is happening. For instance, if there were a *second* explanatory variable (there are many more than one in social science models), then it would simply be an addition column of the **X** matrix and all the calculations would proceed exactly as we have done here.

4.7 Linear Systems of Equations

A basic and common problem in applied mathematics is the search for a solution, **x**, to the system of simultaneous linear equations defined by

$$\mathbf{Ax} = \mathbf{y},$$

Fig. 4.4. RELATIVE INCOME AND SENIOR POVERTY, EU COUNTRIES

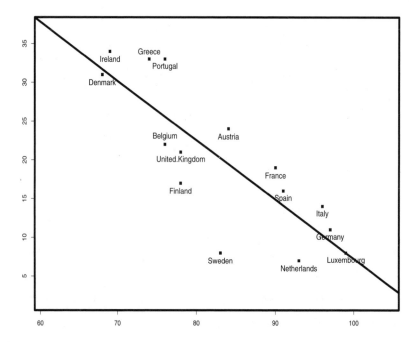

where $\mathbf{A} \in \mathfrak{R}^{p \times q}$, $\mathbf{x} \in \mathfrak{R}^{q}$, and $\mathbf{y} \in \mathfrak{R}^{p}$. If the matrix $\mathbf{A}$ is invertible, then there exists a unique, easy-to-find, solution vector $\mathbf{x} = \mathbf{A}^{-1}\mathbf{y}$ satisfying $\mathbf{A}\mathbf{x} = \mathbf{y}$. Note that this shows the usefulness of a matrix inverse. However, if the system of linear equations in $\mathbf{A}\mathbf{x} = \mathbf{y}$ is not *consistent*, then there exists no solution. Consistency simply means that if a linear relationship exists in the rows of $\mathbf{A}$, it must also exist in the corresponding rows of $\mathbf{y}$. For example, the following simple system of linear equations is consistent:

$$\begin{bmatrix} 1 & 2 \\ 2 & 4 \end{bmatrix} \mathbf{x} = \begin{bmatrix} 3 \\ 6 \end{bmatrix}$$

because the second row is two times the first across $(\mathbf{x}|\mathbf{y})$. This implies that $\mathbf{y}$ is contained in the linear span of the columns (range) of $\mathbf{A}$, denoted as $\mathbf{y} \in R(\mathbf{A})$. Recall that a set of linearly independent vectors (i.e., the columns here) that span a vector subspace is called a basis of that subspace. Conversely, the following system of linear equations is not consistent:

$$\begin{bmatrix} 1 & 2 \\ 2 & 4 \end{bmatrix} \mathbf{x} = \begin{bmatrix} 3 \\ 7 \end{bmatrix},$$

because there is no solution for $\mathbf{x}$ that satisfies both rows. In the notation above this is denoted $\mathbf{y} \notin R(\mathbf{A})$, and it provides no further use without modification of the original problem. It is worth noting, for purposes of the discussion below, that if $\mathbf{A}^{-1}$ exists, then $\mathbf{A}\mathbf{x} = \mathbf{y}$ is always consistent because there exist no linear relationships in the rows of $\mathbf{A}$ that must be satisfied in $\mathbf{y}$. The inconsistent case is the more common *statistically* in that a solution that minimizes the squared sum of the inconsistencies is typically applied (ordinary least squares).

In addition to the possibilities of the general system of equations $\mathbf{A}\mathbf{x} = \mathbf{y}$ having a unique solution and no solution, this arbitrary system of equations can also have an infinite number of solutions. In fact, the matrix $\begin{bmatrix} 1 & 2 \\ 3 & 4 \end{bmatrix}$ above is such a case. For example, we could solve to obtain $\mathbf{x} = (1, 1)'$, $\mathbf{x} = (-1, 2)'$, $\mathbf{x} = (5, -1)'$, and so on. This occurs when the $\mathbf{A}$ matrix is singular: rank$(\mathbf{A})$ = dimension$(R(\mathbf{A})) < q$. When the $\mathbf{A}$ matrix is singular at least one column vector is a linear combination of the others, and the matrix therefore contains redundant information. In other words, there are $q' < q$ independent column vectors in $\mathbf{A}$.

★ **Example 4.7:** **Solving Systems of Equations by Inversion.** Consider the system of equations

$$2x_1 - 3x_2 = 4$$
$$5x_1 + 5x_2 = 3,$$

where $\mathbf{x} = [x_1, x_2]$, $\mathbf{y} = [4, 3]'$, and $\mathbf{A} = \begin{bmatrix} 2 & -3 \\ 5 & 5 \end{bmatrix}$. First invert $\mathbf{A}$:

$$\mathbf{A}^{-1} = \begin{bmatrix} 2 & -3 \\ 5 & 5 \end{bmatrix}^{-1} = \begin{bmatrix} 0.2 & 0.12 \\ -0.2 & 0.08 \end{bmatrix}.$$

Then, to solve for $\mathbf{x}$ we simply need to multiply this inverse by $\mathbf{y}$:

$$\mathbf{A}^{-1}\mathbf{y} = \begin{bmatrix} 0.2 & 0.12 \\ -0.2 & 0.08 \end{bmatrix} \begin{bmatrix} 4 \\ 3 \end{bmatrix} = \begin{bmatrix} 0.16 \\ -0.56 \end{bmatrix},$$

meaning that $\mathbf{x}_1 = 0.16$ and $\mathbf{x}_2 = -0.56$.

4.8 Eigen-Analysis of Matrices

We start this section with a brief motivation. Apparently a single original population undergoes genetic differentiation once it is dispersed into new geographic regions. Furthermore, it is interesting anthropologically to compare the rate of this genetic change with changes in nongenetic traits such as language, culture, and use of technology. Sorenson and Kenmore (1974) explored the genetic drift of proto-agricultural people in the Eastern Highlands of New Guinea with the idea that changes in horticulture and mountainous geography both determined patterns of dispersion. This is an interesting study because it uses biological evidence (nine alternative forms of a gene) to make claims about the relatedness of groups that are geographically distinct but similar ethnohistorically and linguistically. The raw genetic information can be summarized in a large matrix, but the information in this form is not really the primary interest. To see differences and similarities Sorenson and Kenmore transformed these variables into just two individual factors (new composite variables) that appear to explain the bulk of the genetic variation.

Once that is done it is easy to graph the groups in a single plot and then look at similarities geometrically. This useful result is shown in the figure at right, where we see the placement of these linguistic groups according to the similarity in blood-group genetics. The tool they used for turn-

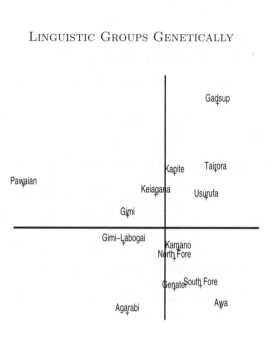

LINGUISTIC GROUPS GENETICALLY

ing the large multidimensional matrix of unwieldy data into an intuitive two-dimensional structure was eigenanalysis.

A useful and theoretically important feature of a given square matrix is the set of **eigenvalues** associated with this matrix. Every $p \times p$ matrix $\mathbf{X}$ has p scalar values, $\lambda_i, i = 1, \ldots, p$, such that

$$\mathbf{X}\mathbf{h}_i = \lambda_i \mathbf{h}_i$$

for some corresponding vector $\mathbf{h}_i$. In this decomposition, λ_i is called an eigenvalue of $\mathbf{X}$ and h_i is called an **eigenvector** of $\mathbf{X}$. These eigenvalues show important structural features of the matrix. Confusingly, these are also called the **characteristic roots** and **characteristic vectors** of $\mathbf{X}$, and the process is also called **spectral decomposition**.

The expression above can also be rewritten to produce the **characteristic**

equation. Start with the algebraic rearrangement

$$(\mathbf{X} - \lambda_i \mathbf{I})\mathbf{h}_i = \mathbf{0}.$$

If the $p \times p$ matrix in the parentheses has a zero determinant, then there exist eigenvalues that are solutions to the equation:

$$|\mathbf{X} - \lambda_i \mathbf{I}| = \mathbf{0}.$$

★ **Example 4.8:** **Basic Eigenanalysis**. A symmetric matrix $\mathbf{X}$ is given by

$$\mathbf{X} = \begin{bmatrix} 1.000 & 0.880 & 0.619 \\ 0.880 & 1.000 & 0.716 \\ 0.619 & 0.716 & 1.000 \end{bmatrix}.$$

The eigenvalues and eigenvectors are found by solving the characteristic equation $|\mathbf{X} - \lambda \mathbf{I}| = 0$. This produces the matrix

$$\lambda \mathbf{I} = \begin{bmatrix} 2.482 & 0.00 & 0.000 \\ 0.000 & 0.41 & 0.000 \\ 0.000 & 0.00 & 0.108 \end{bmatrix}$$

from which we take the eigenvalues from the diagonal. Note the descending order. To see the mechanics of this process more clearly, consider finding the eigenvalues of

$$\mathbf{Y} = \begin{bmatrix} 3 & -1 \\ 2 & 0 \end{bmatrix}.$$

To do this we expand and solve the determinant of the characteristic equation:

$$|\mathbf{Y} - \lambda \mathbf{I}| = (3 - \lambda)(0 - \lambda) - (-2) = \lambda^2 - 3\lambda + 2$$

and the only solutions to this quadratic expression are $\lambda_1 = 1, \lambda_2 = 2$. In fact, for a $p \times p$ matrix, the resulting characteristic equation will be a polynomial of order p. This is why we had a quadratic expression here.

Unfortunately, the eigenvalues that result from the characteristic equation can be zero, repeated (nonunique) values, or even complex numbers. However, all symmetric matrices like the 3×3 example above are guaranteed to have real-valued eigenvalues.

Eigenvalues and eigenvectors are associated. That is, for each eigenvector of a given matrix $\mathbf{X}$ there is exactly one corresponding eigenvalue such that

$$\lambda = \frac{\mathbf{h}'\mathbf{X}\mathbf{h}}{\mathbf{h}'\mathbf{h}}.$$

This uniqueness, however, is asymmetric. For each eigenvalue of the matrix there is an infinite number of eigenvectors, all determined by scalar multiplication: If $\mathbf{h}$ is an eigenvector corresponding to the eigenvalue λ, then $s\mathbf{h}$ is also an eigenvector corresponding to this same eigenvalue where s is any nonzero scalar.

There are many interesting matrix properties related to eigenvalues. For instance, the number of nonzero eigenvalues is the rank of the $\mathbf{X}$, the sum of the eigenvalues is the trace of $\mathbf{X}$, and the product of the eigenvalues is the determinant of $\mathbf{X}$. From these principles it follows immediately that a matrix is singular if and only if it has a zero eigenvalue, and the rank of the matrix is the number of nonzero eigenvalues.

Properties of Eigenvalues for a Nonsingular ($n \times n$) Matrix

$\rightarrowtail$ Inverse Property   If λ_i is an eigenvalue of $\mathbf{X}$, then $\frac{1}{\lambda_i}$ is an eigenvalue of $\mathbf{X}^{-1}$

$\rightarrowtail$ Transpose Property $\mathbf{X}$ and $\mathbf{X}'$ have the same eigenvalues

$\rightarrowtail$ Identity Matrix   For $\mathbf{I}$, $\sum \lambda_i = n$

$\rightarrowtail$ Exponentiation   If λ_i is an eigenvalue of $\mathbf{X}$, then λ_i^k is an eigenvalue of $\mathbf{X}^k$ and k a positive integer

---

It is also true that if there are no zero-value eigenvectors, then the eigenvalues determine a basis for the space determined by the size of the matrix ($\mathfrak{R}^2$, $\mathfrak{R}^3$, etc.). Even more interestingly, symmetric nonsingular matrices have eigenvectors that are perpendicular (see the Exercises).

A notion related to eigenvalues is matrix conditioning. For a symmetric definite matrix, the ratio of the largest eigenvalue to the smallest eigenvalue is the **condition number**. If this number is large, then we say that the matrix is "ill-conditioned," and it usually has poor properties. For example, if the matrix is nearly singular (but not quite), then the smallest eigenvalue will be close to zero and the ratio will be large for any reasonable value of the largest eigenvalue. As an example of this problem, in the use of matrix inversion to solve systems of linear equations, an ill-conditioned $\mathbf{A}$ matrix means that small changes in $\mathbf{A}$ will produce large changes in $\mathbf{A}^{-1}$ and therefore the calculation of x will differ dramatically.

★ **Example 4.9:   Analyzing Social Mobility with Eigens**. Duncan (1966) analyzed social mobility between categories of employment (from the 1962 Current Population Survey) to produce probabilities for blacks and whites [also analyzed in McFarland (1981) from which this discussion is derived]. This well-known finding is summarized in two *transition* matrices, indicating probabilities for changing between *higher white collar, lower white collar, higher manual, lower manual,* and *farm*:

$$
B = \begin{bmatrix}
0.112 & 0.105 & 0.210 & 0.573 & 0.000 \\
0.156 & 0.098 & 0.000 & 0.745 & 0.000 \\
0.094 & 0.073 & 0.120 & 0.684 & 0.030 \\
0.087 & 0.077 & 0.126 & 0.691 & 0.020 \\
0.035 & 0.034 & 0.072 & 0.676 & 0.183
\end{bmatrix}
$$

$$
W = \begin{bmatrix}
0.576 & 0.162 & 0.122 & 0.126 & 0.014 \\
0.485 & 0.197 & 0.145 & 0.157 & 0.016 \\
0.303 & 0.127 & 0.301 & 0.259 & 0.011 \\
0.229 & 0.124 & 0.242 & 0.387 & 0.018 \\
0.178 & 0.076 & 0.214 & 0.311 & 0.221
\end{bmatrix},
$$

where the rows and columns are in the order of employment categories given. So, for instance, 0.576 in the first row and first column of the W matrix means that we expect 57.6% of the children of white higher white collar workers will themselves become higher white collar workers. Contrastingly, 0.573 in the first row and fourth column of the B matrix means that we expect 57.4% of the children of black lower manual workers to become lower manual workers themselves.

A lot can be learned by staring at these matrices for some time, but what tools will let us understand long-run trends built into the data? Since these are transition probabilities, we could multiply one of these matrices to itself a large number of times as a simulation of future events (this is actually the topic of Chapter 9). It might be more convenient for answering simple questions to use eigenanalysis to pull structure out of the matrix instead.

It turns out that the eigenvector produced from $\mathbf{X}\mathbf{h}_i = \lambda_i \mathbf{h}_i$ is the **right eigenvector** because it sits on the right-hand side of $\mathbf{X}$ here. This is the default, so when an eigenvector is referenced without any qualifiers, the form derived above is the appropriate one. However, there is also the less-commonly used **left eigenvector** produced from $\mathbf{h}_i \mathbf{X} = \lambda_i \mathbf{h}_i$ and so-named for the obvious reason. If $\mathbf{X}$ is a symmetric matrix, then the two vectors are identical (the eigenvalues are the same in either case). If $\mathbf{X}$ is not symmetrical, they differ, but the left eigenvector can be produced from using the transpose: $\mathbf{X}'\mathbf{h}_i = \lambda_i \mathbf{h}_i$. The *spectral component* corresponding to the ith eigenvalue is the square matrix produced from the cross product of the right and left eigenvectors over the dot product of the right and left eigenvectors:

$$S_i = h_{i,\text{right}} \times h_{i,\text{left}} / h_{i,\text{right}} \cdot h_{i,\text{left}}.$$

This spectral decomposition into constituent components by eigenvalues is especially revealing for probability matrices like the two above, where the rows necessarily sum to 1.

Because of the probability structure of these matrices, the first eigenvalue is always 1. The associated spectral components are

$$B = \begin{bmatrix} 0.09448605 & 0.07980742 & 0.1218223 & 0.6819610 & 0.02114880 \end{bmatrix}$$

$$W = \begin{bmatrix} 0.4293069 & 0.1509444 & 0.1862090 & 0.2148500 & 0.01840510. \end{bmatrix},$$

where only a single row of this 5×5 matrix is given here because all rows are identical (a result of $\lambda_1 = 1$). The spectral values corresponding to the first eigenvalue give the long-run (stable) proportions implied by the matrix probabilities. That is, if conditions do not change, these will be the eventual population proportions. So if the mobility trends persevere, eventually a little over two-thirds of the black population will be in lower manual occupations, and less than 10% will be in each of the white collar occupational categories (keep in mind that Duncan collected the data before the zenith of the civil rights movement). In contrast, for whites, about 40% will be in the higher white collar category with 15–20% in each of the other nonfarm occupational groups.

Subsequent spectral components from declining eigenvalues give weighted propensities for movement between individual matrix categories. The second eigenvalue produces the most important indicator, followed by the third, and so on. The second spectral components corresponding to the second eigenvalues $\lambda_{2,\text{black}} = 0.177676$, $\lambda_{2,\text{white}} = 0.348045$ are

$$B = \begin{bmatrix} 0.063066 & 0.043929 & 0.034644 & -0.019449 & -0.122154 \\ 0.103881 & 0.072359 & 0.057065 & -0.032037 & -0.201211 \\ -0.026499 & -0.018458 & -0.014557 & 0.008172 & 0.051327 \\ -0.002096 & -0.001460 & -0.001151 & 0.000646 & 0.004059 \\ -0.453545 & -0.315919 & -0.249145 & 0.139871 & 0.878486 \end{bmatrix}$$

$$W = \begin{bmatrix} 0.409172 & 0.055125 & -0.187845 & -0.273221 & -0.002943 \\ 0.244645 & 0.032960 & -0.112313 & -0.163360 & -0.001759 \\ -0.3195779 & -0.043055 & 0.146714 & 0.213396 & 0.002298 \\ -0.6018242 & -0.081080 & 0.276289 & 0.401864 & 0.004328 \\ -1.2919141 & -0.174052 & 0.593099 & 0.862666 & 0.009292 \end{bmatrix}$$

Notice that the full matrix is given here because the rows now differ. McFarland noticed the structure highlighted here with the boxes containing positive values. For blacks there is a tendency for white collar status and higher manual to be self-reinforcing: Once landed in the upper left 2×3 submatrix, there is a tendency to remain and negative influences on leaving. The same phenomenon applies for blacks to manual/farm labor: Once there it is more difficult to leave. For whites the phenomenon is the same, except this barrier effect puts higher manual in the less desirable block. This suggests a racial differentiation with regard to higher manual occupations.

4.9 Quadratic Forms and Descriptions

This section describes a general attribute known as *definiteness*, although this term means nothing on its own. The central question is what properties does an $n \times n$ matrix $\mathbf{X}$ possess when pre- and post-multiplied by a conformable nonzero vector $\mathbf{y} \in \mathfrak{R}^n$. The quadratic form of the matrix $\mathbf{X}$ is given by

$$\mathbf{y}'\mathbf{X}\mathbf{y} = s,$$

where the result is some scalar, s. If $s = 0$ for every possible vector $\mathbf{y}$, then $\mathbf{X}$ can only be the null matrix. But we are really interested in more nuanced properties. The following table gives the standard descriptions.

Properties of the Quadratic, y Non-Null

Non-Negative Definite:

$\longmapsto$ positive definite $\mathbf{y'Xy} > 0$

$\longmapsto$ positive semidefinite $\mathbf{y'Xy} \geq 0$

Non-Positive Definite:

$\longmapsto$ negative definite $\mathbf{y'Xy} < 0$

$\longmapsto$ negative semidefinite $\mathbf{y'Xy} \leq 0$

We can also say that $\mathbf{X}$ is **indefinite** if it is neither nonnegative definite nor nonpositive definite. The big result is worth stating with emphasis:

A positive definite matrix is always nonsingular.

Furthermore, a positive definite matrix is therefore invertible and the resulting inverse will also be positive definite. Positive semidefinite matrices are sometimes singular and sometimes not. If such a matrix is nonsingular, then its inverse is also nonsingular.

One theme that we keep returning to is the importance of the diagonal of a matrix. It turns out that every diagonal element of a positive definite matrix is positive, and every element of a negative definite matrix is negative. In addition, every element of a positive semidefinite matrix is nonnegative, and every element of a negative semidefinite matrix is nonpositive. This makes sense because we can switch properties between "negativeness" and "positiveness" by simply multiplying the matrix by -1.

★ **Example 4.10:   LDU Decomposition.**   In the last chapter we learned about LU decomposition as a way to triangularize matrices. The vague caveat at the time was that this could be done to "many" matrices. The condition, unstated at the time, is that the matrix must be nonsingular. We now know what that means, so it is now clear when LU decomposition is possible. More generally, though, *any* $p \times q$ matrix can be decomposed as follows:

$$\underset{(p\times q)}{\mathbf{A}} = \underset{(p\times p)(p\times q)(q\times q)}{\mathbf{L}\ \mathbb{D}\ \mathbf{U}}, \qquad \text{where} \qquad \mathbb{D} = \begin{bmatrix} \mathbf{D}_{r\times r} & 0 \\ 0 & 0 \end{bmatrix},$$

where $\mathbf{L}$ (lower triangular) and $\mathbf{U}$ (upper triangular) are nonsingular (even given a singular matrix $\mathbf{A}$). The diagonal matrix $\mathbf{D}_{r\times r}$ is unique and has dimension and rank r that corresponds to the rank of $\mathbf{A}$. If $\mathbf{A}$ is positive definite, and symmetric, then $\mathbf{D}_{r\times r} = \mathbb{D}$ (i.e., $r = q$) and $\mathbf{A} = \mathbf{L}\mathbb{D}\mathbf{L}'$ with unique $\mathbf{L}$.

For example, consider the LDU decomposition of the 3×3 unsymmetric, positive definite matrix A:

$$\mathbf{A} = \begin{bmatrix} 140 & 160 & 200 \\ 280 & 860 & 1060 \\ 420 & 1155 & 2145 \end{bmatrix}$$

$$= \begin{bmatrix} 1 & 0 & 0 \\ 2 & 4 & 0 \\ 3 & 5 & 6 \end{bmatrix} \begin{bmatrix} 20 & 0 & 0 \\ 0 & 15 & 0 \\ 0 & 0 & 10 \end{bmatrix} \begin{bmatrix} 7 & 8 & 10 \\ 0 & 9 & 11 \\ 0 & 0 & 12 \end{bmatrix}.$$

Now look at the symmetric, positive definite matrix and its LDL' decomposition:

$$\mathbf{B} = \begin{bmatrix} 5 & 5 & 5 \\ 5 & 21 & 21 \\ 5 & 21 & 30 \end{bmatrix} = \begin{bmatrix} 1 & 0 & 0 \\ 1 & 2 & 0 \\ 1 & 2 & 3 \end{bmatrix} \begin{bmatrix} 5 & 0 & 0 \\ 0 & 4 & 0 \\ 0 & 0 & 1 \end{bmatrix} \begin{bmatrix} 1 & 0 & 0 \\ 1 & 2 & 0 \\ 1 & 2 & 3 \end{bmatrix}',$$

which shows the symmetric principle above.

4.10 New Terminology

Exercises

4.1　For the matrix $\left[\begin{smallmatrix} 3 & 5 \\ 2 & 0 \end{smallmatrix}\right]$, show that the following vectors are or are not in the column space:

$$\begin{bmatrix} 11 \\ 4 \end{bmatrix}, \qquad \begin{bmatrix} 11 \\ 5 \end{bmatrix}.$$

4.2　Demonstrate that two orthogonal vectors have zero-length projections. Use unit vectors to make this easier.

4.3　Obtain the determinant and trace of the following matrix. Think about tricks to make the calculations easier.

$$\begin{bmatrix} 6 & 6 & 1 & 0 \\ 0 & 4 & 0 & 1 \\ 4 & 2 & 1 & 1 \\ 1 & 1 & 0 & 0 \end{bmatrix}$$

4.4　Prove that $\text{tr}(\mathbf{XY}) \neq \text{tr}(\mathbf{X})\text{tr}(\mathbf{Y})$, except for special cases.

4.5　In their formal study of models of group interaction, Bonacich and Bailey (1971) looked at linear and nonlinear systems of equations (their interest was in models that include factors such as free time, psychological compatibility, friendliness, and common interests). One of their conditions for a stable system was that the determinant of the matrix

$$\begin{pmatrix} -r & a & 0 \\ 0 & -r & a \\ 1 & 0 & -r \end{pmatrix}$$

must have a positive determinant for values of r and a. What is the arithmetic relationship that must exist for this to be true.

4.6　Find the eigenvalues of $\mathbf{A} = \begin{bmatrix} 1 & 3 \\ 2 & 4 \end{bmatrix}$ and $\mathbf{A} = \begin{bmatrix} 1 & 4 \\ 2 & -1 \end{bmatrix}$.

4.7   Calculate $|B|$, tr(B), and B^{-1} given $B = \begin{bmatrix} 1 & 0 & 4 \\ 0 & 2 & 0 \\ 0 & 0 & 3 \end{bmatrix}$.

4.8   (Hanushek and Jackson 1977). Given the matrices

$$\mathbf{Y} = \begin{bmatrix} 10 \\ 13 \\ 7 \\ 5 \\ 2 \\ 6 \end{bmatrix}, \quad \mathbf{X}_1 = \begin{bmatrix} 1 & 1 & 2 \\ 1 & 1 & 4 \\ 1 & 1 & 4 \\ 1 & 0 & 1 \\ 1 & 0 & 2 \\ 1 & 0 & 5 \end{bmatrix}, \quad \mathbf{X}_2 = \begin{bmatrix} 0 & 1 & 2 \\ 0 & 1 & 4 \\ 0 & 1 & 4 \\ 1 & 0 & 1 \\ 1 & 0 & 2 \\ 1 & 0 & 5 \end{bmatrix},$$

calculate $b_1 = (\mathbf{X}_1'\mathbf{X}_1)^{-1}\mathbf{X}_1'\mathbf{Y}$ and $b_2 = (\mathbf{X}_2'\mathbf{X}_2)^{-1}\mathbf{X}_2'\mathbf{Y}$. How are these vectors different? Similar?

4.9   Prove that the following matrix is or is not orthogonal:

$$\mathbf{B} = \begin{bmatrix} 1/3 & 2\sqrt{2}/3 & 0 \\ 2/3 & -\sqrt{2}/6 & \sqrt{2}/2 \\ -2/3 & \sqrt{2}/6 & \sqrt{2}/2 \end{bmatrix}.$$

4.10   Determine the rank of the following matrix:

$$\begin{bmatrix} 1 & 2 & 0 & 1 & 0 \\ 2 & 4 & 1 & 0 & 0 \\ 0 & 0 & 1 & -2 & 1 \\ 1 & 2 & 1 & -1 & 1 \end{bmatrix}.$$

4.11   Clogg, Petkova, and Haritou (1995) give detailed guidance for deciding between different linear regression models using the same data. In this work they define the matrices $\mathbf{X}$, which is $n \times (p+1)$ rank $p+1$, and $\mathbf{Z}$, which is $n \times (q+1)$ rank $q+1$, with $p < q$. They calculate the matrix $A = \left[\mathbf{X}'\mathbf{X} - \mathbf{X}\mathbf{Z}(\mathbf{Z}'\mathbf{Z})^{-1}Z'X\right]^{-1}$. Find the dimension and rank of A.

4.12   For each of the following matrices, find the eigenvalues and eigenvectors:

$$\begin{bmatrix} 0 & 1 \\ 0 & 1 \end{bmatrix} \qquad \begin{bmatrix} 1 & 2 \\ -3 & -4 \end{bmatrix} \qquad \begin{bmatrix} 11 & 3 \\ 9 & -4 \end{bmatrix}$$

$$\begin{bmatrix} 2 & 7 & 4 \\ 0 & 3 & 4 \\ 0 & 0 & 4 \end{bmatrix} \qquad \begin{bmatrix} 1 & 4 & 7 \\ 2 & 5 & 8 \\ 3 & 6 & 1 \end{bmatrix} \qquad \begin{bmatrix} 3 & 7 & \pi \\ 3 & e & 4 \\ 1 & 0 & \pi \end{bmatrix}.$$

4.13   Land (1980) develops a mathematical theory of social change based on a model of underlying demographic accounts. The corresponding population mathematical models are shown to help identify and track changing social indicators, although no data are used in the article. Label L_x as the number of people in a population that are between x and $x+1$ years old. Then the square matrix $\mathbf{P}'$ of order $(\omega+1) \times (\omega+1)$ is given by

$$\mathbf{P}' = \begin{bmatrix} 0 & 0 & 0 & 0 & \cdots \\ L_1/L_0 & 0 & 0 & 0 & \cdots \\ 0 & L_2/L_1 & 0 & 0 & \cdots \\ 0 & 0 & L_2/L_1 & 0 & \cdots \\ \vdots & \vdots & & \ddots & \cdots \\ 0 & 0 & 0 & 0 & L_\omega/L_{\omega-1} \end{bmatrix},$$

where ω is the assumed maximum lifespan and each of the nonzero ratios gives the proportion of people living to the next age. The matrix $(\mathbf{I} - \mathbf{P}')$ is theoretically important. Calculate its trace and inverse. The inverse will be a lower triangular form with survivorship probabilities as the nonzero values, and the column sums are standard life expectations in the actuarial sense.

4.14   The Clement matrix is a symmetric, tridiagonal matrix with zero diagonal values. It is sometimes used to test algorithms for computing inverses and eigenvalues. Compute the eigenvalues of the following

4×4 Clement matrix:

$$
\begin{bmatrix}
0 & 1.732051 & 0 & 0 \\
1.732051 & 0 & 2.0 & 0 \\
0 & 2.0 & 0 & 1.732051 \\
0 & 0 & 1.732051 & 0
\end{bmatrix}.
$$

4.15   Consider the two matrices

$$
\mathbf{X_1} =
\begin{bmatrix}
5 & 2 & 5 \\
2 & 1 & 2 \\
3 & 2 & 3 \\
2.95 & 1 & 3
\end{bmatrix}
\qquad
\mathbf{X_2} =
\begin{bmatrix}
5 & 2 & 5 \\
2 & 1 & 2 \\
3 & 2 & 3 \\
2.99 & 1 & 3
\end{bmatrix}.
$$

Given how similar these matrices are to each other, why is $(\mathbf{X_2}'\mathbf{X_2})^{-1}$ so different from $(\mathbf{X_1}'\mathbf{X_1})^{-1}$?

4.16   A Vandermonde matrix is a specialized matrix that occurs in a particular type of regression (polynomial). Find the determinant of the following general Vandermonde matrix:

$$
\begin{bmatrix}
1 & v_1 & v_1^2 & v_1^3 & \cdots & v_1^{n-1} & v_1^n \\
1 & v_2 & v_2^2 & v_2^3 & \cdots & v_2^{n-1} & v_2^n \\
\vdots & \vdots & \vdots & & \vdots & \vdots \\
1 & v_{n-1} & v_{n-1}^2 & v_{n-1}^3 & \cdots & v_{n-1}^{n-1} & v_{n-1}^n \\
1 & v_n & v_n^2 & v_n^3 & \cdots & v_n^{n-1} & v_n^n
\end{bmatrix}.
$$

4.17   A Hilbert matrix has elements $x_{ij} = 1/(i + j - 1)$ for the entry in row i and column j. Is this always a symmetric matrix? Is it always positive definite?

4.18   Verify (replicate) the matrix calculations in the example with EU poverty data on page 155.

4.19   Solve the following systems of equations for x, y, and z:

$$x + y + 2z = 2$$
$$3x - 2y + z = 1$$
$$y - z = 3$$

$$2x + 3y - z = -8$$
$$x + 2y - z = 2$$
$$-x - 4y + z = -6$$

$$x - y + 2z = 2$$
$$4x + y - 2z = 10$$
$$x + 3y + z = 0.$$

4.20   Show that the eigenvectors from the matrix $\begin{bmatrix} 2 & 1 \\ 1 & 2 \end{bmatrix}$ are perpendicular.

4.21   A matrix is an M-matrix if $x_{ij} \leq 0$, $\forall i \neq j$, and all the elements of the inverse (X^{-1}) are nonnegative. Construct an example.

4.22   Williams and Griffin (1964) looked at executive compensation in the following way. An allowable bonus to managers, B, is computed as a percentage of net profit, P, before the bonus and before income taxes, T. But a reciprocal relationship exists because the size of the bonus affects net profit, and vice versa. They give the following example as a system of equations. Solve.

$$B - 0.10P + 0.10T = 0$$
$$0.50B - 0.50P + T = 0$$
$$P = 100,000.$$

4.23   This question uses the following 8×8 matrix $\mathbf{X}$ of fiscal data by country:

	$\mathbf{x}_{.1}$	$\mathbf{x}_{.2}$	$\mathbf{x}_{.3}$	$\mathbf{x}_{.4}$	$\mathbf{x}_{.5}$	$\mathbf{x}_{.6}$	$\mathbf{x}_{.7}$	$\mathbf{x}_{.8}$
Australia	3.3	9.9	5.41	5.57	5.15	5.35	5.72	6.24
Britain	5.8	11.4	4.81	4.06	4.48	4.59	4.79	5.24
Canada	12.1	9.9	2.43	2.24	2.82	4.29	4.63	5.65
Denmark	12.0	12.5	2.25	2.15	2.42	3.66	4.26	5.01
Japan	4.1	2.0	0.02	0.03	0.10	1.34	1.32	1.43
Sweden	2.2	4.9	1.98	2.55	2.17	3.65	4.56	2.20
Switzerland	−5.3	1.2	0.75	0.24	0.82	2.12	2.56	2.22
USA	5.4	6.2	2.56	1.00	3.26	4.19	4.19	5.44

where $\mathbf{x}_{.1}$ is percent change in the money supply a year ago (narrow), $\mathbf{x}_{.2}$ is percent change in the money supply a year ago (broad), $\mathbf{x}_{.3}$ is the 3-month money market rate (latest), $\mathbf{x}_{.4}$ is the 3-month money market rate (1 year ago), $\mathbf{x}_{.5}$ is the 2-year government bond rate, $\mathbf{x}_{.6}$ is the 10-year government bond rate (latest), $\mathbf{x}_{.7}$ is the 10-year government bond rate (1 year ago), and $\mathbf{x}_{.8}$ is the corporate bond rate (source: *The Economist*, January 29, 2005, page 97). We would expect a number of these figures to be stable over time or to relate across industrialized democracies. Test whether this makes the matrix $\mathbf{X}'\mathbf{X}$ ill-conditioned by obtaining the condition number. What is the rank of $\mathbf{X}'\mathbf{X}$. Calculate the determinant using eigenvalues. Do you expect near collinearity here?

4.24   Show that the inverse relation for the matrix $\mathbf{A}$ below is true:

$$\mathbf{A}^{-1} = \begin{bmatrix} a & b \\ c & d \end{bmatrix}^{-1} = \begin{bmatrix} \frac{d}{e} & \frac{-b}{e} \\ \frac{-c}{e} & \frac{a}{e} \end{bmatrix}.$$

Here e is the determinant of $\mathbf{A}$. Now apply this rule to invert the 2×2 matrix $\mathbf{X}'\mathbf{X}$ from the $n \times 2$ matrix $\mathbf{X}$, which has a leading column of 1's and a second column vector: $[x_{11}, x_{12}, \ldots, x_{1n}]$.

4.25   Another method for solving linear systems of equations of the form $A^{-1}y = x$ is **Cramer's rule**. Define A_j as the matrix where y is plugged in for the jth column of A. Perform this for every column $1, \ldots, q$ to produce q of these matrices, and the solution will be the vector $\left[\frac{|A_1|}{A}, \frac{|A_2|}{A}, \ldots \frac{|A_q|}{A} \right]$. Show that performing these steps on the matrix in the example on page 159 gives the same answer.

5

Elementary Scalar Calculus

5.1 Objectives

This chapter introduces the basics of calculus operating on scalar quantities, and most of these principles can be understood quite readily. Many find that the language and imagery of calculus are a lot more intimidating than the actual material (once they commit themselves to studying it). There are two primary tools of calculus, differentiation and integration, both of which are introduced here. A further chapter gives additional details and nuances, as well as an explanation of calculus on nonscalar values like vectors and matrices.

5.2 Limits and Lines

The first important idea on the way to understanding calculus is that of a limit. The key point is to see how functions behave when some value is made: arbitrarily small or arbitrarily large on some measure, or arbitrarily close to some finite value. That is, we are specifically interested in how a function tends to or converges to some point or line in the limit.

Consider the function $f(x) = 3 - (x - 2)^2$ over the domain (support) $[0:4]$. This function is **unimodal**, possessing a single maximum point, and it is **symmetric**, meaning that the shape is mirrored on either side of the line through the middle (which is the mode here). This function is graphed in the figure at the right.

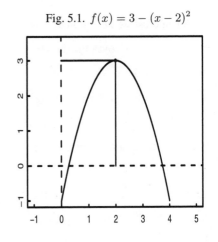

Fig. 5.1. $f(x) = 3 - (x - 2)^2$

What happens as the function approaches this mode from either direction? Consider "creeping up" on the top of the hill from either direction, as tabulated:

	x	1.8000	1.9000	1.9500	1.9900
Left	$f(x)$	2.9600	2.9900	2.9975	2.9999
Right	x	2.2000	2.1000	2.0500	2.0100
	$f(x)$	2.9600	2.9900	2.9975	2.9999

It should be obvious from the graph as well as these listed values that the **limit of the function** as $x \to 2$ is 3, approached from either direction. This is denoted $\lim_{x \to 2} f(x) = 3$ for the general case, as well as $\lim_{x \to 2-} f(x) = 3$ for approaching from the left and $\lim_{x \to 2+} f(x) = 3$ for approaching from the right. The reason that the right-hand limit and the left-hand limit are equal is that the function is continuous at the point of interest. If the function is smooth (continuous at all points; no gaps and no "corners" that cause problems here), then the left-hand limit and the right-hand limit are always identical except for at infinity.

Let us consider a more interesting case. Can a function have a finite limiting value in $f(x)$ as x goes to infinity? The answer is absolutely yes, and this turns out to be an important principle in understanding some functions.

An interesting new function is
$f(x) = 1 + 1/x^2$ over the domain
$(0:\infty^+)$. Note that this function's
range is over the positive real numbers greater than or equal to one because of the square placed here on
x. Again, the function is graphed
in the figure at right showing the
line at $y = 1$. What happens as
this function approaches infinity

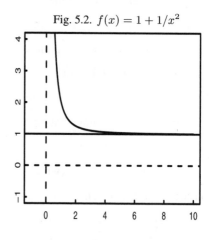

Fig. 5.2. $f(x) = 1 + 1/x^2$

from from the left? Obviously it does not make sense to approach infinity from
the right! Consider again tabulated the values:

x	1	2	3	6	12	24	100
$f(x)$	2.0000	1.2500	1.1111	1.0278	1.0069	1.0017	1.0001

Once again the effect is not subtle. As x gets arbitrarily large, $f(x)$ gets
progressively closer to 1. The curve approaches but never seems to reach
$f(x) = 1$ on the graph above. What occurs at exactly ∞ though? Plug ∞ into
the function and see what results: $f(x) = 1 + 1/\infty = 1$ ($1/\infty$ is defined as zero
because 1 divided by progressively larger numbers gets progressively smaller
and infinity is the largest number). So *in the limit* (and only in the limit) the
function reaches 1, and for every finite value the curve is above the horizontal
line at one. We say here that the value 1 is the **asymptotic value** of the function
$f(x)$ as $x \to \infty$ and that the line $y = 1$ is the **asymptote**: $\lim_{x \to \infty} f(x) = 1$.

There is another limit of interest for this function. What happens at $x = 0$?
Plugging this value into the function gives $f(x) = 1 + 1/0$. This produces
a result that we cannot use because dividing by zero is not defined, so the
function has no allowable value for $x = 0$ but does have allowable values for
every positive x. Therefore the asymptotic value of $f(x)$ with x approaching
zero from the right is infinity, which makes the vertical line $y = 0$ an asymptote

of a different kind for this function: $\lim_{x \to 0+} f(x) = \infty$.

There are specific properties of interest for limits (tabulated here for the variable x going to some arbitrary value X).

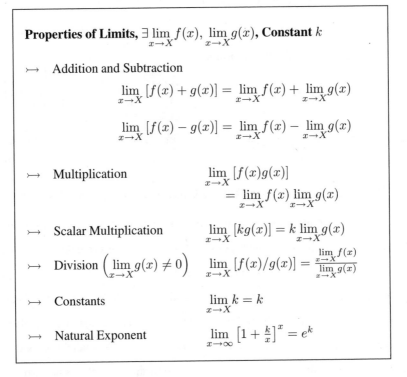

Properties of Limits, $\exists \lim_{x \to X} f(x), \lim_{x \to X} g(x),$ **Constant** k

$\longmapsto$ Addition and Subtraction

$$\lim_{x \to X} [f(x) + g(x)] = \lim_{x \to X} f(x) + \lim_{x \to X} g(x)$$

$$\lim_{x \to X} [f(x) - g(x)] = \lim_{x \to X} f(x) - \lim_{x \to X} g(x)$$

$\longmapsto$ Multiplication

$$\lim_{x \to X} [f(x)g(x)] = \lim_{x \to X} f(x) \lim_{x \to X} g(x)$$

$\longmapsto$ Scalar Multiplication

$$\lim_{x \to X} [kg(x)] = k \lim_{x \to X} g(x)$$

$\longmapsto$ Division $\left(\lim_{x \to X} g(x) \neq 0 \right)$ $\lim_{x \to X} [f(x)/g(x)] = \dfrac{\lim_{x \to X} f(x)}{\lim_{x \to X} g(x)}$

$\longmapsto$ Constants

$$\lim_{x \to X} k = k$$

$\longmapsto$ Natural Exponent

$$\lim_{x \to \infty} \left[1 + \tfrac{k}{x} \right]^x = e^k$$

Armed with these rules we can analyze the asymptotic properties of more complex functions in the following examples.

★ **Example 5.1:**   **Quadratic Expression.**

$$\lim_{x \to 2} \left[\frac{x^2 + 5}{x - 3} \right] = \frac{\lim_{x \to 2} x^2 + 5}{\lim_{x \to 2} x - 3} = \frac{2^2 + 5}{2 - 3} = -9.$$

★ **Example 5.2:**   **Polynomial Ratio.**

$$\lim_{x \to 1} \left[\frac{x^3 - 1}{x - 1} \right] = \lim_{x \to 1} \left[\frac{(x-1)(x+1)(x+1) - x(x-1)}{(x-1)} \right]$$

$$= \lim_{x \to 1} \left[\frac{(x+1)^2 - x}{1} \right] = \lim_{x \to 1} (x+1)^2 - \lim_{x \to 1} (x) = 3.$$

★ **Example 5.3:**   **Fractions and Exponents.**

$$\lim_{x \to \infty} \left[\frac{\left(1 + \frac{k_1}{x}\right)^x}{\left(1 + \frac{k_2}{x}\right)^x} \right] = \frac{\lim_{x \to \infty} \left(1 + \frac{k_1}{x}\right)^x}{\lim_{x \to \infty} \left(1 + \frac{k_2}{x}\right)^x} = \frac{e^{k_1}}{e^{k_2}} = e^{k_1 - k_2}.$$

★ **Example 5.4:**   **Mixed Polynomials.**

$$\lim_{x \to 1} \left[\frac{\sqrt{x} - 1}{x - 1} \right] = \lim_{x \to 1} \left[\frac{(\sqrt{x} - 1)(\sqrt{x} + 1)}{(x - 1)(\sqrt{x} + 1)} \right] = \lim_{x \to 1} \left[\frac{x - 1}{(x - 1)(\sqrt{x} + 1)} \right]$$

$$= \lim_{x \to 1} \left[\frac{1}{(\sqrt{x} + 1)} \right] = \frac{1}{\lim_{x \to 1} \sqrt{x} + 1} = 0.5.$$

5.3   Understanding Rates, Changes, and Derivatives

So why is it important to spend all that time on limits? We now turn to the definition of a derivative, which is based on a limit. To illustrate the discussion we will use a formal model from sociology that seeks to explain thresholds in voluntary racial segregation. Granovetter and Soong (1988) built on the foundational work of Thomas Schelling by mathematizing the idea that members of a racial group are progressively less likely to remain in a neighborhood as the proportion of another racial group rises. Assuming just blacks and whites, we can define the following terms: x is the percentage of whites, R is the "tolerance" of whites for the ratio of whites to blacks, and N_w is the total number of whites living in the neighborhood. In Granovetter and Soong's model, the function $f(x)$ defines a mobility frontier whereby an absolute number of blacks above the frontier causes whites to move out and an absolute number of blacks below the frontier causes whites to move in (or stay). They then developed and justified the function:

$$f(x) = R \left[1 - \frac{x}{N_w} \right] x,$$

which is depicted in the first panel of Figure 5.3 for $N_w = 100$ and $R = 5$ (so $f(x) = 5x - \frac{1}{20}x^2$). We can see that the number of blacks tolerated by whites increases sharply moving right from zero, hits a maximum at 125, and then decreases back to zero. This means that the tolerated level was **monotonically increasing** (constantly increasing or staying the same, i.e., nondecreasing) until the maxima and then **monotonically decreasing** (constantly decreasing or staying the same, i.e., nonincreasing) until the tolerated level reaches zero.

Fig. 5.3. DESCRIBING THE RATE OF CHANGE

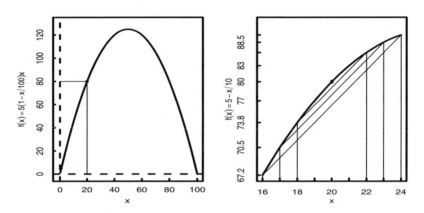

We are actually interested here in the **rate of change** of the tolerated number as opposed to the tolerated number itself: The rate of increase steadily declines from an earnest starting point until it reaches zero; then the rate of decrease starts slowly and gradually picks up until the velocity is zero. This can be summarized by the following table (recall that $\in$ means "an element of").

Region	Speed	Rate of Change
$x \in (0{:}50]$	increasing	decreasing
$x = 50$	maximum	zero
$x \in [50{:}100)$	decreasing	increasing

Say that we are interested in the rate of change *at exactly time* $x = 20$, which is the point designated at coordinates $(20, 80)$ in the first panel of Figure 5.3. How would we calculate this? A reasonable approximation can be made with line segments. Specifically, starting 4 units away from 20 in either direction, go 1 unit along the x-axis toward the point at 20 and construct line segments connecting the points along the curve at these x levels. The slope of the line segment (easily calculated from Section 1.5.1) is therefore an approximation to the instantaneous rate at $x = 20$, "rise-over-run," given by the segment

$$m = \frac{f(x_2) - f(x_1)}{x_2 - x_1}.$$

So the first line segment of interest has values $x_1 = 16$ and $x_2 = 24$. If we call the width of the interval $h = x_2 - x_1$, then the point of interest, x, is at the center of this interval and we say

$$m = \frac{f\left(x + \frac{h}{2}\right) - f\left(x - \frac{h}{2}\right)}{h}$$

$$= \frac{f(x + h) - f(x)}{h}$$

because $f(h/2)$ can move between functions in the numerator. This segment is shown as the lowest (longest) line segment in the second panel of Figure 5.3 and has slope 2.6625.

In fact, this estimate is not quite right, but it is an average of a slightly faster rate of change (below) and a slightly slower rate of change (above). Because this is an estimate, it is reasonable to ask how we can improve it. The obvious idea is to decrease the width of the interval around the point of interest. First go to 27–23 and then 22–18, and construct new line segments and therefore new estimates as shown in the second panel of Figure 5.3. At each reduction in interval width we are improving the estimate of the instantaneous rate of change at $x = 20$. Notice the nonlinear scale on the y-axis produced by the curvature of the function.

When should we stop? The answer to this question is found back in the previous discussion of limits. Define h again as the length of the intervals created as just described and call the expression for the slope of the line segment $m(x)$, to distinguish the slope form from the function itself. The point where $\lim_{h \to 0}$ occurs is the point where we get *exactly* the instantaneous rate of change at $x = 20$ since the width of the interval is now zero, yet it is still "centered" around $(20, 80)$. This instantaneous rate is equal to the slope of the **tangent line** (not to be confused with the tangent trigonometric function from Chapter 2) to the curve at the point x: the line that touches the curve *only at this one point*. It can be shown that there exists a unique tangent line for every point on a smooth curve.

So let us apply this logic to our function and perform the algebra very mechanically:

$$\lim_{h \to 0} m(x) = \lim_{h \to 0} \frac{f(x + h) - f(x)}{h}$$

$$= \lim_{h \to 0} \frac{\left[5(x + h) - \frac{1}{20}(x + h)^2\right] - \left[5x - \frac{1}{20}x^2\right]}{h}$$

$$= \lim_{h \to 0} \frac{5h - \frac{1}{20}(x^2 + 2xh + h^2) + \frac{1}{20}x^2}{h}$$

$$= \lim_{h \to 0} \frac{5h - \frac{2}{20}xh - \frac{1}{20}h^2}{h}$$

$$= \lim_{h \to 0} \left(5 - \frac{1}{10}x - \frac{1}{20}h\right) = 5 - \frac{1}{10}x.$$

This means that for any allowable x point we now have an expression for the instantaneous slope at that point. Label this with a prime to clarify that it is a different, but related, function: $f'(x) = 5 - \frac{1}{10}x$. Our point of interest is 20, so $f'(20) = 3$. Figure 5.4 shows tangent lines plotted at various points on $f(x)$. Note that the tangent line at the maxima is "flat," having slope zero. This is an important principle that we will make extensive use of later.

What we have done here is produce the **derivative** of the function $f(x)$, denoted $f'(x)$, also called **differentiating** $f(x)$. This derivative process is fundamental and has the definition

$$f'(x) = \lim_{h \to 0} \frac{f(x + h) - f(x)}{h}.$$

The derivative expression $f'(x)$ is Euler's version of Newton's notation, but it is often better to use Leibniz's notation $\frac{d}{dx} f(x)$, which resembles the limit derivation we just performed, substituting $\Delta x = h$. The change (delta) in x is

Fig. 5.4. TANGENT LINES ON $f(x) = 5x - \frac{1}{20}x^2$

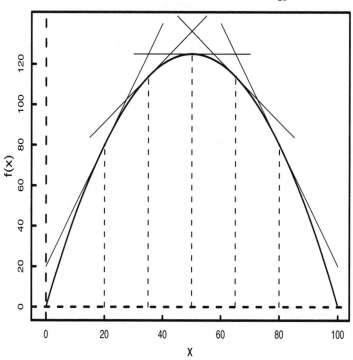

therefore

$$\frac{d}{dx}f(x) = \frac{df(x)}{dx} = \lim_{\Delta x \to 0} \frac{\Delta f(x)}{\Delta x}.$$

This latter notation for the derivative is generally preferred because it better reflects the change in the function $f(x)$ for an infinitesimal change in x, and it is easier to manipulate in more complex problems. Also, note that the fractional form of Leibniz's notation is given in two different ways, which are absolutely equivalent:

$$\frac{d}{dx}u = \frac{du}{dx},$$

for some function $u = f(x)$. Having said all that, Newton's form is more compact and looks nicer in simple problems, so it is important to know each form because they are both useful.

To summarize what we have done so far:

Summary of Derivative Theory

$\longmapsto$ Existence $\qquad$ $f'(x)$ at x exists iff $f(x)$ is continuous at x, and there is no point where the right-hand derivative and the left-hand derivative are different

$\longmapsto$ Definition $\qquad$ $f'(x) = \lim\limits_{h \to 0} \frac{f(x+h)-f(x)}{h}$

$\longmapsto$ Tangent Line $\qquad$ $f'(x)$ is the slope of the line tangent to $f()$ at x; this is the limit of the enclosed secant lines

---

The second existence condition needs further explanation. This is sometimes call the "no corners" condition because these points are geometric corners of the function and have the condition that

$$\lim_{\Delta x \to 0^-} \frac{\Delta f(x)}{\Delta x} \neq \lim_{\Delta x \to 0^+} \frac{\Delta f(x)}{\Delta x}.$$

That is, taking these limits to the left and to the right of the point produces different results. The classic example is the function $f(x) = |x|$, which looks like a "V" centered at the origin. So infinitesimally approaching $(0,0)$ from the left, $\Delta x \to 0^-$, is different from infinitesimally approaching $(0,0)$ from the right, $\Delta x \to 0^+$. Another way to think about this is related to Figure 5.4. Each of the illustrated tangent lines is uniquely determined by the selected point along the function. At a corner point the respective line would be allowed to "swing around" to an infinite number of places because it is resting on a single point (atom). Thus no unique derivative can be specified.

★ **Example 5.5:** **Derivatives for Analyzing Legislative Committee Size.**
Francis (1982) wanted to find criteria for determining "optimal" committee sizes in Congress or state-level legislatures. This is an important question because committees are key organizational and procedural components of American legislatures. A great number of scholars of American politics

have observed the central role that committee government plays, but not nearly as many have sought to understand committee size and subsequent efficiency. Efficiency is defined by Francis as minimizing two criteria for committee members:

- **Decision Costs:** (Y_d) the time and energy required for obtaining policy information, bargaining with colleagues, and actual meeting time.

- **External Costs:** (Y_e) the electoral and institutional costs of producing nonconsensual committee decisions (i.e., conflict).

Francis modeled these costs as a function of committee size in the following partly-linear specifications:

$$Y_d = a_d + b_d X^g, \quad g > 0$$

$$Y_e = a_e + b_e X^k, \quad k < 0,$$

where the a terms are intercepts (i.e., the costs for nonexistence or non-membership), the b terms are slopes (the relative importance of the multiplied term X) in the linear sense discussed in Section 1.5.1, and X is the size of the committee. The interesting terms here are the exponents on X. Since g is necessarily positive, increasing committee size increases decision costs, which makes logical sense. The term k is restricted to be negative, implying that the larger the committee, the closer the representation on the committee is to the full chamber or the electorate and therefore the lower such outside costs of committee decisions are likely to be to a member.

The key point of the Francis model is that committee size is a trade-off between Y_d and Y_e since they move in opposite directions for increasing or decreasing numbers of members. This can be expressed in one single equation by asserting that the two costs are treated equally for members (an assumption that could easily be generalized by weighting the two functions differently) and adding the two cost equations:

$$Y = Y_d + Y_e = a_d + b_d X^g + a_e + b_e X^k.$$

So now we have a single equation that expresses the full identified costs to members as a function of X. How would we understand the effect of changing the committee size? Taking the derivative of this expression with respect to X gives the instantaneous rate of change in these political costs at levels of X, and understanding changes in this rate helps to identify better or worse committee sizes for known or estimated values of a_d, b_d, g, a_e b_e, and also k.

The derivative operating on a polynomial does the following: It multiplies the expression by the exponent, it decreases the exponent by one, and it gets rid of any isolated constant terms. These rules are further explained and illustrated in the next section. The consequence in this case is that the first derivative of the Francis model is

$$\frac{d}{dx}Y = gb_d X^{g-1} + kb_e X^{k-1},$$

which allowed him to see the instantaneous effect of changes in committee size and to see where important regions are located. Francis thus found a minimum point by looking for an X value where $\frac{d}{dx}Y$ is equal to zero (i.e., the tangent line is flat). This value of X (subject to one more qualification to make sure that it is not a maximum) minimizes costs as a function of committee size given the known parameters.

5.4 Derivative Rules for Common Functions

It would be pretty annoying if every time we wanted to obtain the derivative of a function we had to calculate it through the limit as was done in the last section. Fortunately there are a number of basic rules such that taking derivatives on polynomials and other functional forms is relatively easy.

5.4.1 Basic Algebraic Rules for Derivatives

We will provide a number of basic rules here without proof. Most of them are fairly intuitive.

The **power rule** (already introduced in the last example) defines how to treat exponents in calculating derivatives. If n is any real number (including fractions and negative values), then

$$\frac{d}{dx}x^n = nx^{n-1}.$$

Straightforward examples include

$$\frac{d}{dx}x^2 = 2x \qquad \frac{d}{dx}3x^3 = 9x^2 \qquad \frac{d}{dx}x^{1000} = 1000x^{999}$$

$$\frac{d}{dx}x = 1 \qquad \frac{d}{dx}\sqrt{x} = \frac{1}{2}x^{-\frac{1}{2}} \qquad \frac{d}{dx}\left(-\frac{5}{8}x^{-\frac{8}{5}}\right) = x^{-\frac{13}{5}}.$$

This is a good point in the discussion to pause and make sure that the six examples above are well understood by the reader as the power rule is perhaps the most fundamental derivative operation.

The **derivative of a constant** is always zero:

$$\frac{d}{dx}k = 0, \quad \forall k.$$

This makes sense because a derivative is a rate of change and constants do not change. For example,

$$\frac{d}{dx}2 = 0$$

(i.e., there is no change to account for in 2). However, when a constant is multiplying some function of x, it is immaterial to the derivative operation, but it has to be accounted for later:

$$\frac{d}{dx}kf(x) = k\frac{d}{dx}f(x).$$

As an example, the derivative of $f(x) = 3x$ is simply 3 since $\frac{d}{dx}f(x)$ is 1.

The **derivative of a sum** is just the sum of the derivatives, provided that each component of the sum has a defined derivative:

$$\frac{d}{dx}[f(x) + g(x)] = \frac{d}{dx}f(x) + \frac{d}{dx}g(x),$$

and of course this rule is not limited to just two components in the sum:

$$\frac{d}{dx}\sum_{i=1}^{k} f_i(x) = \frac{d}{dx}f_1(x) + \frac{d}{dx}f_2(x) + \cdots + \frac{d}{dx}f_k(x).$$

For example,

$$\frac{d}{dx}\left(x^3 - 11x^2 + 3x - 5\right) = \frac{d}{dx}x^3 - \frac{d}{dx}11x^2 + \frac{d}{dx}3x - \frac{d}{dx}5$$

$$= 3x^2 - 22x + 3.$$

Unfortunately, the **product rule** is a bit more intricate than these simple methods. The product rule is the sum of two pieces where in each piece one of the two multiplied functions is left alone and the other is differentiated:

$$\frac{d}{dx}[f(x)g(x)] = f(x)\frac{d}{dx}g(x) + g(x)\frac{d}{dx}f(x).$$

This is actually not a very difficult formula to remember due to its symmetry. As an example, we now differentiate the following:

$$\frac{d}{dx}(3x^2 - 3)(4x^3 - 2x)$$

$$= (3x^2 - 3)\frac{d}{dx}(4x^3 - 2x) + (4x^3 - 2x)\frac{d}{dx}(3x^2 - 3)$$

$$= (3x^2 - 3)(12x^2 - 2) + (4x^3 - 2x)(6x)$$

$$= (36x^4 - 6x^2 - 36x^2 + 6) + (24x^4 - 12x^2)$$

$$= 60x^4 - 54x^2 + 6$$

(where we also used the sum property). It is not difficult to check this answer by multiplying the functions first and then taking the derivative (sometimes this will be hard, thus motivating the product rule):

$$\frac{d}{dx}(3x^2 - 3)(4x^3 - 2x) = \frac{d}{dx}(12x^5 - 6x^3 - 12x^3 + 6x)$$

$$= 60x^4 - 54x^2 + 6.$$

Unlike the product rule, the **quotient rule** is not very intuitive nor easy to remember:

$$\frac{d}{dx}\left[\frac{f(x)}{g(x)}\right] = \frac{g(x)\frac{d}{dx}f(x) - f(x)\frac{d}{dx}g(x)}{g(x)^2}, \quad g(x) \neq 0.$$

Here is an example using the same component terms:

$$\frac{d}{dx}\left(\frac{3x^2-3}{4x^3-2x}\right) = \frac{(4x^3-2x)\frac{d}{dx}(3x^2-3)-(3x^2-3)\frac{d}{dx}(4x^3-2x)}{(4x^3-2x)(4x^3-2x)}$$

$$= \frac{(4x^3-2x)(6x)-(3x^2-3)(12x^2-2)}{16x^6-16x^4+4x^2}$$

$$= \frac{-6x^4+15x^2-3}{8x^6-8x^4+2x^2}.$$

But since quotients are products where one of the terms is raised to the -1 power, it is generally easier to remember and easier to execute the product rule with this adjustment:

$$\frac{d}{dx}\left[\frac{f(x)}{g(x)}\right] = \frac{d}{dx}\left[f(x)g(x)^{-1}\right]$$

$$= f(x)\frac{d}{dx}g(x)^{-1}+g(x)^{-1}\frac{d}{dx}f(x).$$

This would be fine, but we do not yet know how to calculate $\frac{d}{dx}g(x)^{-1}$ in general since there are nested components that are functions of x: $g(x)^{-1} = (4x^3-2x)^{-1}$. Such a calculation requires the *chain rule*.

The **chain rule** provides a means of differentiating nested functions. In Chapter 1, on page 20, we saw nested functions of the form $f \circ g = f(g(x))$. The case of $g(x)^{-1} = (4x^3-2x)^{-1}$ fits this categorization because the inner function is $g(x) = 4x^3-2x$ and the outer function is $f(u) = u^{-1}$. Typically u is used as a placeholder here to make the point that there is a distinct subfunction. To correctly differentiate such a nested function, we have to account for the actual *order* of the nesting relationship. This is done by the chain rule, which is given by

$$\frac{d}{dx}f(g(x)) = f'(g(x))g'(x),$$

provided of course that $f(x)$ and $g(x)$ are both differentiable functions. We can also express this in the other standard notation. If $y = f(u)$ and $u = g(x)$ are both differentiable functions, then

$$\frac{dy}{dx} = \frac{dy}{du}\frac{du}{dx},$$

which may better show the point of the operation. If we think about this in purely fractional terms, it is clear that du cancels out of the right-hand side, making the equality obvious. Let us use this new tool to calculate the function $g(x)^{-1}$ from above ($g(x) = 4x^3 - 2x$):

$$\frac{d}{dx} g(x)^{-1} = (-1)(4x^3 - 2x)^{-2} \times \frac{d}{dx}(4x^3 - 2x)$$

$$= \frac{-(12x^2 - 2)}{(4x^3 - 2x)^2}$$

$$= \frac{-6x^2 + 1}{8x^6 - 8x^4 + 2x^2}.$$

So we see that applying the chain rule ends up being quite mechanical.

In many cases one is applying the chain rule along with other derivative rules in the context of the same problem. For example, suppose we want the derivative

$$\frac{d}{dy} \left(\frac{y^2 - 1}{y^2 + 1} \right)^3,$$

which clearly requires the chain rule. Now define u such that

$$u = \frac{y^2 - 1}{y^2 + 1} \qquad \text{and} \qquad y = u^3,$$

which redefines the problem as

$$\frac{d}{dy} \left(\frac{y^2 - 1}{y^2 + 1} \right)^3 = \frac{dy}{du} \frac{du}{dy}.$$

We proceed mechanically simply by keeping track of the two components:

$$\frac{dy}{du}\frac{du}{dy} = 3\left(\frac{y^2-1}{y^2+1}\right)^2 \frac{d}{dy}\left[(y^2-1)(y^2+1)^{-1}\right]$$

$$= 3\left(\frac{y^2-1}{y^2+1}\right)^2 \left[2y(y^2+1)^{-1} + (y^2-1)(-1)(y^2+1)^{-2}2y\right]$$

$$= 3\left(\frac{y^2-1}{y^2+1}\right)^2 \left[2y(y^2+1)^{-1} - 2y(y^2-1)(y^2+1)^{-2}\right]$$

$$= 6y\frac{(y^2-1)^2(y^2+1) - (y^2-1)^3}{(y^2+1)^4}$$

$$= 6y\frac{(y^2-1)^2\left[(y^2+1) - (y^2-1)\right]}{(y^2+1)^4}$$

$$= 12y\frac{(y^2-1)^2}{(y^2+1)^4}.$$

Note that another application of the chain rule was required with the inner step because of the term $(y^2+1)^{-1}$. While this is modestly inconvenient, it comes from the more efficient use of the product rule with the second term raised to the -1 power rather than the use of the quotient rule. .

★ **Example 5.6:   Productivity and Interdependence in Work Groups**.

We might ask, how does the productivity of workers affect total organizational productivity differently in environments where there is a great amount of interdependence of tasks relative to an environment where tasks are processed independently? Stinchcombe and Harris (1969) developed a mathematical model to explain such productivity differences and the subsequent effect of greater supervision. Not surprisingly, they found that the effect of additional supervision is greater for work groups that are more interdependent in processing tasks. Define T_1 as the total production when each person's task is independent and T_2 as the total production when *every* task is interdependent. Admittedly, these are extreme cases, but the point is to show differences, so they are likely to be maximally revealing.

In the independent case, the total organizational productivity is

$$T_1 = \sum_{j=1}^{n} bp_j = nb\bar{p},$$

where p_j is the jth worker's performance, b is an efficiency constant for the entire organization that measures how individual performance contributes to total performance, and there are n workers. The notation $\bar{p}$ indicates the average (mean) of all the p_j workers. In the interdependent case, we get instead

$$K \prod_{j=1}^{n} p_j,$$

where K is the total rate of production when everyone is productive. What the product notation (explained on page 12) shows here is that if even one worker is totally unproductive, $p_j = 0$, then the entire organization is unproductive.

Also, productivity is a function of willingness to use ability at each worker's level, so we can define a function $p_j = f(x_j)$ that relates productivity to ability. The premise is that supervision affects this function by motivating people to use their abilities to the greatest extent possible. Therefore we are interested in comparing

$$\frac{\partial T_1}{\partial x_j} \quad \text{and} \quad \frac{\partial T_2}{\partial x_j}.$$

But we cannot take this derivative directly since T is a function of p and p is a function of x. Fortunately the chain rule sorts this out for us:

$$\frac{\partial T_1}{\partial p_j} \frac{\partial p_j}{\partial x_j} = \frac{T_1}{n\bar{p}} \frac{\partial p_j}{\partial x_j}$$

$$\frac{\partial T_2}{\partial p_j} \frac{\partial p_j}{\partial x_j} = \frac{T_2}{p_j} \frac{\partial p_j}{\partial x_j}.$$

The interdependent case is simple because $b = T_1/n\bar{p}$ is how much any one of the individuals contributes through performance, and therefore how much the jth worker contributes. The interdependent case comes from dividing out the p_jth productivity from the total product. The key for comparison was that the second fraction in both expressions $(\partial p_j / \partial x_j)$ is the same, so the effect of different organizations was completely testable as the first fraction only. Stinchcombe and Harris' subsequent claim was that "the marginal productivity of the jth worker's performance is about n times as great in the interdependent case but varies according to his absolute level of performance" since the marginal for the interdependent case wass dependent on a single worker and the marginal for the independent case was dependent only on the average worker. So those with very low performance were more harmful in the interdependent case than in the independent case, and these are the cases that should be addressed first.

5.4.2 Derivatives of Logarithms and Exponents

We have already seen the use of real numbers as exponents in the derivative process. What if the variable itself is in the exponent? For this form we have

$$\frac{d}{dx}n^x = \log(n)n^x \quad \text{and} \quad \frac{d}{dx}n^{f(x)} = \log(n)n^x \frac{df(x)}{dx},$$

where the log function is the natural log (denoted $\log_n()$ or $\ln()$). So the derivative "peels off" a value of n that is "logged." This is especially handy when n is the e value, since

$$\frac{d}{dx}e^x = \log(e)e^x = e^x,$$

meaning that e^x is *invariant* to the derivative operation. But for compound functions with $u = f(x)$, we need to account for the chain rule:

$$\frac{d}{dx}e^u = e^u \frac{du}{dx},$$

for u a function of the x.

Relatedly, the derivatives of the logarithm are given by

$$\frac{d}{dx}\log(x) = \frac{1}{x},$$

for the natural log (recall that the default in the social sciences for logarithms where the base is not identified is a natural log, $\log_n$). The chain rule is

$$\frac{d}{dx}\log(u) = \frac{1}{u}\frac{d}{dx}u.$$

More generally, for other bases we have

$$\frac{d}{dx}\log_b(x) = \frac{1}{x\ln(b)}, \text{ because } \log_b(x) = \frac{\ln(x)}{\ln(b)}$$

with the associated chain rule version:

$$\frac{d}{dx}\log_b(u) = \frac{1}{u\ln(b)}\frac{d}{dx}u.$$

As an additional illustrative example, we find the derivative of the logarithmic function $y = \log(2x^2 - 1)$:

$$\frac{d}{dx}y = \frac{d}{dx}\log(2x^2 - 1)$$

$$= \frac{1}{2x^2 - 1}\frac{d}{dx}(2x^2 - 1)$$

$$= \frac{4x}{2x^2 - 1}.$$

That was pretty simple actually, so now perform a more complicated calculation. The procedure **logarithmic differentiation** uses the log function to make the process of differentiating a difficult function easier. The basic idea is to log the function, take the derivative of this version, and then compensate back at the last step. Start with the function:

$$y = \frac{(3x^2 - 3)^{\frac{1}{3}}(4x - 2)^{\frac{1}{4}}}{(x^2 + 1)^{\frac{1}{2}}},$$

which would be quite involved using the product rule, the quotient rule, and the chain rule. So instead, let us take the derivative of

$$\log(y) = \frac{1}{3}\log(3x^2 - 3) + \frac{1}{4}\log(4x - 2) - \frac{1}{2}\log(x^2 + 1)$$

(note the minus sign in front of the last term because it was in the denominator). Now we take the derivative and solve on this easier metric using the additive property of derivation rather than the product rule and the quotient rule. The left-hand side becomes $\frac{du}{dy}\frac{dy}{dx} = \frac{1}{y}\frac{d}{dx}y$ since it denotes a function of x. We then proceed as

$$\frac{1}{y}\frac{d}{dx}y = \frac{1}{3}\left(\frac{1}{3x^2-3}\right)(6x) + \frac{1}{4}\left(\frac{1}{4x-2}\right)(4) - \frac{1}{2}\left(\frac{1}{x^2+1}\right)(2x)$$

$$= \frac{2x(4x-2)(x^2+1) + (3x^2-3)(x^2+1) - x(3x^2-3)(4x-2)}{(3x^2-3)(4x-2)(x^2+1)}$$

$$= \frac{-x^4 + 2x^3 + 20x - 10x - 3}{(3x^2-3)(4x-2)(x^2+1)}.$$

Now multiply both sides by y and simplify:

$$\frac{d}{dx}y = \frac{-x^4 + 2x^3 + 20x - 10x - 3}{(3x^2-3)(4x-2)(x^2+1)}\frac{(3x^2-3)^{\frac{1}{3}}(4x-2)^{\frac{1}{4}}}{(x^2+1)^{\frac{1}{2}}}$$

$$\frac{d}{dx}y = \frac{-x^4 + 2x^3 + 20x - 10x - 3}{(3x^2-3)^{\frac{2}{3}}(4x-2)^{\frac{3}{4}}(x^2+1)^{\frac{3}{2}}}.$$

So this calculation is made much easier due to the logarithm.

★ **Example 5.7:   Security Trade-Offs for Arms Versus Alliances**. Sorokin (1994) evaluated the decisions that nations make in seeking security through building their armed forces and seeking alliances with other nations. A standard theory in the international relations literature asserts that nations (states) form alliances predominantly to protect themselves from threatening states (Walt 1987, 1988). Thus they rely on their own armed services as well as the armed services of other allied nations as a deterrence from war. However, as Sorokin pointed out, both arms and alliances are costly, and so states will seek a balance that maximizes the security benefit from necessarily limited resources.

How can this be modeled? Consider a state labeled i and its erstwhile ally labeled j. They each have military capability labeled M_i and M_j, correspondingly. This is a convenient simplification that helps to construct an illustrative model, and it includes such factors as the numbers of soldiers, quantity and quality of military hardware, as well as geographic constraints.

It would be unreasonable to say that just because i had an alliance with j it could automatically count on receiving the full level of M_j support if attacked. Sorokin thus introduced the term $T \in [0:1]$, which indicates the "tightness" of the alliance, where higher values imply a higher probability of country j providing M_j military support or the proportion of M_j to be provided. So $T = 0$ indicates no military alliances whatsoever, and values very close to 1 indicate a very tight military alliance such as the heyday of NATO and the Warsaw Pact.

The variable of primary interest is the amount of security that nation i receives from the combination of their military capability and the ally's capability weighted by the tightness of the alliance. This term is labeled S_i and is defined as

$$S_i = \log(M_i + 1) + T \log(M_j + 1).$$

The logarithm is specified because increasing levels of military capability are assumed to give diminishing levels of security as capabilities rise at higher levels, and the 1 term gives a baseline.

So if $T = 0.5$, then one unit of M_i is equivalent to two units of M_j in security terms. But rather than simply list out hypothetical levels for substantive analysis, it would be more revealing to obtain the **marginal effects** of each variable, which are the *individual* contributions of each term. There are three quantities of interest, and we can obtain marginal effect equations for each by taking three individual first derivatives that provide the instantaneous rate of change in security at chosen levels.

Because we have three variables to keep track of, we will use slightly different notation in taking first derivatives. The **partial derivative notation** replaces "d" with "∂" but performs exactly the same operation. The replacement is just to remind us that there are other random quantities in the equation and we have picked just one of them to differentiate with this particular expression (more on this in Chapter 6). The three marginal effects from the security equation are given by

$$\text{marginal effect of } M_i : \quad \frac{\partial S_i}{\partial M_i} = \frac{1}{1 + M_i} > 0$$

$$\text{marginal effect of } M_j : \quad \frac{\partial S_i}{\partial M_j} = \frac{T}{1 + M_j} > 0$$

$$\text{marginal effect of } T : \quad \frac{\partial S_i}{\partial T} = \log(1 + M_j) \geq 0.$$

What can we learn from this? The marginal effects of M_i and M_j are declining with increases in level, meaning that the rate of increase in security decreases. This shows that adding more men and arms has a diminishing effect, but this is exactly the motivation for seeking a mixture of arms under national command and arms from an ally since limited resources will then necessarily leverage more security. Note also that the marginal effect of M_j includes the term T. This means that this marginal effect is defined only at levels of tightness, which makes intuitive sense as well. Of course the reverse is also true since the marginal effect of T depends as well on the military capability of the ally.

5.4.3 L'Hospital's Rule

The early Greeks were wary of zero and the Pythagoreans outlawed it. Zero causes problems. In fact, there have been times when zero was considered an "evil" number (and ironically other times when it was considered proof of the existence of god). One problem, already mentioned, caused by zero is when it ends up in the denominator of a fraction. In this case we say that the fraction is "undefined," which sounds like a nonanswer or some kind of a dodge. A certain conundrum in particular is the case of $0/0$. The seventh-century Indian mathematician Brahmagupta claimed it was zero, but his mathematical heirs, such as Bhaskara in the twelfth century, believed that $1/0$ must be infinite and yet it would be only one unit away from $0/0 = 0$, thus producing a paradox.

Fortunately for us calculus provides a means of evaluating the special case of $0/0$.

Assume that $f(x)$ and $g(x)$ are differentiable functions at a where $f(a) = 0$ and $g(a) = 0$. L'Hospital's rule states that

$$\lim_{x \to a} \frac{f(x)}{g(x)} = \lim_{x \to a} \frac{f'(x)}{g'(x)},$$

provided that $g'(x) \neq 0$. In plainer words, the limit of the ratio of their two functions is equal to the limit of the ratio of the two derivatives. Thus, even if the original ratio is not interpretable, we can often get a result from the ratio of the derivatives. Guillaume L'Hospital was a wealthy French aristocrat who studied under Johann Bernoulli and subsequently wrote the world's first calculus textbook using correspondence from Bernoulli. L'Hospital's rule is thus misnamed for its disseminator rather than its creator.

As an example, we can evaluate the following ratio, which produces $0/0$ at the point 0:

$$\lim_{x \to 0} \frac{x}{\log(1-x)} = \lim_{x \to 0} \frac{\frac{d}{dx} x}{\frac{d}{dx} \log(1-x)}$$

$$= \lim_{x \to 0} \frac{1}{\frac{1}{-(1-x)}} = -1.$$

L'Hospital's rule can also be applied for the form ∞/∞: Assume that $f(x)$ and $g(x)$ are differentiable functions at a where $f(a) = \infty$ and $g(a) = \infty$; then again $\lim_{x \to a} f(x)/g(x) = \lim_{x \to a} f'(x)/g'(x)$.

Here is an example where this is handy. Note the repeated use of the product rule and the chain rule in this calculation:

$$\lim_{x \to \infty} \frac{(\log(x))^2}{x^2 \log(x)} = \lim_{x \to \infty} \frac{\frac{d}{dx}(\log(x))^2}{\frac{d}{dx} x^2 \log(x)}$$

$$= \lim_{x \to \infty} \frac{2\log(x)\frac{1}{x}}{2x \log(x) + x^2 \frac{1}{x}}$$

$$= \lim_{x \to \infty} \frac{\log(x)}{x^2 \log(x) + \frac{1}{2}x^2}.$$

It seems like we are stuck here, but we can actually apply L'Hospital's rule again, so after the derivatives we have

$$= \lim_{x \to \infty} \frac{\frac{1}{x}}{2x \log(x) + x^2 \frac{1}{x} + x}$$

$$= \lim_{x \to \infty} \frac{1}{2x^2 (\log(x) + 1)} = 0.$$

★ **Example 5.8:** **Analyzing an Infinite Series for Sociology Data.** Peterson (1991) wrote critically about sources of bias in models that describe durations: how long some observed phenomena lasts [also called hazard models or event-history models; see Box-Steffensmeier and Jones (2004) for a review]. In his appendix he claimed that the series defined by

$$a_{j,i} = j_i \times \exp(-\alpha j_i), \qquad \alpha > 0, j_i = 1, 2, 3, \ldots,$$

goes to zero in the limit as j_i continues counting to infinity. His evidence is the application of L'Hospital's rule twice:

$$\lim_{j_i \to \infty} \frac{j_i}{\exp(\alpha j_i)} = \lim_{j_i \to \infty} \frac{1}{\alpha \exp(\alpha j_i)} = \lim_{j_i \to \infty} \frac{0}{\alpha^2 \exp(\alpha j_i)}.$$

Did we need the second application of L'Hospital's rule? It appears not, because after the first iteration we have a constant in the numerator and positive values of the increasing term in the denominator. Nonetheless, it is no less true and pretty obvious after the second iteration.

5.4.4 Applications: Rolle's Theorem and the Mean Value Theorem

There are some interesting consequences for considering derivatives of functions that are over bounded regions of the x-axis. These are stated and explained here without proof because they are standard results.

Rolle's Theorem:

- Assume a function $f(x)$ that is continuous on the closed interval $[a:b]$ and differentiable on the open interval $(a:b)$. Note that it would be unreasonable to require differentiability at the endpoints.

- $f(a) = 0$ and $f(b) = 0$.

- Then there is guaranteed to be at least one point $\hat{x}$ in $(a:b)$ such that $f'(\hat{x}) = 0$.

Think about what this theorem is saying. A point with a zero derivative is a minima or a maxima (the tangent line is flat), so the theorem is saying that if the endpoints of the interval are both on the x-axis, then there must be one or more points that are modes or anti-modes. Is this logical? Start at the point $[a, 0]$. Suppose from there the function increased. To get back to the required endpoint at $[b, 0]$ it would have to "turn around" somewhere above the x-axis, thus guaranteeing a maximum in the interval. Suppose instead that the function left $[a, 0]$ and decreased. Also, to get back to $[b, 0]$ it would have to also turn around somewhere below the x-axis, now guaranteeing a minimum. There is one more case that is pathological (mathematicians love reminding people about these). Suppose that the function was just a flat line from $[a, 0]$ to $[b, 0]$. Then every point is a maxima and Rolle's Theorem is still true. Now we have exhausted the possibilities since the function leaving either endpoint has to either increase, decrease, or stay the same. So we have just provided an informal proof! Also, we have stated this theorem for $f(a) = 0$ and $f(b) = 0$, but it is really more general and can be restated for $f(a) = f(b) = k$, with any constant k

Mean Value Theorem:

- Assume a function $f(x)$ that is continuous on the closed interval $[a:b]$ and differentiable on the open interval $(a:b)$.

- There is now guaranteed to be at least one point $\hat{x}$ in $(a:b)$ such that $f(b) - f(a) = f'(\hat{x})(b - a)$.

This theorem just says that between the function values at the start and finish of the interval there will be an "average" point. Another way to think about this is to rearrange the result as

$$\frac{f(b) - f(a)}{b - a} = f'(\hat{x})$$

so that the left-hand side gives a slope equation, rise-over-run. This says that the line that connects the endpoints of the function has a slope that is equal to the derivative somewhere inbetween. When stated this way, we can see that it comes from Rolle's Theorem where $f(a) = f(b) = 0$.

Both of these theorems show that the derivative is a fundamental procedure for understanding polynomials and other functions. Remarkably, derivative calculus is a relatively recent development in the history of mathematics, which is of course a very long history. While there were glimmers of differentiation and integration prior to the seventeenth century, it was not until Newton, and independently Leibniz, codified and integrated these ideas that calculus was born. This event represents a dramatic turning point in mathematics, and perhaps in human civilization as well, as it lead to an explosion of knowledge and understanding. In fact, much of the mathematics of the eighteenth and early nineteenth centuries was devoted to understanding the details and implications of this new and exciting tool. We have thus far visited one-half of the world of calculus by looking at derivatives; we now turn our attention to the other half, which is integral calculus.

5.5 Understanding Areas, Slices, and Integrals

One of the fundamental mathematics problems is to find the area "under" a curve, designated by R. By this we mean the area below the curve given by a smooth, bounded function, $f(x)$, and above the x-axis (i.e., $f(x) \geq 0$, $\forall x \in [a:b]$). This is illustrated in Figure 5.5. Actually, this characterization is a bit too restrictive because other areas in the coordinate axis can also be measured and we will want to treat unbounded or discontinuous areas as well, but we will stick with this setup for now. **Integration** is a calculus procedure for measuring areas and is as fundamental a process as differentiation.

5.5.1 Riemann Integrals

So how would we go about measuring such an area? Here is a really mechanical and fundamental way. First "slice up" the area under the curve with a set of bars that are approximately as high as the curve at different places. This would then be somewhat like a histogram approximation of R where we simply sum up the sizes of the set of rectangles (a very easy task). This method is sometimes referred to as the **rectangle rule** but is formally called **Riemann integration**. It is the simplest but least accurate method for numerical integration. More formally, define n disjoint intervals along the x-axis of width $h = (b - a)/n$ so that the lowest edge is $x_0 = a$, the highest edge is $x_n = b$, and for $i = 2, \ldots, n-1$, $x_i = a + ih$, produces a histogram-like approximation of R. The key point is that for the ith bar the approximation of $f(x)$ over h is $f(a + ih)$.

The only wrinkle here is that one must select whether to employ "left" or "right" Riemann integration:

$$h \sum_{i=0}^{n-1} f(a + ih), \quad \text{left Riemann integral}$$

$$h \sum_{i=1}^{n} f(a + ih), \quad \text{right Riemann integral,}$$

determining which of the top corners of the bars touches the curve. Despite the obvious roughness of approximating a smooth curve with a series of rectangular bars over regular bins, Riemann integrals can be extremely useful as a crude starting point because they are easily implemented.

Figure 5.5 shows this process for both left and right types with the different indexing strategies for i along the x-axis for the function:

$$p(\theta) = \begin{cases} (6 - \theta)^2/200 + 0.011 & \text{for } \theta \in [0 : 6] \\ \mathcal{C}(11, 2)/2 & \text{for } \theta \in [6 : 12], \end{cases}$$

Fig. 5.5. RIEMANN INTEGRATION

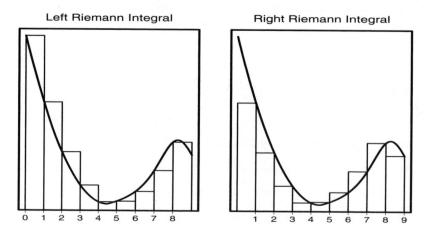

where $C(11, 2)$ denotes the Cauchy (distribution) function for $\theta = 11$ and $\sigma = 2$: $C(x|\theta, \sigma) = \frac{1}{\pi\sigma} \frac{1}{1+\left(\frac{x-\theta}{\sigma}\right)^2}$, $-\infty < x, \theta < \infty, 0 < \sigma$.

It is evident from the two graphs that when the function is downsloping, as it is on the left-hand side, the left Riemann integral overestimates and the right Riemann integral underestimates. Conversely when the function is upsloping, as it is toward the right-hand-side, the left Riemann integral underestimates and the right Riemann integral overestimates. For the values given, the left Riemann integral is too large because there is more downsloping in the bounded region, and the right Riemann integral is too small correspondingly. There is a neat theorem that shows that the actual value of the area for one of these regions is *bounded* by the left and right Riemann integrals. Therefore, the *true* area under the curve is bounded by the two estimates given.

Obviously, because of the inaccuracies mentioned, this is not the best procedure for general use. The value of the left Riemann integral is 0.7794 and the value of the right Riemann integral is 0.6816 for this example, and such a discrepancy is disturbing. Intuitively, as the number of bars used in this process increases, the smaller the regions of curve that we are under- or overestimating. This suggests making the width of the bars (h) very small to improve accuracy.

Such a procedure is always possible since the x-axis is the real number line, and we know that there are an infinite number of places to set down the bars.

It would be very annoying if every time we wanted to measure the area under a curve defined by some function we had to create lots of these bars and sum them up. So now we can return to the idea of limit. As the number of bars increases over a bounded area, then necessarily the width of the bars decreases. So let the width of the bars go to zero in the limit, forcing an infinite number of bars. It is not technically necessary, but continue to assume that all the bars are of equal size, so this limit result holds easily. We now need to be more formal about what we are doing.

For a continuous function $f(x)$ bounded by a and b, define the following limits for left and right Riemann integrals:

$$S_{\text{left}} = \lim_{h \to 0} h \sum_{i=0}^{n-1} f(a + ih)$$

$$S_{\text{right}} = \lim_{h \to 0} h \sum_{i=1}^{n} f(a + ih),$$

where n is the number of bars, h is the width of the bars (and bins), and nh is required to cover the domain of the function, $b - a$. For every subregion the left and right Riemann integrals bound the truth, and these bounds necessarily get progressively tighter approaching the limit. So we then know that

$$S_{\text{left}} = S_{right} = R$$

because of the effect of the limit. This is a wonderful result: The limit of the Riemann process is the true area under the curve. In fact, there is specific terminology for what we have done: The **definite integral** is given by

$$R = \int_{a}^{b} f(x)dx,$$

where the $\int$ symbol is supposed to look somewhat like an "S" to remind us that this is really just a special kind of sum. The placement of a and b indicate the lower and upper limits of the definite integral, and $f(x)$ is now called the **integrand**. The final piece, dx, is a reminder that we are summing over infinitesimal values of x. So while the notation of integration can be intimidating to the uninitiated, it really conveys a pretty straightforward idea.

The integral here is called "definite" because the limits on the integration are defined (i.e., having specific values like a and b here). Note that this use of the word *limit* applies to the range of application for the integral, not a limit, in the sense of limiting functions studied in Section 5.2.

5.5.1.1 Application: Limits of a Riemann Integral

Suppose that we want to evaluate the function $f(x) = x^2$ over the domain $[0:1]$ using this methodology. First divide the interval up into h slices each of width $1/h$ since our interval is 1 wide. Thus the region of interest is given by the limit of a left Riemann integral:

$$R = \lim_{h \to \infty} \sum_{i=1}^{h} \frac{1}{h} f(x)^2 = \lim_{h \to \infty} \sum_{i=1}^{h} \frac{1}{h} (i/h)^2$$

$$= \lim_{h \to \infty} \frac{1}{h^3} \sum_{i=1}^{h} i^2 = \lim_{h \to \infty} \frac{1}{h^3} \frac{h(h+1)(2h+1)}{6}$$

$$= \lim_{h \to \infty} \frac{1}{6} (2 + \frac{3}{h} + \frac{1}{h^2}) = \frac{1}{3}.$$

The step out of the summation was accomplished by a well-known trick. Here it is with a relative, stated generically:

$$\sum_{x=1}^{n} x^2 = \frac{n(n+1)(2n+1)}{6}, \qquad \sum_{x=1}^{n} x = \frac{n(n+1)}{2}.$$

This process is shown in Figure 5.6 using left Riemann sums for 10 and 100 bins over the interval to highlight the progress that is made in going to the limit. Summing up the bin heights and dividing by the number of bins produces 0.384967 for 10 bins and 0.3383167 for 100 bins. So already at 100 bins we are fitting the curve reasonably close to the true value of one-third.

Fig. 5.6. Riemann Sums for $f(x) = x^2$ Over $[0{:}1]$

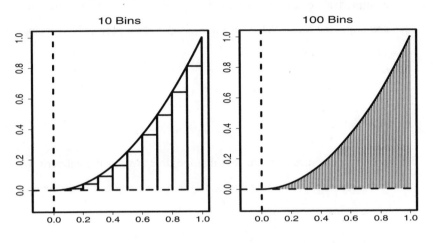

5.6 The Fundamental Theorem of Calculus

We start this section with some new definitions. In the last section principles of Riemann integration were explained, and here we extend these ideas. Since both the left and the right Riemann integrals produce the correct area in the limit as the number of $h_i = (x_i - x_{i-1})$ goes to infinity, it is clear that some point in between the two will also lead to convergence. Actually, it is immaterial which point we pick in the closed interval, due to the effect of the limiting operation. For slices $i = 1$ to H covering the full domain of $f(x)$, define the point $\hat{x}_i$ as an arbitrary point in the ith interval $[x_{i-1}{:}x_i]$. Therefore,

$$\int_a^b f(x)dx = \lim_{h \to 0} \sum_{i=1}^H f(\hat{x})h_i,$$

and this is now called a **Riemann sum** as opposed to a Riemann integral.

We need one more definition before proceeding. The process of taking a derivative has an opposite, the **antiderivative**. The antiderivative corresponding to a specific derivative takes the equation form back to its previous state. So, for example, if $f(x) = \frac{1}{3}x^3$ and the derivative is $f'(x) = x^2$, then the antiderivative of the function $g(x) = x^2$ is $G(x) = \frac{1}{3}x^3$. Usually antiderivatives are designated with a capital letter. Note that the derivative of the antiderivative returns the original form: $F'(x) = f(x)$.

The antiderivative is a function in the regular sense, so we can treat it as such and apply the Mean Value Theorem discussed on page 202 for a single bin within the interval:

$$F(x_i) - F(x_{i-1}) = F'(\hat{x}_i)(x_i - x_{i-1})$$

$$= f(\hat{x}_i)(x_i - x_{i-1}).$$

The second step comes from the fact that the derivative of the antiderivative returns the function back. Now let us do this for *every* bin in the interval, assuming H bins:

$$F(x_1) - F(a) = f(\hat{x}_1)(x_1 - a)$$
$$F(x_2) - F(x_1) = f(\hat{x}_2)(x_2 - x_1)$$
$$F(x_3) - F(x_2) = f(\hat{x}_3)(x_3 - x_2)$$
$$\vdots$$
$$F(x_{H-1}) - F(x_{H-2}) = f(\hat{x}_{H-1})(x_{H-1} - x_{H-2})$$
$$F(x_b) - F(x_{H-1}) = f(\hat{x}_b)(x_b - x_{H-1}).$$

In adding this series of H equations, something very interesting happens on the left-hand side:

$$(F(x_1) - F(a)) + (F(x_2) - F(x_1)) + (F(x_3) - F(x_2)) + \cdots$$

can be rewritten by collecting terms:

$$-F(a) + (F(x_1) - F(x_1)) + (F(x_2) - F(x_2)) + (F(x_3) - F(x_3)) + \cdots$$

It "accordions" in the sense that there is a term in each consecutive parenthetical quantity from an individual equation that cancels out part of a previous parenthetical quantity: $F(x_1) - F(x_1)$, $F(x_2) - F(x_2)$,... $F(x_{H-1}) - F(x_{H-1})$. Therefore the only two parts left are those corresponding to the endpoints, $F(a)$ and $F(b)$, which is a great simplification! The right-hand side addition looks like

$$f(\hat{x}_1)(x_1 - a) + f(\hat{x}_2)(x_2 - x_1) + f(\hat{x}_3)(x_3 - x_2) +$$
$$\cdots + f(\hat{x}_{H-1})(x_{H-1} - x_{H-2}) + f(\hat{x}_b)(x_b - x_{H-1}),$$

which is just $\int_a^b f(x)dx$ from above. So we have now stumbled onto the **Fundamental Theorem of Calculus**:

$$\int_a^b f(x)dx = F(b) - F(a),$$

which simply says that integration and differentiation are opposite procedures: an integral of $f(x)$ from a to b is just the antiderivative at b minus the antiderivative at a. This is really important theoretically, but it is also really important computationally because it shows that we can integrate functions by using antiderivatives rather than having to worry about the more laborious limit operations.

5.6.1 Integrating Polynomials with Antiderivatives

The use of antiderivatives for solving definite integrals is especially helpful with polynomial functions. For example, let us calculate the following definite integral:

$$\int_1^2 (15y^4 + 8y^3 - 9y^2 + y - 3)dy.$$

The antiderivative is

$$F(y) = 3y^5 + 2y^4 - 3y^3 + \frac{1}{2}y^2 - 3y,$$

since

$$\frac{d}{dy}F(y) = \frac{d}{dy}(3y^5 + 2y^4 - 3y^3 + \frac{1}{2}y^2 - 3y) = 15y^4 + 8y^3 - 9y^2 + y - 3.$$

$$8y^3 - 9y^2 + y - 3)dy$$

$$= 3y^5 + 2y^4 - 3y^3 + \frac{1}{2}y^2 - 3y\Big|_{y=1}^{y=2}$$

$$= (3(2)^5 + 2(2)^4 - 3(2)^3 + \frac{1}{2}(2)^2 - 3(2))$$

$$- (3(1)^5 + 2(1)^4 - 3(1)^3 + \frac{1}{2}(1)^2 - 3(1))$$

$$= (96 + 32 - 24 + 2 - 6) - (3 + 2 - 3 + \frac{1}{2} - 3) = 100.5.$$

The notation for substituting in limit values, $\Big|_{y=a}^{y=b}$, is shortened here to $\Big|_a^b$, since the meaning is obvious from the dy term (the distinction is more important in the next chapter, when we study integrals of more than one variable).

Now we will summarize the basic properties of definite integrals.

Properties of Definite Integrals

⟼ Constants $\qquad \int_a^b kf(x)dx = k\int_a^b f(x)dx$
$\qquad\qquad\qquad\qquad$ constant × end product

⟼ Additive Property $\qquad \int_a^b (f(x) + g(x))dx$

$$= \int_a^b f(x)dx + \int_a^b g(x)dx$$
$\qquad\qquad\qquad\qquad$ 1-2 same as 2-3

⟼ Linear Functions $\qquad \int_a^b (k_1 f(x) + k_2 g(x))dx$

$$= k_1 \int_a^b f(x)dx + k_2 \int_a^b g(x)dx$$

⟼ Intermediate Values $\quad$ for $a \le b \le c$:

$$\int_a^c f(x)dx = \int_a^b f(x)dx + \int_b^c f(x)dx$$

⟼ Limit Reversibility $\qquad \int_a^b f(x)dx = -\int_b^a f(x)dx$

Fig. 5.7. INTEGRATING BY PIECES

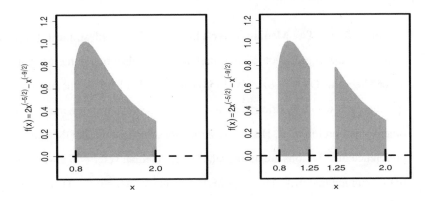

The first two properties are obvious by now and the third is just a combination of the first two. The fourth property is much more interesting. It says that we can split up the definite integral into two pieces based on some intermediate value between the endpoints and do the integration separately. Let us now do this with the function $f(x) = 2x^{-5/2} - x^{-9/2}dx$ integrated over $[0.8:2.0]$ with an intermediate point at 1.25:

$$\int_{0.8}^{2.0} 2x^{-\frac{5}{2}} - x^{-\frac{9}{2}}dx = \int_{0.8}^{1.25} 2x^{-\frac{5}{2}} - x^{-\frac{9}{2}}dx + \int_{1.25}^{2.0} 2x^{-\frac{5}{2}} - x^{-\frac{9}{2}}dx$$

$$= \left[\left(-\frac{2}{3} \right) 2x^{-\frac{3}{2}} - \left(-\frac{2}{7} \right) x^{-\frac{7}{2}} \right] \Bigg|_{0.8}^{1.25}$$

$$+ \left[\left(-\frac{2}{3} \right) 2x^{-\frac{3}{2}} - \left(-\frac{2}{7} \right) x^{-\frac{7}{2}} \right] \Bigg|_{1.25}^{2.0}$$

$$= [-0.82321 - (-1.23948)]$$

$$+ [-0.44615 - (-0.82321)] = 0.79333.$$

This is illustrated in Figure 5.7. This technique is especially handy where it is difficult to integrate the function in one piece (the example here is therefore somewhat artificial). Such cases occur when there are discontinuities or pieces of the area below the x-axis.

★ **Example 5.9:   The Median Voter Theorem.** The simplest, most direct analysis of the aggregation of vote preferences in elections is the Median Voter Theorem. Duncan Black's (1958) early article identified the role of a specific voter whose position in a single issue dimension is at the median of other voters' preferences. His theorem roughly states that if all of the voters' preference distributions are unimodal, then the median voter will always be in the winning majority. This requires two primary restrictions. There must be a single issue dimension (unless the same person is the median voter in all relevant dimensions), and each voter must have a unimodal preference distribution. There are also two other assumptions generally of a less-important nature: All voters participate in the election, and all voters express their true preferences (sincere voting). There is a substantial literature that evaluates the median voter theorem after altering any of these assumptions [see Dion (1992), for example].

The Median Voter Theorem is displayed in Figure 5.8, which is a reproduction of Black's figure (1958, p.15). Shown are the preference curves for five hypothetical voters on an interval measured issue space (the x-axis), where the utility goes to zero at two points for each voter (one can also assume that the utility curves asymptotically approach zero as Black did). In the case given here it is clear that the voter with the mode at O_3 is the median voter for this system, and there is some overlap with the voter whose mode is at O_2. Since overlap represents some form of potential agreement, we might be interested in measuring this area.

These utility functions are often drawn or assumed to be parabolic shapes. The general form used here is

$$f(x) = 10 - (\mu_i - x)^2 \omega_i,$$

where μ_i determines this voter's modal value and ω_i determines how fast their

Fig. 5.8. PLACING THE MEDIAN VOTER

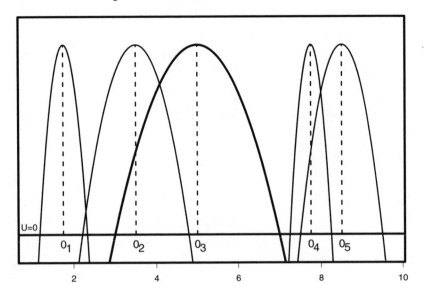

utility diminishes moving away from the mode (i.e., how "fat" the curve is for this voter). For the two voters under study, the utility equations are therefore

$$V_2: f(x) = 10 - (3.5 - x)^2 (6) \qquad V_3: f(x) = 10 - (5 - x)^2 (2.5),$$

so smaller values of ω produce more spread out utility curves. This is a case where we will need to integrate the area of overlap in two pieces, because the functions that define the area from above are different on either side of the intersection point.

The first problem encountered is that we do not have any of the integral limits: the points where the parabolas intersect the x-axis (although we only need two of the four from looking at the figure), and the point where the two parabolas intersect. To obtain the latter we will equate the two forms and solve with the quadratic equation from page 33 (striking out the 10's and the multiplication by -1 here since they will cancel each other anyway). First expand the squares:

$$y = (3.5 - x)^2(6) \qquad\qquad y = (5 - x)^2(2.5)$$

$$y = 6x^2 - 42x + 73.5 \qquad\qquad y = 2.5x^2 - 25x + 62.5.$$

Now equate the two expressions and solve:

$$6x^2 - 42x + 73.5 = 2.5x^2 - 25x + 62.5$$

$$3.5x^2 - 17x + 11 = 0$$

$$x = \frac{-(-17) \pm \sqrt{(-17)^2 - 4(3.5)(11)}}{2(3.5)} = 4.088421 \text{ or } 0.768721.$$

This is a quadratic form, so we get two possible answers. To find the one we want, plug both potential values of x into one of the two parabolic forms and observe the y values:

$$y = 10 - 2.5(5 - (4.0884))^2 = 7.9226$$

$$y = 10 - 2.5(5 - (0.7687))^2 = -34.7593.$$

Because we want the point of intersection that exists above the x-axis, the choice between the two x values is now obvious to make. To get the roots of the two parabolas (the points where $y = 0$), we can again apply the quadratic equation to the two parabolic forms (using the original form):

$$x_2 = \frac{-(42) \pm \sqrt{(42)^2 - 4(-6)(-63.5)}}{2(-6)} = 2.209 \text{ or } 4.79$$

$$x_2 = \frac{-(25) \pm \sqrt{(25)^2 - 4(-2.5)(-52.5)}}{2(-2.5)} = 3 \text{ or } 7.$$

We know that we want the greater root of the first parabola and the lesser root of the second parabola (look at the picture), so we will use 3 and 4.79 as limits on the integrals.

The area to integrate now consists of the following two-part problem, solved by the antiderivative method:

$$A = \int_{3}^{4.0884} (-6x^2 + 42x - 63.5)dx + \int_{4.0884}^{4.79} (-2.5x^2 + 25x - 52.5)dx$$

$$= \left(-2x^3 + 21x^2 - 63.5x \right) \Big|_{3}^{4.0884} + \left(-\frac{5}{6}x^3 + \frac{25}{2}x^2 - 52.5x \right) \Big|_{4.0884}^{4.79}$$

$$= ((-45.27343) - (-55.5)) + ((-56.25895) - (-62.65137))$$

$$= 16.619.$$

So we now know the area of the overlapping region above the x-axis between voter 2 and voter 3. If we wanted to, we could calculate the other overlapping regions between voters and compare as a measure of utility similarity on the issue space.

5.6.2 Indefinite Integrals

Indefinite integrals are those that lack specific limits for the integration operation. The consequence of this is that there must be an arbitrary constant (labeled k here) added to the antiderivative to account for the constant component that would be removed by differentiating:

$$\int f(x)dx = F(x) + k.$$

That is, if $F(x) + k$ is the antiderivative of $f(x)$ and we were to calculate $\frac{d}{dx}(F(x) + k)$ with defined limits, then any value for k would disappear. The logic and utility of indefinite integrals is that we use them to relate functions rather than to measure specific areas in coordinate space, and the further study of this is called *differential equations*.

As an example of calculating indefinite integrals, we now solve one simple problem:

$$\int (1 - 3x)^{\frac{1}{2}} dx = -\frac{2}{9}(1 - 3x)^{\frac{3}{2}} + k.$$

Instead of a numeric value, we get a defined relationship between the functions $f(x) = (1 - 3x)^{\frac{1}{2}}$ and $F(x) = -\frac{2}{9}(1 - 3x)^{\frac{3}{2}}$.

5.6.3 Integrals Involving Logarithms and Exponents

We have already seen that the derivative of exponentials and logarithms are special cases: $\frac{d}{dx}e^x = e^x$ and $\frac{d}{dx}\log(x) = \frac{1}{x}$. For the most part, these are important rules to memorize, particularly in statistical work. The integration process with logarithms and exponents is only slightly more involved.

Recall that the chain rule applied to the exponential function takes the form

$$\frac{d}{dx}e^u = e^u \frac{du}{dx}.$$

This means that the form of the u function remains in the exponent but its derivative comes down. So, for example,

$$\frac{d}{dx}e^{3x^2-x} = e^{3x^2-x}(6x - 1),$$

which is simple if one can remember the rule. For integration it is essential to keep track of the "reverse chain rule" that comes from this principle:

$$\int e^u du = e^u + k.$$

This means that the u function must be incorporated into the limit definition to reverse $\frac{du}{dx}$. In addition, we have to add a constant k that could have been there but was lost due to the derivative function operating on it ($\frac{d}{dx}(k) = 0$).

In the following example the function in the exponent is $f(x) = -x$, so we alter the limit multiplying by -1 so that the exponent value and limit are identical and the regular property of e applies:

$$\int_0^2 e^{-x} dx = -\int_0^2 e^{-x} d(-x) = -e^{-x}\Big|_0^2 = -e^{-2} - (-e^0) = 0.8646647.$$

Now consider a more complicated example:

$$\int \frac{e^x}{1+e^x}dx,$$

which seems very difficult until we make a substitution. First define $u = 1+e^x$, which changes the integral to

$$\int \frac{e^x}{u}dx.$$

This does not seem to help us much until we notice that $\frac{d}{dx}(1+e^x) = e^x = du$, meaning that we can make following second substitution:

$$\int \frac{e^x}{1+e^x}dx = \int \frac{du}{u}, \qquad \text{where } u = 1+e^x \text{ and } du = \frac{d}{dx}(1+e^x) = e^x.$$

So the seemingly difficult integral now has a very simple antiderivative (using the rule $\frac{d}{dy}\log(y) = 1/y$), which we can perform and then substitute back to the quantity of interest:

$$\int \frac{e^x}{1+e^x}dx = \int \frac{du}{u} = \log(u) + k = \log(1 + e^x) + k.$$

What this demonstrates is that the rules governing exponents and logarithms for derivatives can be exploited when going in the opposite direction. When these sorts of substitutions are less obvious or the functions are more complicated, the next tool required is *integration by parts*.

5.6.4 Integration by Parts

So far we have not developed a method for integrating functions that are products, although we did see that differentiating products is quite straightforward. Suppose we have an integral of the form

$$\int f(x)g(x)dx.$$

Often it is not always easy to see the structure of the antiderivative here. We will now derive a method, **integration by parts**, that gives a method for unwinding the product rule. The trick is to recharacterize part of the function into the $d()$ argument.

We will start with a basic derivation. Suppose first that we label $f(x) = u$ and $g(x) = v$, and note the shorthand versions of the derivatives $\frac{d}{dx}v = v'$ and $\frac{d}{dx}u = u'$. We can also rewrite these expressions as

$$dv = v'dx \qquad du = u'dx,$$

which will prove to be convenient. So the product rule is given by

$$\frac{d}{dx}(uv) = u\frac{d}{dx}v + v\frac{d}{dx}u = uv' + vu'.$$

Now integrate both sides of this equation with respect to x; simplify the left-hand side:

$$\int \frac{d}{dx}(uv)dx = \int uv'dx + \int vu'dx$$

$$uv = \int u(v'dx) + \int v(u'dx),$$

and plug in the definitions $dv = v'dx$, $du = u'dx$:

$$= \int udv + \int vdu.$$

By trivially rearranging this form we get the formula for integration by parts:

$$\int udv = uv - \int vdu.$$

This means that if we can rearrange the integral as a product of the function u and the derivative of another function dv, we can get uv, which is the product of u and the integral of dv minus a new integral, which will hopefully be easier to handle. If the latter integral requires it, we can repeat the process with new terms for u and v. We also need to readily obtain the integral of dv to get uv, so it is possible to choose terms that do not help.

As the last discussion probably foretells, there is some "art" associated with integration by parts. Specifically, how we split up the function to be integrated must be done strategically so that get more simple constituent parts on the right-hand side. Here is the classic textbook example:

$$\int x\log(x)dx,$$

which would be challenging without some procedure like the one described. The first objective is to see how we can split up $x \log(x)dx$ into udv. The two possibilities are

$$[u][dv] = [x][\log(x)]$$

$$[u][dv] = [\log(x)][x],$$

where the choice is clear since we cannot readily obtain $v = \int dv dx = \int \log(x)dx$. So picking the second arrangement gives the full mapping:

$$
\begin{array}{cc}
u = \log(x) & dv = xdx \\
du = \dfrac{1}{x}dx & v = \dfrac{1}{2}x^2.
\end{array}
$$

This physical arrangement in the box is not accidental; it helps to organize the constituent pieces and their relationships. The top row multiplied together should give the integrand. The second row is the derivative and the antiderivative of each of the corresponding components above. We now have all of the pieces mapped out for the integration by parts procedure:

$$\int udv = uv - \int vdu.$$

$$= (\log(x))\left(\frac{1}{2}x^2\right) - \int \left(\frac{1}{2}x^2\right)\left(\frac{1}{x}dx\right)$$

$$= \frac{1}{2}x^2 \log(x) - \int \frac{1}{2}xdx$$

$$= \frac{1}{2}x^2 \log(x) - \frac{1}{2}(\frac{1}{2}x^2) + k$$

$$= \frac{1}{2}x^2 \log(x) - \frac{1}{4}x^2 + k.$$

We benefited from a very simple integral in the second stage, because the antiderivative of $\frac{1}{2}x$ is straightforward. It can be the case that this integral is *more* difficult than the original one, which means that the choice of function assignment needs to be rethought.

5.6.4.1 Application: The Gamma Function

The **gamma function** (also called *Euler's integral*) is given by

$$\Gamma(\omega) = \int_0^\infty t^{\omega-1} e^{-t} dt, \quad \omega > 0.$$

Here t is a "dummy" variable because it integrates away (it is a placeholder for the limits). The gamma function is a generalization of the factorial function that can be applied to any positive real number, not just integers. For integer values, though, there is the simple relation: $\Gamma(n) = (n-1)!$. Since the result of the gamma function for any given value of ω is finite, the gamma function shows that finite results can come from integrals with limit values that include infinity.

Suppose we wanted to integrate the gamma function for a known value of ω, say 3. The resulting integral to calculate is

$$\int_0^\infty t^2 e^{-t} dt.$$

There are two obvious ways to split the integrand into u and dv. Consider this one first:

$$u = e^{-t} \qquad dv = t^2$$
$$du = -e^{-t} \qquad v = \frac{1}{3} t^3.$$

The problem here is that we are moving up ladders of the exponent of t, thus with each successive iteration of integration by parts we are actually making the subsequent $\int v \, du$ integral *more* difficult. So this will not do. The other logical split is

$$u = t^2 \qquad dv = e^{-t}$$
$$du = 2t \qquad v = -e^{-t}.$$

So we proceed with the integration by parts (omitting the limits on the integral for the moment):

$$\Gamma(3) = uv - \int v\,du$$

$$= (t^2)(-e^{-t}) - \int(-e^{-t})(2t)dt$$

$$= -e^{-t}t^2 + 2\int e^{-t}t\,dt.$$

Of course we now need to repeat the process to calculate the new integral on the right-hand side, so we will split this new integrand ($e^{-t}t$) up in a similar fashion:

$$\begin{array}{ll} u = t & dv = e^{-t} \\ du = 1 & v = -e^{-t}. \end{array}$$

The antiderivative property of e makes this easy (and repetitive). Now finish the integration:

$$\Gamma(3) = -e^{-t}t^2 + 2\int_0^\infty e^{-t}t\,dt$$

$$= -e^{-t}t^2 + 2\left[(t)(-e^{-t}) - \int_0^\infty(-e^{-t})(1)dt\right]$$

$$= \left[-e^{-t}t^2 - 2e^{-t}t - 2e^{-t}\right]\Big|_0^\infty$$

$$= [0 - 0 - 0] - [0 - 0 - 2] = 2,$$

which makes sense because we know that $\Gamma(3) = 2! = 2$. Observe also that the limits on the function components $-e^{-t}t^2$ and $2e^{-t}t$ needed to be calculated with L'Hospital's rule.

★ **Example 5.10:** **Utility Functions from Voting**. Back in Chapter 1, in Example 1.3, we saw an important mathematical model of voting developed by Riker and Ordeshook (1968). In that same article they looked at the "utility" that a particular voter receives from having her preferred candidate receive a specific number of votes. Call x the number of votes for her preferred candidate, v the total number of voters (participating), and $u(x)$ the utility for x. Obviously this last term ranges from a maximum of $u(v)$, where all voters select this candidate, to $u(0)$, where no voters select this candidate. For this example, assume that utility increases linearly with proportion, x/v, and so these minimum and maximum utility values are really zero and one.

They next specify a value x_0 that is the respondent's estimate of what might happen in the election when they do *not* vote. There is a function $g(x - x_0)$ that for a single specified value x gives the subjectively estimated probability that her vote changes the outcome. So when $g(x - x_0)$ is high our potential voters feels that there is a reasonable probability that she can affect the election, and vice versa. The expected value of some outcome x is then $u(x)g(x - x_0)$ in the same sense that the expected value of betting \$1 on a fair coin is 50¢. Probability and expectation will be covered in detail in Chapter 7, but here it is sufficient to simply talk about them colloquially.

All this means that the expected value for the election before it occurs, given that our potential voter does not vote, is the integral of the expected value where the integration occurs over all possible outcomes:

$$EV = \int_0^v u(x)g(x - x_0)dx = \int_0^v \frac{x}{v}g(x - x_0)dx,$$

which still includes her subjective estimate of x_0, and we have plugged in the linear function $u(x) = x/v$ in the second part. Actually, it might be more appropriate to calculate this with a sum since v is discrete, but with a large value it will not make a substantial difference and the sum would be much harder. This formulation means that the rate of change in utility for a change in x_0 (she votes) is

$$\frac{\partial EV}{\partial x_0} = -\frac{1}{v}\int_0^v x\frac{\partial}{\partial x_0}g(x - x_0)dx,$$

which requires some technical "regularity" conditions to let the derivative pass inside the integral. To solve this integral, integration by parts is necessary where $x = u$ and $dv = \frac{\partial}{\partial x_0} g(x - x_0) dx$. This produces

$$\frac{\partial EV}{\partial x_0} = -\frac{1}{v}(vg(x - x_0)dx - 1).$$

This means that as $g(x-x_0)$ goes to zero (the expectation of actually affecting the election) voting utility simplifies to $1/v$, which returns us to the paradox of participation that resulted from the model on page 5. After developing this argument, Riker and Ordeshook saw the result as a refutation of the linear utility assumption for elections because a utility of $1/v$ fails to account for the reasonable number of people that show up at the polls in large elections.

5.7 Additional Topics: Calculus of Trigonometric Functions

This section contains a set of trigonometry topics that are less frequently used in the social sciences but may be useful as references. As before, readers may elect to skip this section.

5.7.1 Derivatives of Trigonometric Functions

The trigonometric functions do not provide particularly intuitive derivative forms, but fortunately the two main results are incredibly easy to remember. The derivative forms for the sine and cosine function are

$$\frac{d}{dx}\sin(x) = \cos(x) \qquad \frac{d}{dx}\cos(x) = -\sin(x).$$

So the only difficult part to recall is that there is a change of sign on the derivative of the cosine. Usually, this operation needs to be combined with the chain rule, because it is more common to have a compound function, $u = g(x)$, rather than just x. The same rules incorporating the chain rule are given by

$$\frac{d}{dx}\sin(u) = \cos(u)\frac{d}{dx}u \qquad \frac{d}{dx}\cos(u) = -\sin(u)\frac{d}{dx}u.$$

The derivative forms for the other basic trigonometric functions are given in the same notation by

$$\frac{d}{dx}\csc(u) = -\csc(u)\cot(u)\frac{d}{dx}u \qquad \frac{d}{dx}\sec(u) = \sec(u)\tan(u)\frac{d}{dx}u$$

$$\frac{d}{dx}\tan(u) = \sec^2(u)\frac{d}{dx}u \qquad\qquad \frac{d}{dx}\cot(u) = -\csc^2(u)\frac{d}{dx}u.$$

It is better not to worry about memorizing these and most people (other than undergraduates taking math exams) tend to look them up when necessary. Some numerical examples are helpful:

$$\frac{d}{dx}\sin(\frac{1}{2}\pi x) = \frac{1}{2}\pi\cos(\frac{1}{2}\pi x) \qquad \frac{d}{dy}\cot(y^2 - y) = -\csc^2(y^2 - y)(2y - 1).$$

5.7.2 Integrals of Trigonometric Functions

The integrals of the basic trigonometric functions are like the derivative forms: easy to understand, annoying to memorize, and simple to look up (don't sell this book!). They can be given as either definite or indefinite integrals.

The two primary forms are

$$\int \sin(x)dx = -\cos(x) + k \qquad\qquad \int \cos(x)dx = \sin(x) + k.$$

It is also important to be able to manipulate these integrals for the reverse chain rule operation, for instance, $\int \sin(u)du = -\cos(u) + k$. The other four basic forms are more complicated. They are (in reverse chain rule notation)

$$\int \csc(u)du = \log|\csc(u) - \cot(u)| + k$$

$$\int \cot(u)du = \log|\sin(u)| + k.$$

$$\int \tan(u)du = -\log|\cos(u)| + k$$

$$\int \sec(u)du = \log|\sec(u) + \tan(u)| + k$$

Eight other fundamental trigonometric formulas are worth noting. These involve products and are given by

$$\int \sin^2(u)du = \frac{1}{2}u - \frac{1}{4}\sin(2u) + k$$

$$\int \cos(u)^2 du = \frac{1}{2}u + \frac{1}{4}\sin(2u) + k$$

$$\int \csc^2(u)du = -\cot(u) + k$$

$$\int \sec^2(u)du = \tan(u) + k$$

$$\int \tan^2(u)du = \tan(u) - u + k$$

$$\int \cot^2(u)du = -\cot(u) - u + k$$

$$\int \csc(u)\cot(u)du = -\csc(u) + k$$

$$\int \sec(u)\tan(u)du = \sec(u) + k.$$

There are actually many, many more of these and reference books abound with integral formulas that range from the basic (such as these) to the truly exotic.

5.8 New Terminology

Exercises

5.1 Find the following finite limits:

$$\lim_{x \to 4} \left[x^2 - 6x + 4 \right] \qquad\qquad \lim_{x \to 0} \left[\frac{x - 25}{x + 5} \right]$$

$$\lim_{x \to 4} \left[\frac{x^2}{3x - 2} \right] \qquad\qquad \lim_{y \to 1} \left[\frac{y^4 - 1}{y - 1} \right].$$

5.2 Given

$$\lim_{y \to 0} f(y) = -2 \quad \text{and} \quad \lim_{y \to 0} g(y) = 2,$$

find

$$\lim_{y \to 0} \left[f(y) - 3f(y)g(y) \right].$$

5.3 Find the following infinite limits and graph:

$$\lim_{x \to \infty} \left[\frac{9x^2}{x^2 + 3} \right] \qquad \lim_{x \to \infty} \left[\frac{3x - 4}{x + 3} \right] \qquad \lim_{x \to \infty} \left[\frac{2^x - 3}{2^x + 1} \right].$$

5.4 Marshall and Stahura (1979) modeled racial mixes in U.S. suburbs over a 10-year period and found that changes between white and black proportions can be described with one of two functional forms: linear and quadratic:

Population Change, 1960 to 1970, White (y)
as a Function of Black (x), by Suburb Size

Suburb	$y = 0.330 - 0.024x$
Under 25K	$y = 0.295 - 0.102x + 0.033x^2$
Suburb	$y = 0.199 - 0.112x$
25K–50K	$y = 0.193 - 0.144x + 0.103x^2$
Suburb	$y = 0.100 - 0.045x$
Over 50K	$y = 0.084 - 0.114x + 0.026x^2$

Comparing each suburb size separately, which of these two forms implies the greatest instantaneous change in y at $b = 0.5$? What is the interpretation on the minus sign for each coefficient on x and a positive coefficient for each coefficient on x^2?

5.5   Calculate the following derivatives:

$$\frac{d}{dx}3x^{\frac{1}{3}} \qquad\qquad \frac{d}{dt}(14t-7)$$

$$\frac{d}{dy}(y^3+3y^2-12) \qquad\qquad \frac{d}{dx}\left(\frac{1}{100}x^{25}-\frac{1}{10}x^{0.25}\right)$$

$$\frac{d}{dx}(x^2+1)(x^3-1) \qquad\qquad \frac{d}{dy}(y^3-7)\left(1+\frac{1}{y^2}\right)$$

$$\frac{d}{dy}(y-y^{-1})(y-y^{-2}) \qquad\qquad \frac{d}{dx}\left(\frac{4x-12x^2}{x^3-4x^2}\right)$$

$$\frac{d}{dy}\exp[y^2-3y+2] \qquad\qquad \frac{d}{dx}\log(2\pi x^2).$$

5.6   Stephan and McMullin (1981) considered transportation issues and
time minimization as a determinant of the distribution of county seats
in the United States and elsewhere. The key trade-off is this: If territories are too small, then there may be insufficient economic resources to
sustain necessary services, and if territories are too large, then travel
distances swamp economic advantages from scale. Define s as the
average distance to traverse, v as the average speed, h as the total
maintenance time required (paid for by the population), and p as the
population size. The model for time proposed is $T = s/v + h/p$.
Distance is proportional to area, so substitute in $s = g\sqrt{a}$ and $p = ad$,
where g is a proportionality constant and a is area. Now find the condition for a that minimizes time by taking the first derivative of T with
respect to a, setting it equal to zero, and solving. Show that this is a
minimum by taking an additional (second) derivative with respect to
a and noting that it must be positive.

5.7   Calculate the derivative of the following function using logarithmic
differentiation:

$$y = \frac{(2x^3-3)^{\frac{5}{2}}}{(x^2-1)^{\frac{2}{3}}(9x^2-1)^{\frac{1}{2}}}.$$

5.8   Use L'Hospital's rule to evaluate the following limits:

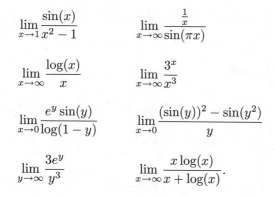

$$\lim_{x\to 1}\frac{\sin(x)}{x^2-1} \qquad\qquad \lim_{x\to\infty}\frac{\frac{1}{x}}{\sin(\pi x)}$$

$$\lim_{x\to\infty}\frac{\log(x)}{x} \qquad\qquad \lim_{x\to\infty}\frac{3^x}{x^3}$$

$$\lim_{x\to 0}\frac{e^y\sin(y)}{\log(1-y)} \qquad\qquad \lim_{x\to 0}\frac{(\sin(y))^2-\sin(y^2)}{y}$$

$$\lim_{y\to\infty}\frac{3e^y}{y^3} \qquad\qquad \lim_{x\to\infty}\frac{x\log(x)}{x+\log(x)}.$$

5.9   Using the limit of Riemann integrals, calculate the following integrals. Show steps.

$$R=\int_2^3\sqrt{x}\,dx \qquad\qquad R=\int_1^9\frac{1}{1+y^2}\,dy$$

$$R=\int_0^{0.1}x^2\,dx \qquad\qquad R=\int_1^9 1\,dx.$$

5.10   Solve the following definite integrals using the antiderivative method.

$$\int_6^8 x^3\,dx \qquad\qquad \int_1^9 2y^5\,dy \qquad\qquad \int_{-1}^0(3x^2-1)\,dx$$

$$\int_{-1}^1(14+x^2)\,dx \qquad\qquad \int_1^2\frac{1}{t^2}\,dt \qquad\qquad \int_2^4 e^y\,dy$$

$$\int_{-1}^2 x\sqrt{1+x^2}\,dx \qquad \int_{-100}^{100}(x^2-2/x)\,dx \qquad \int_2^4\sqrt{t}\,dt.$$

5.11   Calculate the area of the following function that lies above the x-axis and over the domain $[-10, 10]$:

$$f(x)=4x^2+12x-18.$$

5.12   In Figure 5.8, the fourth and fifth voters have ideal points at 7.75 and 8.5, respectively. Calculate the area of the overlapping region above the x-axis.

5.13   Calculate the following indefinite integrals:

$$\int (2 + 12x^2)^{3/2} dx \qquad \int (x^2 - x^{-\frac{1}{2}}) dx \qquad \int \frac{y}{\sqrt{9 + 3y^3}} dy$$

$$\int 360 t^6 dt \qquad \int \frac{x^2}{1 - x^2} dx \qquad \int (11 - 21y^9)^2 dy.$$

5.14   Calculate the following integrals using integration by parts:

$$\int x \cos(x) dx \qquad \int x \log(x^2 + 1) dx \qquad \int e^x x^{-2} dx$$

$$\int 2x \log(x)^2 dx \qquad \int \sec(x)^3 dx \qquad \int x e^{(3x^2 - 3)} dx.$$

5.15   For the gamma function (Section 5.6.4.1):

(a) Prove that $\Gamma(1) = 1$.

(b) Express the binomial function, $\binom{n}{y} = \frac{n!}{y!(n-y)!}$, in terms of the gamma function instead of factorial notation for integers.

(c) What is $\Gamma\left(\frac{1}{2}\right)$?

5.16   Another version of the factorial function is the **double factorial**, with odd and even versions:

$$(2n)!! = (2n) \cdot (2n - 2) \cdots (2n - 4) \cdots 6 \cdot 4 \cdot 2$$
$$(2n - 1)!! = (2n - 1) \cdot (2n - 3) \cdots (2n - 5) \cdots 5 \cdot 3 \cdot 1$$
$$= \pi^{-\frac{1}{2}} 2^n \Gamma\left(n + \frac{1}{2}\right).$$

Show that $(2n)!! = 2^n n!$ and $(2n - 1)!! = \frac{(2n-1)!}{2^n n!}$.

5.17   Blackwell and Girshick (1954) derived the result below in the context of mixed strategies in game theory. Game theory is a tool in the social sciences where the motivations, strategies, and rewards to hypothesized competing actors are analyzed mathematically to make predictions or explain observed behavior. This idea originated formally with von Neumann and Morgenstern's 1944 book. Simplified, an actor employs a mixed strategy when she has a set of alternative actions each with a known or assumed probability of success, and the choice of actions is made by randomly selecting one with that associated probability. Thus if there are three alternatives with success probabilities $\frac{1}{2}, \frac{1}{3}, \frac{1}{6}$, then there is a 50% chance of picking the first, and so on. Blackwell and Girshick (p.54) extended this idea to continuously measured alternatives between zero and one (i.e., a smooth function rather than a discrete listing). The first player accordingly chooses value $x \in [0:1]$, and the second player chooses value $y \in [0:1]$, and the function that defines the "game" is given by $M(x,y) = f(x-y)$, where

$$
f(t) = \begin{cases} t(1-t), & \text{for } 0 \geq t \geq 1 \\ f(t+1), & \text{for } -1 \geq t \geq 0. \end{cases}
$$

In other words, it matters which of x and y is larger in this game. Here is the surprising part. For any fixed value of y (call this y_0), the expected value of the game to the first player is $\frac{1}{6}$. To show this we integrate over a range of alternatives available to this player:

$$
\int_0^1 M(x,y)dx = \int_0^1 f(x-y_0)dx
$$

$$
= \underbrace{\int_0^{y_0} f(x-y_0)dx}_{x<y_0} + \underbrace{\int_{y_0}^1 f(x-y_0)dx}_{x>y_0},
$$

where breaking the integral into two pieces is necessary because the first one contains the case where $-1 \geq t \geq 0$ and the second one contains the case where $0 \geq t \geq 1$. Substitute in the two function values (t or $t+1$) and integrate over x to obtain exactly $\frac{1}{6}$.

5.18   Calculate the following derivatives of trigonometric functions:

$$\frac{d}{dx}\tan(9x) \qquad\qquad \frac{d}{dy}(\cos(3y) - \sin(2y))$$

$$\frac{d}{dx}\csc(\sin(x/2)) \qquad\qquad \frac{d}{dx}\cot(1 - x^2)$$

$$\frac{d}{dy}\tan(y)^2 \qquad\qquad \frac{d}{dy}\left(\frac{\tan(y) - \sin(y)}{\tan(y) + \sin(y)}\right)^{\frac{1}{3}}$$

$$\frac{d}{dx}\left(9x^2 + \csc(x)^3 - \tan(2x)\right) \quad \frac{d}{dx}(x + \sec(3x)).$$

5.19   Show that the Mean Value Theorem is a special case of Rolle's Theorem by generalizing the starting and stopping points.

5.20   Calculate $f(x) = x^3$ over the domain $[0:1]$ using limits only (no power rule), as was done for $f(x) = x^2$ on page 208.

5.21   From the appendix to Krehbiel (2000), take the partial derivative of

$$\frac{50((M^2 - M/2 + \delta)^2 + 100(1 - M/2 + \delta) - M)}{M((1 - M/2 + \delta) - (M/2 + \delta))}$$

with respect to M and show that it is decreasing in $M \in (0:1)$ (i.e., as M increases) for all values $\delta \in (0:1)$.

6

Additional Topics in Scalar and Vector Calculus

6.1 Objectives

This chapter presents additional topics in basic calculus that go beyond that of the introductory material in Chapter 5. These topics include more advanced uses of derivatives like partial derivatives and higher order partial derivatives; root finding (locating an important point along some function of interest); analyzing function minima, maxima, and inflection points (points where derivatives change); integrals on functions of multiple variables; and, finally, the idea of an abstract series. In general, the material extends that of the last chapter and demonstrates some applications in the social sciences. A key distinction made in this chapter is the manner in which functions of multiple variables are handled with different operations.

6.2 Partial Derivatives

A **partial derivative** is a regular derivative, just as we have already studied, except that the operation is performed on a function of multiple variables where the derivative is taken only with respect to one of them and the others are treated constants. We start with the generic function

$$u = f(x, y, z)$$

specified for the three variables, x, y, and z. We can now define the three partial derivatives

$$\frac{\partial u}{\partial x} = \frac{\partial}{\partial x} f(x, y, z) = g_1(x, y, z)$$

$$\frac{\partial u}{\partial y} = \frac{\partial}{\partial y} f(x, y, z) = g_2(x, y, z)$$

$$\frac{\partial u}{\partial z} = \frac{\partial}{\partial z} f(x, y, z) = g_3(x, y, z),$$

where the resulting functions are labeled as $g_i()$, $i = 1, 2, 3$, to indicate that not only are they different from the original function, they are also distinct from each other because different variables are manipulated with the derivative processes. As an example, consider the function

$$f(x, y, z) = x \exp(y) \log(z),$$

which has the three partial derivatives

$$\frac{\partial}{\partial x} f(x, y, z) = \exp(y) \log(z) \frac{\partial}{\partial x} x = \exp(y) \log(z)$$

$$\frac{\partial}{\partial y} f(x, y, z) = x \log(z) \frac{\partial}{\partial y} \exp(y) = x \exp(y) \log(z)$$

$$\frac{\partial}{\partial z} f(x, y, z) = x \exp(y) \frac{\partial}{\partial z} \log(z) = x \exp(y) \frac{1}{z}.$$

Notice that the variables that are not part of the derivation process are simply treated as constants in these operations.

We can also evaluate a more complex function with additional variables:

$$f(u_1, u_2, u_3, u_4, u_5) = u_1^{u_2 u_3} \sin\left(\frac{u_1}{2}\right) \log\left(\frac{u_4}{u_5}\right) u_3^2,$$

which produces

$$\frac{\partial}{\partial u_1} f(u_1, u_2, u_3, u_4, u_5) = \left[u_1^{u_2 u_3} \log\left(\frac{u_4}{u_5}\right) u_3^2 \right]$$

$$\times \left[\frac{u_2 u_3}{u_1} \sin\left(\frac{u_1}{2}\right) + \frac{1}{2} \cos\left(\frac{u_1}{2}\right) \right]$$

$$\frac{\partial}{\partial u_2} f(u_1, u_2, u_3, u_4, u_5) = \log(u_1) u_1^{u_2 u_3} \sin\left(\frac{u_1}{2}\right) \log\left(\frac{u_4}{u_5}\right) u_3^3$$

$$\frac{\partial}{\partial u_3} f(u_1, u_2, u_3, u_4, u_5) = u_1^{u_2 u_3} \sin\left(\frac{u_1}{2}\right) \log\left(\frac{u_4}{u_5}\right) u_3 \left[u_2 \log(u_1) u_3 + 2 \right]$$

$$\frac{\partial}{\partial u_4} f(u_1, u_2, u_3, u_4, u_5) = u_1^{u_2 u_3} \sin\left(\frac{u_1}{2}\right) \frac{u_3^2}{u_4}$$

$$\frac{\partial}{\partial u_5} f(u_1, u_2, u_3, u_4, u_5) = -u_1^{u_2 u_3} \sin\left(\frac{u_1}{2}\right) \frac{u_3^2}{u_5}.$$

★ **Example 6.1:** **The Relationship Between Age and Earnings.** Rees and Schultz (1970) analyzed the relationship between workers' ages and their earnings with the idea that earnings increase early in a worker's career but tend to decrease toward retirement. Thus the relationship is parabolic in nature according to their theory. Looking at maintenance electricians, they posited an additive relationship that affects income (in units of $1,000) according to

$$Income = \beta_0 + \beta_1(Seniority) + \beta_2(School.Years)$$
$$+ \beta_3(Experience) + \beta_4(Training)$$
$$+ \beta_5(Commute.Distance) + \beta_6(Age) + \beta_7(Age^2),$$

where the β values are scalar values that indicate how much each factor individually affects *Income* (produced by linear regression, which is not critical to our discussion here). Since *Age* and *Age*^{2} are both included in the analysis, the effect of the workers' age is parabolic, which is exactly as the authors intended: rising early, cresting, and then falling back. If we take the first partial derivative with respect to age, we get

$$\frac{\partial}{\partial Age} Income = \beta_6 + 2\beta_7 Age,$$

where $\beta_6 = 0.031$ and $\beta_7 = -0.00032$ (notice that all the other causal factors disappear due to the additive specification). Thus at age 25 the incremental effect of one additional year is $0.031 + 2(-0.00032)(25) = 0.015$, at age 50 it is $0.031 + 2(-0.00032)(50) = -0.001$, and at 75 it is $0.031 + 2(-0.00032)(75) = -0.017$.

★ **Example 6.2:   Indexing Socio-Economic Status (SES)**. Any early measure of socio-economic status by Gordon (1969) reevaluated conventional compilation of various social indicators as a means of measuring "the position of the individual in some status ordering as determined by the individual's characteristics–his education, income, position, in the community, the market place, etc." The basic idea is to combine separate collected variables into a single measure because using any one single measure does not fully provide an overall assessment of status. The means by which these indicators are combined can vary considerably: additive or multiplicative, scaled or unscaled, weighted according to some criteria, and so on. Gordon proposed an alternative multiplicative causal expression of the form for an individual's socio-economic status:

$$SES = AE^b I^c M^d,$$

where
A = all terms not explicitly included in the model

E = years of education

I = amount of income

M = percent of time employed annually

and b, c, d are the associated "elasticities" providing a measure of strength for each causal term. The marginal (i.e., incremental) impacts on SES for each of the three terms of interest are given by partial derivatives with respect to the term of interest:

$$\frac{\partial SES}{\partial E} = AbE^{b-1}I^c M^d$$

$$\frac{\partial SES}{\partial I} = AcE^b I^{c-1} M^d$$

$$\frac{\partial SES}{\partial M} = AdE^b I^c M^{d-1}.$$

The point is that individual effects can be pulled from the general multiplicative specification with the partial derivatives. Note that due to the multiplicative nature of the proposed model, the marginal impacts are still dependent on levels of the other variables in a way that a strictly additive model would not produce: $SES = A + E^b + I^c + M^d$.

6.3 Derivatives and Partial Derivatives of Higher Order

Derivatives of higher order than one (what we have been doing so far) are simply iterated applications of the derivative process. The **second derivative** of a function with respect to x is

$$\frac{\partial^2 f(x)}{\partial x^2} = \frac{\partial}{\partial x}\left(\frac{\partial}{\partial x} f(x)\right),$$

also denoted $f''(x)$ for functions of only one variable (since $f''(x, y)$ would be ambiguous). It follows then how to denote, calculate, and notate higher order derivatives:

$$\frac{\partial^3 f(x)}{\partial x^3}, \quad \frac{\partial^4 f(x)}{\partial x^4}, \quad \frac{\partial^5 f(x)}{\partial x^5},$$

(i.e., $f'''(x)$, $f''''(x)$, and $f'''''(x)$, although this notation gets cumbersome). Note the convention with respect to the order designation here, and that it differs by placement in the numerator (∂^5) and denominator (∂x^5). Of course at some point a function will cease to support new forms of the higher order derivatives when the degree of the polynomial is exhausted. For instance, given the function

$f(x) = 3x^3,$

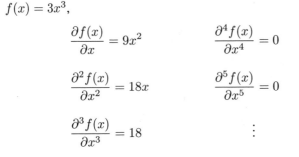

$$\frac{\partial f(x)}{\partial x} = 9x^2 \qquad\qquad \frac{\partial^4 f(x)}{\partial x^4} = 0$$

$$\frac{\partial^2 f(x)}{\partial x^2} = 18x \qquad\qquad \frac{\partial^5 f(x)}{\partial x^5} = 0$$

$$\frac{\partial^3 f(x)}{\partial x^3} = 18 \qquad\qquad \vdots$$

Thus we "run out" of derivatives eventually, and all derivatives of order four or higher remain zero.

So how do we interpret higher order derivatives? Because the first derivative is the rate of change of the original function, the second derivative is the rate of change for the rate of that change, and so on. Consider the simple example of the velocity of a car. The first derivative describes the rate of change of this velocity: very high when first starting out from a traffic light, and very low when cruising on the highway. The second derivative describes how fast this rate of change is changing. Again, the second derivative is very high early in the car's path as it increases speed rapidly but is low under normal cruising conditions. Third-order and higher derivatives work in exactly this same way on respective lower orders, but the interpretation is often less straightforward.

Higher order derivation can also be applied to partial derivatives. Given the function $f(x, y) = 3x^3 y^2$, we can calculate

$$\frac{\partial^2}{\partial x \partial y} f(x, y) = \frac{\partial}{\partial y}(9x^2 y^2) = 18x^2 y$$

and

$$\frac{\partial^3}{\partial x^2 \partial y} f(x, y) = \frac{\partial^2}{\partial x \partial y}(9x^2 y^2)$$

$$= \frac{\partial}{\partial y}(18xy^2)$$

$$= 36xy.$$

Thus the order hierarchy in the denominator gives the "recipe" for how many derivatives of each variable to perform, but the sequence of operations does not change the answer and therefore should be done in an order that makes the problem as easy as possible. Obviously there are other higher order partial derivatives that could be calculated for this function. In fact, if a function has k variables each of degree n, the number of derivatives of order n is given by $\binom{n+k-1}{n}$.

6.4 Maxima, Minima, and Root Finding

Derivatives can be used to find points of interest along a given function. One point of interest is the point where the "curvature" of the function changes, given by the following definition:

- **[Inflection Point.]** For a given function, $y = f(x)$, a point (x^*, y^*) is called an **inflection point** if the second derivative immediately on one side of the point is signed oppositely to the second derivative immediately on the other side.

So if x^* is indeed an inflection point, then for some small interval around x^*, $[x^* - \delta, x^* + \delta]$, $f''(x)$ is positive on one side and negative on the other. Interestingly, if $f''(x)$ is continuous at the inflection point $f(x^*)$, then $f''(x^*) = 0$. This makes intuitive sense since on one side $f'(x)$ is increasing so that $f''(x)$ must be positive, and on the other side $f'(x)$ is decreasing so that $f''(x)$ must be negative. Making δ arbitrarily small and decreasing it toward zero, x^* is the point where δ vanishes and the second derivative is neither positive nor negative and therefore must be zero.

Graphically, the tangent line at the inflection point crosses the function such that it is on one side before the point and on the other side afterward. This is a consequence of the change of sign of the second derivative of the function and is illustrated in Figure 6.1 with the function $f(x) = (x^3 - 15x^2 + 60x + 30)/15$. The function (characteristically) curves away from the tangent line on one side

Fig. 6.1. ILLUSTRATING THE INFLECTION POINT

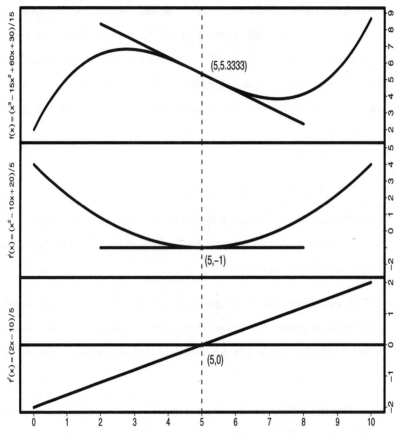

and curves away in the opposite direction on the other side. In the first panel of this figure the function itself is plotted with the tangent line shown. In the second panel the first derivative function, $f'(x) = (x^2 - 10x + 20)/5$, is plotted with the tangent line shown at the corresponding minima. Finally the third panel shows the second derivative function, $f''(x) = (2x - 10)/5$, with a horizontal line where the function crosses zero on the y-axis. Note that having a zero second derivative is a necessary but not sufficient condition for being an inflection point since the function $f'(5)$ has a zero second derivative, but $f'''(5)$ does not change sign just around 5.

★ **Example 6.3:** **Power Cycle Theory.** Sometimes inflection points can be substantively helpful in analyzing politics. Doran (1989) looked at critical changes in relative power between nations, evaluating *power cycle theory*, which asserts that war is caused by changes in the gap between state power and state interest. The key is that when dramatic differences emerge between relative power (capability and prestige) and systematic foreign policy role (current interests developed or allowed by the international system), existing balances of power are disturbed. Doran particularly highlighted the case where a nation ascendent in both power and interest, with power in excess of interest, undergoes a "sudden violation of the prior trend" in the form of an inflection point in their power curve.

Fig. 6.2. POWER/ROLE GAP CHANGES INDUCED BY THE INFLECTION POINT

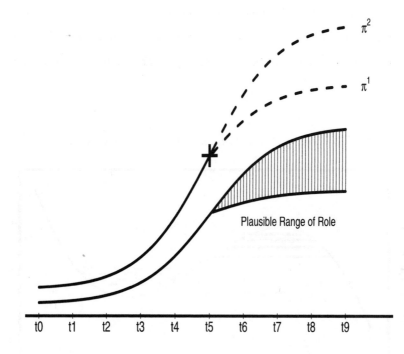

This is illustrated in Figure 6.2, where the inflection point at time $t5$ in the power curve introduces uncertainty in the anticipated decline in increasing power (i.e., the difference in π^1 and π^2 in the figure) and the subsequent potential differences between power and the range of plausible roles. Thus the problem introduced by the inflection point is that it creates changes in the slope difference and thus changes in the gap between role and power that the state and international system must account for.

The function $f(x) = (x^3 - 15x^2 + 60x + 30)/15$ in Figure 6.1 has a single inflection point in the illustrated range because there is on point where the concave portion of the function meets the convex portion. If a function (or portion of a function) is **convex** (also called **concave upward**), then every possible chord is above the function, except for their endpoints. A **chord** is just a line segment connecting two points along a curve. If a function (or portion of a function) is **concave** (or **concave downward**), then every possible chord is below the function, except for their endpoints. Figure 6.3 shows chords over the concave portion of the example function, followed by chords over the convex portion.

Fig. 6.3. Concave and Convex Portions of a Function

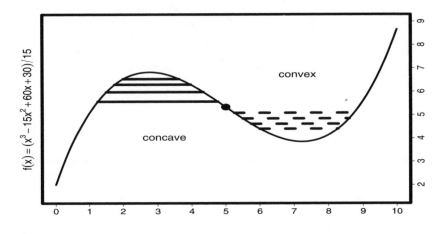

There is actually a more formal determination of concave and conv

If a function $f(x)$ is twice differentiable and concave over some open

then $f''(x) \leq 0$, and if a function $f(x)$ is twice differentiable and convex

over some open interval then $f''(x) \geq 0$. The reverse statement is also true:

A twice differentiable function that has a nonpositive second derivative over

some interval is concave over that interval, and a twice differentiable function

that has a nonnegative derivative over some interval is convex over that interval.

So the sign of the second derivative gives a handy test, which will apply in the

next section.

6.4.1 Evaluating Zero-Derivative Points

Repeated application of the derivative also gives us another general test: the

second derivative test. We saw in Chapter 5 (see, for instance, Figure 5.4

on page 186) that points where the first derivatives are equal to zero are either

a maxima or a minima of the function (modes or anti-modes), but without

graphing how would we know which? Visually it is clear that the rate of

change of the first derivative declines, moving away from a relative maximum

point in both directions, and increases, moving away from a relative minimum

point. The term "relative" here reinforces that these functions may have multiple

maxima and minima, and we mean the behavior in a small neighborhood around

the point of interest. This rate of change observation of the first derivative means

that we can test with the second derivative: If the second derivative is negative

at a point where the first derivative is zero, then the point is a relative maximum,

and if the second derivative is positive at such a point, then the point is a relative

minimum.

Higher order polynomials often have more than one mode. So, for example,

we can evaluate the function

$$f(x) = \frac{1}{4}x^4 - 2x^3 + \frac{11}{2}x^2 - 6x + \frac{11}{4}.$$

The first derivative is

$$f'(x) = x^3 - 6x^2 + 11x - 6,$$

which can be factored as

$$= (x^2 - 3x + 2)(x - 3)$$
$$= (x - 1)(x - 2)(x - 3).$$

Since the critical values are obtained by setting this first derivative function equal to zero and solving, it is apparent that they are simply 1, 2, and 3. Substituting these three x values into the original function shows that at the three points $(1, 0.5), (2, 0.75), (3, 0.5)$ there is a function maximum or minimum. To determine whether each of these is a maximum or a minimum, we must first obtain the second derivative form,

$$f''(x) = 3x^2 - 12x + 11,$$

and then plug in the three critical values:

$$f''(1) = 3(1)^2 - 12(1) + 11 = 2$$

$$f''(2) = 3(2)^2 - 12(2) + 11 = -1$$

$$f''(3) = 3(3)^2 - 12(3) + 11 = 2.$$

This means that $(1, 0.5)$ and $(3, 0.5)$ are minima and $(2, 0.75)$ is a maximum. We can think of this in terms of Rolle's Theorem from the last chapter. If we modified the function slightly by subtracting $\frac{1}{2}$ (i.e., add $\frac{9}{4}$ instead of $\frac{11}{4}$), then two minima would occur on the x-axis. This change does not alter the fundamental form of the function or its maxima and minima; it just shifts the function up or down on the y-axis. By Rolle's Theorem there is guaranteed to be another point in between where the first derivative is equal to zero; the point at $x = 2$ here is the only one from the factorization. Since the points at $x = 1$

and $x = 3$ are minima, then the function increases away from them, which means that $x = 2$ has to be a maximum.

6.4.2 Root Finding with Newton-Raphson

A **root** of a function is the point where the function crosses the x-axis: $f(x) = 0$. This value is a "root" of the function $f()$ in that it provides a solution to the polynomial expressed by the function. It is also the point where the function crosses the x-axis in a graph of x versus $f(x)$. A discussion of polynomial function roots with examples was given on page 33 in Chapter 1.

Roots are typically substantively important points along the function, and it is therefore useful to be able to find them without much trouble. Previously, we were able to easily factor such functions as $f(x) = x^2 - 1$ to find the roots. However, this is not always realistically the case, so it is important to have a more general procedure. One such procedure is **Newton's method** (also called **Newton-Raphson**). The general form of Newton's method also (to be derived) is a series of steps according to

$$x_1 \cong x_0 - \frac{f(x_0)}{f'(x_0)},$$

where we move from a starting point x_0 to x_1, which is closer to the root, using characteristics of the function itself.

Newton's method exploits the **Taylor series expansion**, which gives the relationship between the value of a mathematical function at the point x_0 and the function value at another point, x_1, given (with continuous derivatives over the relevant support) as

$$f(x_1) = f(x_0) + (x_1 - x_0)f'(x_0) + \frac{1}{2!}(x_1 - x_0)^2 f''(x_0)$$
$$+ \frac{1}{3!}(x_1 - x_0)^3 f'''(x_0) + \cdots,$$

where f' is the first derivative with respect to x, f'' is the second derivative with respect to x, and so on. Infinite precision between the values $f(x_1)$ and $f(x_0)$ is achieved with the infinite extending of the series into higher order derivatives and higher order polynomials:

$$f(x_1) = f(x_0) + (x_1 - x_0)f'(x_0) + \frac{1}{2!}(x_1 - x_0)^2 f''(x_0) + \cdots$$
$$+ \cdots \frac{1}{\infty!}(x_1 - x_0)^\infty f^{(\infty)}(x_0)$$

(of course the factorial component in the denominator means that these are rapidly decreasing increments).

We are actually interested in finding a root of the function, which we will suppose exists at the undetermined point x_1. What we know so far is that for any point x_0 that we would pick, it is possible to relate $f(x_1)$ and $f(x_0)$ with the Taylor series expansion. This is simplified in two ways. First, note that if x_1 is a root, then $f(x_1) = 0$, meaning that the left-hand side of the two above equations is really zero. Second, while we cannot perfectly relate the $f(x_0)$ to the function evaluated at the root because the expansion can never by **fully** evaluated, it should be obvious that using some of the first terms at least gets us closer to the desired point. Since the factorial function is increasing rapidly, let us use these last two facts and assert that

$$0 \cong f(x_0) + (x_1 - x_0)f'(x_0),$$

where the quality of the approximation can presumably be improved with better guesses of x_0. Rearrange the equation so that the quantity of interest is on the left-hand side:

$$x_1 \cong x_0 - \frac{f(x_0)}{f'(x_0)},$$

to make this useful for candidate values of x_0. If this becomes "algorithmic" because x_0 is chosen arbitrarily, then repeating the steps with successive approximations gives a process defined for the $(j + 1)$th step:

$$x_{j+1} \cong x_j - \frac{f(x_j)}{f'(x_j)},$$

so that progressively improved estimates are produced until $f(x_{j+1})$ is sufficiently close to zero. The process exploits the principle that the first terms of the Taylor series expansion get qualitatively better as the approximation gets closer and the remaining (ignored) steps get progressively less important.

Newton's method converges quadratically in time (number of steps) to a solution provided that the selected starting point is reasonably close to the solution, although the results can be very bad if this condition is not met. The key problem with distant starting points is that if $f''(x)$ changes sign between this starting point and the objective, then the algorithm may even move *away* from the root (diverge).

As a simple example of Newton's method, suppose that we wanted a numerical routine for finding the square root of a number, μ. This is equivalent to finding the root of the simple equation $f(x) = x^2 - \mu = 0$. The first derivative is just $\frac{\partial}{\partial x} f(x) = 2x$. If we insert these functions into the $(j+1)$th step:

$$x_{j+1} = x_j - \frac{f(x_j)}{f'(x_j)},$$

we get

$$x_{j+1} = x_j - \frac{(x_j)^2 - \mu}{2x_j} = \frac{1}{2}(x_j + \mu x_j^{-1}).$$

Recall that μ is a constant here defined by the problem and x_j is an arbitrary value at the jth step. A very basic algorithm for implementing this in software or on a hand calculator is

```
delta = 0.0000001
x = starting.value
DO:
        x.new = 0.5*(x + mu/x)
        x = x.new
UNTIL:
        abs(x^2 - mu) < delta
```

where `abs()` is the absolute value function and `delta` is the accuracy threshold that we are willing to accept. If we are interested in getting the square root of 99 and we run this algorithm starting at the obviously wrong point of $x = 2$, we get:

Iteration	x	x^2
0	2.0	4.0
1	25.75	663.0625
2	14.7973300970874	218.960978002168
3	10.7438631130069	115.430594591030
4	9.97921289277379	99.5846899593026
5	9.94991749815775	99.0008582201457
6	9.94987437115967	99.00000000186

where further precision could be obtained with more iterations.

6.5 Multidimensional Integrals

As we have previously seen, the integration process measures the area under some function for a given variable. Because functions can obviously have multiple variables, it makes sense to define an integral as measuring the area (volume actually) under a function in more than one dimension. For two variables, the **iterated integral** (also called the **repeated integral**), is given in definite form here by

$$V = \int_a^b \int_c^d f(x, y) \, dy \, dx,$$

where x is integrated between constants a and b, and y is integrated between constants c and d. The best way to think of this is by its inherent "nesting" of operations:

$$V = \int_a^b \left[\int_c^d f(x, y) \, dy \right] dx,$$

so that after the integration with respect to y there is a single integral left with respect to x of some *new* function that results from the first integration:

$$V = \int_a^b g(x) \, dx,$$

where $g(x) = \int_c^d f(x, y) \, dy$. That is, in the first (inner) step x is treated as a constant, and once the integration with respect to y is done, y is treated as a constant in the second (outer) step. In this way each variable is integrated

Fig. 6.4. ILLUSTRATION OF ITERATED INTEGRATION OF VOLUMES

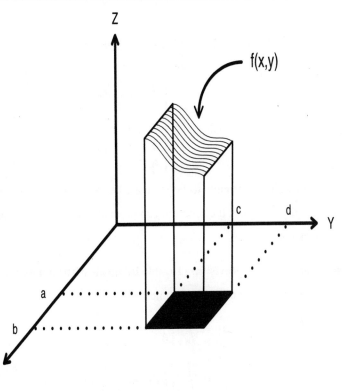

separately with respect to its limits. The idea of integrating under a surface with an iterated intregral is illustrated in Figure 6.4, where the black rectangle shows the region and the stripped region shows $f(x, y)$. The integration provides the volume between this plan and this surface.

★ **Example 6.4:** **Double Integral with Constant Limits.** In the following simple integral we first perform the operation for the variable y:

$$\int_2^3 \int_0^1 x^2 y^3 dy dx = \int_2^3 \left[\frac{1}{4} x^2 y^4 \Big|_{y=0}^{y=1} \right] dx$$

$$= \int_2^3 \left[\frac{1}{4} x^2 (1)^4 - \frac{1}{4} x^2 (0)^4 \right] dx$$

$$= \int_2^3 \frac{1}{4} x^2 dx = \frac{1}{12} x^3 \Big|_{x=2}^{x=3} = \frac{19}{12}.$$

It turns out that it is not important which variable we integrate first. Therefore, in our case,

$$V = \int_a^b \int_c^d f(x,y)\, dy\, dx$$

$$= \int_a^b \left[\int_c^d f(x,y)\, dy \right] dx$$

$$= \int_c^d \left[\int_a^b f(x,y)\, dx \right] dy.$$

Sometimes though it pays to be strategic as to which variable integration to perform first, because the problem can be made more or less complicated by this decision.

★ **Example 6.5:** **Revisiting Double Integrals with Constant Limits**. Now integrate x first with the same function:

$$\int_0^1 \int_2^3 x^2 y^3\, dx\, dy = \int_0^1 \left[\frac{1}{3} x^3 y^3 \Big|_{x=2}^{x=3} \right] dy$$

$$= \int_0^1 \left[\frac{1}{3}(3)^3 y^3 - \frac{1}{3}(2)^3 y^3 \right] dy = \int_0^1 \frac{19}{3} y^3\, dy$$

$$= \frac{19}{12} y^4 \Big|_{y=0}^{y=1} = \frac{19}{12}.$$

So far all the limits of the integration have been constant. This is not particularly realistic because it assumes that we are integrating functions over rectangles only to measure the volume under some surface described by $f(x, y)$. More generally, the region of integration is a function of x and y. For instance, consider the unit circle centered at the origin defined by the equation $1 = x^2 + y^2$. The limits of the integral in the x and the y dimensions now depend on the other variable, and an iterated integral over this region measures the cylindrical volume under a surface defined by $f(x, y)$. Thus, we need a means of performing the integration in two steps as before but accounting for this dependency. To generalize the iterated integration process above, we first express the limits of the integral in terms of a single variable. For the circle example we could use either of

$$y = g_y(x) = \sqrt{1 - x^2} \qquad x = g_x(y) = \sqrt{1 - y^2},$$

depending on our order preference. If we pick the first form, then the integral limits in the inner operation are the expression for y in terms of x, so we label this as the function $g_y(x)$.

Fig. 6.5. INTEGRATING $f(x, y) = 2x^3y$ OVER PART OF THE UNIT CIRCLE

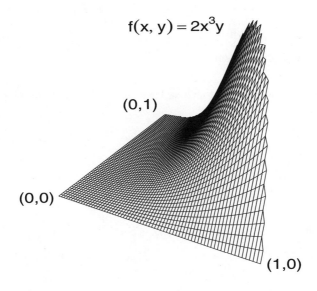

$$f(x, y) = 2x^3y$$

(0,1)

(0,0)

(1,0)

★ **Example 6.6: Double Integral with Dependent Limits**. We want to integrate the function $f(x, y) = 2x^3y$ over the quarter of the unit circle in the first quadrant (x and y both positive), as illustrated in Figure 6.5. Selecting to integrate y in the inner operation, we have the limits on the integral as 0 and $\sqrt{1-x^2}$. Thus the process proceeds as

$$V = \int_0^1 \int_0^{\sqrt{1-x^2}} 2x^3 y\, dy\, dx$$

$$= \int_0^1 x^3 y^2 \Big|_{y=0}^{y=\sqrt{1-x^2}} dx$$

$$= \int_0^1 x^3(1-x^2)dx = \int_0^1 x^3 - x^5 dx$$

$$= \frac{1}{4}x^4 - \frac{1}{6}x^6 \Big|_{x=0}^{x=1} = \frac{1}{12}.$$

In the above example we would get identical (and correct) results integrating x first with the limits $(0, \sqrt{1-x^2})$. This leads to the following general theorem.

Iterated Integral Theorem:

- A two-dimensional area of interest, denoted $\mathfrak{A}$, is characterized by either

$$a \le x \le b, \qquad g_{y1}(x) \le y g_{y2}(x)$$

or

$$c \le y \le d, \qquad g_{x1}(y) \le x g_{x2}(y).$$

- The function to be integrated, $f(x, y)$, is continuous for all of $\mathfrak{A}$.
- Then the double integral over $\mathfrak{A}$ is equivalent to either of the iterated integrals:

$$\iint_{\mathfrak{A}} f(x, y)d\mathfrak{A} = \int_a^b \int_{g_{y1}(x)}^{g_{y2}(x)} f(x, y)dy\, dx = \int_c^d \int_{g_{x1}(y)}^{g_{x2}(y)} f(x, y)dx\, dy.$$

This theorem states that, like the case with constant limits, we can switch the order of integration if we like, and that in both cases the result is equivalent to the motivating double integral.

★ **Example 6.7:   More Complicated Double Integral.** Consider the problem of integrating the function $f(x, y) = 3 + x^2$ over the region $\mathfrak{A}$, determined by the intersection of the function $f_1(x) = (x-1)^2$ and the function

Fig. 6.6. IRREGULAR REGION DOUBLE INTEGRAL

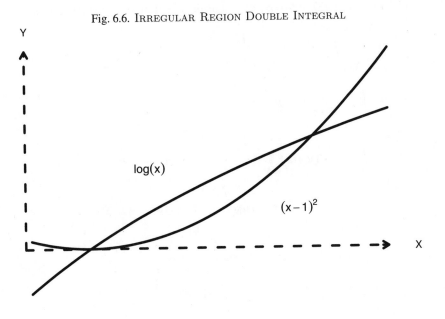

$f_2(x) = \log(x)$, as depicted in Figure 6.6. This integral is

$$V = \int_a^b \int_{(x-1)^2}^{\log(x)} 3 + x^2 \, dy dx,$$

where a is obviously from the point $(1, 0)$, but it is not clear how to determine b. One way to obtain this point is to define the difference equation and its first derivative:

$$f_d(x) = x^2 - 2x + 1 - \log(x), \qquad f'_d(x) = 2x - 2 - \frac{1}{x},$$

which comes from expanding the square and subtracting $\log(x)$. Now we can apply the Newton-Raphson algorithm quite easily, and the result is the point

$(1.7468817, 0.5578323)$ (try it!). Thus the integration procedure becomes

$$\int_1^{1.74...} \int_{(x-1)^2}^{\log(x)} 3 + x^2 \, dy dx$$

$$= \int_1^{1.74...} 3y + x^2 y \Big|_{y=(x-1)^2}^{y=\log(x)} dx$$

$$= \int_1^{1.74...} \left(3\log(x) - 3(x-1)^2 + x^2 \log(x) - x^2(x-1)^2\right) dx$$

$$= \int_1^{1.74...} \left(x^2 \log(x) + 3\log(x) - x^4 + 2x^3 - 4x^2 + 6x - 3\right) dx$$

$$= \frac{1}{9}x^3(3\log(x) - 1) + 3(x\log(x) - x) - \frac{1}{5}x^5 + \frac{1}{2}x^4$$

$$- \frac{4}{3}x^3 + 3x^2 - 3x \Big|_1^{1.7468817}$$

$$= 0.02463552 - (-0.1444444) = 0.1690799,$$

where the antiderivative of $x^2 \log(x)$ comes from the rule

$$\int u^n \log(u) du = \frac{u^{n+1}}{(n+1)^2}[(n+1)\log(u) - 1] + k$$

(k is again an arbitrary constant in the case of indefinite integrals).

6.6 Finite and Infinite Series

The idea of finite and infinite series is very important because it underlies many theoretical principles in mathematics, and because some physical phenomena can be modeled or explained through a series. The first distinction that we care about is whether a series converges or diverges. We will also be centrally concerned here with the idea of a limit as discussed in Section 5.2 of Chapter 5.

★ **Example 6.8:** **The Nazification of German Sociological Genetics.** The Hitlerian regime drove out or killed most of the prominent German sociologists of the time (a group that had enormous influence on the discipline).

The few remaining German sociologists apparently supported Nazi principles of heredity even though these were wrong and the correct chromosonal theory of inheritance had been published and supported in Germany since 1913 (Hager 1949). The motivation was Hitler's fascination with **Reinrassen** (pure races) as opposed to **Mischrassen** (mixed races), although such distinctions have no scientific basis in genetics whatsoever. These sociologists prescribed to Galton's (1898) theory that "the two parents, between them, contribute *on average* one half each inherited faculty,..." and thus a person's contributed genetics is related to a previous ancestor by the series

$$\frac{1}{2}, \frac{1}{4}, \frac{1}{8}, \frac{1}{16}, \frac{1}{32}, \cdots$$

(which interestingly sums to 1). This incorrect idea of heredity supported Hitler's goal of passing laws forbidding mixed marriages (i.e., "Aryan" and "non-Aryan" in this case) because then eventually German society could become 100% Aryan since the fraction above goes to zero in the limit (recall that it was claimed to be a "thousand year Reich").

★ **Example 6.9:** **Measuring Small Group Standing.** Some sociologists care about the relative standing of individuals in small, bounded groups. This can be thought of as popularity, standing, or esteem, broadly defined. Suppose there are N members of the group and $\mathbf{A}$ is the $N \times N$ matrix where a 1 for a_{ij} indicates that individual i (the row) chooses to associate with individual j (the column), and 0 indicates the opposite choice. For convenience, the diagonal values are left to be zero (one cannot choose or not choose in this sense). The early literature (Moreno 1934) posited a ranking of status that simply added up choice reception by individual, which can be done by multiplying the $\mathbf{A}$ matrix by an appropriate unit vector to sum by columns, for instance,

$$\text{status}_1 = \mathbf{A}'u = \begin{bmatrix} 0 & 0 & 1 & 0 \\ 1 & 0 & 0 & 0 \\ 1 & 1 & 0 & 0 \\ 1 & 1 & 1 & 0 \end{bmatrix}' \begin{bmatrix} 1 \\ 1 \\ 1 \\ 1 \end{bmatrix} = \begin{bmatrix} 3 \\ 2 \\ 2 \\ 0 \end{bmatrix}.$$

Later it was proposed (Katz 1953) that indirect associations also led to increased standing, so a means of incorporating indirect paths throughout this matrix needed to be included. Of course we would not want to require that indirect paths be equal in weight to direct paths, so we include a weighting factor, $0 < \alpha < 1$, that discounts distance. If we include every possible path, then the matrix that keeps track of these is given by the *finite matrix series*:

$$B = \alpha \mathbf{A} + \alpha^2 \mathbf{A}'\mathbf{A} + \alpha^3 \mathbf{A}\mathbf{A}'\mathbf{A} + \alpha^4 \mathbf{A}'\mathbf{A}\mathbf{A}'\mathbf{A} + \ldots + \alpha^N \mathbf{A}'\mathbf{A} \cdots \mathbf{A}'\mathbf{A}$$

(assuming N is even) so that the Katz measure of standing for the example above is now $\text{status}_2 = B'u =$

$$= \left(0.5 \begin{bmatrix} 0 & 0 & 1 & 0 \\ 1 & 0 & 0 & 0 \\ 1 & 1 & 0 & 0 \\ 1 & 1 & 1 & 0 \end{bmatrix} + 0.5^2 \begin{bmatrix} 3 & 2 & 1 & 0 \\ 2 & 2 & 1 & 0 \\ 1 & 1 & 2 & 0 \\ 0 & 0 & 0 & 0 \end{bmatrix} \right.$$

$$\left. + 0.5^3 \begin{bmatrix} 1 & 1 & 2 & 0 \\ 3 & 2 & 1 & 0 \\ 5 & 4 & 2 & 0 \\ 6 & 5 & 4 & 0 \end{bmatrix} + 0.5^4 \begin{bmatrix} 14 & 11 & 7 & 0 \\ 11 & 9 & 6 & 0 \\ 7 & 6 & 6 & 0 \\ 0 & 0 & 0 & 0 \end{bmatrix} \right)' \begin{bmatrix} 1 \\ 1 \\ 1 \\ 1 \end{bmatrix}$$

$$= \begin{bmatrix} 1.7500 & 1.3125 & 1.4375 & 0.0000 \\ 2.0625 & 1.3125 & 0.7500 & 0.0000 \\ 1.8125 & 1.6250 & 1.1250 & 0.0000 \\ 1.2500 & 1.1250 & 1.0000 & 0.0000 \end{bmatrix}' \begin{bmatrix} 1 \\ 1 \\ 1 \\ 1 \end{bmatrix}$$

$$= \begin{bmatrix} 6.8750 \\ 5.3750 \\ 4.3125 \\ 0.0000 \end{bmatrix}.$$

These calculations obviously used $\alpha = 0.5$. The final column vector shows relative standing that includes these other paths. This new measure apparently improves the standing of the second person.

6.6.1 Convergence

The key point of a series is that the consecutively produced values are generated by some sort of a rule or relationship. This can be anything from simply adding some amount to the previous value or a complex mathematical form operating on consecutive terms. Notationally, start with an **infinite series**:

$$S_\infty = \sum_{i=1}^{\infty} x_i = x_1 + x_2 + x_3 + \cdots,$$

which is just a set of enumerated values stretching out to infinity. This is not to say that any one of these values is itself equal to infinity or even that their sum is necessarily infinite, but rather that the *quantity* of them is infinite. Concurrently, we can also define a **finite series** of length n:

$$S_n = \sum_{i=1}^{n} x_i = x_1 + x_2 + x_3 + \cdots + x_n,$$

which is a series that terminates with the nth value: x_n. This may also simply be the first n values of an infinite series and in this context is called an **nth partial sum** of the larger infinite sequence. The difference in subscript of S on the left-hand side emphasizes that the length of these summations differs.

A series is **convergent** if the limit as n goes to infinity is bounded (noninfinite itself):

$$\lim_{n\to\infty} S_n = \mathfrak{A}, \text{ where } \mathfrak{A} \text{ is bounded.}$$

A series is **divergent** if it is not convergent, that is, if $\mathfrak{A}$ above is positive or negative infinity. Another test is stated in the following theorem.

Integral Test for Series Convergence:

- If S_n converges, then $\lim_{n\to\infty} x_n = 0$, and if $\lim_{n\to\infty} x_n \neq 0$, then S_n diverges.
- If S_n is a series with all positive terms and $f(x)$ is the corresponding function that must be decreasing and everywhere continuous for values of $x \geq 1$, then the series S_n and the integral $\int_1^\infty f(x)dx$ both converge or diverge.

It is important to think about these statements carefully. It is *not* true that a zero limit of x_n shows convergence (the logic only goes in one direction). For instance, a harmonic series (see the Exercises) has the property that x_n goes to zero in the limit, but it is a well-known divergent series. Convergence is a handy result because it means that the infinite series can be approximated by a reasonable length finite series (i.e., additional values become unimportant at some point). So how does this test work? Let us now evaluate the limiting term of the series:

$$\sum_{i=1}^{n} \frac{i-1}{i+1} = 0 + \frac{1}{3} + \frac{2}{4} + \frac{3}{5} + \cdots .$$

We could note that the values get larger, which is clearly an indication of a diverging series. The integral test also shows this, because

$$\lim_{n\to\infty} \frac{n-1}{n+1} = \lim_{n\to\infty} \frac{1-\frac{1}{n}}{1+\frac{1}{n}} = 1,$$

which is not zero, indicating divergence of the series. The integral part of the statement above relates the characteristic of a series with an integral, so that if we can obtain convergence of one, we can establish convergence of the other.

Consider the simple series and associated integral

$$S_\infty = \sum_{i=1}^{\infty} \frac{1}{i^3}, \qquad I_\infty = \int_1^{\infty} \frac{1}{x^3}\,dx.$$

The integral quantity is $\frac{1}{2}$, so we know that the series converges.

Here are some famous examples along with their convergence properties.

★ **Example 6.10:** **Consecutive Integers.** Given $x_k = x_{k-1} + 1$, then $S_\infty = \sum_{i=1}^{\infty} i = 1 + 2 + 3 + \cdots$. This is a divergent series.

★ **Example 6.11:** **Telescoping Sum.** Assume $S_n = \sum_{i=1}^{n} \left(\frac{1}{i} - \frac{1}{i+1} \right)$. On quick inspection, there seems to be no obvious reason why this sum should converge in the limit, but note that it can be reexpressed as

$$
\begin{aligned}
S_n &= \sum_{i=1}^{n} \left(\frac{1}{i} - \frac{1}{i+1} \right) \\
&= \left(\frac{1}{1} - \frac{1}{2} \right) + \left(\frac{1}{2} - \frac{1}{3} \right) + \left(\frac{1}{3} - \frac{1}{4} \right) + \cdots + \left(\frac{1}{i} - \frac{1}{i+1} \right) \\
&= 1 + \left(-\frac{1}{2} + \frac{1}{2} \right) + \left(-\frac{1}{3} + \frac{1}{3} \right) + \cdots + \left(-\frac{1}{i} + \frac{1}{i} \right) + \frac{1}{i+1} \\
&= 1 + \frac{1}{i+1}.
\end{aligned}
$$

So this series gets its name from the way that it expands or contracts with the cancellations like an old-style telescope. Now if we take n to infinity, the result is obvious:

$$
\begin{aligned}
S_\infty &= \lim_{n \to \infty} S_n \\
&= \lim_{n \to \infty} \left(1 + \frac{1}{n+1} \right) \\
&= 1
\end{aligned}
$$

since no matter how big n becomes, adjacent terms cancel except for the first and last. Notice also that the limit of the nth term is zero, as per the integral test.

★ **Example 6.12:   Geometric Series.** Suppose for some positive integer k and real number r, we have the series

$$S_n = \sum_{i=0}^{n} kr^i = k + kr + kr^2 + kr^3 + \cdots + kr^n.$$

Specific cases include

$$k = 1, r = -1: \qquad 1 - 1 + 1 - 1 \cdots$$

$$k = 1, r = 2: \qquad 1 + 2 + 4 + 8 + 16 + \cdots$$

$$k = 2, r = \frac{1}{2}: \qquad 2 + \frac{1}{2} + \frac{1}{4} + \frac{1}{8} + \frac{1}{16} + \cdots.$$

It turns out that the geometric series converges to $S_n = \frac{k}{1-r}$ if $|r| < 1$ but diverges if $|r| > 1$. The series also diverges for $r = 1$ since it is then simply the sum $k + k + k + k + \cdots$.

★ **Example 6.13:   Repeating Values as a Geometric Series.** Consider the repeating number

$$0.123123123\ldots = \frac{123}{1000^1} + \frac{123}{1000^2} + \frac{123}{1000^3} + \cdots$$

which is expressed in the second form as a geometric series with $k = 123$ and $r = 0.001$. Clearly this sequence converges because r is (much) less than one.

Because it can sometimes be less than obvious whether a series is convergent, a number of additional tests have been developed. The most well known are listed below for the infinite series $\sum_{i=1}^{\infty} a_i$.

- **Ratio Test.** If every $a_i > 0$ and $\lim_{i \to \infty} \frac{a_{i+1}}{a_i} = A$, then the series converges for $A < 1$, diverges for $A > 1$, and may converge or diverge for $A = 1$.

- **Root Test.** If every $a_i > 0$ and $\lim_{i \to \infty} (a_i)^{\frac{1}{i}} = A$, then the series converges for $A < 1$, diverges for $A > 1$, and may converge or diverge for $A = 1$.

- **Comparison Test.** If there is a convergent series $\sum_{i=1}^{\infty} b_i$ and a positive (finite) integer value J such that $a_i \le b_i \; \forall i \ge J$, then $\sum_{i=1}^{\infty} a_i$ converges.

Some Properties of Convergent Series

⟼ Limiting Values $\lim\limits_{n\to\infty} a_n = 0$

(if $\lim\limits_{n\to\infty} a_n! = 0$, then $\sum_{i=1}^{\infty} a_i$ diverges)

⟼ Summation $\sum_{i=1}^{\infty} a_i + \sum_{i=1}^{\infty} b_i = \sum_{i=1}^{\infty}(a_i + b_i)$

⟼ Scalar Multiplication $\sum_{i=1}^{\infty} ka_i = k \sum_{i=1}^{\infty} a_i$

★ **Example 6.14:** **An Equilibrium Point in Simple Games.** Consider the basic prisoner's dilemma game, which has many variants, but here two parties obtain $10 each for both cooperating, $15 dollars for acting opportunistically when the other acts cooperatively, and only $5 each for both acting opportunistically. What is the value of this game to a player who intends to act opportunistically at all iterations and expects the other player to do so as well? Furthermore, assume that each player discounts the future value of payoffs by 0.9 per period. Then this player expects a minimum payout of

$$\$5(0.9^0 + 0.9^1 + 0.9^2 + 0.9^3 + \ldots + 0.9^\infty).$$

The component in parentheses is a geometric series where $r = 0.9 < 1$, so it converges giving $5\frac{1}{1-0.9} = \$50$. Of course the game might be worth slightly more to our player if the opponent was unaware of this strategy on the first or second iteration (presumably it would be quite clear after that).

6.6.1.1 Other Types of Infinite Series

Occasionally there are special characteristics of a given series that allow us to assert convergence. A series where adjacent terms are alternating in sign for the whole series is called an **alternating series**. An alternating series converges if the same series with absolute value terms also convergences. So if $\sum_{i=1}^{\infty} a_i$ is an alternating series, then it converges if $\sum_{i=1}^{\infty} |a_i|$ converges. For instance, the alternating series given by

$$\sum_{i=1}^{\infty} \frac{(-1)^{i+1}}{i^2}$$

converges if $\sum_{i=1}^{\infty} \frac{1}{i^2}$ converges since the latter is always greater for some given i value. This series converges if the integral is finite

$$\int_1^{\infty} \frac{1}{x^2} dx = -x^{-1} \Big|_1^{\infty} = -\frac{1}{\infty} - \left(-\frac{1}{1}\right) = 1,$$

so the second series converges and thus the original series converges.

Another interesting case is the **power series**, which is a series defined for x of the form

$$\sum_{i=1}^{\infty} a_i x^i,$$

for scalar values $a_1, a_2, \ldots, a_\infty$. A special case is defined for the difference operator $(x - x_0)$:

$$\sum_{i=1}^{\infty} a_i (x - x_0)^i.$$

This type of power series has the characteristic that if it converges for the given value of $x_0 \neq 0$, then it converges for $|x| < |x_0|$. Conversely, if the power series diverges at x_0, then it also diverges for $|x| > |x_0|$. There are three power series that converge in important ways:

$$\sum_{i=1}^{\infty} \frac{x^i}{i!} = e^x$$

$$\sum_{i=1}^{\infty} \frac{(-1)^i x^{2i+1}}{(2i+1)!} = \sin(x)$$

$$\sum_{i=1}^{\infty} \frac{(-1)^i x^{2i}}{(2i)!} = \cos(x).$$

The idea here is bigger than just these special cases (as interesting as they are). It turns out that if a function can be expressed in the form $f(x) = \sum_{i=1}^{\infty} a_i (x - x_0)^i$, then it has derivatives of all orders and a_i can be expressed as the ith derivative divided by the ith factorial. Note that the converse is not necessarily true in terms of guaranteeing the existence of a series expansion. Thus the function can be expressed as

$$f(x) = \frac{1}{0!}(x - x_0)^0 f(x_0) + \frac{1}{1!}(x - x_0)^1 f'(x_0) + \frac{1}{2!}(x_1 - x_0)^2 f''(x_0)$$
$$+ \frac{1}{3!}(x - x_0)^3 f'''(x_0) + \cdots,$$

which is just the **Taylor series** discussed in Section 6.4.2.

The trick of course is expressing some function of interest in terms of such a series including the sequence of increasing derivatives. Also, the ability to express a function in this form does not guarantee convergence for particular values of x; that must be proven if warranted.

A special case of the Taylor series is the **Maclaurin series**, which is given when $x_0 = 0$. Many well-known functions can be rewritten as a Maclaurin series. For instance, now express $f(x) = \log(x)$ as a Maclaurin series and compare at $x = 2$ to $x = 1$ where $f(x) = 0$. We first note that

$$f'(x) = \frac{1}{x}$$

$$f''(x) = \frac{-1}{x^2}$$

$$f'''(x) = \frac{2}{x^3}$$

$$f''''(x) = \frac{-6}{x^4}$$

$$\vdots$$

which leads to the general order form for the derivative

$$f^{(i)}(x) = \frac{(-1)^{i+1}(i-1)!}{x^i}.$$

So the function of interest can be expressed as follows by plugging in the derivative term and simplifying:

$$\log(x) = \sum_{i=0}^{\infty} \frac{1}{i!}(x - x_0)^i f^{(i)}(x_0)$$

$$= \sum_{i=0}^{\infty} \frac{1}{i!}(x - x_0)^i \left(\frac{(-1)^{i+1}(i-1)!}{x_0^i} \right)$$

$$= \sum_{i=0}^{\infty} (-1)^{i+1} \frac{1}{i} \frac{(x - x_0)^i}{x_0^i}.$$

Now set $x_0 = 1$ and $x = 2$:

$$\log(2) = \sum_{i=0}^{\infty} \frac{(-1)^{i+1}}{i} = 1 - \frac{1}{2} + \frac{1}{3} - \frac{1}{4} \cdots,$$

which converges to the (correct) value of 0.6931472.

6.7 The Calculus of Vector and Matrix Forms

This last section is more advanced than the rest of the chapter and may be skipped as it is not integral to future chapters. A number of calculus techniques operate or are notated differently enough on matrices and vectors that a separate section is warranted (if only a short one). Sometimes the notation is confusing when one misses the point that derivatives and integrals are operating on these larger, nonscalar structures.

6.7.1 Vector Function Notation

Using standard (Hamiltonian) notation, we start with two orthogonal unit vectors **i** and **j** starting at the origin and following along the x-axis and y-axis correspondingly. Any vector in two-space ($\Re^2$) can be expressed as a scalar-weighted sum of these two **basis vectors** giving the horizontal and vertical progress:

$$\mathbf{v} = a\mathbf{i} + b\mathbf{j}.$$

So, for example, to characterize the vector from the point $(3, 1)$ to the point $(5, 5)$ we use $\mathbf{v} = (5 - 3)\mathbf{i} + (5 - 1)\mathbf{j} = 2\mathbf{i} + 4\mathbf{j}$. Now instead of the scalars a

and b, substitute the real-valued functions $f_1(t)$ and $f_2(t)$ for $t \in \mathfrak{R}$. Now we can define the **vector function**:

$$\mathbf{f}(t) = f_1(t)\mathbf{i} + f_2(t)\mathbf{j},$$

which gives the x and y vector values $\mathbf{f}(t) = (x, y)$. The parametric representation of the line passing through $(3, 1)$ and $(5, 5)$ is found according to

$$x = x_0 + t(x_1 - x_0) \qquad\qquad y = y_0 + t(y_1 - y_0)$$

$$x = 3 + 2t \qquad\qquad y = 1 + 4t,$$

meaning that for some value of t we have a point on the line. To get the expression for this line in standard slope-intercept form, we first find the slope by getting the ratio of differences $(5 - 1)/(5 - 3) = 2$ in the standard fashion and subtracting from one of the two points to get the y value where x is zero: $(0, -5)$. Setting $x = t$, we get $y = -5 + 2x$.

So far this setup has been reasonably simple. Now suppose that we have some curvilinear form in $\mathfrak{R}$ given the functions $f_1(t)$ and $f_2(t)$, and we would like to get the slope of the tangent line at the point $t_0 = (x_0, y_0)$. This, it turns out, is found by evaluating the ratio of first derivatives of the functions

$$\mathbf{R}'(t_0) = \frac{f_2'(t_0)}{f_1'(t_0)},$$

where we have to worry about the restriction that $f_1'(t_0) \neq 0$ for obvious reasons. Why does this work? Consider what we are doing here; the derivatives are producing incremental changes in x and y separately by the construction with $\mathbf{i}$ and $\mathbf{j}$ above. Because of the limits, this ratio is the instantaneous change in y for a change in x, that is, the slope. Specifically, consider this logic in the notation:

$$\lim_{\Delta t \to 0} \frac{\Delta y}{\Delta x} = \frac{\lim_{\Delta t \to 0} \frac{\Delta y}{\Delta t}}{\lim_{\Delta t \to 0} \frac{\Delta x}{\Delta t}} = \frac{\frac{\partial y}{\partial t}}{\frac{\partial x}{\partial t}} = \frac{\partial y}{\partial t}\frac{\partial t}{\partial x} = \frac{\partial y}{\partial x}.$$

For example, we can find the slope of the tangent line to the curve $x =$

$3t^3 + 5t^2 + 7$, $y = t^2 - 2$, at $t = 1$:

$$f_1'(1) = 9t^2 + 10t\Big|_{t=1} = 19$$

$$f_2'(1) = 2t\Big|_{t=1} = 2$$

$$\mathbf{R}'(1) = \frac{2}{19}.$$

We can also find all of the horizontal and vertical tangent lines to this curve by a similar calculation. There are horizontal tangent lines when $f_1'(t) = 9t^2 + 10t = 0$. Factoring this shows that there are horizontal tangents when $t = 0$, $t = -\frac{10}{9}$. Plugging these values back into $x = 3t^3 + 5t^2 + 7$ gives horizontal tangents at $x = 7$ and $x = 9.058$. There are vertical horizontal lines when $f_2'(t) = 2t = 0$, which occurs only at $t = 0$, meaning $y = -2$.

6.7.2 Differentiation and Integration of a Vector Function

The vector function $\mathbf{f}(t)$ is differentiable with domain t if the limit

$$\lim_{\Delta t \to 0} \frac{\mathbf{f}(t + \Delta t) - \mathbf{f}(t)}{\Delta t}$$

exists and is bounded (finite) for all specified t. This is the same idea we saw for scalar differentiation, except that by consequence

$$\mathbf{f}'(t) = f_1'(t)\mathbf{i} + f_2'(t)\mathbf{j},$$

which means that the function can be differentiated by these orthogonal pieces. It follows also that if $\mathbf{f}'(t)$ meets the criteria above, then $\mathbf{f}''(t)$ exists, and so on. As a demonstration, let $\mathbf{f}(t) = e^{5t}\mathbf{i} + \sin(t)\mathbf{j}$, so that

$$\mathbf{f}'(t) = 5e^5 t\mathbf{i} + \cos(t)\mathbf{j}.$$

Not surprisingly, integration proceeds piecewise for the vector function just as differentiation was done. For $\mathbf{f}(t) = f_1(t)\mathbf{i} + f_2(t)\mathbf{j}$, the integral is

$$\begin{cases} \int \mathbf{f}(t)dt = \left[\int f_1'(t)dt\right]\mathbf{i} + \left[\int f_2'(t)dt\right]\mathbf{j} + \mathbf{K} & \text{for the indefinite form,} \\ \int_a^b \mathbf{f}(t)dt = \left[\int_a^b f_1'(t)dt\right]\mathbf{i} + \left[\int_a^b f_2'(t)dt\right]\mathbf{j} & \text{for the definite form.} \end{cases}$$

Incidently, we previously saw an arbitrary constant k for indefinite integrals of scalar functions, but that is replaced here with the more appropriate vector-valued form $\mathbf{K}$. This "splitting" of the integration process between the two dimensions can be tremendously helpful in simplifying difficult dimensional problems.

Consider the trigonometric function $\mathbf{f}(t) = \tan(t)\mathbf{i} + \sec^2(t)\mathbf{j}$. The integral over $[0:\pi/4]$ is produced by

$$\int_0^{\pi/4} \mathbf{f}(t)dt = \left[\int_0^{\pi/4} \tan(t)dt\right]\mathbf{i} + \left[\int_0^{\pi/4} \sec^2(t)dt\right]\mathbf{j}$$

$$= \left[-\log(|\cos(t)|)\Big|_0^{\pi/4}\right]\mathbf{i} + \left[\tan(t)\Big|_0^{\pi/4}\right]\mathbf{j}$$

$$= 0.3465736\mathbf{i} + 0.854509\mathbf{j}.$$

Indefinite integrals sometimes come with additional information that makes the problem more complete. If $\mathbf{f}'(t) = t^2\mathbf{i} - t^4\mathbf{j}$, and we know that $\mathbf{f}(0) = 4\mathbf{i} - 2\mathbf{j}$, then a full integration starts with

$$\mathbf{f}(t) = \int \mathbf{f}'(t)dt$$

$$= \int t^2 dt\mathbf{i} - \int t^4 dt\mathbf{j}$$

$$= \frac{1}{3}t^3\mathbf{i} + \frac{1}{5}t^5\mathbf{j} + \mathbf{K}.$$

Since $\mathbf{f}(0)$ is the function value when the components above are zero, except for $\mathbf{K}$ we can substitute this for $\mathbf{K}$ to complete

$$\mathbf{f}(t) = \left(\frac{1}{3}t^3 + 4\right)\mathbf{i} + \left(\frac{1}{5}t^5 - 2\right)\mathbf{j}.$$

In statistical work in the social sciences, a scalar-valued vector function is important for maximization and description. We will not go into the theoretical derivation of this process (maximum likelihood estimation) but instead will describe the key vector components. Start with a function: $y = f(\mathbf{x}) = f(x_1, x_2, x_3 \ldots, x_k)$ operating on the k-length vector $\mathbf{x}$. The vector of partial derivatives with respect to each x_i is called the **gradient**:

$$
\mathbf{g} = \frac{\partial f(\mathbf{x})}{\partial \mathbf{x}} =
\begin{bmatrix}
\partial y/\partial x_1 \\
\partial y/\partial x_2 \\
\partial y/\partial x_3 \\
\vdots \\
\partial y/\partial x_k
\end{bmatrix},
$$

which is given by convention as a column vector. The second derivative for this setup is taken in a different manner than one might suspect; it is done by differentiating the complete gradient vector by each x_i such that the result is a $k \times k$ matrix:

$$
\mathbf{H} = \left[\frac{\partial}{\partial x_1}\left(\frac{\partial f(\mathbf{x})}{\partial \mathbf{x}}\right), \frac{\partial}{\partial x_2}\left(\frac{\partial f(\mathbf{x})}{\partial \mathbf{x}}\right), \right.
$$

$$
\left. \frac{\partial}{\partial x_3}\left(\frac{\partial f(\mathbf{x})}{\partial \mathbf{x}}\right), \cdots \frac{\partial}{\partial x_k}\left(\frac{\partial f(\mathbf{x})}{\partial \mathbf{x}}\right) \right]
$$

$$
=
\begin{bmatrix}
\frac{\partial^2 f(\mathbf{x})}{\partial x_1 \partial x_1} & \frac{\partial^2 f(\mathbf{x})}{\partial x_1 \partial x_2} & \frac{\partial^2 f(\mathbf{x})}{\partial x_1 \partial x_3} & \cdots & \frac{\partial^2 f(\mathbf{x})}{\partial x_1 \partial x_k} \\[2ex]
\frac{\partial^2 f(\mathbf{x})}{\partial x_2 \partial x_1} & \frac{\partial^2 f(\mathbf{x})}{\partial x_2 \partial x_2} & \frac{\partial^2 f(\mathbf{x})}{\partial x_2 \partial x_3} & \cdots & \frac{\partial^2 f(\mathbf{x})}{\partial x_2 \partial x_k} \\[2ex]
\frac{\partial^2 f(\mathbf{x})}{\partial x_3 \partial x_1} & \frac{\partial^2 f(\mathbf{x})}{\partial x_3 \partial x_2} & \frac{\partial^2 f(\mathbf{x})}{\partial x_3 \partial x_3} & \cdots & \frac{\partial^2 f(\mathbf{x})}{\partial x_3 \partial x_k} \\[2ex]
\vdots & \vdots & \vdots & \ddots & \vdots \\[2ex]
\frac{\partial^2 f(\mathbf{x})}{\partial x_k \partial x_1} & \frac{\partial^2 f(\mathbf{x})}{\partial x_k \partial x_2} & \frac{\partial^2 f(\mathbf{x})}{\partial x_k \partial x_3} & \cdots & \frac{\partial^2 f(\mathbf{x})}{\partial x_k \partial x_k}
\end{bmatrix}
$$

$$
= \frac{\partial^2 f(\mathbf{x})}{\partial \mathbf{x} \partial \mathbf{x}}.
$$

Note that the partial derivatives in the last (most succinct) form are done on vector quantities. This matrix, called the **Hessian** after its inventor/discover the German mathematician Ludwig Hesse, is square and symmetrical. In the course of normal statistical work it is also positive definite, although serious problems arise if for some reason it is not positive definite because it is necessary to invert the Hessian in many estimation problems.

6.8 Constrained Optimization

This section is considerably more advanced than the previous and need not be covered on the first read-through of the text. It is included because constrained optimization is a standard tool in some social science literatures, notably economics.

We have already seen a similar example in the example on page 187, where a cost function was minimized subject to two terms depending on committee size. The key feature of these methods is using the first derivative to find a point where the slope of the tangent line is zero. Usually this is substantively interesting in that it tells us where some x value leads to the greatest possible $f(x)$ value to maximize some quantity of interest: money, utility, productivity, cooperation, and so on. These problems are usually more useful in higher dimensions, for instance, what values of x_1, x_2, and x_3 simultaneously provide the greatest value of $f(x_1, x_2, x_3)$?

Now let us revisit the optimization problem but requiring the additional *constraint* that the values of x_1, x_2, and x_3 have to conform to some predetermined relationship. Usually these constraints are expressed as inequalities, say $x_1 > x_2 > x_3$, or with specific equations like $x_1 + x_2 + x_3 = 10$. The procedure we will use is now called **constrained optimization** because we will optimize the given function but with the constraints specified in advance. There is one important underlying principle here. The constrained solution will never be a better solution than the unconstrained solution because we are requiring certain relationships among the terms. At best these will end up being trivial constraints and the two solutions will be identical. Usually, however, the constraints lead to a suboptimal point along the function of interest, and this is done by substantive necessity.

Our task will be to maximize a k-dimensional function $f(\mathbf{x})$ subject to the arbitrary constraints expressed as m functions:

$$c_1(\mathbf{x}) = r_1, \ c_2(\mathbf{x}) = r_2, \ldots, \ c_m(\mathbf{x}) = r_m,$$

where the $r_1, r_2, \ldots, r_m$ values are stipulated constants. The trick is to deliberately include these constraint functions in the maximization process. This method is called the **Lagrange multiplier** , and it means substituting for the standard function, $f(\mathbf{x})$, a modified version of the form

$$L(\mathbf{x}, \boldsymbol{\lambda}) = f(\mathbf{x}) + \lambda_1(c_1(\mathbf{x}) - r_1) + \lambda_2(c_2(\mathbf{x}) - r_2) + \ldots + \lambda_m(c_m(\mathbf{x}) - r_m)$$

$$= f(\mathbf{x}) + \underset{1 \times m}{\boldsymbol{\lambda}'} \underset{m \times k}{\mathbf{c}(\mathbf{x})},$$

where the second form is just a restatement in vector form in which the $-r$ terms are embedded ($\boldsymbol{\lambda}'$ denotes a transpose not a derivative). Commonly these $r_1, r_2, \ldots, r_m$ values are zero (as done in the example below), which makes the expression of $L(\mathbf{x}, \boldsymbol{\lambda})$ cleaner. The λ terms in this expression are called Lagrange multipliers, and this is where the name of the method comes from.

Now we take two (multidimensional) partial derivatives and set them equal to zero just as before, except that we need to keep track of $\boldsymbol{\lambda}$ as well:

$$\frac{d}{d\mathbf{x}} L(\mathbf{x}, \boldsymbol{\lambda}) = \frac{d}{d\mathbf{x}} f(\mathbf{x}) + \boldsymbol{\lambda}' \frac{d}{d\mathbf{x}} \mathbf{c}(\mathbf{x}) \equiv \mathbf{0} \quad \Rightarrow \quad \frac{d}{d\mathbf{x}} f(\mathbf{x}) = -\boldsymbol{\lambda}' \frac{d}{d\mathbf{x}} \mathbf{c}(\mathbf{x})$$

$$\frac{d}{d\boldsymbol{\lambda}} L(\mathbf{x}, \boldsymbol{\lambda}) = \mathbf{c}(\mathbf{x}) \equiv \mathbf{0}.$$

The derivative with respect to $\boldsymbol{\lambda}$ is simple because there are no λ values in the first term. The term $\frac{d}{d\mathbf{x}}\mathbf{c}(\mathbf{x})$ is just the matrix of partial derivatives of the constraints, and it is commonly abbreviated $\mathbf{C}$. Expressing the constraints in this way also means that the Lagrange multiplier component $-\boldsymbol{\lambda}'\frac{d}{d\mathbf{x}}\mathbf{c}(\mathbf{x})$ is now just $-\boldsymbol{\lambda}'\mathbf{C}$, which is easy to work with. It is interesting to contrast the final part of the first line $\frac{d}{d\mathbf{x}}f(\mathbf{x}) = -\boldsymbol{\lambda}\frac{d}{d\mathbf{x}}\mathbf{c}(\mathbf{x})$ with unconstrained optimization at this step, $\frac{d}{d\mathbf{x}}f(\mathbf{x}) = \mathbf{0}$, because it clearly shows the imposition of the constraints on the function maximization. Finally, after taking these derivatives, we solve for the values of $\mathbf{x}$ and $\boldsymbol{\lambda}$ that result. This is our constrained answer.

Just about every econometrics book has a numerical example of this process, but it is helpful to have a simple one here. Suppose we have "data" according to the following matrix and vector:

$$\omega = \begin{bmatrix} 1 & 2 & 3 \end{bmatrix} \qquad \Omega = \begin{bmatrix} 5 & 1 & 5 \\ 4 & 5 & 5 \\ 1 & 5 & 5 \end{bmatrix},$$

and we want to maximize the quadratic function:

$$f(\mathbf{x}) = \mathbf{x}'\Omega\mathbf{x} - 2\omega'\mathbf{x} + 5.$$

This is great justification for using matrix algebra because the same function $f(\mathbf{x})$ written out in scalar notation is

$$f(\mathbf{x}) = 5x_1^2 + 5x_2^2 + 5x_3^2 + 5x_1x_2 + 6x_1x_3 + 10x_2x_3 + 2x_1 + 4x_2 + 6x_3 + 5.$$

We now impose the two constraints:

$$2x_1 + x_2 = 0 \qquad x_1 - x_2 - x_3 = 0,$$

which gives

$$\mathbf{c}(\mathbf{x}) = \begin{bmatrix} c_1(\mathbf{x}) \\ c_2(\mathbf{x}) \end{bmatrix} = \begin{bmatrix} 2x_1 & x_2 & 0 \\ x_1 & -x_2 & 0 \end{bmatrix}$$

Taking the partial derivatives $\frac{d}{d\mathbf{x}}\mathbf{c}(\mathbf{x})$ (i.e., with respect to x_1, x_2, and x_3) produces the $\mathbf{C}$ matrix:

$$\mathbf{C} = \begin{bmatrix} 2 & 1 & 0 \\ 1 & -1 & -1 \end{bmatrix},$$

which is just the matrix-collected multipliers of the $\mathbf{x}$ terms in the constraints since there were no higher order terms to worry about here. This step can be somewhat more involved with more complex (i.e., nonlinear constraints).

With the specified constraints we can now specify the Lagrange multiplier version of the function:

$$L(\mathbf{x}, \boldsymbol{\lambda}) = f(\mathbf{x}) + \boldsymbol{\lambda}'\mathbf{c}(\mathbf{x})$$

$$= \underset{(1\times3)(3\times3)(3\times1)}{\mathbf{x}'\ \Omega\ \mathbf{x}} - \underset{(1\times3)(3\times1)}{2\ \omega'\ \mathbf{x}} + 5 + \underset{(1\times2)(2\times3)(3\times1)}{\boldsymbol{\lambda}'\ \mathbf{C}\ \mathbf{x}}.$$

Note that $m = 2$ and $k = 3$ in this example. The next task is to take the two derivatives and set them equal to zero:

$$\frac{d}{dx}L(\mathbf{x}, \lambda) = 2\mathbf{x}'\Omega - 2\omega' + \lambda'\mathbf{C} \equiv 0 \quad \Rightarrow \quad \mathbf{x}'\Omega + \frac{1}{2}\lambda'\mathbf{C} = \omega'$$

$$\frac{d}{d\lambda}L(\mathbf{x}, \lambda) = \mathbf{c}(\mathbf{x}) = \mathbf{C}\mathbf{x} \equiv 0,$$

where $\mathbf{c}(\mathbf{x}) = \mathbf{C}\mathbf{x}$ comes from the simple form of the constraints here. This switch can be much more intricate in more complex specifications of restraints. These final expressions allow us to stack the equations (they are multidimensional anyway) into the following single matrix statement:

$$\begin{bmatrix} \Omega' & \frac{1}{2}\mathbf{C}' \\ \mathbf{C} & 0 \end{bmatrix} \begin{bmatrix} \mathbf{x} \\ \lambda \end{bmatrix} = \begin{bmatrix} \omega \\ 0 \end{bmatrix}$$

where we used the transpose property such that $(\lambda'\mathbf{C})' = \mathbf{C}'\lambda$ and $(\mathbf{x}'\Omega)' = \Omega'\mathbf{x}$ (given on page 116) since we want the column vector ω:

$$\omega' = \mathbf{x}'\Omega + \frac{1}{2}\lambda'\mathbf{C}$$

$$\omega = (\mathbf{x}'\Omega + \frac{1}{2}\lambda'\mathbf{C})' = \Omega'\mathbf{x} + \frac{1}{2}\mathbf{C}'\lambda$$

$$= \begin{bmatrix} \Omega' & \frac{1}{2}\mathbf{C}' \end{bmatrix} \begin{bmatrix} \mathbf{x} \\ \lambda \end{bmatrix}$$

(the second row is done exactly the same way). This order of multiplication on the left-hand side is essential so that the known quantities are in the matrix and the unknown quantities are in the first vector. If we move the matrix to the right-hand side by multiplying both sides by its inverse (presuming it is nonsingular of course), then all the unknown quantities are expressed by the known quantities. So a solution for $[\mathbf{x} \ \lambda]'$ can now be obtained by matrix inversion and then pre-multiplication:

$$
\begin{bmatrix} \mathbf{x} \\ \lambda \end{bmatrix} = \begin{bmatrix} \Omega' & \frac{1}{2}C' \\ C & 0 \end{bmatrix}^{-1} \begin{bmatrix} \omega \\ 0 \end{bmatrix}
$$

$$
= \begin{bmatrix} 5 & 4 & 1 & 1.0 & 0.5 \\ 1 & 5 & 5 & 0.5 & -0.5 \\ 5 & 5 & 5 & 0.0 & -0.5 \\ 2 & 1 & 0 & 0.0 & 0.0 \\ 1 & -1 & -1 & 0.0 & 0.0 \end{bmatrix}^{-1} \begin{bmatrix} 1 \\ 2 \\ 3 \\ 0 \\ 0 \end{bmatrix}
$$

$$
= \begin{bmatrix} \frac{1}{18} & -\frac{1}{9} & \frac{1}{6} & -\frac{1}{6} & \frac{1}{3} \\ -\frac{1}{9} & \frac{2}{9} & -\frac{1}{3} & \frac{4}{3} & -\frac{2}{3} \\ \frac{1}{6} & -\frac{1}{3} & \frac{1}{2} & -\frac{3}{2} & 0 \\ \frac{4}{9} & \frac{10}{9} & -\frac{2}{3} & -\frac{4}{3} & \frac{8}{3} \\ \frac{10}{9} & -\frac{20}{9} & \frac{4}{3} & \frac{10}{3} & -\frac{10}{3} \end{bmatrix} \begin{bmatrix} 1 \\ 2 \\ 3 \\ 0 \\ 0 \end{bmatrix}
$$

$$
= \begin{bmatrix} \frac{1}{3}, -\frac{2}{3}, 1, \frac{2}{3}, \frac{2}{3} \end{bmatrix}',
$$

meaning that $x_1 = \frac{1}{3}$, $x_2 = -\frac{2}{3}$, $x_3 = 1$, and $\lambda' = [\frac{2}{3}, \frac{2}{3}]$. Since the λ values are nonzero, we know that the constraints changed the optimization solution. It is not essential, but we can check that the solution conforms to the constraints:

$$
2\left(\frac{1}{3}\right) + \left(-\frac{2}{3}\right) = 0 \qquad \left(\frac{1}{3}\right) - \left(-\frac{2}{3}\right) - (1) = 0.
$$

Suppose we now impose just one constraint: $3x_1 + x_2 - x_3 = 0$. Thus the C matrix is a vector according to $[3, 1, -1]$ and the Ω matrix is smaller. The calculation of the new values is

$$
\begin{bmatrix}
5 & 1 & 5 & -0.5 \\
1 & 5 & 5 & 0.5 \\
5 & 5 & 5 & -0.5 \\
3 & 1 & -1 & 0.0
\end{bmatrix}^{-1}
\begin{bmatrix}
1 \\
2 \\
3 \\
0
\end{bmatrix}
$$

$$
=
\begin{bmatrix}
\frac{1}{5} & -\frac{7}{20} & \frac{1}{4} & -\frac{3}{10} \\
-\frac{9}{25} & \frac{17}{25} & -\frac{2}{5} & \frac{26}{25} \\
\frac{6}{25} & -\frac{37}{100} & \frac{7}{20} & -\frac{43}{50} \\
\frac{4}{5} & -\frac{2}{5} & 0 & -\frac{6}{5}
\end{bmatrix}
\begin{bmatrix}
1 \\
2 \\
3 \\
0
\end{bmatrix}
$$

$$
=
\begin{bmatrix}
\frac{1}{4} \\
-\frac{1}{5} \\
\frac{11}{20} \\
0
\end{bmatrix}.
$$

Notice that the $\lambda = 0$ here. What this means is that our restriction actually made no impact: The solution above is the unconstrained solution. So we imposed a constraint that would have been satisfied anyway.

The Lagrange multiplier method is actually more general than is implied here. We used very simple constraints and only a quadratic function. Much more complicated problems can be solved with this approach to constrained optimization.

6.9 New Terminology

Exercises

6.1   For the following functions, determine the interval over which the function is convex or concave (if at all), and identify any inflection points:

$$f(x) = \frac{1}{x} \qquad\qquad\qquad f(x) = x^3$$

$$f(x) = x^2 + 4x + 8 \qquad\qquad f(x) = -x^2 - 9x + 16$$

$$f(x) = \frac{1}{1 + x^2} \qquad\qquad f(x) = \frac{\exp(x)}{(1 + \exp(x))}$$

$$f(x) = 1 - \exp(-\exp(x)) \qquad f(x) = \frac{x^{7/2}}{2 + x^2}$$

$$f(x) = (x - 1)^4 (x + 1)^3 \qquad f(x) = \log(x).$$

6.2   Using Newton's method, find one root of each of the following functions:

$$f(x) = x^2 - 5, x > 0 \qquad\qquad f(x) = x^2 + 4x - 8$$

$$f(x) = \log(x^2), x < 0 \qquad\qquad f(x) = x^4 - x^3 - 5$$

$$f(x) = x^2 - 2\sqrt{x}x > 0 \qquad\qquad f(x) = x^5 - 2\tan(x).$$

6.3   To test memory retrieval, Kail and Nippold (1984) asked 8-, 12-, and 21-year-olds to name as many animals and pieces of furniture as possible in separate 7–minute intervals. They found that this number increased across the tested age range but that the rate of retrieval slowed down as the period continued. In fact, the responses often came in "clusters" of related responses ("lion," "tiger," "cheetah," etc.), where the relation of time in seconds to cluster size was fitted to be $cs(t) = at^3 + bt^2 + ct + d$, where time is t, and the others are estimated parameters (which differ by topic, age group, and subject). The researchers were very interested in the inflection point of this function because it suggests a change of cognitive process. Find it for the unknown parameter values analytically by taking the second derivative. Verify that it is an inflection point and not a maxima or minima. Now graph this function for the points supplied in the authors' graph of one particular case for an 8-year-old: $cs(t) = [1.6, 1.65, 2.15, 2.5, 2.67, 2.85, 3.1, 4.92, 5.55]$ at the points $t = [2, 3, 4, 5, 6, 7, 8, 9, 10]$. They do not give parameter values for this case, but plot the function on the same graph for the values $a = 0.04291667$, $b = -0.7725$, $c = 4.75$, and $d = -7.3$. Do these values appear to satisfy your result for the inflection point?

6.4   For the function $f(x, y) = \frac{\sin(xy)}{\cos(x+y)}$, calculate the partial derivatives with respect to x and y.

6.5   Smirnov and Ershov (1992) chronicled dramatic changes in public opinion during the period of "Perestroika" in the Soviet Union (1985 to 1991). They employed a creative approach by basing their model on the principles of thermodynamics with the idea that sometimes an encapsulated liquid is immobile and dormant and sometimes it becomes turbulent and pressured, literally letting off steam. The catalyst for change is hypothesized to be radical economic reform confronted by conservative counter-reformist policies. Define p as some policy on a metric $[-1:1]$ representing different positions over this range from conservative ($p < 1$) to liberal ($p > 1$). The resulting public opinion support, S, is a function that can have single or multiple modes over this range, inflection points and monotonic areas, where the number and variety of these reflect divergent opinions in the population. Smirnov and Ershov found that the most convenient mathematical form here was

$$S(p) = \sum_{i=1}^{4} \lambda_i p^i,$$

where the notation on p indicates exponents and the λ_i values are a series of specified scalars. Their claim was that when there are two approximately equal modes (in $S(p)$), this represents the situation where "the government ceases to represent the majority of the electorate." Specify λ_i values to give this shape; graph over the domain of p; and use the first and second derivatives of $S(p)$ to identify maxima, minima, and inflection points.

6.6   Derive the five partial derivatives for $u_1 \ldots u_5$ from the function on page 236. Show all steps.

6.7   For the function $f(u, v) = \sqrt{u + v^2}$, calculate the partial derivatives with respect to u and v and provide the value of these functions at the point $(\frac{1}{2}, \frac{1}{3})$.

6.8   Using the function

$$f(x, y, z) = zy^4 - xy^3 + x^3 yz^2,$$

show that

$$\frac{\partial^3}{\partial x \partial y \partial z} f(x, y, z) = \frac{\partial^3}{\partial z \partial y \partial x} f(x, y, z).$$

6.9   Obtain the first, second, and third derivatives of the following functions:

$$f(x) = 5x^4 + 3x^3 - 11x^2 + x - 7 \qquad h(z) = 111z^3 - 121z$$

$$f(y) = \sqrt{y} + \frac{1}{y^{\frac{7}{2}}} \qquad\qquad\qquad f(x) = (x^9)^{-2}$$

$$h(u) = \log(u) + k \qquad\qquad\qquad g(z) = \sin(z) - \cos(z).$$

6.10   Graph the function given on page 245, the first derivative function, and the second derivative function over $[0:4]$. Label the three points of interest.

6.11 Evaluate the following iterated integrals:

$$\int_2^4 \int_3^5 dy\,dx \qquad\qquad \int_0^1 \int_0^1 x^{\frac{3}{2}} y^{\frac{2}{3}}\,dx\,dy$$

$$\int_1^3 \int_1^x \frac{x}{y}\,dy\,dx \qquad\qquad \int_0^\pi \int_0^x y\cos(x)\,dy\,dx$$

$$\int_0^1 \int_0^y (x+y^2)\,dx\,dy \qquad\qquad \int_1^2 \int_1^{\sqrt{2-y}} y\,dx\,dy$$

$$\int_0^1 \int_0^1 \int_0^1 \sqrt{1-x-y-z}\,dx\,dy\,dz \qquad \int_2^e \int_e^3 \frac{1}{u}\frac{1}{v}\,du\,dv$$

$$\int_0^1 \int_0^{2-2x} \int_0^{x^2 y^2} dz\,dy\,dx \qquad\qquad \int_{-1}^1 \int_0^{1-y/3} xy\,dx\,dy.$$

6.12 A well-known series is the **harmonic series** defined by

$$S_\infty = \sum_{i=1}^\infty \frac{1}{i} = 1 + \frac{1}{2} + \frac{1}{3} + \frac{1}{4} + \cdots.$$

Prove that this sequence diverges. Does this series converge for $\frac{1}{i^k}$, for all $k > 1$?

6.13 Show whether the following series are convergent or divergent. If the series is convergent, find the sum.

$$\sum_{i=0}^\infty \frac{1}{3^i} \qquad \sum_{r=0}^\infty \frac{1}{(r+1)(r+2)} \qquad \sum_{i=1}^\infty \frac{1}{100i}$$

$$\sum_{k=1}^\infty k^{-\frac{1}{2}} \qquad \sum_{i=i}^\infty \left(\frac{i}{i-1}\right)^{\frac{1}{i}} \qquad \sum_{r=1}^\infty \sin\left(\frac{1}{r}\right)$$

$$\sum_{i=1}^\infty \frac{i^3 + 2i^2 - i + 3}{2i^5 + 3i - 3} \qquad \sum_{r=1}^\infty \frac{2r+1}{(\log(r)^r} \qquad \sum i = 1^\infty \frac{2^i}{i^2}$$

6.14 Calculate the area between $f(x) = x^2$ and $f(x) = x^3$ over the domain $[0:1]$. Be careful about the placement of functions of x in y's integral. Plot this area.

6.15   Write the following repeating decimals forms in series notation:

$0.3333\ldots$ $0.43114311\ldots$ $0.484848\ldots$

$0.1234512345\ldots$ $555551555551\ldots$ $0.221222223221222223\ldots$.

6.16   Evaluate the Maclaurin series for

- e^x at 1.
- $\sqrt{x}$ at 4.
- $\log(x)$ at 7.389056.

6.17   Find the Maclaurin series for $\sin(x)$ and $\cos(x)$. What do you observe?

6.18   The Mercator series is defined by

$$\log(1+x) = x - \frac{x^2}{2} + \frac{x^3}{3} - \frac{x^4}{4} + \cdots.$$

which converges for $-1 < x \geq 1$. Write a general expression for this series using summation notation.

6.19   Find the vertical and horizontal tangent lines to the ellipse defined by

$$x = 6 + 3\cos(t) \qquad y = 5 + 2\sin(t).$$

6.20   Express a hyperbola with $a = 9$ and $b = 8$ in $\mathbf{f}(t) = f_1(t)\mathbf{i} + f_2(t)\mathbf{j}$ notation, and give the slope-intercept forms for the two vertical tangents.

6.21   Given $\mathbf{f}(t) = \frac{1}{t}\mathbf{i} + \frac{1}{t^3}$, find the first three orders of derivatives. Solve for $t = 2$.

6.22   For the function $\mathbf{f}(t) = e^{-2t}\mathbf{i} + \cos(t)\mathbf{j}$, calculate the integral from 1 to 2.

6.23   A number of seemingly counterintuitive voting principles can actually be proven mathematically. For instance, Brams and O'Leary (1970) claimed that "If three kinds of votes are allowed in a voting body, the probability that two randomly selected members disagree on a roll call will be maximized when one-third of the members vote 'yes,' one-third 'no,' and one third 'abstain.'" The proof of this statement rests on the premise that their probability of disagreement function is maximized when $y = n = a = t/3$, where y is the number voting yes, n is the number voting no, a is the number abstaining, and these are assumed to divide equally into the total number of voters t. The disagreement function is given by

$$p(DG) = \frac{2(yn + ya + na)}{(y + n + a)(y + n + a - 1)}.$$

Use the Lagrange multiplier method to demonstrate their claim by first taking four partial derivatives of $p(DG) - \lambda(t - y - n - a)$ with respect to y, n, a, λ (the Lagrange multiplier); setting these equations equal to zero; and solving the four equations for the four unknowns.

6.24 Doreian and Hummon (1977) gave applications of differential equation models in empirical research in sociology with a focus transforming the data in useful ways. Starting with their equation (14):

$$\frac{X_2 - X_{20}}{q} = \frac{X_1 - X_{10}}{p} \cos \varphi - \left[1 - \frac{(X_1 - X_{10})^2}{p} \right]^{\frac{1}{2}} \sin \varphi,$$

substitute in

$$p = \frac{\beta_4^2 - \beta_0}{\beta_1 - \beta_2^2} + X_{10}^2 \qquad q = p\beta_1^{\frac{1}{2}} \qquad \cos \varphi = -\frac{\beta_2}{\beta_1^{\frac{1}{2}}}$$

$$X_{20} = \frac{\beta_2\beta_3 - \beta_1\beta_4}{\beta_1 - \beta_2^2} \qquad X_{10} = \frac{\beta_2\beta_4 - \beta_3}{\beta_1 - \beta_2^2}$$

to produce an expression with only β and X terms on the left-hand side and zero on the right-hand side. Show the steps.

7

Probability Theory

7.1 Objectives

We study probability for a variety of reasons. First, probability provides a way of systematically and rigorously treating uncertainty. This is an important idea that actually developed rather late in human history. Despite major contributions from ancient and medieval scholars, the core of what we use today was developed in the seventeenth and eighteenth centuries in continental Europe due to an intense interest in gambling by various nobles and the mathematicians they employed. Key scholars of this period included Pascal, Fermat, Jacob Bernoulli, Johann Bernoulli, de Moivre, and later on Euler, Gauss, Lagrange, Poisson, Laplace, and Legendre. See Stigler (1986, 1999) or Dale (1991) for fascinating accounts of this period. In addition, much of the axiomatic rigor and notation we use today is due to Keynes (1921) and Kolmogorov (1933).

Interestingly, humans often think in probabilistic terms (even when not gambling), whether we are conscious of it or not. That is, we decide to cross the street when the probability of being run over by a car is sufficiently low, we go fishing at the lakes where the probability of catching something is sufficiently high, and so on. So, even when people are wholly unfamiliar with the mathematical formalization of probability, there is an inclination to frame uncertain future events in such terms.

Third, probability theory is a precursor to understanding statistics and various fields of applied mathematics. In fact, probability theory could be described as "mathematical models of uncertain reality" because it supports the use of uncertainty in these fields. So to study quantitative political methodology, game theory, mathematical sociology, and other related social science subfields, it is important to understand probability theory in rigorous notation.

There are actually two interpretations of probability. The idea of **subjective probability** is *individually* defined by the conditions under which a person would make a bet or assume a risk in pursuit of some reward. In other words, probability differs by person but becomes apparent in the terms under which a person is willing to wager. Conversely, **objective probability** is defined as a limiting relative frequency: the long-run behavior of a nondeterministic outcome or just an observed proportion in a population. So objectivity is a function of physical observations over some period of time. In either case, the ideas discussed in this chapter apply equally well to both interpretations of probability.

7.2 Counting Rules and Permutations

It seems strange that there could be different and even complicated ways of counting events or contingencies. Minor complexities occur because there are two different features of counting: whether or not the order of occurrence matters, and whether or not events are counted more than once. Thus, in combining these different considerations there are four basic versions of counting rules that are commonly used in mathematical and statistical problems.

To begin, observe that the number of ways in which n individual units can be ordered is governed by the use of the factorial function from Chapter 1 (page 37):

$$n(n-1)(n-2)\cdots(2)(1) = n!.$$

This makes sense: There are n ways to select the first object in an ordered list, $n - 1$ ways to pick the second, and so on, until we have one item left and there is only one way to pick that one item. For example, consider the set $\{A, B, C\}$. There are three (n) ways to pick the first item: A, B, or C. Once we have done this, say we picked C to go first, then there are two ways $(n - 1)$ to pick the second item: either A or B. After that pick, assume A, then there is only one way to pick the last item $(n - 2)$: B.

To continue, how do we organize and consider a range of possible choices given a set of characteristics? That is, if we are selecting from a group of people, we can pick male vs. female, young vs. old, college educated vs. non-college educated, and so on. Notice that we are now thinking about *counting* objects rather than just *ordering* objects as done above. So, given a list of known features, we would like a method for enumerating the possibilities when picking from such a population. Fortunately there is a basic and intuitive theorem that guides such counting possibilities. Intuitively, we want to "cross" each possibility from each characteristic to obtain every possible combination.

The Fundamental Theorem of Counting:

- If there are k distinct decision stages to an operation or process,
- each with its own n_k number of alternatives,
- then there are $\prod_{i=1}^{k} n_k$ possible outcomes.

What this formal language says is that if we have a specific number of individual steps, each of which has some set of alternatives, then the total number of alternatives is the product of those at each step. So for $1, 2, \ldots, k$ different characteristics we multiply the corresponding $n_1, n_2, \ldots, n_k$ number of features.

As a simple example, suppose we consider cards in a deck in terms of suit $(n_1 = 4)$ and whether they are face cards $(n_2 = 2)$. Thus there are 8 possible countable outcomes defined by crossing [Diamonds, Hearts, Spades, Clubs] with [Face, NotFace]:

$$
\begin{array}{cccc}
\mathbf{D} & \mathbf{H} & \mathbf{S} & \mathbf{C}
\end{array}
$$

$$
\begin{array}{c}
\mathbf{F} \\
\mathbf{NF}
\end{array}
\left(
\begin{array}{cccc}
F,D & F,H & F,S & F,C \\
NF,D & NF,H & NF,S & NF,C
\end{array}
\right).
$$

In general, though, we are interested in the number of ways to draw a subset from a larger set. So how many five-card poker hands can be drawn from a 52-card deck? How many ways can we configure a committee out of a larger legislature? And so on. As noted, this counting is done along two criteria: with or without tracking the order of selection, and with or without replacing chosen units back into the pool for future selection. In this way, the general forms of choice rules combine *ordering* with *counting*.

The first, and easiest method, to consider is **ordered, with replacement**. If we have n objects and we want to pick $k < n$ from them, and replace the choice back into the available set each time, then it should be clear that on each iteration there are always n choices. So by the Fundamental Theorem of Counting, the number of choices is the product of k values of n alternatives:

$$
n \times n \times \cdots n = n^k,
$$

(just as if the factorial ordering rule above did not decrement).

The second most basic approach is **ordered, without replacement**. This is where the ordering principle discussed above comes in more obviously. Suppose again we have n objects and we want to pick $k < n$ from them. There are n ways to pick the first object, $n-1$ ways to pick the second object, $n-2$ ways to pick the third object, and so on until we have k choices. This decrementing of choices differs from the last case because we are not replacing items on each iteration. So the general form of ordered counting, without replacement using the two principles is

$$
n \times (n-1) \times (n-2) \times \cdots \times (k+1) \times k = \frac{n!}{(n-k)!},
$$

Here the factorial notation saves us a lot of trouble because we can express this list as the difference between $n!$ and the factorial series that starts with $k - 1$. So the denominator, $(n - k)!$, strips off terms lower than k in the product.

A slightly more complicated, but very common, form is **unordered, without replacement**. The best way to think of this form is that it is just like ordered without replacement, except that we cannot see the order of picking. For example, if we were picking colored balls out of an urn, then *red,white,red* is equivalent to *red,red,white* and *white,red,red*. Therefore, there are $k!$ fewer choices than with ordered, without replacement since there are $k!$ ways to express this redundancy. So we need only to modify the previous form according to

$$\frac{n!}{(n - k)!k!} = \binom{n}{k}.$$

Recall that this is the "choose" notation introduced on page 31 in Chapter 1. The abbreviated notation is handy because unordered, without replacement is an extremely common sampling procedure. We can derive a useful generalization of this idea by first observing that

$$\binom{n}{k} = \binom{n - 1}{k} + \binom{n - 1}{k - 1}$$

(the proof of this property is a chapter exercise). This form suggests successively peeling off $k - 1$ iterates to form a sum:

$$\binom{n}{k} = \sum_{i=0}^{k} \binom{n - 1 - i}{k - i}.$$

Another generalization of the choose notation is found by observing that we have so far restricted ourselves to only two subgroups: those chosen and those not chosen. If we instead consider J subgroups labeled $k_1, k_2, \ldots, k_J$ with the property that $\sum_{j=1}^{J} k_j = n$, then we get the more general form

$$\frac{n!}{\prod_{j=1}^{J} k_j!} = \binom{n}{k_1}\binom{n - k_1}{k_2}\binom{n - k_1 - k_2}{k_3}$$

$$\ldots \binom{n - k_1 - k_2 - \cdots - k_{J-2}}{k_{J-1}}\binom{k_J}{k_J},$$

which can be denoted $\left(\begin{smallmatrix} n \\ k_1,k_2,...,k_J \end{smallmatrix}\right)$.

The final counting method, **unordered, with replacement** is terribly unintuitive. The best way to think of this is that unordered, without replacement needs to be adjusted upward to reflect the increased number of choices. This form is best expressed again using choose notation:

$$\frac{(n+k-1)!}{(n-1)!k!} = \binom{n+k-1}{k}.$$

★ **Example 7.1:** **Survey Sampling.** Suppose we want to perform a small survey with 15 respondents from a population of 150. How different are our choices with each counting rule? The answer is, quite different:

Ordered, with replacement: $\qquad n^k = 150^{15} = 4.378939 \times 10^{32}$

Ordered, without replacement: $\qquad \frac{n!}{(n-k)!} = \frac{150!}{135!} = 2.123561 \times 10^{32}$

Unordered, without replacement: $\qquad \binom{n}{k} = \binom{150}{15} = 1.623922 \times 10^{20}.$

Unordered, with replacement: $\qquad \binom{n+k-1}{k} = \binom{164}{15} = 6.59974 \times 10^{20}.$

So, even though this seems like quite a small survey, there is a wide range of sampling outcomes which can be obtained.

7.2.1 The Binomial Theorem and Pascal's Triangle

The most common mathematical use for the choose notation is in the following theorem, which relates exponentiation with counting.

Binomial Theorem:

- Given any real numbers X and Y and a nonnegative integer n,

$$(X + Y)^n = \sum_{k=0}^{n} \binom{n}{k} x^k y^{n-k}.$$

An interesting special case occurs when $X = 1$ and $Y = 1$:

$$2^n = \sum_{k=0}^{n} \binom{n}{k},$$

which relates the exponent function to the summed binomial. Euclid (around 300 BC to 260 BC) apparently knew about this theorem for the case $n = 2$ only. The first recorded version of the full Binomial Theorem is found in the 1303 book by the Chinese mathematician Chu Shï-kié, and he speaks of it as being quite well known at the time. The first European appearance of the more general form here was due to Pascal in 1654.

To show how rapidly the binomial expansion increases in polynomial terms, consider the first six values of n:

$(X + Y)^0 = 1$

$(X + Y)^1 = X + Y$

$(X + Y)^2 = X^2 + 2XY + Y^2$

$(X + Y)^3 = X^3 + 3X^2Y + 3XY^2 + Y^3$

$(X + Y)^4 = X^4 + 4X^3Y + 6X^2Y^2 + 4XY^3 + Y^4$

$(X + Y)^5 = X^5 + 5X^4Y + 10X^3Y^2 + 10X^2Y^3 + 5XY^4 + Y^5.$

Note the symmetry of these forms. In fact, if we just display the coefficient values and leave out exponents and variables for the moment, we get **Pascal's Triangle**:

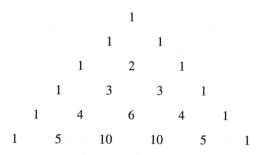

which gives a handy form for summarizing binomial expansions (it can obviously go on further than shown here). There are many interesting features of

Pascal's Triangle. Any value in the table is the sum of the two values diagonally above. For instance, 10 in the third cell of the bottom row is the sum of the 4 and 6 diagonally above. The sum of the kth row (counting the first row as the zero row) can be calculated by $\sum_{j=0}^{k} \binom{k}{j} = 2^k$. The sum of the diagonals from left to right: $\{1\}, \{1\}, \{1,1\}, \{1,2\}, \{1,3,1\}, \{1,4,3\}, \ldots$, give the Fibonacci numbers $(1,2,3,5,8,13,\ldots)$. If the first element in a row after the 1 is a prime number, then every number in that row is divisible by it (except the leading and trailing 1's). If a row is treated as consecutive digits in a larger number (carrying multidigit numbers over to the left), then each row is a power of 11:

$$1 = 11^0$$

$$11 = 11^1$$

$$121 = 11^2$$

$$1331 = 11^3$$

$$14641 = 11^4$$

$$161051 = 11^5,$$

and these are called the "magic 11's." There are actually many more mathematical properties lurking in Pascal's Triangle, but these are some of the more famous.

7.3 Sets and Operations on Sets

Sets are holding places. A **set** is a bounded collection defined by its contents (or even by its lack thereof) and is usually denoted with curly braces. So the set of even positive integers less than 10 is

$$\{2, 4, 6, 8\}.$$

We can also define sets without necessarily listing all the contents if there is some criteria that defines the contents. For example,

$$\{X : 0 \leq X \leq 10, X \in \Re\}$$

defines the set of all the real numbers between zero and 10 inclusive. We can read this statement as "the set that contains all values labeled X such that X is greater than or equal to zero, less than or equal to 10, and part of the real numbers." Clearly sets with an infinite number of members need to be described in this fashion rather than listed out as above.

The "things" that are contained within a set are called **elements**, and these can be individual units or multiple units. An **event** is any collection of possible outcomes of an experiment, that is, any subset of the full set of possibilities, including the full set itself (actually "event" and "outcome" are used synonymously). So $\{H\}$ and $\{T\}$ are outcomes for a coin flipping experiment, as is $\{H, T\}$. Events and sets are typically, but not necessarily, labeled with capital Roman letters: A, B, T, etc.

Events can be abstract in the sense that they may have not yet happened but are imagined, or outcomes can be concrete in that they are observed: "A occurs." Events are also defined for more than one individual subelement (odd numbers on a die, hearts out of a deck of cards, etc.). Such defined groupings of individual elements constitute an event in the most general sense.

★ **Example 7.2:**   **A Single Die.** Throw a single die. The event that an even number appears is the set $A = \{2, 4, 6\}$.

Events can also be referred to when they do *not* happen. For the example above we can say "if the outcome of the die is a 3, then A did not occur."

7.3.1 General Characteristics of Sets

Suppose we conduct some experiment, not in the stereotypical laboratory sense, but in the sense that we roll a die, toss a coin, or spin a pointer. It is useful to have some way of describing not only a single observed outcome, but also the full list of possible outcomes. This motivates the following set definition. The **sample space** S of a given experiment is the set that consists of all possible outcomes (events) from this experiment. Thus the sample space from flipping a coin is $\{H, T\}$ (provided that we preclude the possibility that the coin lands on its edge as in the well-known *Twilight Zone* episode).

Sets have different characteristics such as countability and finiteness. A **countable set** is one whose elements can be placed in one-to-one correspondence with the positive integers. A **finite set** has a noninfinite number of contained events. Countability and finiteness (or their opposites) are not contradictory characteristics, as the following examples show.

★ **Example 7.3:** **Countably Finite Set**. A single throw of a die is a countably finite set,

$$S = \{1, 2, 3, 4, 5, 6\}.$$

★ **Example 7.4:** **Multiple Views of Countably Finite**. Tossing a pair of dice is also a countably finite set, but we can consider the sample space in three different ways. If we are just concerned with the sum on the dice (say for a game like craps), the sample space is

$$S = \{2, 3, 4, 5, 6, 7, 8, 9, 10, 11, 12\}.$$

If the individual values matter, then the sample space is extended to a large set:

$$
\begin{array}{cccccc}
\{1, 1\}, & \{1, 2\}, & \{1, 3\}, & \{1, 4\}, & \{1, 5\}, & \{1, 6\}, \\
 & \{2, 2\}, & \{2, 3\}, & \{2, 4\}, & \{2, 5\}, & \{2, 6\}, \\
 & & \{3, 3\}, & \{3, 4\}, & \{3, 5\}, & \{3, 6\}, \\
 & & & \{4, 4\}, & \{4, 5\}, & \{4, 6\}, \\
 & & & & \{5, 5\}, & \{5, 6\}, \\
 & & & & & \{6, 6\}.
\end{array}
$$

Also, if we have some way of distinguishing between the two dice, such as using different colors, then the sample space is even larger because it is now possible to distinguish order:

$$
\begin{array}{cccccc}
\{1,1\}, & \{1,2\}, & \{1,3\}, & \{1,4\}, & \{1,5\}, & \{1,6\}, \\
\{2,1\}, & \{2,2\}, & \{2,3\}, & \{2,4\}, & \{2,5\}, & \{2,6\}, \\
\{3,1\}, & \{3,2\}, & \{3,3\}, & \{3,4\}, & \{3,5\}, & \{3,6\}, \\
\{4,1\}, & \{4,2\}, & \{4,3\}, & \{4,4\}, & \{4,5\}, & \{4,6\}, \\
\{5,1\}, & \{5,2\}, & \{5,3\}, & \{5,4\}, & \{5,5\}, & \{5,6\}, \\
\{6,1\}, & \{6,2\}, & \{6,3\}, & \{6,4\}, & \{6,5\}, & \{6,6\}.
\end{array}
$$

Note that however we define our sample space here, that definition does not affect the probabilistic behavior of the dice. That is, they are not responsive in that they do not change physical behavior due to the game being played.

★ **Example 7.5:** **Countably Infinite Set**. The number of coin flips until two heads in a row appear is a countably infinite set:

$$S = \{1, 2, 3, \ldots\}.$$

★ **Example 7.6:** **Uncountably Infinite Set**. Spin a pointer and look at the angle in radians. Given a hypothetically infinite precision measuring instrument, this is an uncountably infinite set:

$$S = [0{:}2\pi).$$

We can also define the **cardinality** of a set, which is just the number of elements in the set. The finite set A has cardinality given by $n(A)$, $\bar{A}$, or $\|A\|$, where the first form is preferred. Obviously for finite sets the cardinality is an integer value denoting the quantity of events (exclusive of the null set). There are, unfortunately, several ways that the cardinality of a nonfinite set is denoted. The cardinality of a countably infinite set is denoted by $\aleph_0$ (the Hebrew aleph character with subscript zero), and the cardinality of an uncountably infinite set is denoted similarly by $\aleph_1$.

7.3.2 A Special Set: The Empty Set

One particular kind of set is worth discussing at length because it can seem confusing when encountered for the first time. The **empty set**, or **null set**, is a set with no elements, as the names imply. This seems a little paradoxical since if there is nothing in the set, should not the set simply go away? Actually, we *need* the idea of an empty set to describe certain events that do not exist and, therefore the empty set is a convenient thing to have around. Usually the empty set is denoted with the Greek letter phi: ϕ.

An analogy is helpful here. We can think of a set as a suitcase and the elements in the set are contents like clothes and books. Therefore we can define various events for this set, such as the suitcase has all shirts in it, or some similar statement. Now we take these items out of the suitcase one at a time. When there is only one item left in the set, the set is called a **singleton**. When this last item is removed the suitcase still exists, despite being empty, and it is also available to be filled up again. Thus the suitcase is much like a set and can contain some number of items or simply be empty but still defined. It should be clear, however, that this analogy breaks down in the presence of infinite sets.

7.3.3 Operations on Sets

We can perform basic operations on sets that define new sets or provide arithmetic and boolean (true/false) results. The first idea here is the notion of containment, which specifies that a set is composed entirely of elements of another set. Set A is a **subset** of set B if every element of A is also an element of B. We also say that A is contained in B and denote this as $A \subset B$ or $B \supset A$. Formally,

$$A \subset B \iff \forall X \in A, X \in B,$$

which reads "A is a subset of B if and only if all values X that are in A are also in B." The set A here is a **proper subset** of B if it meets this criteria *and* $A \neq B$. Some authors distinguish proper subsets from the more general kind where equality is allowed by using $\subset$ to denote only proper subsets and $\subseteq$ to denote the more general kind. Unfortunately this notation is not universal.

Subset notation is handy in many ways. We just talked about two sets being equal, which intuitively means that they must contain exactly the same elements. To formally assert that two sets are equal we need to claim, however, that both $A \subset B$ and $B \subset A$ are true so that the contents of A exactly match the contents of B:

$$A = B \iff A \subset B \text{ and } B \subset A.$$

Sets can be "unioned," meaning that they can be combined to create a set that is the same size or larger. Specifically, the **union** of the sets A and B, $A \cup B$, is the new set that contains all of the elements that belong to either A or B. The key word in this definition is "or," indicating that the new set is inclusive. The union of A and B is the set of elements X whereby

$$A \cup B = \{X : X \in A \text{ or } X \in B\}.$$

The union operator is certainly not confined to two sets, and we can use a modification of the "$\cup$" operator that resembles a summation operator in its application:

$$A_1 \cup A_2 \cup \ldots \cup A_n = \bigcup_{i=1}^{n} A_i.$$

It is sometimes convenient to specify ranges, say for $m < n$, with the union operator:

$$A_1 \cup A_2 \cup \ldots \cup A_m = \bigcup_{i \leq m} A_i.$$

There is an obvious relationship between unions and subsets: An individual set is always a subset of the new set defined by a union with other sets:

$$A_1 \subset A \iff A = \bigcup_{i=1}^{n} A_i,$$

and this clearly works for other constituent sets besides A_1. We can also talk about nested subsets:

$$A_n \uparrow A \Longrightarrow A_1 \subset A_2 \subset \ldots A_n, \text{ where } A = \bigcup_{i=1}^{n} A_i$$

$$A_n \downarrow A \Longrightarrow A_n \subset A_{n-1} \subset \ldots A_1, \text{ where } A = \bigcup_{i=1}^{n} A_i.$$

So, for example, if A_1 is the ranking minority member on the House appropriations committee, A_2 is the minority party membership on the House appropriations committee, A_3 is the minority party membership in the House, A_4 is the full House of Representatives, A_5 is Congress, and A is the government, then we can say $A_n \uparrow A$.

We can also define the **intersection** of sets, which contains only those elements found in both (or all for more than two sets of interest). So $A \cap B$ is the new set that contains all of the elements that belong to A and B. Now the key word in this definition is "and," indicating that the new set is exclusive. So the elements of the intersection do not have the luxury of belonging to one set or the other but must now be a member of both. The intersection of A and B is the set elements X whereby

$$A \cap B = \{X : X \in A \text{ and } X \in B\}.$$

Like the union operator, the intersection operator is not confined to just two sets:

$$A_1 \cap A_2 \cap \ldots \cap A_n = \bigcap_{i=1}^{n} A_i.$$

Again, it is convenient to specify ranges, say for $m < n$, with the intersection operator:

$$A_1 \cap A_2 \cap \ldots \cap A_m = \bigcap_{i \leq m} A_i.$$

Sets also define complementary sets by the definition of their existence. The **complement** of a given set is the set that contains all elements not in the original set. More formally, the complement of A is the set A^C (sometimes denoted A' or $\bar{A}$) defined by

$$A^C = \{X : X \notin A\}.$$

A special feature of complementation is the fact that the complement of the null set is the sample space, and vice versa:

$$\phi^C = \mathcal{S} \quad \text{and} \quad \mathcal{S}^C = \phi.$$

This is interesting because it highlights the roles that these special sets play: The complement of the set with everything has nothing, and the complement of the set with nothing has everything.

Another common operator is the **difference operator**, which defines which portion of a given set is *not* a member of the other. The difference of A relative to B is the set of elements X whereby

$$A \setminus B = \{X : X \in A \text{ and } X \notin B\}.$$

The difference operator can also be expressed with intersection and complement notation:

$$A \setminus B = A \cap B^C.$$

Note that the difference operator as defined here is not symmetric: It is not necessarily true that $A \setminus B = B \setminus A$. There is, however, another version called the **symmetric difference** that further restricts the resulting set, requiring the operator to apply in both directions. The symmetric difference of A relative to B and B relative to A is the set

$$A \bigtriangleup B = \{X : X \in A \text{ and } X \notin B \text{ or } X \in B \text{ and } B \notin A\}.$$

Because of this symmetry we can also denote the symmetric difference as the union of two "regular" differences:

$$A \bigtriangleup B = (A \setminus B) \cup (B \setminus A) = (A \cap B^{\complement}) \cup (B \cap A^{\complement}).$$

★ **Example 7.7:** **Single Die Experiment**. Throw a single die. For this experiment, define the following sample space and accompanying sets:

$$S = \{1, 2, 3, 4, 5, 6\}$$
$$A = \{2, 4, 6\}$$
$$B = \{4, 5, 6\}$$
$$C = \{1\}.$$

So A is the set of even numbers, B is the set of numbers greater than 3, and C has just a single element. Using the described operators, we find that

$$A^{\complement} = \{1, 3, 5\} \quad A \cup B = \{2, 4, 5, 6\} \quad A \cap B = \{4, 6\}$$
$$B \cap C = \phi \quad (A \cap B)^{\complement} = \{1, 2, 3, 5\} \quad A \setminus B = \{2\}$$
$$B \setminus A = \{5\} \quad A \bigtriangleup B = \{2, 5\} \quad (A \cap B) \cup C = \{1, 4, 6\}.$$

Figure 7.1 illustrates set operators using a **Venn diagram** of three sets where the "universe" of possible outcomes (S) is given by the surrounding box. Venn diagrams are useful tools for describing sets in a two-dimensional graph. The intersection of A and B is the dark region that belongs to both sets, whereas the union of A and B is the lightly shaded region that indicates elements in A or B (including the intersection region). Note that the intersection of A or B with C is ϕ, since there is no overlap. We could, however, consider the nonempty sets $A \cup C$ and $B \cup C$. The complement of $A \cup B$ is all of the nonshaded region, including C. Consider the more interesting region $(A \cap B)^{\complement}$. This would be every part of S *except* the intersection, which could also be expressed as those elements that are in the complement of A *or* the complement of B, thus ruling out the intersection (one of de Morgan's Laws; see below). The portion of A

Fig. 7.1. THREE SETS

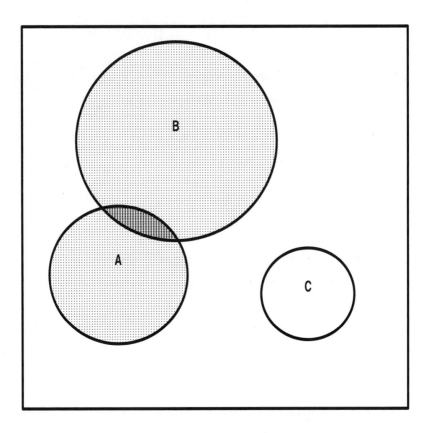

that does not overlap with B is denoted $A \backslash B$, and we can also identify $A \vartriangle B$ in the figure, which is either A or B (the full circles) but not both.

There are formal properties for unions, intersections, and complement operators to consider.

Properties For Any Three Sets A, B, and C, in $\mathcal{S}$

⟼ Commutative Property $\quad A \cup B = B \cup A$

$A \cap B = B \cap A$

⟼ Associative Property $\quad A \cup (B \cup C) = (A \cup B) \cup C$

$A \cap (B \cap C) = (A \cap B) \cap C$

⟼ Distributive Property $\quad A \cap (B \cup C) = (A \cap B) \cup (A \cap C)$

$A \cup (B \cap C) = (A \cup B) \cap (A \cup C)$

⟼ de Morgan's Laws $\quad (A \cup B)^{\complement} = A^{\complement} \cap B^{\complement}$

$(A \cap B)^{\complement} = A^{\complement} \cup B^{\complement}$

As an illustration we will prove $A \cup (B \cap C) = (A \cup B) \cap (A \cup C)$ by demonstrating inclusion (subsetting) in both directions to establish the equality.

- First show $A \cup (B \cap C) \subset (A \cup B) \cap (A \cup C)$ by demonstrating that some element in the first set is also in the second set:

    Suppose $X \in A \cup (B \cap C)$, so $X \in A$ or $X \in (B \cap C)$

    If $X \in A$, then $X \in (A \cup B)$ and $X \in (A \cup C)$

    $\quad \therefore X \in (A \cup B) \cap (A \cup C)$

    Or if $X \notin A$, then $X \in (B \cap C)$ and $X \in B$ and $X \in C$

    $\quad \therefore X \in (A \cup B) \cap (A \cup C)$

- Now show $A \cup (B \cap C) \supset (A \cup B) \cap (A \cup C)$ by demonstrating that some element in the second set is also in the first set:

Suppose $X \in (A \cup B) \cap (A \cup C)$ so $X \in (A \cup B)$ and $X \in (A \cup C)$

If $X \in A$, then $X \in A \cup (B \cap C)$

Or if $X \notin A$, then $X \in B$ and $X \in C$,

since it is in the two unions but not in A.

$\therefore X \in A \cup (B \cap C)$

- Since $A \cup (B \cap C) \subset (A \cup B) \cap (A \cup C)$ *and* $A \cup (B \cap C) \supset (A \cup B) \cap (A \cup C)$, then every element in the first set is in the second set, and every element in the second set is in the first set. So the sets must be equal.

The case where two sets do not have an intersection (say A and C in Figure 7.1) is important enough that it has a special name. Two sets A and B are **disjoint** when their intersection is empty: $A \cap B = \phi$. This is generalizable as well. The k sets $A_1, A_2, \ldots, A_k$ are **pairwise disjoint**, also called **mutually exclusive**, if $A_i \cap A_j = \phi \; \forall i \neq j$. In addition, if $A_1, A_2, \ldots, A_k$ are pairwise disjoint and we add the condition that $\bigcup_{i=1}^{k} A_i = S$ (i.e., that they cover the sample space completely), then we say that the $A_1, A_2, \ldots, A_k$ are a **partition** of the sample space. For instance, the outcomes $\{1, 2, 3, 4, 5, 6\}$ form a partition of S for throwing a single die because they are pairwise distinct and nothing else can occur. More formally, $A_1, A_2, \ldots, A_k$ are a partition of S iff

- $A_i \cap A_j = \phi \; \forall i \neq j$.
- $\bigcup_{i=1}^{k} A_i = S$.

★ **Example 7.8:   Overlapping Group Memberships**. Sociologists are often interested in determining connections between distinct social networks. Bonacich (1978) used set theory to explore overlapping group memberships such as sports teams, clubs, and social groups in a high school. The data are given by the following cross-listing of 18 community members and 14 social events they could possibly have attended. An "X" indicated that the individual on that row attended the social event indexed by the column. The idea is that the more social events two selected individuals have in common, the closer they are in a social network.

| | Event | | | | | | | | | | | | |
Ind.	A	B	C	D	E	F	G	H	I	J	K	L	M	N
1	X	X	X	X	X	X		X	X					
2	X	X	X		X		X	X						
3		X	X	X	X	X	X	X	X					
4	X		X	X	X	X	X	X						
5		X	X	X		X								
6		X		X	X		X							
7				X	X	X	X							
8					X			X	X					
9					X		X	X	X					
10							X	X	X			X		
11							X	X	X	X		X		
12							X	X	X			X	X	X
13						X	X	X	X			X	X	X
14						X	X		X	X	X	X	X	X
15							X	X		X	X	X		
16								X	X					
17									X		X			
18									X		X			

We can see that there are two relatively distinct groups here, with reasonable overlap to complicate things. Counting the social events as sets, we can ask some specific questions and make some observations. First, observe that only $M = N$; they have the same members: $\{12, 13, 14\}$. A number of sets are disjoint, such as (A, J), (B, L), (D, M), and others. Yet, the full group of sets, $A : N$, clearly does not form a partition due to the many nonempty intersections. In fact, there is no subset of the social events that forms a partition. How do we know this? Consider that either I or K would have to be included in the formed partition because they are the only two that include individuals 17 and 18. The set K lacks individual 16, necessitating inclusion of H or I, but these overlap with K elsewhere. Similarly, I lacks individual 15, but each of the five sets that include this individual overlap somewhere with I. Thus no subset can be configured to form a partition. Let's now test out the first de Morgan's Law for the sets E and G:

$$(E \cup G)^C = (\{1,2,3,4,5,6,7,9\} \cup \{2,3,4,5,7,9,10,13,14,15\})^C$$

$$= (\{1,2,3,4,5,6,7,9,10,13,14,15\})^C$$

$$= \{8,11,12,16,17,18\}$$

$$E^C \cap G^C = \{1,2,3,4,5,6,7,9\}^C \cap \{2,3,4,5,7,9,10,13,14,15\}^C$$

$$= \{8,10,11,12,13,14,15,16,17,18\}$$

$$\cap \{1,6,8,11,12,16,17,18\}$$

$$= \{8,11,12,,16,17,18\},$$

which demonstrates the property.

★ **Example 7.9:   Approval Voting.** This example derives from the review of formal models of voting in Gill and Gainous (2002). In approval voting, voters are allowed to vote for (approve of) as many candidates as they want but cannot cast more than one vote for each candidate. Then the candidate with the most of these approval votes wins the election. Obviously this system gives voters a wide range of strategies, and these can be analyzed with a formal (mathematical) model.

Given $K \geq 3$ candidates, it appears that there are 2^K possible strategies, from the counting rules in Section 7.2, but because an abstention has the same net effect as voting for every candidate on the ballot, the actual number of different choices is $2^K - 1$. We can formalize approval voting as follows:

- Let w, x, y, z be the individual candidates from which a group of voters can choose, and let wPx represent a given voter's strict preference for w over x. A multicandidate strict preference order is denoted $wPxPyPz$.

- No preference between w and x is denoted by wIx, meaning that the voter is indifferent or ambivalent between the two.

- Strict preference and indifference have transitive relations, $wPx, xPy \rightarrow wPz$ and $wIx, xIy \rightarrow wIy$.

- Every possible grouped ordering can be separated into ℓ nonempty subsets where

$$[w_1, w_2, \ldots], [x_1, x_2, \ldots], [y_1, y_2, \ldots], [z_1, z_2, \ldots], \ldots, [\ell_1, \ell_2, \ldots]$$

, denoted as $W, X, Y, Z, \ldots, L$, and the voter is indifferent among the candidates within any single such subset while still strictly preferring every member of that subset to any of the other candidate subsets lower in the preference ordering.

When $\ell = 1$, the voter is called *unconcerned* and has no strict preference between any candidates. If $\ell = 2$, then the voter is called *dichotomous*, *trichotomous* if $\ell = 3$, and finally *multichotomous* if $\ell \geq 4$. If all voters have a dichotomous preference, then an approval voting system always produces an election result that is majority preferred, but when all preferences are not dichotomous, the result can be different. In such cases there are multiple *admissible voter strategies*, meaning a strategy that conforms to the available options among k alternatives and is not uniformly dominated (preferred in all aspects by the voter) by another alternative.

As an example, the preference order wPx with xPy has two admissible sincere strategies where the voter may have given an approval vote for only the top alternative w or for the two top alternatives w, x. Also, with multiple alternatives it is possible for voters to cast *insincere* (strategic) votes: With $wPxPy$ she prefers candidate w but might select only candidate x to make x close to w without helping y.

For two given subsets A and B, define the union $A \cup B = \{a : a \in A$ or $a \in B\}$. A subset that contains only candidate w is denoted as $\{w\}$, the subset that contains only candidate x is denoted as $\{x\}$, the subset containing only candidates w and x is denoted as $\{w, x\}$, and so on. A *strategy*, denoted by S, is defined as voting for some specified set of candidates regardless of actual approval or disapproval. Now consider the following set-based assumptions for a hypothetical voter:

- P: If wPx, then $\{w\}P\{w, x\}P\{x\}$.
- I: If $A \cup B$ and $B \cup C$ are nonempty, and if wIx, xIy, and wIy for all $w \in A$, $x \in B$, $y \in C$, then $(A \cup B)I(B \cup C)$.
- $M(P) = A_1$ is the subset of the most-preferred candidates under P, and $L(P) = A_n$, the subset of the least-preferred candidates under P.

Suppose we look once again at the voter who has the preference order $wPxPyPz$, while all other voters have dichotomous preferences, with some being sequentially indifferent (such as wIx and yIz), and some strictly prefer w and x to y and z, while the rest prefer y and z to w and x. Each of the other voters uses their unique admissible strategy, so that the aggregated preference for w is equal to that of x , $f(w) = f(x)$, and the aggregated preference for y is equal to that of z, $f(y) = f(z)$. Now assume that the voter with preference $wPxPyPz$ is convinced that there is at least a one-vote difference between w and y, $f(w) \geq f(y) + 1$; therefore, $\{w, y\}$ is a good strategy for this voter because a vote for w ensures that w will receive at least one more vote than x, and a vote for y ensures that y will receive at least one more vote than z. Therefore, $\{w, y\}$ ensures that the $wPxPyPz$ voter's most-preferred candidate gets the greatest votes and $wPxPyPz$ voter's least-preferred candidate gets the fewest votes.

7.4 The Probability Function

The idea of a probability function is very basic and very important. It is a mapping from a defined event (or events) onto a metric bounded by zero (it cannot happen) and one (it will happen with absolute certainty). Thus a probability function enables us to discuss various *degrees of likelihood of occurrence* in a systematic and practical way. Some of the language here is a bit formal, but it is important to discuss probability using the terminology in which it was codified so that we can be precise about specific meanings.

A collection of subsets of the sample space S is called a **sigma-algebra** (also called a **sigma-field**), and denoted $\mathfrak{F}$ (a fancy looking "F"), if it satisfies the following three properties:

(i) **Null Set Inclusion.** It contains the null set: $\phi \in \mathfrak{F}$.

(ii) **Closed Under Complementation.** If $A \in \mathfrak{F}$, then $A^{C} \in \mathfrak{F}$.

(iii) **Closed Under Countable Unions.** If $A_1, A_2, \ldots \in \mathfrak{F}$ then $\bigcup_{i=1}^{\infty} A_i \in \mathfrak{F}$.

So if A is any identified subset of S, then an associated (minimal size) sigma-algebra is $\mathfrak{F} = \{\phi, A, A^{C}, S\}$. Why do we have these particular elements? We need ϕ in there due to the first condition, and we have identified A as a subset. So by the second condition we need S and A^{C}. Finally, does taking unions of any of these events ever take us out of S. Clearly not, so this is a sigma-algebra. Interesting enough, so is $\mathfrak{F}' = \{\phi, A, A^{C}, A, A, S, A^{C}\}$ because there is no requirement that we not repeat events in a sigma-algebra. But this is not terribly useful, so it is common to specify the minimal size sigma-algebra as we have originally done. In fact such a sigma-algebra has a particular name: a **Borel-field**. These definitions are of course inherently discrete in measure. They do have corresponding versions over continuous intervals, although the associated mathematics get much more involved [see Billingsley (1995) or Chung (2000) for definitive introductions].

★ **Example 7.10:** **Single Coin Flip**. For this experiment, flip a coin once.

This produces
$$S = \{H, T\}$$
$$\mathfrak{F} = \{\phi, H, T, (H, T)\}.$$

Given a sample space S and an associated sigma-algebra $\mathfrak{F}$, a **probability function** is a mapping, p, from the domain defined by $\mathfrak{F}$ to the interval $[0:1]$. This is shown in Figure 7.2 for an event labeled A in the sample space S.

Fig. 7.2. THE MAPPING OF A PROBABILITY FUNCTION

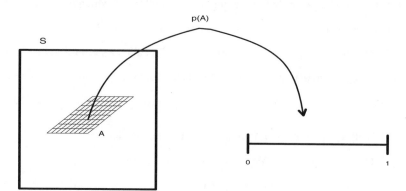

The **Kolmogorov probability axioms** specify the conditions for a proper probability function:

- The probability of any realizable event is between zero and one: $p(A_i) \in [0{:}1] \; \forall a_i \in \mathfrak{F}$.
- Something happens with probability one: $p(\mathcal{S}) = 1$.
- The probability of unions of n pairwise disjoint events is the sum of their individual probabilities: $P\left(\bigcup_{i=1}^{n} A_i\right) = \sum_{i=1}^{n} p(A_i)$ (even if $n = \infty$).

It is common to identify an experiment or other probabilistic setup with the **triple** (also called a probability space or a probability measure space) consisting of $(\mathcal{S}, \mathfrak{F}, P)$, to fully specify the sample space, sigma-algebra, and probability function applied.

7.5 Calculations with Probabilities

The manipulation of probability functions follows logical and predictable rules. The probability of a union of two sets is no smaller than the probability of an intersection of two sets. These two probabilities are equal if one set is a subset of another. It also makes intuitive sense that subsets have no greater probability than the enclosing set:

$$\text{If } A \subset B, \text{ then } p(A) \leq p(B).$$

The general rules for probability calculation are straightforward:

Calculations with Probabilities for A, B, and C, in $\mathcal{S}$

⟼ Probability of Unions

$$p(A \cup B)$$
$$= p(A) + p(B) - p(A \cap B)$$

⟼ Probability of Intersections

$$p(A \cap B)$$
$$= p(A) + p(B) - p(A \cup B)$$
(also denoted $p(A, B)$)

⟼ Probability of Complements

$$p(A^{\complement}) = 1 - p(A),$$
$$p(A) = 1 - p(A^{\complement})$$

⟼ Probability of the Null Set $p(\phi) = 0$

⟼ Probability of the Sample Space $p(\mathcal{S}) = 1$

⟼ Boole's Inequality $p(\bigcup_j A_j) \leq \sum_j p(A_j)$

Either of the first two rules can also be restated as $p(A \cup B) + p(A \cap B) = p(A) + p(B)$, which shows that the intersection is "double-counted" with naive addition. Note also that the probability of the intersection of A and B is also called the joint probability of the two events and denoted $p(A, B)$.

We can also now state a key result that is quite useful in these types of calculations.

The Theorem of Total Probability:

• Given any events A and B,

- $p(A) = p(A \cap B) + p(A \cap B^{\complement})$.

This intuitively says that the probability of an event A can be decomposed into to parts: one that intersects with another set B and the other that intersects with the complement of B, as shown in Figure 7.3. If there is no intersection or if B is a subset of A, then one of the two parts has probability zero.

Fig. 7.3. THEOREM OF TOTAL PROBABILITY ILLUSTRATED

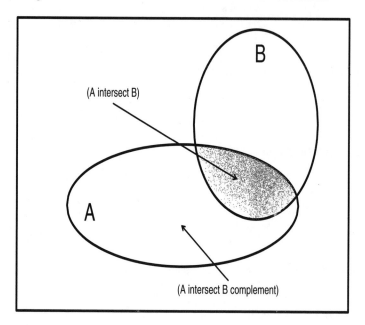

More generally, if $B_1, B_2, \ldots, B_n$ is a partition of the sample space, then

$$p(A) = p(A \cap B_1) + p(A \cap B_2) + \ldots + p(A \cap B_n).$$

★ **Example 7.11:   Probabilistic Analysis of Supreme Court Decisions.**
Probability statements can be enormously useful in political science research. Since political actors are rarely deterministic enough to predict with certainty, using probabilities to describe potential events or actions provides a means of making claims that include uncertainty.

Jeffrey Segal (1984) looked at Supreme Court decisions to review search and seizure cases from lower courts. He constructed a model using data from all 123 Fourth Amendment cases from 1962 to 1981 to explain why the Court upheld the lower court ruling versus overturning it. The objective was to make probabilistic statements about Supreme Court decisions given specific aspects of the case and therefore to make predictive claims about future actions. Since his multivariate statistical model simultaneously incorporates all these variables, the probabilities described are the effects of individual variables holding the effects of all others constant.

One of his first findings was that a police search has a 0.85 probability of being upheld by the Court if it took place at the home of another person and only a 0.10 probability of being upheld in the detainee's own home. This is a dramatic difference in probability terms and reveals considerable information about the thinking of the Court. Another notable difference occurs when the search takes place with no property interest versus a search on the actual person: 0.85 compared to 0.41. Relatedly, a "stop and frisk" search case has a 0.70 probability of being upheld whereas a full personal search has a probability of 0.40 of being upheld. These probabilistic findings point to an underlying distinction that justices make in terms of the personal context of the search.

Segal also found differences with regard to police possession of a warrant or probable cause. A search sanctioned by a warrant had a 0.85 probability of being upheld but only a 0.50 probability in the absence of such prior authority. The probability that the Court would uphold probable cause searches (where the police notice some evidence of illegality) was 0.65, whereas those that were not probable cause searches were upheld by the Court with probability 0.53. This is not a great difference, and Segal pointed out that it is confounded with other criteria that affect the overall reasonableness of the search. One such criteria noted is the status of the arrest. If the search is performed subject to a lawful arrest, then there is a (quite impressive) 0.99 probability of being upheld, but only a 0.50 probability if there is no arrest, and all the way down to 0.28 if there is an unlawful arrest.

What is impressive and useful about the approach taken in this work is that the author translates extensive case study into probability statements that are intuitive to readers. By making such statements, underlying patterns of judicial thought on Fourth Amendment issues are revealed.

7.6 Conditional Probability and Bayes Law

Conditional probability statements recognize that some prior information bears on the determination of subsequent probabilities. For instance, a candidate's probability of winning office are almost certain to change if the opponent suffers a major scandal or drops out of the race. We would not want to ignore information that alters probability statements and **conditional probability** provides a means of systematically including other information by changing "$p(A)$" to "$p(A|B)$" to mean the probability that A occurs given that B has occurred.

★ **Example 7.12:   Updating Probability Statements**. Suppose a single die is rolled but it cannot be seen. The probability that the upward face is a four is obviously one-sixth, $p(x = 4) = \frac{1}{6}$. Further suppose that you are told that the value is greater than three. Would you revise your probability statement? Obviously it would be appropriate to update since there are now only three possible outcomes, one of which is a four. This gives $p(x = 4|x > 3) = \frac{1}{3}$, which is a substantially different statement.

There is a more formal means of determining conditional probabilities. Given two outcomes A and B in $\mathcal{S}$, the probability that A occurs given that B occurs is the probability that A and B both occur divided by the probability that B occurs:

$$p(A|B) = \frac{p(A \cap B)}{p(B)},$$

provided that $p(B) \neq 0$.

★ **Example 7.13:** **Conditional Probability with Dice**. In rolling two dice labeled X and Y, we are interested in whether the sum of the up faces is four, given that the die labeled X shows a three. The unconditional probability is given by

$$p(X+Y=4) = p(\{1,3\},\{2,2\},\{3,1\}) = \frac{1}{12},$$

since there are 3 defined outcomes here out of 36 total. The conditional probability, however, is given by

$$p(X+Y=4|X=3) = \frac{p(X+Y=4,X=3)}{p(X=3)}$$

$$= \frac{p(\{3,1\})}{p(\{3,1\},\{3,2\},\{3,3\}\{3,4\},\{3,5\},\{3,6\})}$$

$$= \frac{1}{6}.$$

We can rearrange $p(A|B) = \frac{p(A \cap B)}{p(B)}$ to get $p(A|B)p(B) = p(A \cap B)$. Similarly, for the set B^C, we get $p(A|B^C)p(B^C) = p(A \cap B^C)$. For any set B we know that A has two components, one that intersects with B and one that does not (although either could be a null set). So the set A can be expressed as the sum of conditional probabilities:

$$p(A) = p(A|B)p(B) + p(A|B^C)p(B^C).$$

Thus the Theorem of Total Probability can also be reexpressed in conditional notation, showing that the probability of any event can be decomposed into conditional statements about any other event. It is possible to further extend this with an additional conditional statement. Suppose now that we are interested in decomposing $p(A|C)$ with regard to another event, B and B^C. We start with the definition of conditional probability, expand via the most basic form of the

Theorem of Total Probability, and then simplify:

$$p(A|C) = \frac{p(A \cap C)}{p(C)}$$

$$= \frac{p(A \cap B \cap C) + p(A \cap B^{C} \cap C)}{p(C)}$$

$$= \frac{p(A|B \cap C)p(B \cap C) + p(A|B^{C} \cap C)p(B^{C} \cap C)}{p(C)}$$

$$= p(A|B \cap C)p(B|C) + p(A|B^{C} \cap C)p(B^{C}|C).$$

It is important to note here that the conditional probability is order-dependent: $p(A|B) \neq p(B|A)$. As an illustration, apparently in California the probability that a highway motorist was in the left-most lane given they subsequently received a speeding ticket is about 0.93. However, it is certainly not true that the probability that one receives a speeding ticket given they are in the left lane is also 0.93 (or this lane would be quite empty!). But can these conditional probabilities be related somehow?

We can manipulate the conditional probability statements in parallel:

$$p(A|B) = \frac{p(A \cap B)}{p(B)} \qquad\qquad p(B|A) = \frac{p(B \cap A)}{p(A)}$$

$$p(A \cap B) = p(A|B)p(B) \qquad p(B \cap A) = p(B|A)p(A).$$

Wait a minute! We know that $p(A \cap B) = p(B \cap A)$, so we can equate

$$p(A|B)p(B) = p(B|A)p(A)$$

$$p(A|B) = \frac{p(A)}{p(B)}p(B|A)$$

$$= \frac{p(A)p(B|A)}{p(A)p(B|A) + p(A^{C})p(B|A^{C})},$$

where the last step uses the Total Probability Theorem. This means that we have a way of relating the two conditional probability statements. In fact, this is so useful that it has a name, **Bayes Law**, for its discoverer, the Reverend Thomas Bayes (published posthumously in 1763).

Any joint probability can be decomposed into a series of conditional probabilities followed by a final unconditional probability using the **multiplication rule**. This is a generalization of the definition of conditional probability. The joint distribution of k events can be reexpressed as

$$p(A_1, A_2, \ldots, A_k) = p(A_k | A_{k-1}, A_{k-2}, \ldots, A_2, A_1)$$
$$\times p(A_{k-1} | A_{k-2}, \ldots, A_2, A_1) \cdots p(A_3 | A_2, A_1) p(A_2 | A_1) p(A_1).$$

So we can "reassemble" the joint distribution form starting from the right-hand side using the definition of conditional probability, giving

$$p(A_2 | A_1) p(A_1) = p(A_1, A_2)$$
$$p(A_3 | A_2, A_1) p(A_2, A_1) = p(A_1, A_2, A_3)$$
$$p(A_4 | A_3, A_2, A_1) p(A_3, A_2, A_1) = p(A_1, A_2, A_3, A_4),$$

and so on.

7.6.1 Simpson's Paradox

Sometimes conditioning on another event actually provides *opposite* results from what would normally be expected. Suppose, for example, a state initiated a pilot job training program for welfare recipients with the goal of improving skill levels to presumably increase the chances of obtaining employment for these individuals. The investigators assign half of the group to the job placement program and leave the other half out as a control group. The results for the full group and a breakdown by sex are provided in Table 7.1.

Looking at the full group, those receiving the job training are somewhat more likely to land employment than those who did not. Yet when we look at these same people divided into men and women, the results are the opposite! Now

Table 7.1. ILLUSTRATION OF SIMPSON'S PARADOX: JOB TRAINING

		Job	No Job	Placement Rate
Full Group, $n = 400$	Training	100	100	50%
	No Training	80	120	40%
Men, $n = 200$	Training	90	60	60%
	No Training	35	15	70%
Women, $n = 200$	Training	10	40	20%
	No Training	45	105	30%

it appears that it is better not to participate in the job training program for both sexes. This surprising result is called **Simpson's Paradox**.

How can something that is good for the full group be bad for all of the component subgroups? A necessary condition for this paradox to arise is for Training and Job to be correlated with each other, *and* Male to be correlated with both Training and Job. So more men received job training and more men got jobs. In other words, treatment (placement in the program) is confounded with sex. Therefore the full group analysis "masks" the effect of the treatment by aggregating the confounding effect out. This is also called **aggregation bias** because the average of the group averages is not the average of the full population.

We can also analyze this using the conditional probability version of the Total Probability Theorem. Label the events J for a job, T for training, and M for male. Looking at the table it is easy to observe that the $p(J|T) = 0.5$ since a total of 200 individuals got the training and 100 acquired jobs. Does this comport with the conditioning variable?

$$p(J|T) = p(J|M \cap T)p(M|T) + p(J|M^{\complement} \cap T)p(M^{\complement}|T)$$

$$= (0.6)\left(\frac{90 + 60}{100 + 100}\right) + (0.2)\left(\frac{10 + 40}{100 + 100}\right)$$

$$= 0.5.$$

Thus the explanation for why $p(J|T) > p(J|T^{\complement})$ but $p(J|M \cap T) < p(J|M \cap T^{\complement})$ and $p(J|M^{\complement} \cap T) < p(J|M^{\complement} \cap T^{\complement})$ is the unequal weighting between men and women.

7.7 Independence

In the last section we found that certain events will change the probability of other events and that we are advised to use the conditional probability statement as a way of updating information about a probability of interest. Suppose that the first event does *not* change the probability of the second event. For example, if we observe that someone drives a blue car, it does not change the probability that they will vote for the Republican candidate in the next election. Conversely, if we knew that this person voted for the Republican candidate in the last election, we would certainly want to update our unconditional probability.

So how do we treat the first case when it does not change the subsequent probability of interest? If all we are interested in is the probability of voting Republican in the next election, then it is obviously reasonable to ignore the information about car color and continue to use whatever probability we had originally assigned. But suppose we are interested in the probability that an individual votes Republican (event A) *and* owns a blue car (event B)? This joint probability is just the product of the unconditional probabilities and we say that A and B are **independent** if

$$p(A \cap B) = p(A)p(B).$$

So the subject's probability of voting for the Republican and driving a blue car is just the probability that she votes for the Republican times the probability that she owns a blue car. Put another way, the intersection occurs by chance, not by some dependent process.

The idea of independence can be generalized to more than two events. A set of events $A_1, A_2, \ldots, A_k$ is **pairwise independent** if

$$p(A_i \cap A_j) = p(A_i)p(A_j) \quad \forall i \neq j.$$

This means that if we pick any two events out of the set, they are independent of each other. Pairwise independence does *mean* the same thing as general independence, though it is a property now attached to the pairing operation. As an example, Romano and Siegel (1986) give the following three events for two tosses of a fair coin:

- **Event A:** Heads appears on the first toss.
- **Event B:** Heads appears on the second toss.
- **Event C:** Exactly one heads appears in the two tosses.

It is clear that each event here has probability of $\frac{1}{2}$. Also we can ascertain that they are each pairwise independent:

$$p(A \cap B) = \frac{1}{4} = p(A)p(B) = \left(\frac{1}{2}\right)\left(\frac{1}{2}\right)$$

$$p(B \cap C) = \frac{1}{4} = p(B)p(C) = \left(\frac{1}{2}\right)\left(\frac{1}{2}\right)$$

$$p(A \cap C) = \frac{1}{4} = p(A)p(C) = \left(\frac{1}{2}\right)\left(\frac{1}{2}\right),$$

but they are not independent as a group because

$$p(A \cap B \cap C) = 0 \neq p(A)p(B)p(C) = \frac{1}{8}.$$

So independence is a property that changes with group constituency. In addition, independence can be conditional on a third event.

Events A and B are **conditionally independent** on event C:

$$p(A \cap B|C) = p(A|C)p(B|C).$$

Returning to the example above, A and B are not conditionally independent either if the condition is C because

$$p(A \cap B|C) = 0,$$

but

$$p(A|C) = \frac{1}{2}, \qquad p(B|C) = \frac{1}{2},$$

and their product is clearly not zero.

An important theorem states that if A and B are independent, then functions of A and B operating on the same domain are also independent. As an example, suppose we can generate random (equally likely) integers from 1 to 20 (usually done on computers). Define A as the event that a prime number occurs except the prime number 2:

$$p(A) = p(x \in \{1, 3, 5, 7, 11, 13, 17, 19\}) = \frac{8}{20},$$

and B as the event that the number is greater than 10:

$$p(B) = p(x > 10) = \frac{10}{20}.$$

Since there are 4 odd primes above and below 10, A and B are independent:

$$p(A \cap B) = \frac{4}{20} = p(A)p(B) = \frac{8}{20}\frac{1}{2}.$$

For example, use the simple functions $p(g(A)) = p(A^C) = \frac{12}{20}$ and $p(h(B)) = p(B^C) = \frac{1}{2}$. Then $\frac{12}{20} \times \frac{1}{2} = \frac{3}{10} = p(g(A) \cap (h(B)))$.

★ **Example 7.14:** **Analyzing Politics with Decision Trees.** Another way of looking at conditional probabilities is with game or decision trees (depending on the specific application). Bueno de Mesquita, Newman, and Rabushka (1985) suggested this method for forecasting political events and applied it to the test case of Hong Kong's reversal to China (PRC). The decision tree in Figure 7.4 shows the possible decisions and results for a third party's decision to support either the challenger or the government in an election, given that they have ruled out doing nothing. Suppose we were trying to anticipate the behavior of this party and the resulting impact on the election (presumably the support of this party matters).

Hypothetical probabilities of each event at the nodes are given in the figure. For instance, the probability that the challenger wins is 0.03 and the probability that the challenger loses is 0.97, *after the third party has already*

Fig. 7.4. MARGINAL CONTRIBUTION OF THIRD PARTIES

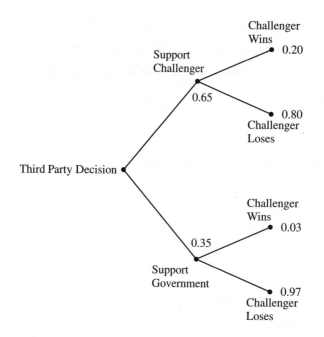

thrown its support behind the government. Correspondingly, the probability that challenger wins is 0.20 and the probability that the challenger loses is 0.80, *after the third party has already thrown its support behind the challenger.* So these are conditional probabilities exactly as we have studied before but now show diagrammatically. In standard notation these are

$$p(C|SC) = 0.20 \qquad\qquad p(G|SC) = 0.80$$

$$p(C|SG) = 0.03 \qquad\qquad p(G|SG) = 0.97,$$

where we denote C as challenger wins, G as government wins, SG for the third party supports the government, and SC for the third party supports the challenger. As an analyst of future Hong Kong elections, one might be estimating the probability of either action on the part of the third party, and these are given here as $p(SC) = 0.65$ and $p(SG) = 0.35$. In other words, our study indicates that this party is somewhat more inclined to support the opposition. So what does this mean for predicting the eventual outcome?

We have to multiply the probability of getting to the first node of interest times the probability of getting to the outcome of interest, and we have to do this for the entire tree to get the full picture.

Looking at the first (top) path of the tree, the probability that the challenger wins when the third party supports them is $(0.20)(0.65) = 0.13$. Conceptually we can rewrite this in the form $p(C|SC)p(SC)$, and we know that this is really $p(C, SC) = p(C|SC)p(SC)$ from the definition of conditional probability on page 312. So the probabilities at the nodes in the tree figure are only "local" in the sense that they correspond to events that can happen at that geographic point only since they assume that the tree has been traversed already to that point. This makes a nice point about conditional probability. As we condition on events we are literally walking down a tree of possibilities, and it is easy to see that such trees can be much wider (more decisions at each node) and much deeper (more steps to the final event of interest).

7.8 Odds

Sometimes probability statements are reexpressed as **odds**. In some academic fields this is routine and researchers view these to be more intuitive than standard probability statements. To simplify for the moment, consider a sample space with only two outcomes: success and failure. These can be defined for any social event we like: wars, marriages, group formations, crimes, and so on. Defining the probability of success as $p = p(S)$ and the probability of failure as $q = 1 - p = p(F)$, the odds of success are

$$\text{odds}(S) = \frac{p}{q}.$$

Notice that while the probability metric is confined to $[0\!:\!1]$, odds are positive but unbounded. Often times odds are given as integer comparisons: "The odds of success are 3 to 2" and notated $3 : 2$, and if it is convenient, making the second number 1 is particularly intuitive. Converting probabilities to odds does not lose any information and probability information can be recovered. For instance, with only two events, if the odds are $3:2$, then $p(S) = \frac{3}{5}$ and $p(F) = \frac{2}{5}$. More generally, if $odds(S) = \alpha:\beta$, then the two probabilities are

$$p(S) = \frac{\alpha}{\alpha + \beta} \qquad p(F) = \frac{\beta}{\alpha + \beta}.$$

These calculations are more involved but essentially the same for more than two possible outcomes.

★ **Example 7.15:   Parental Involvement for Black Grandmothers**. Pearson et al. (1990) researched the notion that black grandparents, typically grandmothers, living in the same household are more active in parenting their grandchildren than their white counterparts. The authors were concerned with testing differences in extended family systems and the roles that members play in child rearing. They obtained data on 130 black families where the grandmother lived in the house and with reported levels of direct parenting for the grandchildren.

Three dichotomous (yes/no) effects were of direct interest here. *Supportive behavior* was defined as reading bedtime stories, playing games, or doing a pleasant outing with the child. This was the main variable of interest to the researchers. The first supporting variable was *punishment behavior*, which was whether or not the grandmother punished the child on misbehavior. The second supporting variable was *controlling behavior*, which meant that the grandmother established the rules of behavior for the child.

Pearson et al. looked at a wide range of explanations for differing levels of grandmother involvement, but the two most interesting findings related to these variables. Grandmothers who took the punishment behavior role versus not taking on this role had an odds ratio of $2.99:1$ for exhibiting supportive behavior. Furthermore, grandmothers who took the controlling behavior role versus not doing so had an odds ratio of $5.38:1$ for exhibiting supportive behavior. Therefore authoritarian behavior strongly predicts positive parenting interactions.

7.9 New Terminology

aggregation bias, 316

Bayes Law, 315

Binomial Theorem, 289

Borel-field, 307

cardinality, 294

complement, 298

conditional probability, 312

conditionally independent, 318

countable set, 293

difference operator, 298

disjoint, 302

elements, 292

empty set, 295

event, 292

finite set, 293

Fundamental Theorem of Counting, 286

independent, 317

intersection, 297

Kolmogorov probability axioms, 308

multiplication rule, 315

mutually exclusive, 302

null set, 295

odds, 321

objective probability, 285

ordered, with replacement, 287

ordered, without replacement, 287

pairwise disjoint, 302

pairwise independent, 317

partition, 302

Pascal's Triangle, 290

probability function, 307

proper subset, 295

sample space, 292

set, 291

sigma-algebra, 307

sigma-field, 307

Simpson's Paradox, 316

singleton, 295

subjective probability, 285

subset, 295

symmetric difference, 298

Theorem of Total Probability, 309

triple, 308

union, 296

unordered, with replacement, 289

unordered, without replacement, 288

Venn diagram, 299

Exercises

7.1 A fair coin is tossed 20 times and produces 20 heads. What is the probability that it will give a tails on the 21st try?

7.2 At the end of a legislative session there is time to vote on only three more bills. Pending there are 12 bills total: 6 on foreign policy, 4 on judicial affairs, and 2 on energy policy. Given equally likely selection, what is the probability that

- exactly one foreign policy bill will receive a vote?
- all three votes will be on foreign policy?
- one of each type will receive a vote?
- no judicial affairs bills will receive a vote?

7.3 Prove that $\binom{n}{k} = \binom{n-1}{k} + \binom{n-1}{k-1}$.

7.4 Develop two more rows to the Pascal's Triangle given on page 290 and show that the "magic 11" property holds.

7.5 Suppose you had a pair of four-sided dice (they exist), so the set of possible outcomes from summing the results from a single toss is $\{2, 3, 4, 5, 6, 7, 8\}$. Determine the probability of each of these outcomes.

7.6 For some set A, explain $A \cup A$ and $A \cap A$.

7.7 Prove de Morgan's Laws for two sets A and B.

7.8 The probability that marriage A lasts 20 years is 0.4, the probability that marriage B lasts 20 years is 0.25, and the probability that marriage C lasts 20 years is 0.8. Under the assumption of independence, calculate the probability that they all last 20 years, the probability that none of them last 20 years, and the probability that at least one lasts 20 years.

7.9 If $(D|H) = 0.5$, $p(D) = 1$, and $p(H) = 0.1$, what is the probability that H is true given D?

7.10 In rolling two dice labeled X and Y, what is the probability that the sum of the up faces is four, given that either X or Y shows a three.

7.11 Show that the Theorem of Total Probability also works when either of the two sets is the null set.

7.12 You are trying to form a coalition cabinet from the six major Italian political parties (given by just initials here). There are three senior members of DC, five senior members of the PCI, four senior members of PSI, two senior members of PSDI, five senior members of PRI, and three senior members of PLI, all vying for positions in the cabinet. How many ways could you choose a cabinet composed of two from each party?

7.13 If events A and B are independent, prove that A^C and B^C are also independent. Can you say that A and A^C are independent? Show your logic.

7.14 Suppose we roll a single die three times. What is the probability of:

(a) three sixes?

(b) exactly one six?

(c) the sum of the three rolls is 4?

(d) the sum of the three rolls is a prime number?

7.15 Use this joint probability distribution

		X		
		0	1	2
	0	0.10	0.10	0.01
Y	1	0.02	0.10	0.20
	2	0.30	0.10	0.07

to compute the following:

(a) $p(X < 2)$.

(b) $p(X < 2 | Y < 2)$.

(c) $p(Y = 2 | X \leq 1)$.

(d) $p(X = 1 | Y = 1)$.

(e) $p(Y > 0 | X > 0)$.

7.16   Al and George want to have a "town hall" style debate. There are only 100 undecided voters in the entire country from which to choose an audience. If they want 90 of these people, how many different sets of 90 can be chosen (unordered, without replacement)?

7.17   Someone claims they can identify four different brands of beer by taste. An experiment is set up (off campus of course) to test her ability in which she is given each of the four beers one at a time without labels or any visual identification.

  (a) How many different ways can the four beers be presented to her one at a time?

  (b) What is the probability that she will correctly identify all four brands simply by guessing?

  (c) What is the probability that she will incorrectly identify only one beer simply by guessing (assume she does not duplicate an answer)?

  (d) Is the event that she correctly identifies the second beer disjoint with the event that she incorrectly identifies the fourth beer?

7.18   A company has just placed an order with a supplier for two different products. Let

    E = the event that the first product is out of stock

    F = the event that the second product is out of stock

  Suppose that $p(E) = 0.3, p(F) = 0.2$, and the probability that at least one is out of stock is 0.4.

  (a) What is the probability that both are out of stock?

  (b) Are E and F independent events?

(c) Given that the first product is in stock, what is the probability that the second is also?

7.19 Suppose your professor of political theory put 17 books on reserve in the library. Of these, 9 were written by Greek philosophers and the rest were written by German philosophers. You have already read all of the Greeks, but none of the Germans, and you have to ask for the books one at a time. Assuming you left the syllabus at home, and you have to ask for the books at random (equally likely) by call letters:

(a) What is the probability that you have to ask for at least three books before getting a German philosopher?

(b) What is the highest possible number of times you would have to ask for a book before receiving a German philosopher?

7.20 Suppose you first flipped a quarter, then flipped a dime, and then flipped a nickel.

(a) What is the probability of getting a heads on the nickel *given* you get tails on the quarter and heads on the dime?

(b) Are the events getting a tails on the quarter and getting a tails on the nickel disjoint?

(c) Are the events getting a tails on the dime and a heads on the dime independent?

7.21 In a given town, 40% of the voters are Democrats and 60% are Republican. The president's budget is supported by 50% of the Democrats and 90% of the Republicans. If a randomly (equally likely) selected voter is found to support the president's budget, what is the probability that they are a Democrat?

7.22 At Cafe Med on Telegraph Avenue, 60% of the customers prefer regular coffee and 40% prefer decaffeinated.

(a) Among 10 randomly (equally likely) selected customers, what is the probability that at most 8 prefer regular coffee?

(b) Cafe Med is about to close and only has 7 cups of regular left but plenty of decaffeinated. What is the probability that all 10 remaining customers get their preference?

7.23   Assume that 2% of the population of the United States are members of some extremist militia group, $(p(M) = 0.02)$, a fact that some members might not readily admit to an interviewer. We develop a survey that is 95% accurate on positive classification, $p(C|M) = 0.95$, and 97% accurate on negative classification, $p(C^C|M^C) = 0.97$. Using Bayes' Law, derive the probability that someone positively classified by the survey as being a militia member really is a militia member. (Hint: Draw a Venn diagram to get $p(C)$ and think about the Theorem of Total Probability).

7.24   Suppose we have two urns containing marbles. The first urn contains 6 red marbles and 4 green marbles, and the second urn contains 9 red marbles and 1 green marble. Take one marble from the first urn (without looking at it) and put it in the second urn. Then take one marble from the second urn (again without looking at it) and put it in the first urn. What is the probability of now drawing a red marble from the first urn?

7.25   Corsi (1981) examined political terrorism, responses to terrorist acts, and the counter-response of the terrorists for 1970 to 1974. For the type of events where a target is seized and held at an unknown site (like kidnapping) he found that 55.6% ($n = 35$) of the time the government involved capitulated. Given that this happened, 2.9% of the time the terrorists increased their demands, 91.4% of the time there was no change in these demands, and 5.7% of the time contact is lost. Of these three events, the number of times that there was known to be no damage or death was 1, 31, and 1, respectively. Construct a tree diagram that contains the conditional probabilities at each level.

7.26   Suppose there are three possible outcomes for an experiment: A, B, and C. If the odds of A over B are $9:1$ and the odds of B over C are $3:2$, what are the probabilities of the three events?

8

Random Variables

8.1 Objectives

This chapter describes the means by which we label and treat known and unknown values. Basically there are two types of observable data, and the abstract terminology for yet-to-be observed values should also reflect this distinction. We first talk here about the levels of measurement for observed values where the primary distinction is discrete versus continuous. We will then see that the probability functions used to describe the distribution of such variables preserves this distinction. Many of the topics here lead to the use of statistical analysis in the social sciences.

8.2 Levels of Measurement

It is important to classify data by the precision of measurement. Usually in the social sciences this is an inflexible condition because many times we must take data "as is" from some collecting source. The key distinction is between **discrete data**, which take on a set of categorical values, and **continuous data**, which take on values over the real number line (or some bounded subset of it). The difference can be subtle. While discreteness requires *countability*, it can be infinitely countable, such as the set of positive integers. In contrast, a continuous random variable takes on uncountably infinite values, even if only in some range of the real number line, like $[0:1]$, because any interval of the real line, finitely bounded or otherwise, contains an infinite number of rational and irrational numbers.

To see why this is an uncountably infinite set, consider any two points on the real number line. It is always possible to find a third point between them. Now consider finding a point that lies between the first point and this new point; another easy task. Clearly we can continue this process infinitely and can therefore never fully count the number of values between any two points on the real number line.

It is customary to divide levels of measurement into four types, the first two of which are discrete and the second two of which are either continuous or discrete. Stevens (1946, 1951) introduced the following (now standard) language to describe the four differing measurement precisions for observed data.

Nominal. Nominal data are purely categorical in that there is no logical way to order a set of events. The classic example is religions of the world: Without specifying some additional criteria (such as age, origin, or number of adherents) there is no nonnormative way to rank them. A synonym for nominal is **polychotomous**, and sometimes just "categorical" is used as well, but this latter term can be confusing in this context because there are two types of categorical data types. In addition, dichotomous (yes/no, on/off, etc.) data are also considered nominal, because with two outcomes ordering does not change any interpretive value. Examples of nominal data include

- male/female
- war/peace
- regions of the U.S.
- political parties
- football jersey numbers
- telephone numbers.

Ordinal. Ordinal data are categorical (discrete) like nominal data, but with the key distinction that they can be ranked (i.e., ordered). While we could treat ordinal data as if they were just nominal, both are discrete, we would be ignoring important qualitative information about how to relate categories. Examples include

- seniority in Congress (it is naive to treat years in office more literally);
- lower/middle/upper socio-economic class;
- Likert scales (agree/no opinion/disagree, and other variants);
- Guttman scale (survey respondents are presented with increasingly hard-to-agree-with statements until they disagree);
- levels of democratization.

Often ordinal data are the result, not of directly measured data, but artificial indices created by researchers to measure some latent characteristic. For instance, sociologists are sometimes concerned with measuring tolerance within societies. This may be tolerance of different races, cultures, languages, sexual orientations, or professions. Unfortunately it is not possible to measure such underlying attitudes directly either by observation or a single survey query. So it is common to ask a multitude of questions and combine the resulting information into an index: multi-item measures from accumulating scores to create a composite variable. Political scientists do this to a slightly lesser extent when they are concerned with levels of freedom, volatility, political sophistication, ideology, and other multifaceted phenomenon.

Interval. The key distinction between interval data and ordinal data is that interval data have equal spacing between ordered values. That is, the difference between 1 and 2 is exactly the difference between 1001 and 1002. In this way the ordering of interval data has a higher level of measurement, allowing more precise comparisons of values. Consider alternatively the idea of measuring partisanship in the U.S. electorate from a survey. It may or may not be the case that the difference between **somewhat conservative** and **conservative** is the same as the distance between **conservative** and **extremely conservative**. Therefore it would incorrect, in general, to treat this as interval data.

Interval data can be discrete or continuous, but if they are measured on the real number line, they are obviously continuous. Examples of interval measured data include

- temperature measured in Fahrenheit or Celsius;
- a "feeling thermometer" from 0 to 100 that measures how survey respondents feel about political figures;
- size of legislature (it does not exist when $n = 0$);
- time in years (0 AD is a construct).

Ratio. Ratio measurement is exactly like interval measurement except that the point at zero is "meaningful." There is nothing in the definition of interval measure that asserts that zero (if even included in the set of possible values) is really an indicator of a true lack of effect. For example, Fahrenheit and Celsius both have totally arbitrary zero points. Zero Fahrenheit is attributed to the coldest level that the Dutch scientist Daniel Fahrenheit could make a water and salt solution in his lab (he set 100 degrees as his own measured body temperature at that same time). Zero Celsius was established a bit more scientifically by the Swedish astronomer Anders Celsius as the point where water alone freezes (and, as is generally known, 100 degrees Celsius is the point where water boils). While the zero point in both cases has some physical basis, the choice of water and salt is completely arbitrary. Suppose we were to meet developed creatures from Jupiter. It is likely that their similarly constructed scales would be based on ammonia, given the dominant chemical content of the Jovian atmosphere. So what does this limitation to interval measure mean for these two scales? It means that **ratios** are meaningless: 80 degrees is not twice as hot as 40 degrees (either scale) because the reference point of true zero does not exist. Is there a measure of temperature that is ratio? Fortunately, yes; zero degrees Kelvin is the point at which all molecular motion in matter stops. It is an absolute zero because there can be no lower temperature.

Ratio measurement is useful specifically because it does allow direct *ratio* comparison. That is, 10 Kelvin is twice as "warm" as 5 Kelvin. More relevant examples include

- appropriations
- votes
- crime rates
- war deaths
- unemployment
- group membership.

Ratio measurement, like interval measurement, can be either discrete or continuous. There is also a subtle distinction between interval and ratio measurement that sometimes gets ignored. Previously the example of the size of a legislature was given as interval rather than ratio. Although zero has some meaning in this context, a legislature with zero members does not exist as a legislature and this then voids the utility of the zero point so that it has no practical meaning.

Notice that the scale of measurement here is ascending in precision (and actually in desirability as well). This direction is easy to remember with the mnemonic NOIR, as the French word for the color black. Any level of measurement, except nominal, can always be reduced to a lower one simply by ignoring some information. This makes sense at times when the defining characteristic is suspicious or perhaps measured poorly.

8.3 Distribution Functions

Distribution functions are central in statistical and probabilistic analyses. They provide a description of how we believe that some data-generating process is operating. Since all models are simplifications of reality, probability statements are really just rough simplifications of the way things actually work. Nobody believes that events like wars, marriages, or suicides occur for underlying *mathematical* reasons. Yet, we can learn a lot about natural, social, and political phenomenon by fitting a parsimonious description based on probability statements.

What do we mean by the word **random** here? We will shortly review a formal and rigorous definition, but it helps to first think intuitively about the meaning. Everyone is accustomed to the idea that some events are more likely to occur than others. We are more likely to eat lunch today than to win the lottery; it is more likely to rain on a given Glasgow winter day than to be sunny; the stock market is more likely to rise on good economic news than to fall. The key idea here is the expression of *relative difference* between the likelihood of events. Probability formalizes this notion by standardizing such comparisons to exist between zero and one inclusive, where zero means the event will absolutely not occur and one means that the event will certainly occur.† Every other assignment of probability represents some measure of uncertainty and is between these two extreme values, where higher values imply a greater likelihood of occurrence. So probability is no more than a conventional standard for comparisons that we all readily make.

★ **Example 8.1:** **Measuring Ideology in the American Electorate**. As a simple example, consider a question from the 2002 American National Election Study that asks respondents to identify their ideology on a seven-point scale that covers extremely liberal, liberal, slightly liberal, moderate, slightly conservative, conservative, and extremely conservative. A total of 1245 in the survey placed themselves on this scale (or a similar one that was merged), and we will assume for the moment that it can be treated as an interval measure. Figure 8.1 shows a histogram of the ideology placements in the first panel. This histogram clearly demonstrates the multimodality of the ideology placements with three modes at liberal, moderate, and conservative.

The second panel of Figure 8.1 is a "smoothed" version of the histogram, called a *density plot*. The y-axis is now rescaled because the area under this curve is normalized to integrate to one. The point of this density plot is to estimate an underlying probability structure that supposedly governs the placement of ideology. The key point is that we do not really believe that a mathematical law of some sort determines political ideology, but hopefully

† There is actually a subtlety here. Impossible events have probability zero and exceedingly, exceedingly unlikely events also have probability zero for various reasons. The same logic exists for probability one events. For our purposes these distinctions are not important, however.

Fig. 8.1. SELF-IDENTIFIED IDEOLOGY, ANES 2002

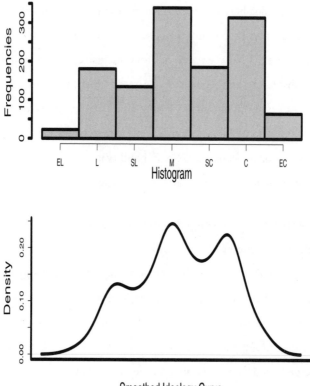

by constructing this density plot we have captured an accurate probabilistic description of the underlying structure that determines the observed phenomenon. So a probability function can be taken as a description of the long-run relative frequencies.

There is actually an old simmering controversy behind the interpretation of these probability functions. One group, who are called "frequentists," believe that probability statements constitute a long-run likelihood of occurrence for specific events. Specifically, they believe that these are objective, permanent statements about the likelihood of certain events relative to the likelihood of other events. The other group, who are usually termed "Bayesians" or "subjectivists," believe that all probability statements are inherently subjective in the sense that they constitute a certain "degree of belief" on the part of the person making the probability statement. More literally, this last interpretation constitutes the odds with which one would be willing to place a bet with his or her own money. There are strong arguments for both perspectives, but to a great degree this discussion is more philosophical than practical.

8.3.1 Randomness and Variables

Randomness does not actually mean what many (nonconcerned) people think that it means. Colloquially "random" is synonymous with equally likely outcomes, and that is how we explicitly treated randomness in part of the last chapter. So it may be common to describe the experiment of rolling a single fair die as random because each of the six sides are equally likely. But think about how restrictive this definition would be if that was the only type of uncertainty allowed: All countries are equally likely to go to war, all eligible citizens in a given country are equally likely to vote in the next election, every surveyed household is equally likely to be below the poverty level.

What randomness really means is that the outcome of some experiment (broadly defined) is not *deterministic*: guaranteed to produce a certain outcome. So, as soon as the probability for some described event slips below one or above zero, it is a random occurrence. Thus if the probability of getting a jackpot on some slot machine is 0.001 for a given pull of the handle, then it is still a random event.

Random variables describe unoccurred events abstractly for pedagogical purposes. That is, it is often convenient to describe the results of an experiment *before it has actually occurred*. In this way we may state that the outcome of a coin flip is designated as X. So for a fair coin we can now say that the probability that X is going to be a heads on the next flip is 0.5.

Formally, a random variable, often denoted with a capital Latin letter such as X or Y, is a function that maps the sample space on which it is "created" to a subset of the real number line (including possibly the whole real number line itself). So we now have a new sample space that corresponds not to the physical experiment performed but to the possible outcomes of the random variable itself. For example, suppose our experiment is to flip a coin 10 times ($n = 10$). The random variable X is defined to be the number of heads in these 10 tosses. Therefore, the sample space of a single iteration of the experiment is $\{H, T\}$, and the sample space of X is $\{0, 1, 2, \ldots, 10\}$.

Random variables provide the connection between events and probabilities because they give the abstraction necessary for talking about uncertain and unobserved events. Sometimes this is as easy as mapping a probability function to a set of discrete outcomes in the sample space of the random variable. To continue the example, we can calculate (more details below) the probability that X takes on each possible value in the sample space determined by 10 flips of a fair coin:

X	0	1	2	3	4
$p(X)$	0.0010	0.0098	0.0439	0.1172	0.2051
X	5	6	7	8	9	10
$p(X)$	0.2461	0.2051	0.1172	0.0439	0.0098	0.0010

Here each possible event for the random variable X, from 0 heads to 10 heads, is paired with a specific probability value. These probability values necessarily sum to unity because one of the 11 values *must* occur.

8.3.2 Probability Mass Functions

When the state space is discrete, we can assign probability values to each single event, even if the state space is countably infinite (discrete with an infinite number of distinct outcomes). So, for example, in the case of flipping a possibly unfair coin, we can assign a probability to heads, $p(H)$, and therefore a complementary probability to tails, $p(T)$.

The essence of a **probability mass function** is that it assigns probabilities to each unique event, such that the Kolmogorov Axioms still apply. It is common to abbreviate the expression "probability mass function" with "PMF" as a shorthand. We denote such PMF statements

$$f(x) = p(X = x),$$

meaning that the PMF $f(x)$ is a function which assigns a probability for the random variable X equaling the specific numerical outcome x. This notation often confuses people on introduction because of the capital and lower case notation for the same letter. It is important to remember that X is a random variable that can take on multiple discrete values, whereas x denotes a hypothetical single value. Customarily, the more interesting versions of this statement insert actual values for x. So, for instance, the coin-flipping statements above are more accurately given as:

$$p(X = H) = 1 - p(X = T).$$

Notice that in this setup the coin need not be "fair" in the sense that the probability expression accommodates weighted versions such as $p(X = H) = 0.7$ and $p(X = T) = 0.3$.

8.3.3 Bernoulli Trials

The coin-flipping example above is actually much more general than it first appears. Suppose we are studying various political or social phenomenon such as whether a coup occurs, whether someone votes, cabinet dissolution or continuation, whether a new person joins some social group, if a bill passes or fails, and so on. These can all be modeled as **Bernoulli outcomes** whereby the occurrence of the event is assigned the value "1," denoting success, and the nonoccurrence of the event is assigned the value "0," denoting failure. Success and failure can be an odd choice of words when we are talking about coups or wars or other undesirable events, but this vocabulary is inherited from statistics and is quite well entrenched.

The basic premise behind the **Bernoulli PMF** is that the value one occurs with probability p and the value zero occurs with probability $1 - p$. Thus these outcomes form a partition of the sample space and are complementary. If x denotes the occurrence of the event of interest, then

$$p(x) = p \quad \text{and} \quad p(x^{\complement}) = 1 - p.$$

So it is natural to want to estimate p given some observations. There are many ways to do this, but the most direct is to take an average of the events (this process actually has substantial theoretical support, besides being quite simple). So if we flip a coin 10 times and get 7 heads, then a reasonable estimate of p is 0.7.

8.3.4 Binomial Experiments

The **binomial PMF** is an extension to the Bernoulli PMF whereby we simultaneously analyze multiple Bernoulli trials. This is historically called an experiment because it was originally applied to controlled tests. The random variable is no longer binary but instead is the sum of the observed binary Bernoulli events and is thus a count: $Y = \sum_{i=1}^{n} X_i$. A complication to this Bernoulli extension is figuring out how to keep track of all of the possible sets of results leading to a particular sum.

To make things easy to start with, suppose we are studying three senior legislators who may or may not be retiring at the end of the current term. We believe that there is an underlying shared probability p governing their independent decisions and denote the event of retiring with R. We thus have a number of events E dictated by the three individual values and their ordering, which produce a sum bounded by zero (no retirements) and three (all retirements). These events are given in the first column of Table 8.1 with their respective sums in the second column.

Table 8.1. BINOMIAL OUTCOMES AND PROBABILITIES

E	Y	$p(Y = y)$	
$\{R^C, R^C, R^C\}$	0	$(1-p)(1-p)(1-p)$	$p^0(1-p)^{3-0}$
$\{R, R^C, R^C\}$	1	$(p)(1-p)(1-p)$	$p^1(1-p)^{3-1}$
$\{R^C, R, R^C\}$	1	$(1-p)(p)(1-p)$	$p^1(1-p)^{3-1}$
$\{R^C, R^C, R\}$	1	$(1-p)(1-p)(p)$	$p^1(1-p)^{3-1}$
$\{R, R, R^C\}$	2	$(p)(p)(1-p)$	$p^2(1-p)^{3-2}$
$\{R, R^C, R\}$	2	$(p)(1-p)(p)$	$p^2(1-p)^{3-2}$
$\{R^C, R, R\}$	2	$(1-p)(p)(p)$	$p^2(1-p)^{3-2}$
$\{R, R, R\}$	3	$(p)(p)(p)$	$p^3(1-p)^{3-3}$

The third column of Table 8.1 gives the probabilities for each of these events, which is simply rewritten in the fourth column to show the structure relating Y and the number of trials, 3. Since the retirement decisions are assumed independent, we can simply multiply the underlying individual probabilities according the definition given on page 317 in Chapter 7 to get the joint probability of occurrence. If we lump these together by the term Y, it is easy to see that there is one way to get zero retirements with probability $(1-p)^3$, three ways to get one retirement with probability $p(1-p)^2$, three ways to get to two retirements with probability $p^2(1-p)$, and one way to get three retirements with probability p^3. Recalling that this is really choosing by unordered selection without replacement (page 288), we can note that the ways to get each of these events is given by the expression $\binom{3}{y}$.

There is also a clear pattern to binomial distribution probabilities. The outcome that receives the highest probability is the one that corresponds to $n \times p$ (more on this calculation below), and probabilities slope down in both directions from this modal point. A particularly elegant picture results from experiments with so-called "fair" probabilities. Suppose we flip such a fair coin 10 times. What is the full probability outcome for the number of heads? We can obviously make these calculations in exactly the same way that was done in the example above. If such probabilities were then graphed with a barplot, the result would look like Figure 8.2.

This is really useful because we can now state the binomial PMF for this particular "experiment" for the sum of retirement events:

$$p(Y = y) = \binom{3}{y} p^y (1 - p)^{3-y},$$

which has the more general form for n Bernoulli trials:

$$p(Y = y | n, p) = \binom{n}{y} p^y (1 - p)^{n-y}, \quad n \geq y, \ n, y \in \mathcal{I}^+, \ p \in [0{:}1].$$

We can denote this general form or any specific case with the shorthand $\mathcal{B}(n, p)$. So in this way we define a general form for the binomial PMF and a mechanism for specifying specific cases, that is, $\mathcal{B}(10, 5)$, $\mathcal{B}(100, 75)$, and so on.

★ **Example 8.2:** **Binomial Analysis of Bill Passage.** Suppose we know that a given legislature has a 0.7 probability of passing routine bills (perhaps from historical analysis). If 10 routine bills are introduced in a given week, what is the probability that:

(i) Exactly 5 bills pass? We can simply plug three values into the binomial

Fig. 8.2. EXAMPLE BINOMIAL PROBABILITIES

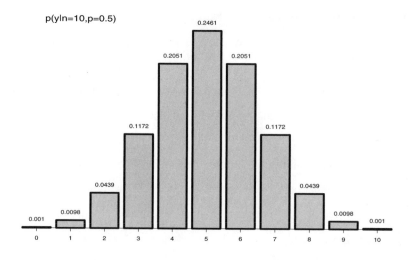

p(y|n=10,p=0.5)

PMF for this question:

$$p(Y = 5|n = 10, p = 0.7) = \binom{10}{5}(0.7)^5(1 - 0.7)^{10-5}$$

$$= (252)(0.16807)(0.00243) = 0.10292.$$

(ii) Less than three bills pass? The most direct method is to add up the three probabilities associated with zero, one, and two occurrences:

$$p(Y < 3|10, 0.7) = p(Y = 0|10, 0.7) + p(Y = 1|10, 0.7)$$
$$+ p(Y = 2|10, 0.7)$$

$$= \binom{10}{0}(0.7)^0(1 - 0.7)^{10-0} + \binom{10}{1}(0.7)^1(1 - 0.7)^{10-1}$$

$$+ \binom{10}{2}(0.7)^2(1 - 0.7)^{10-2}$$

$$= 0.0000059049 + 0.000137781 + 0.001446701 = 0.00159.$$

(iii) Nine or less bills pass? The obvious, but time-consuming way to answer this question is the way the last answer was produced, by summing up all (nine here) applicable individual binomial probabilities. However, recall that because this binomial PMF is a probability function, the sum of the probability of all possible events must be one. So this suggests the following trick:

$$p(Y \le 9|10, 0.7) = \sum_{i=1}^{9} p(Y = i|10, 0.7)$$

$$= \sum_{i=1}^{10} p(Y = i|10, 0.7) - p(Y = 10|10, 0.7)$$

$$= 1 - p(Y = 10|10, 0.7)$$

$$= 1 - \binom{10}{10} (0.7)^{10} (1 - 0.7)^{10-10}$$

$$= 1 - 0.02825 = 0.97175.$$

8.3.5 Poisson Counts

Suppose that instead of counting the number of successes out of a fixed number of trials, we were concerned with the number of events (which can still be considered successes, if one likes) without an upper bound. That is, we might consider the number of wars on a continent, the number of alliances between protest groups, or the number of cases heard by a court. While there may be some practical upper limit imposed by the number of hours in day, these sorts of events are usually counted as if there is no upper bound because the number of attempts is unknown a priori. Another way of thinking of such count data is in terms of durations: the length of time waiting for some prescribed event. If the probability of the event is proportional to the length of the wait, then the length of wait can be modeled with the **Poisson PMF**. This discrete distributional form is given by

$$p(y|\lambda) = \frac{e^{-\lambda} \lambda^y}{y!}, \quad y \in I^+, \ \lambda \in \mathfrak{R}^+.$$

The assumption of proportionality is usually quite reasonable because over longer periods of time the event has more "opportunities" to occur. Here the single PMF parameter λ is called the intensity parameter and gives the expected number of events. This parametric form is very useful but contains one limiting feature: λ is also assumed to be the dispersion (variance, defined on page 366) of the number of events.

★ **Example 8.3:** **Poisson Counts of Supreme Court Decisions.** Recent Supreme Courts have handed down roughly 8 unanimous decisions per term. If we assume that $\lambda = 8$ for the next Court, then what is the probability of observing:

(i) Exactly 6 decisions? Plugging these values into the Poisson PMF gives

$$p(Y = 6|\lambda = 8) = \frac{e^{-8}8^6}{6!} = 0.12214.$$

(ii) Less than three decisions? Here we can use a sum of three events:

$$p(Y < 3|\lambda = 8) = \sum_{i=0}^{2} \frac{e^{-8}8^{y_i}}{y_i!}$$

$$= 0.00034 + 0.00268 + 0.01073 = 0.01375.$$

(iii) Greater than 2 decisions? The easiest way to get this probability is with the following "trick" using the quantity from above:

$$p(Y > 2|\lambda = 8) = 1 - p(Y < 3|\lambda = 8)$$

$$= 1 - 0.01375 = 0.98625.$$

The Poisson distribution is quite commonly applied to events in international systems because of the discrete nature of many studied events. The two examples that follow are typical of simple applications. To directly apply the Poisson distribution two assumptions are required:

- Events in different time periods are independent.
- For small time periods, the probability of an event is proportional to the length of time passed in the period so far, and not dependent on the number of previous events in this period.

These are actually not as restrictive as it might appear. The first condition says that rates of occurrence in one time period are not allowed to influence subsequent rates in another. So if we are measuring conflicts, the outset of a widespread war will certainly influence the number of actual battles in the next period, and this thus obviates the continued use of the same Poisson parameterization as was used prior to the war. The second condition means that time matters in the sense that, for some bounded slice of time, as the waiting time increases, the probability of the event increases. This is intuitive; if we are counting arrivals at a traffic light, then it is reasonable to expect more arrivals as the recording period is extended.

★ **Example 8.4:** **Modeling Nineteenth-Century European Alliances.** McGowan and Rood (1975) looked at the frequency of alliance formation from 1814 to 1914 in Europe between the "Great Powers:" Austria-Hungary, France, Great Britain, Prussia-Germany, and Russia. They found 55 alliances during this period that targeted behavior within Europe between these powers and argued that the observed pattern of occurrence follows the Poisson distribution. The mean number of alliances per year total is 0.545, which they used as their empirical estimate of the Poisson parameter, $\lambda = 0.545$. If we use this value in the Poisson PMF, we can compare observed events against predicted events:

Alliances/Year	$y = 0$	$y = 1$	$y = 2$	$y \geq 3$
Observed	61	31	6	3
Predicted	58.6	31.9	8.7	1.8

This seems to fit the data reasonably well in terms of prediction. It is important to recall that $\lambda = 0.545$ is the intensity parameter for *five* countries to enter into alliances, so assuming that each country is equally likely, the intensity parameter for an individual country is $\lambda_i = 0.545/5 = 0.109$.

★ **Example 8.5:** **Poisson Process Model of Wars.** Houweling and Kuné (1984) looked at wars as discrete events in a paper appropriately titled "Do

Outbreaks of War Follow a Poisson-Process?" They compared 224 events of international and civil wars from 1816 to 1980 to that predicted by estimating the Poisson intensity parameter with the empirical mean: $\lambda = 1.35758$. Evidence from Figure 8.3 indicates that the Poisson assumption fits the data quite nicely (although the authors quibbled about the level of statistical significance).

Fig. 8.3. POISSON PROBABILITIES OF WAR

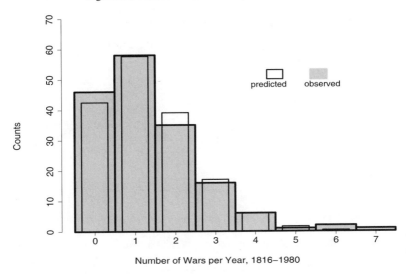

Interestingly, the authors found that the Poisson assumption fits less well when the wars were disaggregated by region. The events in the Western Hemisphere continue to fit, while those in Europe, the Middle East, and Asia deviate from the expected pattern. They attribute this latter effect to not meeting the second condition above.

8.3.6 The Cumulative Distribution Function: Discrete Version

If X is a discrete random variable, then we can define the sum of the probability mass to the left of some point $X = x$: the mass associated with values less than X. Thus the function

$$F(x) = p(X \leq x)$$

defines the **cumulative distribution function** (CDF) for the random variable X. A couple of points about notation are worth mentioning here. First, note that the function uses a capital "F" rather than the lower case notation given for the PMF. Sometimes the CDF notation is given with a random variable subscript, $F_X(x)$, to remind us that this function corresponds to the random variable X.

If the values that X can take on are indexed by order: $x_1 < x_2 < \cdots < x_n$, then the CDF can be calculated with a sum for the chosen point x_j:

$$F(x_j) = \sum_{i=1}^{j} p(x_i).$$

That is, $F(x_j)$ is the sum of the probability mass for events less than or equal to x_j. Using this definition of the random variable, it follows that

$$F(x < x_1) = 0 \quad \text{and} \quad F(x \geq x_n) = 1.$$

Therefore, CDF values are bounded by $[0:1]$ under all circumstances, even if the random variable is not indexed in this convenient fashion. In fact, we can now state technically the three defining properties of a CDF:

- **[Cumulative Distribution Function Definition.]** $F(x)$ is a CDF for the random variable X iff it has the following properties:

  - **bounds:** $\lim_{x \to -\infty} F(x) = 0$ and $\lim_{x \to +\infty} F(x) = 1$,
  - **nondecreasing:** $F(x_i) \leq F(x_j)$ for $x_i < x_j$,
  - **right-continuous:** $\lim_{x \downarrow x_i} F(x) = x_i$ for all x_i defined by $f(x)$.

The idea of a **right-continuous function** is best understood with an illustration. Suppose we have a binomial experiment with $n = 3$ trials and $p = 0.5$. Therefore the sample space is $S = \{0, 1, 2, 3\}$, and the probabilities associated with each event are $[0.125, 0.375, 0.375, 0.125]$. The graph of $F(x)$ is given in Figure 8.4, where the discontinuities reflect the discrete nature of a binomial random variable. The solid circles on the left-hand side of each interval emphasize that this value at the integer belongs to that CDF level, and the lack of such a circle on the right-hand side denotes otherwise. The function is right-continuous because for each value of x_i ($i = 0, 1, 2, 3$) the limit of the function reaches x_i moving from the right. The arrows pointing left and right at 0 and 1, respectively, are just a reminder that the CDF is defined towards negative and positive infinity at these values. Note also that while the values are cumulative, the jumps between each level correspond to the PMF values $f(x_i)$, $i = 0, 1, 2, 3$.

Fig. 8.4. BINOMIAL CDF PROBABILITIES, $n = 3, p = 0.5$

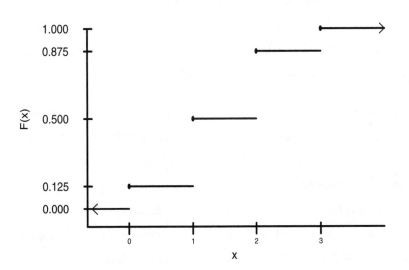

It is important to know that a CDF fully defines a probability function, as does a PMF. Since we can readily switch between the two by noting the step sizes (CDF→PMF) or by sequentially summing (PMF→CDF), then the one we use is completely a matter of convenience.

8.3.7 Probability Density Functions

So far the random variables have only taken on discrete values. Clearly it would be a very limiting restriction if random variables that are defined over some interval of the real number line (or even the entire real number line) were excluded. Unfortunately, the interpretation of probability functions for continuous random variables is a bit more complicated.

As an example, consider a spinner sitting flat on a table. We can measure the direction of the spinner relative to some reference point in radians, which vary from 0 to 2π (Chapter 2). How many outcomes are possible? The answer is infinity because the spinner can theoretically take on any value on the real number line in $[0:2\pi]$. In reality, the number of outcomes is limited to our measuring instrument, which is by definition discrete. Nonetheless, it is important to treat continuous random variables in an appropriate manner.

For continuous random variables we replace the probability mass function with the **probability density function** (PDF). Like the PMF, the PDF assigns probabilities to events in the sample space, but because there is an infinite number of alternatives, we cannot say $p(X = x)$ and so just use $f(x)$ to denote the function value at x. The problem lies in questions such as, if we survey a large population, what is the probability that the average income were $65,123.97? Such an event is sufficiently rare that its probability is essentially zero. It goes to zero as a measurement moves toward being truly continuous (money in dollars and cents is still discrete, although granular enough to be treated as continuous in most circumstances). This seems ultimately frustrating, but the solution lies in the ability to replace probabilities of specific events with probabilities of ranges of events. So instead with our survey example we may ask questions such as, what is the probability that the average income amongst respondents is greater than $65,000?

Fig. 8.5. EXPONENTIAL PDF FORMS

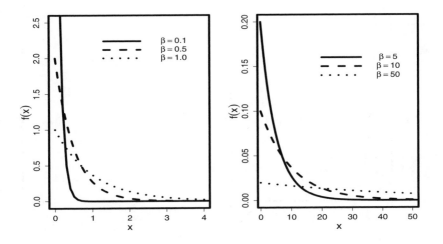

8.3.8 Exponential and Gamma PDFs

The **exponential PDF** is a very general and useful functional form that is often used to model durations (how long "things last"). It is given by

$$f(x|\beta) = \frac{1}{\beta} \exp[-x/\beta], \quad 0 \le x < \infty, \quad 0 < \beta,$$

where, similar to the Poisson PMF, the function parameter (β here) is the mean or expected duration. One reason for the extensive use of this PDF is that it can be used to model a wide range of forms. Figure 8.5 gives six different parameterizations in two frames. Note the broad range of spread of the distribution evidenced by the different axes in the two frames. For this reason β is called a **scale parameter**: It affects the scale (extent) of the main density region.

Although we have praised the exponential distribution for being flexible, it is still a special case of the even more flexible **gamma PDF**. The gamma distribution adds a **shape parameter** that changes the "peakedness" of the distribution: how sharply the density falls from a modal value. The gamma PDF is given by

$$f(x|\alpha, \beta) = \frac{1}{\Gamma(\alpha)\beta^\alpha} x^{\alpha-1} \exp[-x/\beta], \quad 0 \le x < \infty, \quad 0 < \alpha, \beta,$$

Fig. 8.6. GAMMA PDF FORMS

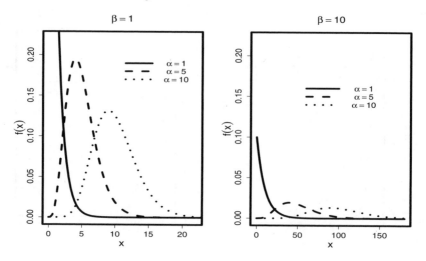

where α is the new shape parameter, and the mean is now $\alpha\beta$. Note the use of the gamma function (hence the name of this PDF). Figure 8.6 shows different forms based on varying the α and β parameters where the y-axis is fixed across the two frames to show a contrast in effects.

An important special case of the gamma PDF is the χ^2 distribution, which is used in many statistical tests, including the analysis of tables. The χ^2 distribution is a gamma where $\alpha = \frac{df}{2}$ and $\beta = 2$, and df is a positive integer value called the **degrees of freedom**.

★ **Example 8.6:   Characterizing Income Distributions**. The gamma distribution is particularly well suited to describing data that have a mode near zero and a long right (positive) skew. It turns out that income data fit this description quite closely. Pareto (1897) first noticed that income in societies, no matter what kind of society, follows this pattern, and this effect is sometimes called **Pareto's Law**. Subsequent studies showed that the gamma distribution could be easily tailored to describe a range of income distributions.

Salem and Mount (1974) looked at family income in the United States from 1960 to 1969 using survey data from the Current Population Report

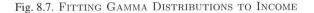

Fig. 8.7. FITTING GAMMA DISTRIBUTIONS TO INCOME

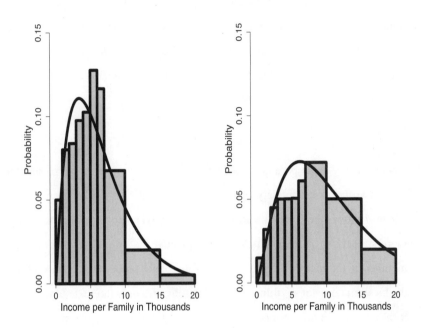

Series (CPS) published by the Census Bureau and fit gamma distributions to categories. Figure 8.7 shows histograms for 1960 and 1969 where the gamma distributions are fit according to

$$f_{1960}(income) = \mathcal{G}(2.06, 3.2418) \quad \text{and}$$
$$f_{1969}(income) = \mathcal{G}(2.43, 4.3454)$$

(note: Salem and Mount's table contains a typo for β_{1969}, and this is clearly the correct value given here, as evidenced from their graph and the associated fit).

The unequal size categories are used by the authors to ensure equal numbers of sample values in each bin. It is clear from these fits that the gamma distribution can approximately represent the types of empirical forms that income data takes.

8.3.9 Normal PDF

By far the most famous probability distribution is the **normal PDF**, some-times also called the **Gaussian PDF** in honor of its "discoverer," the German mathematician Carl Friedrich Gauss. In fact, until replacement with the Euro currency on January 1, 2002, the German 10 Mark note showed a plot of the normal distribution and gave the mathematical form

$$f(x|\mu, \sigma^2) = \frac{1}{\sqrt{2\pi\sigma^2}} \exp\left[-\frac{1}{2\sigma^2}(x-\mu)^2\right], \qquad -\infty < x, \mu < \infty, 0 < \sigma^2,$$

where μ is the mean parameter and σ^2 is the dispersion (variance) parameter. These two terms completely define the shape of the particular normal form where μ moves the modal position along the x-axis, and σ^2 makes the shape more spread out as it increases. Consequently, the normal distribution is a member of the **location-scale family** of distributions because μ moves only the location (and not anything else) and σ^2 changes only the scale (and not the location of the center or modal point). Figure 8.8 shows the effect of varying these two parameters individually in two panels.

Fig. 8.8. NORMAL PDF FORMS

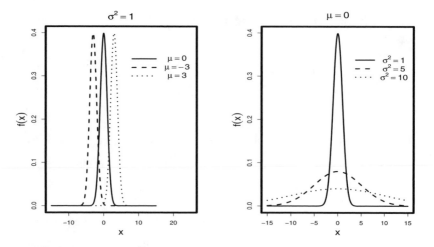

The reference figure in both panels of Figure 8.8 is a normal distribution with

$\mu = 0$ and $\sigma^2 = 1$. This is called a **standard normal** and is of great practical as well as theoretical significance. The PDF for the standard normal simplifies to

$$f(x) = \frac{1}{\sqrt{2\pi}} \exp\left[-\frac{1}{2}x^2\right], \qquad -\infty < x < \infty.$$

The primary reason that this is an important form is that, due to the location-scale characteristic, any other normal distribution can be transformed to a standard normal and then back again to its original form. As a quick example, suppose $x \sim \mathcal{N}(\mu, \sigma^2)$; then $y = (x - \mu)/\sigma^2 \sim \mathcal{N}(0, 1)$. We can then return to x by substituting $x = y\sigma^2 + \mu$. Practically, what this means is that textbooks need only include one normal table (the standard normal) for calculating tail values (i.e., integrals extending from some point out to infinity), because all other normal forms can be transformed to the standard normal in this way.

One additional note relates to the normal distribution. There are quite a few other common distributions that produce unimodal symmetric forms that appear similar to the normal. Some of these, however, have quite different mathematical properties and thus should not be confused with the normal. For this reason it is not only lazy terminology, but it is also very confusing to refer to a distribution as "bell-shaped."

★ **Example 8.7:** **Levels of Women Serving in U.S. State Legislatures.** Much has been made in American politics about the role of women in high level government positions (particularly due to "the year of the woman" in 1992). The first panel of Figure 8.9 shows a histogram of the percent of women in legislatures for the 50 states with a normal distribution ($\mu = 21, \sigma = 8$) superimposed (source: Center for American Women and Politics).

The obvious question is whether the data can be considered normally distributed. The normal curve appears to match well the distribution given in the histogram. The problem with relying on this analysis is that the shape of a histogram is greatly affected by the number of bins selected. Consequently,

Fig. 8.9. FITTING THE NORMAL TO LEGISLATIVE PARTICIPATION

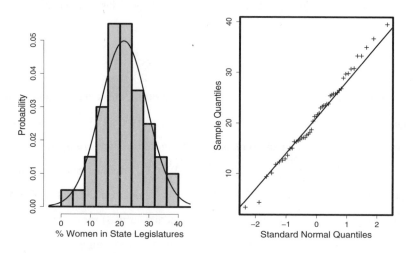

the second panel of Figure 8.9 is a "qqplot" that plots the data against standard normal quantiles (a set of ordered values from the standard normal PDF of length equal to the evaluated vector). The closer the data points are to the line, the closer they are to being normally distributed. We can see here that the fit is quite close with just a little bit of deviation in the tails. Asserting that these data are actually normal is useful in that it allows us to describe typical or atypical cases more precisely, and perhaps to make predictive claims about future legislatures.

8.3.10 The Cumulative Distribution Function: Continuous Version

If X is a continuous random variable, then we can also define the sum of the probability mass to the left of some point $X = x$: the density associated with all values less than X. Thus the function

$$F(x) = p(X \leq x) = \int_{-\infty}^{x} f(x)dx$$

defines the cumulative distribution function (CDF) for the continuous random variable X. Even though this CDF is given with an integral rather than a sum, it retains the three key defining properties, see page 308. The difference is that instead of being a step function (as shown in Figure 8.4), it is a smooth curve monotonically nondecreasing from zero to one.

★ **Example 8.8:** **The Standard Normal CDF: Probit Analysis.** The CDF of the standard normal is often abbreviated $\Phi(X)$ for $\mathcal{N}(X \leq x|\mu = 0, \sigma^2 = 1)$ (the associated PDF notation is $\phi(X)$). One application that occurs in empirical models is the idea that while people may make dichotomous choices (vote/not vote, purchase/not purchase, etc.), the underlying mechanism of decision is really a smooth, continuous preference or utility function that describes more subtle thinking. If one event (usually the positive/action choice) is labeled as "1" and the opposite event as "0," and if there is some interval measured variable X that affects the choice, then $\Phi(X) = p(X = 1)$ is called the **probit model.** In the basic formulation higher levels of X are assumed to push the subject toward the "1" decision, and lower levels of X are assumed to push the subject toward the "0" decision (although the opposite effect can easily be modeled as well).

Fig. 8.10. Probit Models for Partisan Vote Choice

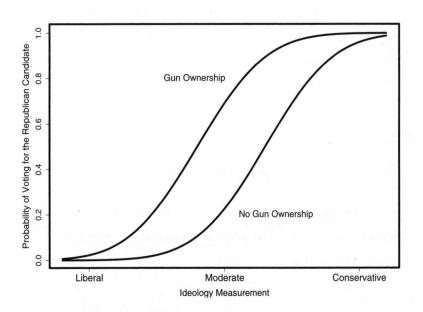

To give a concrete example, consider the dichotomous choice outcome of voting for a Republican congressional candidate against an interval measured explanatory variable for political ideology. One certainly would not be surprised to observe that more conservative individuals tend to vote Republican and more liberal individuals tend not to vote Republican. We also obtain a second variable indicating whether the respondent owns a gun. A simple probit model is specified for these data with no directly indicated interaction term:

$$p(Y_i = 1) = \Phi(IDEOLOGY_i + GUN_i).$$

Here $IDEOLOGY_i$ is the political ideology value for individual i, GUN_i is a dichotomous variable equaling one for gun ownership and zero otherwise (it is common to weight these two values in such models, but we can skip it here without losing the general point). This model is depicted in Figure 8.10 where gun owners and nongun owners are separated. Figure 8.10 shows that gun ownership shifts the curve affecting the probability of voting for the Republican candidate by making it more likely at more liberal levels of ideology. Also, for very liberal and very conservative respondents, gun ownership does not really affect the probability of voting for the Republican. Yet for respondents without a strong ideological orientation, gun ownership matters considerably: a difference of about 50% at the center.

8.3.11 The Uniform Distributions

There is an interesting distributional form that accommodates both discrete and continuous assumptions. The **uniform distribution** is a perfectly flat form that can be specified in either manner:

k-Category Discrete Case (PMF):

$$p(Y = y|k) = \begin{cases} \frac{1}{k}, & \text{for } y = 1, 2, \ldots, k \\ 0, & \text{otherwise;} \end{cases}$$

Continuous Case (PDF):

$$f(y|a, b) = \begin{cases} \frac{1}{b-a}, & \text{for } a \leq y \leq b \\ 0, & \text{otherwise.} \end{cases}$$

The discrete case specifies k outcomes (hence the conditioning on k in $p(Y = y|k)$) that can be given any range desired (obviously greater ranges make $\frac{1}{k}$ smaller for fixed k), and the continuous case just gives the bounds (a and b), which are often zero and one. So the point is that each outcome has equal individual probability (PMF) or equal density (PDF). This distribution is sometimes used to reflect great uncertainty about outcomes (although it is definitely saying something specific about the probability of events). The continuous case with $a = 0$ and $b = 1$ is particularly useful in modeling probabilities.

★ **Example 8.9: Entropy and the Uniform Distribution.** Suppose we wanted to identify a particular voter by serial information on this person's characteristics. We are allowed to ask a consecutive set of yes/no questions (i.e., like the common guessing game). As we get answers to our series of questions we gradually converge (hopefully, depending on our skill) on the desired voter. Our first question is, does the voter reside in California? Since about 13% of voters in the United States reside in California, a yes answer gives us different information than a no answer. Restated, a yes answer reduces our uncertainty more than a no answer because a yes answer eliminates 87% of the choices whereas a no answer eliminates 13%. If P_i is the probability of the ith event (residing in California), then the improvement in information as defined by Shannon (1948) is defined as

$$I_{P_i} = \log_2\left[\frac{1}{P_i}\right] = -\log_2 P_i.$$

The probability is placed in the denominator here because the smaller the probability, the greater the investigative information supplied by a yes answer. The log function is required to obtain some desired properties (discussed below) and is justified by various limit theorems. The logarithm is base-2 because there are only two possible answers to our question (yes and no), making the units of information bits. In this example,

$$H_i = -\log_2(0.13) = 2.943416$$

bits, whereas if we had asked, does the voter live in the state of Arkansas? then an affirmative reply would have increased our information by

$$H_i = -\log_2(0.02) = 5.643856$$

bits, or about twice as much. However, there is a much smaller probability that we would have gotten an affirmative reply had the question been asked about Arkansas. What Slater (1939) found, and Shannon (1948) later refined, was the idea that the "value" of the question was the information returned by a positive response times the probability of a positive response. So if the value of the ith binary-response question is

$$H_i = f_i \log_2 \left[\frac{1}{f_i} \right] = -f_i \log_2 f_i,$$

then the value of a series of n of these questions is

$$\sum_{i=1}^{n} H_i = k \sum_{i=1}^{n} f_i \log_2 \left[\frac{1}{f_i} \right] = -k \sum_{i=1}^{n} f_i \log_2 f_i,$$

where f_i is the frequency distribution of the ith yes answer and k is an arbitrary scaling factor that determines choice of units. This is called the **Shannon entropy** or **information entropy** form. The arbitrary scaling factor here makes the choice of base in the logarithm unimportant because we can change this base by manipulating the constant. For instance, if this form were expressed in terms of the natural log, but $\log_2$ was more appropriate for the application (such as above), then setting $k = \frac{1}{\ln 2}$ converts the entropy form to base 2.

We can see that the total improvement in information is the additive value of the series of individual information improvements. So in our simple example we might ask a series of questions narrowing down on the individual of interest. Is the voter in California? Is the voter registered as a Democrat? Does the voter reside in an urban area? Is the voter female? The total information supplied by this vector of yes/no responses is the total information improvement in units of bits because the response space is binary. Its important to remember that the information obtained is defined only with regard to a well-defined question having finite, enumerated responses

The uniform prior distribution as applied provides the greatest entropy because no single event is more likely to occur than any others:

$$H = -\sum \frac{1}{n} \ln\left(\frac{1}{n}\right) = \ln(n),$$

and entropy here increases logarithmically with the number of these equally likely alternatives. Thus the uniform distribution of events is said to provide the minimum information possible with which to decode the message. This application of the uniform distribution does not imply that this is a "no information" assumption because equally likely outcomes are certainly a type of information. A great deal of controversy and discussion has focused around the erroneous treatment of the uniform distribution as a zero-based information source. Conversely, if there is certainty about the result, then a degenerate distribution describes the m_i, and the message does not change our information level:

$$H = -\sum_{i=1}^{n-1}(0) - \log(1) = 0.$$

8.4 Measures of Central Tendency: Mean, Median, and Mode

The first and most useful step in summarizing observed data values is determining its **central tendency**: a measure of where the "middle" of the data resides on some scale. Interestingly, there is more than one definition of what constitutes the center of the distribution of the data, the so-called average. The most obvious and common choice for the average is the mean. For n data points $x_1, x_2, \ldots, x_n$, the mean is

$$\bar{x} = \frac{1}{n} \sum_{i=1}^{n} x_i,$$

where the bar notation is universal for denoting a mean average. The mean average is commonly called just the "average," although this is a poor convention in the social sciences because we use other averages as well.

The median average has a different characteristic; it is the point such that as many cases are greater as are less: For n data points $x_1, x_2, \ldots, x_n$, the median is X_i such that $i = \lceil n/2 \rceil$ (even n) or $i = \frac{n+1}{2}$ (odd n). This definition suits an odd size to the dataset better than an even size, but in the latter case we just split the difference and define a median point that is halfway between the two central values. More formally, the median is defined as

$$M_x = X_i: \int_{-\infty}^{x_i} f_x(X) dx = \int_{x_i}^{\infty} f_x(X) = \frac{1}{2}.$$

Here $f_x(X)$ denotes the **empirical distribution** of the data, that is, the distribution observed rather than that obtained from some underlying mathematical function generating it (see Chapter 7).

The mode average has a totally different flavor. The mode is the most frequently observed value. Since all observed data are countable, and therefore discrete, this definition is workable for data that are actually continuously measured. This occurs because even truly continuous data generation processes, which should be treated as such, are measured or observed with finite instruments. The mode is formally given by the following:

$$m_x = X_i: n(X_i) > n(X_j) \; \forall j \neq i,$$

where the notation "$n()$" means "number of" values equal to the X stipulated in the cardinality sense (page 294).

★ **Example 8.10:   Employment by Race in Federal Agencies**. Table 8.2 gives the percent of employment across major U.S. government agencies by four racial groups. Scanning down the columns it is clear that there is a great deal of similarity across agencies, yet there exist some interesting dissimilarities as well.

Table 8.2. PERCENT EMPLOYMENT BY RACE, 1998

Agency	Black	Hispanic	Asian	White
Agriculture	10.6	5.6	2.4	81.4
Commerce	18.3	3.4	5.2	73.1
DOD	14.2	6.2	5.4	74.3
Army	15.3	5.9	3.7	75.0
Navy	13.4	4.3	9.8	72.6
Air Force	10.6	9.5	3.1	76.8
Education	36.3	4.7	3.3	55.7
Energy	11.5	5.2	3.8	79.5
EOP	24.2	2.4	4.2	69.3
HHS	16.7	2.9	5.1	75.4
HUD	34.0	6.7	3.2	56.1
Interior	5.5	4.3	1.6	88.6
Justice	16.2	12.2	2.8	68.9
Labor	24.3	6.6	2.9	66.5
State	14.9	4.2	3.7	77.1
Transportation	11.2	4.7	2.9	81.2
Treasury	21.7	8.4	3.3	66.4
VA	22.0	6.0	6.7	65.4
GSA	28.4	5.0	3.4	63.2
NASA	10.5	4.6	4.9	80.1
EEOC	48.2	10.6	2.7	38.5

Source: Office of Personnel Management

The mean values by racial group are $\bar{X}_{Black} = 19.43$, $\bar{X}_{Hispanic} = 5.88$, $\bar{X}_{Asian} = 4.00$, and $\bar{X}_{White} = 70.72$. The median values differ somewhat: $M_{Black} = 16.2$, $M_{Hispanic} = 5.2$, $M_{Asian} = 3.4$, and $M_{White} = 73.1$. Cases where the mean and median differ noticeably are where the data are skewed (asymmetric) with the longer "tail" in the direction of the mean. For example, the white group is negatively skewed (also called left-skewed) because the mean is noticeably less than the median.

These data do not have a modal value in unrounded form, but we can look at modality through a **stem and leaf plot**, which groups data values by leading digits and looks like a histogram that is turned on its side. Unlike a histogram, though, the bar "heights" contain information in the form of the lower digit values. For these data we have the following four stem and leaf plots (with rounding):

Black:

The decimal point is 1 digit to the right of the |

```
0|6
1|111123455678
2|2244
2|8
3|4
3|6
4|
4|8
```

Hispanic:

The decimal point is at the |

```
 2|49
 3|4
 4|233677
 5|0269
 6|0267
 7|
 8|4
 9|5
10|6
11|
12|2
```

Asian:

The decimal point is at the |

```
1|6
2|47899
3|12334778
4|29
5|124
6|7
7|
8|
9|8
```

White:

The decimal point is 1 digit to the right of the |

```
3|9
4|
5|66
6|356799
7|3345577
8|00119
```

Due to the level of measurement and the relatively small number of agency cases (21), we do not have an exact modal value. Nonetheless, the stem and leaf plot shows that values tend to clump along a single modal region in each case. For instance, if we were to round the Asian values to integers (although this would lose information), then the mode would clearly be 2%.

One way to consider the utility of the three different averages is to evaluate their resistance to large outliers. The **breakdown bound** is the proportion of data values that can become unbounded (go to plus or minus infinity) before the statistic of interest becomes unbounded itself. The mean has a breakdown bound of 0 because even one value of infinity will take the sum to infinity. The median is much more resistant because almost half the values on either side can become unbounded before the median itself goes to infinity. In fact, it is customary to give the median a breakdown bound of 0.5 because as the data size increases, the breakdown bound approaches this value. The mode is much more difficult to analyze in this manner as it depends on the relative placement of values. It is possible for a high proportion of the values to become unbounded provided a higher proportion of the data is concentrated at some other point. If these points are more spread out, however, the infinity point may become the mode and thus the breakdown bound lowers. Due to this uncertainty, the mode cannot be given a definitive breakdown bound value.

8.5 Measures of Dispersion: Variance, Standard Deviation, and MAD

The second most important and common data summary technique is calculating a measure of spread, how dispersed are the data around a central position? Often a measure of centrality and a measure of spread are all that are necessary to give researchers a very good, general view of the behavior of the data. This is particularly true if we know something else, such as that the data are unimodal and symmetric. Even when we do not have such complementary information, it is tremendously useful to know how widely spread the data points are around some center.

The most useful and common measure of dispersion is the **variance**. For n data points $x_1, x_2, \ldots, x_n$, the variance is given by

$$\mathrm{Var}(X) = \frac{1}{n-1} \sum_{i=1}^{n} (x_i - \bar{x})^2.$$

The preceding fraction, $\frac{1}{n-1}$, is slightly surprising given the more intuitive $\frac{1}{n}$ for the mean. It turns out that without the -1 component the statistic is **biased**: not quite right on average for the true underlying population quantity. A second closely related quantity is the **standard deviation**, which is simply the square root of the variance:

$$SD(X) = \sqrt{\mathrm{Var}(X)} = \sqrt{\frac{1}{n-1} \sum_{i=1}^{n} (x_i - \bar{x})^2}.$$

Since the variance and the standard deviation give the same information, the choice of which one to use is often a matter of taste. There are times, however, when particular theoretical discussions need to use one form over the other.

A very different measure of dispersion is the **median absolute deviation** (MAD). This is given by the form

$$MAD(X) = median(|x_i - median(x)|),$$

for $i = 1, 2, \ldots, n$. That is, the MAD is the median of the absolute deviations from the data median. Why is this useful? Recall our discussion of resistance. The variance (and therefore the standard deviation) is very sensitive to large outliers, more so even than the mean due to the squaring. Conversely, the MAD obviously uses medians, which, as noted, are far more resistant to atypical values. Unfortunately, there are some differences in the way the MAD is specified. Sometimes a mean is used instead of the innermost median, for instance, and sometimes there is a constant multiplier to give asymptotic properties. This is irritating because it means that authors need to say which version they are providing.

★ **Example 8.11:**   **Employment by Race in Federal Agencies, Continued**. Returning to the values in Table 8.2, we can calculate the three described measures of dispersion for the racial groups. It is important to remember that none of these three measures is necessarily the "correct" view of dispersion in the absolute sense, but rather that they give different views of it.

Table 8.3. MEASURES OF DISPERSION, RACE IN AGENCIES

	Black	Hispanic	Asian	White
variance	107.20	6.18	3.16	122.63
standard deviation	10.35	2.49	1.78	11.07
MAD	5.60	1.00	0.60	6.60

8.6 Correlation and Covariance

A key question in evaluating data is to what extent two variables vary together. We expect income and education to vary in the same direction: Higher levels of one are associated with higher levels of the other. That is, if we look at a particular case with a high level of education, we expect to see a high income. Note the use of the word "expect" here, meaning that we are allowing for cases to occur in opposition to our notion without necessarily totally disregarding the general idea. Of course, if a great many cases did not reflect the theory, we would be inclined to dispense with it.

Covariance is a measure of variance with two paired variables. Positive values mean that there is positive varying effect between the two, and negative values mean that there is negative varying effect: High levels of one variable are associated with low levels of another. For two variables of the same length, $x_1, x_2, \ldots, x_n$ and $y_1, y_2, \ldots, y_n$, the covariance is given by

$$\text{Cov}(X, Y) = \frac{1}{n-1} \sum_{i=1}^{n} (x_i - \bar{x})(y_i - \bar{y}).$$

This is very useful because it gives us a way of determining if one variable tends to vary positively or negatively with another. For instance, we would expect income and education levels to vary positively together, and income and prison time to vary negatively together. Furthermore, if there is no relationship between two variables, then it seems reasonable to expect a covariance near zero. But there is one problem with the covariance: We do not have a particular scale for saying what is large and what is small for a given dataset.

What happens if we calculate the covariance of some variable with itself? Let's take $\text{Cov}(X, Y)$ and substitute in $Y = X$:

$$\text{Cov}(X, X) = \frac{1}{n-1} \sum_{i=1}^{n} (x_i - \bar{x})(x_i - \bar{x})$$

$$= \frac{1}{n-1} \sum_{i=1}^{n} (x_i - \bar{x})^2$$

$$= \text{Var}(X).$$

This means that the covariance is a direct generalization of the variance where we have two variables instead of one to consider. Therefore, while we do not generally know the context of the magnitude of the covariance, we can compare it to the magnitude of the variance for X as a reference. So one solution to the covariance scale problem is to measure the covariance in terms of units of the variance of X:

$$\text{Cov}^*(X, Y) = \frac{\frac{1}{n-1} \sum_{i=1}^{n} (x_i - \bar{x})(y_i - \bar{y})}{\frac{1}{n-1} \sum_{i=1}^{n} (x_i - \bar{x})^2}.$$

In this way units of the covariance are expressed in units of the variance that we can readily interpret. This seems unfair to the Y variable as there may not be anything special about X that deserves this treatment. Now instead let us measure the covariance in units of the standard deviation of X and Y:

$$\text{Cov}^{**}(X, Y) = \frac{\frac{1}{n-1} \sum_{i=1}^{n} (x_i - \bar{x})(y_i - \bar{y})}{\sqrt{\frac{1}{n-1} \sum_{i=1}^{n} (x_i - \bar{x})^2} \sqrt{\frac{1}{n-1} \sum_{i=1}^{n} (y_i - \bar{y})^2}}.$$

The reason we use the standard deviation of X and Y in the denominator is it scales this statistic conveniently to be bounded by $[-1 : 1]$. That is, if we re-performed our trick of substituting $Y = X$ (or equivalently $X = Y$), then the statistic would be equal to one. In substantive terms, a value of one means that Y covaries *exactly* as X covaries. On the other hand, if we substituted

$Y = -X$ (or conversely $X = -Y$), then the statistic would be equal to negative one, meaning that Y covaries in exactly the opposite manner as X. Since these are the limits of the ratio, any value inbetween represents lesser degrees of absolute scaled covariance. This statistic is important enough to have a name: It is the **correlation coefficient** between X and Y (more formally, it is *Pearson's Product Moment Correlation Coefficient*), and is usually denoted $cor(X, Y)$ or r_{XY}.

★ **Example 8.12:** **An Ethnoarchaeological Study in the South American Tropical Lowlands.** Siegel (1990) looked at the relationship between the size of buildings and the number of occupants in a South Amerindian tropical-forest community located in the upper Essequibo region of Guyana. In such communities the household is the key structural focus in social, economic, and behavioral terms. The substantive point is that the overall settlement area of the community is a poor indicator of ethnographic context in terms of explaining observed relationships, but other ethnoarchaeological measures are quite useful in this regard. Siegel points out that ethnographic research tends not to provide accurate and useful quantitative data on settlement and building dimensions. Furthermore, understanding present-day spatial relationships in such societies has the potential to add to our understanding in historical archaeological studies.

The main tool employed by Siegel was a correlational analysis between floor area of structures and occupational usage. There are four types of structures: residences, multipurpose work structures, storage areas, and community buildings. In these tribal societies it is common for extended family units to share household space including kitchen and storage areas but to reserve a component of this space for the nuclear family. Thus there is a distinction between *households* that are encompassing structures, and the individual *residences* within. Table 8.4 gives correlation coefficients between the size of the floor area for three definitions of space and the family unit for the village of Shefariymo where **Total** is the sum of **Multipurpose** space, **Residence** space, and **Storage** space.

Table 8.4. CORRELATION COEFFICIENT OF FAMILY UNIT VS. SPACE

Structure Type	Family Unit	Cases	Correlation
Multipurpose	Nuclear	16	0.137
Residence	Nuclear	24	0.662
Total	Nuclear	24	0.714
Multipurpose	Extended	12	0.411
Residence	Extended	11	0.982
Total	Extended	11	0.962

What we see from this analysis is that there exists a positive but weak relationship between the size of the nuclear family and the size of the multi-purpose space (0.137). Conversely, there are relatively strong relationships between the size of these same nuclear families and the size of their residences (0.662) and the total family space (0.714). A similar pattern emerges when looking at the size of the extended families occupying these structures except that the relationships are now noticeably stronger. Not surprisingly, the size of the extended family is almost perfectly correlated with residence size and total size.

8.7 Expected Value

Expected value is essentially a probability-weighted average over possible events. Thus, with a fair coin, there are 5 *expected* heads in 10 flips. This does not mean that 5 heads will necessarily occur, but that we would be inclined to bet on 5 rather than any other number. Interestingly, with real-life interval measured data you *never* get the expected value in a given experiment because the probability of any one point on the real number line is zero.

The discrete form of the expected value of some random variable X is

$$E[X] = \sum_{i=1}^{k} X_i p(X_i),$$

for k possible events in the discrete sample space $\{X_1, X_2, \ldots, X_k\}$. The continuous form is exactly the same except that instead of summing we need to integrate:

$$E[X] = \int_{-\infty}^{\infty} X p(X) dX,$$

where the integral limits are adjusted if the range is restricted for this random variable, and these are often left off the integral form if these bounds are obvious. Intuitively, this is easier to understand initially for the discrete case. Suppose someone offered you a game that consisted of rolling a single die with the following payoffs:

die face	1	2	3	4	5	6
X, in dollars	0	1	1	1	2	2

Would you be inclined to play this game if it costs $2? The expected value of a play is calculated as

$$E[X] = \sum_{i=1}^{6} X_i p(X_i) = \frac{1}{6}(0) + \frac{1}{6}(1) + \frac{1}{6}(1) + \frac{1}{6}(1) + \frac{1}{6}(2) + \frac{1}{6}(2)$$

$$= \$1.67 \text{ (rounded)}.$$

Therefore it would not make sense to pay $2 to play this game! This is exactly how all casinos around the world function: They calculate the expected value of a play for each of the games and make sure that it favors them. This is not to say that any one person cannot beat the casino, but *on average* the casino always comes out ahead.

So far we have just looked at the expected value of X, but it is a simple matter to evaluate the expected value of some *function* of X. The process inserts the function of X into the calculation above instead of X itself. Discrete and continuous forms are given by

$$E[f(X)] = \sum_{i=1}^{k} f(X_i) p(X_i), \qquad E[f(X)] = \int_{-\infty}^{\infty} f(X) p(X) dX.$$

For instance, if we have the function $f(X) = X^2$, then, given a continuous random variable, $E[X^2] = \int X^2 p(X) dX$.

The calculation of expected value for vectors and matrices is only a little bit more complicated because we have to keep track of the dimension. A $k \times 1$ vector $\mathbf{X}$ of discrete random variables has the expected value $E[\mathbf{X}] = \sum \mathbf{X}p(\mathbf{X})$. For the expected value of a function of the continuous random vector it is common to use the *Riemen-Stieltjes integral* form:

$$E[f(\mathbf{X})] = \int f(\mathbf{X})dF(\mathbf{X}),$$

where $F(\mathbf{X})$ denotes the joint distribution of the random variable vector $\mathbf{X}$.

In much statistical work expected value calculations are "conditional" in the sense that the average for the variable of interest is taken conditional on another. For instance, the discrete form for the expected value of Y given a specific level of X is

$$E[Y|X] = \sum_{i=1}^{k} Y_i p(Y_i|X).$$

Sometimes expectations are given subscripts when there are more than one random variables in the expression and it is not obvious to which one the expectation holds:

$$\text{Var}_x[E_y[Y|X]] = \text{Var}_x \left[\sum_{i=1}^{k} Y_i p(Y_i|X) \right]$$

8.8 Some Handy Properties and Rules

Since expectation is a summed quantity, many of these rules are obvious, but some are worth thinking about. Let X, Y, and Z be random variables defined in $\Re$ (the real number line), whose expectations are finite.

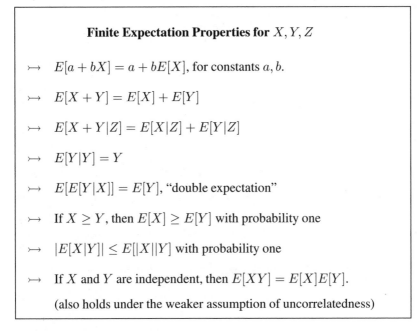

Finite Expectation Properties for X, Y, Z

$\mapsto$ $E[a + bX] = a + bE[X]$, for constants a, b.

$\mapsto$ $E[X + Y] = E[X] + E[Y]$

$\mapsto$ $E[X + Y|Z] = E[X|Z] + E[Y|Z]$

$\mapsto$ $E[Y|Y] = Y$

$\mapsto$ $E[E[Y|X]] = E[Y]$, "double expectation"

$\mapsto$ If $X \geq Y$, then $E[X] \geq E[Y]$ with probability one

$\mapsto$ $|E[X|Y]| \leq E[|X||Y]$ with probability one

$\mapsto$ If X and Y are independent, then $E[XY] = E[X]E[Y]$.

(also holds under the weaker assumption of uncorrelatedness)

The fifth rule, labeled as double expectation, is also called the **law of iterated expectation**, and can be given more generally for functions of Y: $E[E[f(Y)|X]] = E[f(Y)]$. There is also a related set of properties for the variance function:

Finite Variance Properties for X **and** Y

$\mapsto$ Without assuming independence (or uncorrelatedness):
$\text{Cov}[X, Y] = E[XY] - E[X]E[Y]$

$\mapsto$ $\text{Var}[X] = E[X^2] - (E[X])^2$

$\mapsto$ $\text{Var}[X|Y] = E[X^2|Y] - (E[X|Y])^2$

$\mapsto$ $\text{Cov}[X, Y] = \text{Cov}[X, E[Y|X]]$

$\mapsto$ $\text{Var}[Y] = \text{Var}_x[E_y[Y|X]] + E_x[\text{Var}_y[Y|X]]$, "decomposition"

★ **Example 8.13:** **Craps in a Casino.** In this example we review the rules and winning probabilities at the game craps as a way to illustrate expected value. The key principle guiding casino management is that every game has negative expected value to the customer. However, craps has many bets that are very nearly "fair" in that the probability of winning is just below 0.5. This tends to attract the more "sophisticated" gamblers, but of course craps still makes money for the house.

The basic process of a craps game is that one person (the shooter) rolls two dice and people bet on the outcome. The most common bet is a "pass," meaning that the player has an unconditional win if the result is 7 or 11 and an unconditional loss if the result is 2, 3, or 12 (called craps). If the result, however, is 4, 5, 6, 8, 9, or 10, then the outcome is called a "point" and the shooter repeats until either the outcome is repeated (a win) or a 7 appears (a loss).

The probabilities associated with each of the 11 possible sums on any given role are

Result	2	3	4	5	6	7	8	9	10	11	12
Probability	$\frac{1}{36}$	$\frac{2}{36}$	$\frac{3}{36}$	$\frac{4}{36}$	$\frac{5}{36}$	$\frac{6}{36}$	$\frac{5}{36}$	$\frac{4}{36}$	$\frac{3}{36}$	$\frac{2}{36}$	$\frac{1}{36}$

So the probability of winning on the first roll is

$$p(7) + p(11) = \frac{6}{36} + \frac{2}{36} = 0.2222222\ldots,$$

and the probability of losing on the first roll is

$$p(2) + p(3) + p(12) = \frac{1}{36} + \frac{2}{36} + \frac{1}{36} = 0.1111111\ldots.$$

Whereas the probability of winning with the point is slightly more complicated:

$$p(\text{point}) \times p(\text{repeating point before 7})$$

$$= \frac{24}{36} p(\text{repeating point before 7})$$

$$= \frac{24}{36} \Big[p(4 \text{ or } 10 | \text{point}) p(4 \text{ or } 10 \text{ before 7})$$

$$+ p(5 \text{ or } 9 | \text{point}) p(5 \text{ or } 9 \text{ before 7})$$

$$+ p(6 \text{ or } 8 | \text{point}) p(6 \text{ or } 8 \text{ before 7}) \Big]$$

$$= \frac{24}{36} \left[\frac{1}{4} \frac{3/36}{(3+6)/36} + \frac{1}{3} \frac{4/36}{(4+6)/36} + \frac{5}{12} \frac{5/36}{(5+6)/36} \right]$$

$$= 0.270707.$$

This means that the probability of winning including the pass is $0.270707 + 0.2222222 = 0.4929292$. So the expected value of a \$5 bet is the expected winnings minus the cost to play: $10 \times 0.4929292 + 0 \times 0.5070708 - 5 = -0.070708$, meaning about negative seven cents. A player can also play "don't pass bar 12," which is the opposite bet except that 12 is considered a tie (the gamblers bet is returned). The probability of winning on this bet is

$$1 - p(\text{pass}) - \frac{1}{2} p(12) = 1 - 0.4929292 - \frac{1}{2} \left(\frac{1}{36} \right) = 0.4931818,$$

which has for a \$5 bet the expected value $10 \times 0.4931818 - 5 = -0.068182$, which is slightly better than a pass. Two variants are the "come" bet where the player starts a pass bet in the middle of the shooter's sequence, and the "don't come" bet where the player starts a don't pass bar 12 in the middle of the shooter's sequence. Predictably these odds are identical to the pass and don't pass bar 12 bets, respectively. Another common bet is the "field," which bets that a 2, 3, 4, 8, 10, 11, or 12 occurs, with the probability of winning: $p(2) + p(3) + p(4) + p(9) + p(10) + p(11) + p(12) = 0.4444444$, but a 2 or 12 pays double, thereby increasing the total expected value: $1.5p(2) + 1p(3) + 1p(4) + 1p(9) + 1p(10) + 1p(11) + 1.5p(12) = 0.4722222$.

The probability of winning with a "big six" or "big eight" bet (6 or 8 comes up before 7) is $\frac{5/36}{(5+6)/36} = 0.4545454$. It is also possible to bet on a specific value for the next roll, and the house sets differing payoffs according to

Probability	Payoff Odds	Expected Value per 0.50
$p(2) = \frac{1}{36}$	$29 - 1$	$\frac{(29+1)(1)}{2(36)} = 0.4166667$
$p(3) = \frac{2}{36}$	$14 - 1$	$\frac{(14+1)(2)}{2(36)} = 0.4166667$
$p(7) = \frac{6}{36}$	$4 - 1$	$\frac{(4+1)(6)}{2(36)} = 0.4166667$
$p(11) = \frac{2}{36}$	$14 - 1$	$\frac{(14+1)(2)}{2(36)} = 0.4166667$
$p(12) = \frac{1}{36}$	$29 - 1$	$\frac{(29+1)(1)}{2(36)} = 0.4166667$

Obviously these are very poor bets. Another interesting but ill-advised bet is the "hard way," where the player bets that specified doubles occur before the same number in nondoubled form (i.e., the "easy way") or a 7. The associated probabilities are

$$p[(2, 2) \text{ before } 7 \text{ or } (3, 1), (1, 3)] = \left(\frac{1}{9}\right)\frac{7 + 1}{2} = 0.4444444$$

$$p[(3, 3) \text{ before } 7 \text{ or } (4, 2), (2, 4), (5, 1), (1, 5)] = \left(\frac{1}{11}\right)\frac{9 + 1}{2} = 0.4545455$$

$$p[(4, 4) \text{ before } 7 \text{ or } (5, 3), (3, 5), (6, 2), (2, 6)] = \left(\frac{1}{11}\right)\frac{9 + 1}{2} = 0.4545455$$

$$p[(10, 10) \text{ before } 7 \text{ or } (6, 4), (4, 6)] = \left(\frac{1}{9}\right)\frac{7 + 1}{2} = 0.4444444$$

Note that the payouts used above may differ by casino/area/country/etc. Another bet in this category is "any craps," which means betting on the occurrence of 2, 3, or 12. The payoff is $7/1$, so

$$p(2, 3, 12) = \left(\frac{4}{36}\right)\frac{7 + 1}{2} = 0.4444444,$$

and the expected value of a $5 bet is $10 \times 0.4444444 - 5 = -0.55556$.

The really interesting bet is called "odds," which is sometime billed falsely as giving even money to the player. This bet is allowed only during an ongoing pass, don't pass, come, or don't come bet, and the actual bet takes place *during* a point. Sometimes an equal or smaller bet compared to the original bet only is allowed, but some casinos will let you double here. The actual bet is that the point value re-occurs before a 7, and one can also bet the "contrary" bet that it won't (evidence of fairness for the second component of the bet). What does this mean in terms of probabilities and payoffs? The "old" game continues with the same probability of winning that benefits the house (0.4929292), but now a new game begins with new odds and the same rules as the point part of a pass play. A new betting structure starts with the payoffs

4 or 10 before $7 : 2-1$, 5 or 9 before $7 : 1.5-1$, 6 or 8 before $7 : 1.2-1$.

The probabilities of each point value occurring before 7 (recall that you have *one* of these) are

$$p(4\,\text{before}\,7) = \frac{3}{3+6} = \left(\frac{1}{3}\right) \qquad p(10\,\text{before}\,7) = \frac{3}{3+6} = \left(\frac{1}{3}\right)$$

$$p(5\,\text{before}\,7) = \frac{4}{4+6} = \left(\frac{2}{5}\right) \qquad p(9\,\text{before}\,7) = \frac{4}{4+6} = \left(\frac{2}{5}\right)$$

$$p(6\,\text{before}\,7) = \frac{5}{5+6} = \left(\frac{5}{11}\right) \qquad p(8\,\text{before}\,7) = \frac{5}{5+6} = \left(\frac{5}{11}\right).$$

So what are the odds on this new game (betting $1)? They are

$$4, 10 : \quad \left(\frac{1}{3}\right)\left(\frac{2+1}{2}\right) = \frac{1}{2}$$

$$5, 9 : \quad \left(\frac{2}{5}\right)\left(\frac{1.5+1}{2}\right) = \frac{1}{2}$$

$$6, 8 : \quad \left(\frac{5}{11}\right)\left(\frac{1.2+1}{2}\right) = \frac{1}{2}.$$

The house still comes out ahead because you cannot play the even-money game independently, so the total probability is the average of 0.4929292 and 0.5, which is still below 0.5 (weighted by the relative bets). Also, the second half of pass bet when you are on the points has the probabilities $p(4, 5, 6, 8, 9, 10$ before $7) = 0.40606\ldots$ and $p(7$ first$) = 0.59393\ldots$. But apparently most craps players aren't sophisticated enough to use this strategy anyway.

8.9 Inequalities Based on Expected Values

There are a number of "famous" inequalities related to expected values that are sometimes very useful. In all cases X and Y are random variables with expected values that are assumed to exist and are finite. The positive constants k and ℓ are also assumed finite. These assumptions are actually important and the compelling book by Romano and Siegel, *Counterexamples in Probability and Statistics* (1986), gives cases where things can go awry otherwise. A classic reference on just inequalities is *Inequalities* by Hardy, Littlewood, and Polya (1988).

- **Chebychev's Inequality**. If $f(X)$ is a positive and nondecreasing function on $[0, \infty]$, then for all (positive) values of k

$$p(f(X) > k) \leq E[f(X)/k].$$

A more common and useful form of Chebychev's inequality involves μ and σ, the mean and standard deviation of X (see Section 8.5). For k greater than or equal to 1:

$$p(|X - \mu| \geq k\sigma) \leq 1/k^2.$$

To relate these two forms, recall that μ is the expected value of X.

- **Markov Inequality**. Similar to Chebychev's Inequality:

$$P[|X| \geq k] \leq E[|X|^\ell]/k^\ell.$$

- **Jensen's Inequality**. If $f(X)$ is a concave function (open toward the x-axis, like the natural log function), then

$$E[f(X)] \leq f(E[X]).$$

Conversely, if $f(X)$ is a convex function (open away from the x-axis, like the absolute value function), then

$$E[f(X)] \geq f(E[X]).$$

- **Minkowski's Inequality.** For $k > 1$,

$$(E[|X + Y|^k])^{1/k} \leq (E[|X|^k])^{1/k} + (E[|Y|^k])^{1/k}.$$

- **Hölder's Inequality.** For $\frac{1}{k} + \frac{1}{\ell} = 1$,

$$|E[XY]| \leq E[|XY|] \leq (E[|X|]^k)^{1/k}(E[|Y|^\ell])^{1/\ell}.$$

- **Schwarz Inequality.** An interesting special case of Hölder's Inequality where $k = \ell = \frac{1}{2}$:

$$E[|XY|] \leq \sqrt{E[X^2]E[Y^2]}$$

- **Liapounov's Inequality.** For $1 < k < \ell$,

$$(E[|X|]^k)^{1/k} \leq (E[|X|]^\ell)^{1/\ell}.$$

- **Cramer-Rao Inequality.** Given a PDF or PMF conditional on a parameter vector, $f(\mathbf{X}|\boldsymbol{\theta})$, define the *information matrix* as

$$I(\boldsymbol{\theta}) = E\left[\frac{\partial}{\partial \boldsymbol{\theta}} \log(f(\mathbf{X}|\boldsymbol{\theta}))' \frac{\partial}{\partial \boldsymbol{\theta}} \log(f(\mathbf{X}|\boldsymbol{\theta}))\right],$$

and define the vector quantity

$$\alpha = \frac{\partial}{\partial \boldsymbol{\theta}} E[f(\mathbf{X}|\boldsymbol{\theta})].$$

Then

$$\text{Var}(f(\mathbf{X}|\boldsymbol{\theta})) \geq \alpha I(\boldsymbol{\theta})\alpha.$$

- **Berge Inequality.** Suppose $E[X] = E[Y] = 0$, $\text{Var}[X] = \text{Var}[Y] = 1$, and $\sigma^2 = \text{Cov}[X, Y]$. In other words, these are *standardized* random variables. Then for (positive) k

$$P[\max(|X|, |Y|) \geq k] \leq (1 + \sqrt{1 - \text{Cov}(X, Y)^2})/k^2.$$

Note also that these inequalities apply for conditional expectations as well. For instance, the statement of Liapounov's Inequality conditional on Y is $(E[|X|]^k|Y)^{1/k} \leq (E[|X|]^\ell|Y)^{1/\ell}$.

8.10 Moments of a Distribution

Most (but not all) distributions have a series of **moments** that define important characteristics of the distribution. In fact, we have already seen the first moment, which is the mean or expected value of the distribution. The general formula for the kth moment is based on the expected value:

$$m_k = E[X^k] = \int_X x^k dF(x)$$

for the random variable X with distribution $f(X)$ where the integration takes place over the appropriate support of X. It can also be expressed as

$$m_k = \int_X e^{kx} dF(x),$$

which is more useful in some circumstances. The kth **central moment** is (often called just the "kth moment")

$$m'_k = E[(X - m_1)^k] = \int_X (x - m_1)^k dF(x).$$

So the central moment is defined by a deviation from the mean. The most obvious and important central moment is the variance: $\sigma^2 = E[(X - \bar{X})^2]$. We can use this second central moment to calculate the variance of a PDF or

PMF. This calculation for the exponential is

$$\mathrm{Var}[X] = E[(X - E[X])^2]$$

$$= \int_0^\infty (X - E[X])^2 f(x|\beta)dx$$

$$= \int_0^\infty (X - \beta)^2 \frac{1}{\beta} \exp[-x/\beta]dx$$

$$= \int_0^\infty (X^2 - 2X\beta + \beta^2)\frac{1}{\beta} \exp[-x/\beta]dx$$

$$= \int_0^\infty X^2 \frac{1}{\beta} \exp[-x/\beta]dx$$
$$+ \int_0^\infty 2X \exp[-x/\beta]dx + \int_0^\infty \beta \exp[-x/\beta]dx$$

$$= (0 - 2\beta^2) + (2\beta^2) + (\beta^2)$$

$$= \beta^2,$$

where we use integration by parts and L'Hospital's Rule to do the individual integrations.

An important theory says that a distribution function is "determined" by its moments of all orders (i.e., all of them), and some distributions have an infinite number of moments defined. The normal distribution actually has an infinite number of moments. Conversely, the Cauchy PDF has no finite moments at all, even though it is "bell shaped" and looks like the normal (another reason not to use that expression). The **Cauchy distribution]** has the PDF

$$f(x|\beta) = \frac{1}{\beta}\frac{1}{1 + (x - \beta)^2}, \qquad -\infty < x, \beta < \infty.$$

Calculating the first moment with integration by parts gives

$$E[X] = \int_{-\infty}^{\infty} \frac{1}{\beta} \frac{x}{1 + (x - \beta)^2} dx$$

$$= \left[x\arctan(x - \beta) - (x - \beta)\arctan(x - \beta) + \frac{1}{2}\log(1 + x^2) \right] \Bigg|_{-\infty}^{\infty}$$

$$= \beta\arctan(x - \beta) \Bigg|_{-\infty}^{\infty} + \frac{1}{2}\log(1 + x^2) \Bigg|_{-\infty}^{\infty}.$$

While the first term above is finite because $\arctan(\pm\infty) = \pm\frac{1}{2}\pi$, the second term is clearly infinite. It is straightforward to show that higher moments are also infinite and therefore undefined (an exercise), and clearly every central moment is also infinite as they all include m_1.

8.11 New Terminology

8.1   Indicate the level of measurement and which measure(s) of central tendency can be used for the following:

   (a) college education: none, AA, BA/BS, JD, MD/DVM/DDO, Ph.D.;

   (b) letter grades;

   (c) income given as 0–10K, 10–20K, 30–50K, 50–80K, 100K+;

   (d) distance of commute from home to work;

   (e) marital status: single, married, widowed, divorced;

   (f) working status: employed, unemployed, retired, student;

   (g) governmental level: local, state, federal, international;

   (h) party: Democrat, Republican, Green, Bull Moose.

8.2   The following data are exam grade percentages: 37, 39, 28, 73, 50, 59, 41, 57, 46, 41, 62, 28, 26, 66, 53, 54, 37, 46, 25.

   (a) What is the level of measurement for these data?

   (b) Suppose we change the data to create a new dataset in the following way: values from 25 to 45 are assigned "Low," values from 45 to 60 are assigned "Medium," and values from 60 to 75 are assigned "High." Now what is the level of measurement for these data?

   (c) Now suppose we take the construction from (b) and assign "Low" and "High" to "Atypical" and assign "Medium" to "Typical." What is the level of measurement of this new dataset?

   (d) Calculate the mean and standard deviation of each of the three datasets created above.

8.3   Morrison (1977) gave the following data for Supreme Court vacancies from 1837 to 1932:

Number of Vacancies/Year	0	1	2	3	4+
Number of Years for Event	59	27	9	1	0

Fit a distribution to these data, estimating any necessary parameters. Using this model, construct a table of expected versus observed frequencies by year.

8.4   The National Taxpayers Union Foundation (NTUF), an interest group that advocates reduced government spending, scores House members on the budgetary impact of their roll call votes. A "spending" vote is one in favor of a bill or amendment that increases federal outlays and a "saving" vote is one that specifically decreases federal spending (i.e., program cuts). The fiscal impact of each House member's vote is cross-indexed and calculated as the total increase to the budget or the total decrease to the budget. The NTUF supplies these values along with a ranking of each member's "fiscal responsibility," calculated by adding all positive and negative fiscal costs of each bill voted on by each member and then ranking members by total cost. What is the level of measurement of the NTUF fiscal responsibility scale? Since House members' values are compared in NTUF public statements, is there a different level of measurement being implied?

8.5   Suppose you had a Poisson process with intensity parameter $\lambda = 5$. What is the probability of getting exactly 7 events? What is the probability of getting exactly 3 events? These values are the same distance from the expected value of the Poisson distribution, so why are they different?

8.6   Given the following PMF:

$$f(x) = \begin{cases} \frac{3!}{x!(3-x)!} \left(\frac{1}{2}\right)^3 & x = 0, 1, 2, 3 \\ 0 & \text{otherwise,} \end{cases}$$

(a) prove that this *is* in fact a PMF;

(b) find the expected value;

(c) find the variance;

(d) Derive the CDF.

8.7   Let X be the event that a single die is rolled and the resulting number is even. Let Y be the event describing the actual number that results from the roll (1–6). Prove the independence or nonindependence of these two events.

8.8   Suppose X_1 and X_2 are independent identically distributed (iid) random variables according to the PMF Bernoulli, $p = \frac{1}{2}$. Are $Y_1 = X_1 + X_2$ and $Y_2 = |X_1 - X_2|$ correlated? Are they independent?

8.9   Suppose we have a PMF with the following characteristics: $p(X = -2) = \frac{1}{5}$, $p(X = -1) = \frac{1}{6}$, $p(X = 0) = \frac{1}{5}$, $p(X = 1) = \frac{1}{15}$, and $p(X = 2) = \frac{11}{30}$. Define the random variable $Y = X^2$. Derive the PMF of Y and prove that it is a PMF. Calculate the expected value and variance of Y.

8.10   Charles Manski (1989) worried about missing data when the outcome variable of some study had missing values rather than when the variables assumed to be causing the outcome variable had missing values, which is the more standard concern. Missing values can cause series problems in making probabilistic statements from observed data. His first concern was notated this way: "Suppose each member of a population is characterized by a triple (y, x, z) where y is a real number, z is a binary indicator, and x is a real number vector." The problem is that, in collecting these data, (z, x) are always observed, but y is observed only when $z = 1$. The quantity of interest is $E(y|x)$. Use the Theorem of Total Probability to express this conditional probability when the data only provide $E(y|x, z = 1)$ and we cannot assume mean independence: $E(y|x) = E(y|x, z = 1) = E(y|x, z = 0)$.

8.11   Twenty developing countries each have a probability of military coup of 0.01 in any given year. We study these countries over a 10-year period.

   (a) How many coups do you expect in total?

   (b) What is the probability of four coups?

(c) What is the probability that there will be no coups during this period?

8.12 Show that the full parameter normal PDF $f(X|\mu, \sigma^2)$ reduces to the standard normal PDF when $\mu = 0$ and $\sigma^2 = 1$.

8.13 Use the exponential PDF to answer the following questions.

(a) Prove that the exponential form *is* a PDF.

(b) Derive the CDF.

(c) Prove that the exponential distribution is a special case of the gamma distribution.

8.14 Use the normal PDF to answer the following questions.

(a) If a normal distribution has $\mu = 25$ and $\sigma = 25$, what is the 91st percentile of the distribution?

(b) What is the 6th percentile of the distribution of part (a)?

(c) The width of a line etched on an integrated circuit chip is normally distributed with mean $3.000\mu m$ and standard deviation 0.150. What width value separates the widest 10% of all such lines from the other 90%?

8.15 A function that can be used instead of the probit function is the logit function: $\Lambda(X) = \frac{\exp(X)}{1+\exp(X)}$. Plot both the logit function and the probit function in the same graph and compare. What differences do you observe?

8.16 The **beta function** is defined for nonnegative values a and b as:

$$B(a, b) = \int_0^1 x^{a-1}(1 - x)^{b-1} dx.$$

This form is used in some statistical problems and elsewhere. The relationship between the beta and gamma functions is given by

$$B(a, b) = \frac{\Gamma(a)\Gamma(b)}{\Gamma(a + b)}.$$

Prove this using the properties of PDFs.

8.17 Prove that $E[Y|Y] = Y$.

8.18 Suppose that the performance of test-takers is normally distributed around a mean, μ. If we observe that 99% of the students are within 0.194175 of the mean, what is the value of σ?

8.19 Calculate the entropy of the distribution $\mathcal{B}(n = 5, p = 0.1)$ and the distribution $\mathcal{B}(n = 3, p = 0.5)$. Which one is greater? Why?

8.20 We know that the reaction time of subjects to a specific visual stimuli is distributed gamma with $\alpha = 7$ and $\beta = 3$, measured in seconds.

   (a) What is the probability that the reaction time is greater that 12 seconds?

   (b) What is the probability that the reaction time will be between 15 and 21 seconds?

   (c) What is the 95th percentile value of this distribution?

8.21 Show that the second moment of the Cauchy distribution is infinite and therefore undefined.

8.22 The following data are temperature measurements in Fahrenheit. Use these data answer the following questions.

38.16	52.68	53.47	50.18	49.13

   (a) Is the median bigger or smaller than the mean?

   (b) Calculate the mean and standard deviation.

   (c) What is the level of measurement for these data?

   (d) Suppose we transformed the data in the following way: Values from 0 to 40 are assigned "Cold," values from 41 to 70 are assigned "Medium," and values above 71 are assigned "Hot." Now what is the level of measurement for these data?

   (e) Suppose we continue to transform the data in the following way: "Cold" and "Hot" are combined into "Uncomfortable," and "Medium" is renamed "Comfortable." What is the level of measurement for these data?

8.23 The following is a stem and leaf plot for 20 different observations (stem = tens digit). Use these data to answer the questions.

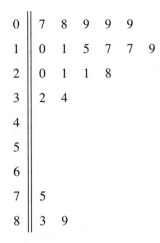

0	7 8 9 9 9
1	0 1 5 7 7 9
2	0 1 1 8
3	2 4
4	
5	
6	
7	5
8	3 9

(a) Is the median bigger or smaller than the mean?

(b) Calculate the 10% trimmed mean.

(c) Make a frequency distribution with relative *and* relative cumulative frequencies.

(d) Calculate the standard deviation.

(e) Identify the IQR.

8.24 Nine students currently taking introductory statistics are randomly selected, and both the first midterm score (x) and the second midterm score (y) are determined. Three of the students have the class at 8 A.M., another three have it at noon, and the remaining three have a night class.

8 A.M.	(70,60)	(72,83)	(94,85)
Noon	(80,72)	(60,74)	(55,58)
Night	(45,63)	(50,40)	(35,54)

(a) Calculate the sample correlation coefficient for the nine (x, y) pairs.

(b) Let $\bar{x}_1$ = the average score on the first midterm for the 8 A.M. students and $\bar{y}_1$ = the average score on the second midterm for these students. Let $\bar{x}_2$ and $\bar{y}_2$ be these averages for the noon students, and $\bar{x}_3$ and $\bar{y}_3$ be these averages for the evening students. Calculate r for these three $(\bar{x}, \bar{y})$ pairs.

(c) Construct a scatterplot of the nine (x, y) pairs and construct another one of the three $(\bar{x}, \bar{y})$ pairs. Does this suggest that a correlation coefficient based on averages (an "ecological" correlation) might be misleading? Explain.

8.25   The *Los Angeles Times* (Oct. 30, 1983) reported that a typical customer of the 7-Eleven convenience stores spends $3.24. Suppose that the average amount spent by customers of 7-Eleven stores is the reported value of $3.24 and that the standard deviation for the amount of sale is $8.88.

(a) What is the level of measurement for these data?

(b) Based on the given mean and standard deviation, do you think that the distribution of the variable *amount of sale* could have been symmetric in shape? Why or why not?

(c) What can be said about the proportion of all customers that spend more than $20 on a purchase at 7-Eleven?

8.26   The following are Grunfeld's General Electric data (see Maddala 1977) with the following variables: GEI = "Gross investment GE," GEC = "Lagged Capital Stock GE," and GEF = "Lagged Value of GE shares."

Year	GEI	GEC	GEF
1935	33.1	1170.6	97.8
1936	45.0	2015.8	104.4
1937	77.2	2803.3	118.0
1938	44.6	2039.7	156.2
1939	48.1	2256.2	172.6
1940	74.4	2132.2	186.6
1941	113.0	1834.1	220.9
1942	91.9	1588.0	287.8
1943	61.3	1749.4	319.9
1944	56.8	1687.2	321.3
1945	93.6	2007.7	319.6
1946	159.9	2208.3	346.0
1947	147.2	1656.7	456.4
1948	146.3	1604.4	543.4
1949	98.3	1431.8	618.3
1950	93.5	1610.5	647.4
1951	135.2	1819.4	671.3
1952	157.3	2079.7	726.1
1953	179.5	2371.6	800.3
1954	189.6	2759.9	888.9

(a) Calculate the variance and the MAD of each of the three variables.

(b) Calculate the correlation coefficients. Truncate the variables such that there are no values to the right of the decimal point and recalculate the correlation coefficients. Do you see a difference? Why or why not?

9

Markov Chains

9.1 Objectives

This chapter introduces an underappreciated topic in the social sciences that lies directly in the intersection of matrix algebra (Chapters 3 and 4) and probability (Chapter 7). It is an interesting area in its own right with many applications in the social sciences, but it is also a nice reinforcement of important principles we have already covered. Essentially the idea is relevant to the things we study in the social sciences because Markov chains specifically condition on the current status of events. Researchers find that this is a nice way to describe individual human decision making and collective human determinations.

So Markov chains are very practical and useful. They model how social and physical phenomena move from one state to another. The first part of this chapter introduces the mechanics of Markov chains through the kernel. This is the defining mechanism that "moves" the Markov chain around. The second part of the chapter describes various properties of Markov chains and how such chains can differ in how they behave. The first few properties are elementary, and the last few properties are noticeably more advanced and may be skipped by the reader who only wants an introduction.

9.2 Defining Stochastic Processes and Markov Chains

Markov chains sound like an exotic mathematical idea, but actually the principle is quite simple. Suppose that your decision-making process is based only on a current state of affairs. For example, in a casino wagering decisions are usually dictated only by the current state of the gambler: the immediate confronting decision (which number to bet on, whether to take another card, etc.) and the available amount of money. Thus these values at a previous point in time are irrelevant to future behavior (except perhaps in the psychological sense). Similarly, stock purchase decisions, military strategy, travel directions, and other such trajectories can often successfully be described with Markov chains.

What is a Markov chain? It is a special kind of stochastic process that has a "memoryless" property. That does not help much, so let us be specific. A **stochastic process** is a consecutive series of observed random variables. It is a random variable defined in exactly the standard way with a known or unknown distribution, except that the order of events is recordable. So for some state space, Θ, the random variable θ is defined by $\theta^{[t]} \sim F(\theta)$, $t \in T$, where t is some index value from the set T. Actually it is almost always more simple than this general definition of indexing since it is typical to define T as the positive integers so $t = 0, 1, 2, 3, \ldots$. The implication from this simplification is that time periods are evenly spaced, and it is rare to suppose otherwise.

The state space that a stochastic process is defined on must be identified. This is exactly like the support of a probability mass function (PMF) or probability density function (PDF) in that it defines what values $\theta^{[t]}$ can take on any point in time t. There are two types of state spaces: discrete and continuous. In general, discrete state spaces are a lot more simple to think about and we will therefore focus only on these here.

Suppose that we had a cat locked in a classroom with square tiles on the floor. If we defined the room as the state space (the cat cannot leave) and each square tile as a discrete state that the cat can occupy, then the path of the cat walking throughout the room is a stochastic process where we record the grid numbers of the tiles occupied by the cat over time. Now suppose that the walking decisions made by the cat are governed only by where it is at any given moment: The cat does not care where it has been in the past. To anyone who knows cats, this seems like a reasonable assumption about feline psychology. So the cat forgets previous states that it has occupied and wanders based only on considering where it is at the moment. This property means that the stochastic process in question is now a special case called a Markov chain.

More formally, a **Markov chain** is a stochastic process with the property that any specified state in the series, $\theta^{[t]}$, is dependent only on the previous state, $\theta^{[t-1]}$. But wait, yesterday's value ($\theta^{[t-1]}$) is then also conditional on the day before that's value ($\theta^{[t-2]}$), and so on. So is it not then true that $\theta^{[t]}$ is conditional on every previous value: $0, 1, 2, \ldots, t-1$? Yes, in a sense, but *conditioned on $\theta^{[t-1]}$, $\theta^{[t]}$ is independent of all previous values.* This is a way of saying that all information that was used to determine the current step was contained in the previous step, and therefore if the previous step is considered, there is no additional information of importance in any of the steps before that one. This "memoryless" property can be explicitly stated in the probability language from Chapter 7. We say that $\theta^{[t]}$ is *conditionally independent* on all values previous to $\theta^{[t-1]}$ if

$$p(\theta^{[t]} \in A | \theta^{[0]}, \theta^{[1]}, \ldots, \theta^{[t-2]}, \theta^{[t-1]}) = p(\theta^{[t]} \in A | \theta^{[t-1]}),$$

where A is any identified set (an event or range of events) on the complete state space (like our set of tiles in the classroom). Or, more colloquially, "a Markov chain wanders around the state space remembering only where it has been in the last period." Now that *does* sound like a cat! A different type of stochastic process that sometimes gets mentioned in the same texts is a **martingale**. A martingale is defined using expectation instead of probability:

$$E(\theta^{[t]} \in A | \theta^{[0]}, \theta^{[1]}, \ldots, \theta^{[t-2]}, \theta^{[t-1]}) = \theta^{[t-1]},$$

meaning that the expected value that the martingale is in the set A in the next period is the value of the current position. Note that this differs from the Markov chain in that there is a stable iterative process based on this expectation rather than on Markovian probabilistic exploration.

Also, since the future at time $t+1$ and the past at time t are independent given the state at time t, the Markovian property does not care about the direction of time. This seems like a weird finding, but recall that time here is not a physical characteristic of the universe; instead it is a series of our own construction. Interestingly, there are Markov chains that are defined to work backward through "time," such as those in *coupling from the past* (see Propp and Wilson 1996).

In general interest is restricted here to discrete-time, homogeneous Markov chains. By **discrete time**, we simply mean that the counting process above, $t = 0, 1, \ldots, T$, is recordable at clear, distinguishable points. There is a corresponding study of continuous-time Markov processes, but it is substantially more abstract and we will not worry about it here. A **homogeneous** Markov chain is one in which the process of moving (i.e., the *probability* of moving) is independent of current time. Stated another way, move decisions at time t are independent of t.

★ **Example 9.1:** **Contraception Use in Barbados**. Ebanks (1970) looked at contraception use by women of lower socio-economic class in Barbados and found a stable pattern in the 1950s and a different stable pattern emerged in the late 1960s. This is of anthropological interest because contraception and reproduction are key components of family and social life in rural areas. His focus was on the stability and change of usage, looking at a sample from family planning programs at the time. Using 405 respondents from 1955 and another 405 respondents from 1967, he produced the following change probabilities where the row indicates current state and the column indicates the next state (so, for instance, the probability of moving from "Use" at the current state to "Not Use" in the next state for 1955 is 0.52):

1955	Use	Not Use		**1967**	Use	Not Use
Use	0.48	0.52		Use	0.89	0.11
Not Use	0.08	0.92		Not Use	0.52	0.48

The first obvious pattern that emerges is that users in the 1950s were nearly equally likely to continue as to quit and nonusers were overwhelming likely to continue nonuse. However, the pattern is reversed in the late 1960s, whereby users were overwhelmingly likely to continue and nonusers were equally likely to continue or switch to use.

If we are willing to consider these observed (empirical) probabilities as enduring and stable indications of underlying behavior, then we can "run" a Markov chain to get anticipated future behavior. This is done very mechanically by treating the 2×2 tables here as matrices and multiplying repeatedly. What does this do? It produces expected cell values based on the probabilities in the last iteration: the Markovian property. There are (at least) two interesting things we can do here. Suppose we were interested in predicting contraception usage for 1969, that is, two years into the future. This could be done simply by the following steps:

$$\begin{bmatrix} 0.89 & 0.11 \\ 0.52 & 0.48 \end{bmatrix} \times \begin{bmatrix} 0.89 & 0.11 \\ 0.52 & 0.48 \end{bmatrix} = \underbrace{\begin{bmatrix} 0.85 & 0.15 \\ 0.71 & 0.29 \end{bmatrix}}_{1968}$$

$$\begin{bmatrix} 0.85 & 0.15 \\ 0.71 & 0.29 \end{bmatrix} \times \begin{bmatrix} 0.89 & 0.11 \\ 0.52 & 0.48 \end{bmatrix} = \underbrace{\begin{bmatrix} 0.83 & 0.17 \\ 0.78 & 0.22 \end{bmatrix}}_{1969}.$$

This means that we would *expect* to see an increase in nonusers converting to users if the 1967 rate is an underlying trend. Secondly, we can test Ebanks' assertion that the 1950s were stable. Suppose we take the 1955 matrix of transitions and apply it iteratively to get a predicted distribution across the four cells for 1960. We can then compare it to the actual distribution seen in 1960, and if it is similar, then the claim is supportable (the match will not be exact, of course, due to sampling considerations). Multiplying the 1955 matrix four times gives

$$
\begin{bmatrix} 0.48 & 0.52 \\ 0.08 & 0.92 \end{bmatrix}^4 = \begin{bmatrix} 0.16 & 0.84 \\ 0.13 & 0.87 \end{bmatrix}.
$$

This suggests the following empirical distribution, given the marginal numbers of users for 1959 in the study:

1959-1960 predicted	Use	Not Use
Use	7	41
Not Use	46	311

which can be compared with the actual 1960 numbers from that study:

1959-1960 actual	Use	Not Use
Use	27	21
Not Use	39	318

These are clearly dissimilar enough to suggest that the process is not Markovian as claimed. More accurately, it can perhaps be described as a martingale since the 1955 actual numbers are $\left[\begin{smallmatrix} 24 & 26 \\ 28 & 327 \end{smallmatrix}\right]$. What we are actually seeing here is a question of whether the 1955 proportions define a transaction kernel for the Markov chain going forward. The idea of a transaction kernel is explored more fully in the next section.

9.2.1 The Markov Chain Kernel

We know that a Markov chain moves based only on its current position, but using that information, how does the Markov chain decide? Every Markov chain is defined by two things: its state space (already discussed) and its **transition kernel,** $K()$. The transition kernel is a general mechanism for describing the probability of moving to other states based on the current chain status. Specifically, $K(\theta, A)$ is a defined probability measure for all θ points in the state space to the set $A \in \Theta$: It maps potential transition events to their probability of occurrence.

The easiest case to understand is when the state space is discrete and **K** is just a matrix mapping: a $k \times k$ matrix for k discrete elements in that exhaust the allowable state space, A. We will use the notation θ_i, meaning the ith state of the space. So a Markov chain that occupies subspace i at time t is designated $\theta_i^{[t]}$.

Each individual cell defines the probability of a state transition from the first term to all possible states:

$$
\mathbf{K} = \begin{bmatrix}
p(\theta_1, \theta_1) & p(\theta_1, \theta_2) & \cdots & p(\theta_1, \theta_{k-1}) & p(\theta_1, \theta_k) \\
p(\theta_2, \theta_1) & p(\theta_2, \theta_2) & \cdots & p(\theta_2, \theta_{k-1}) & p(\theta_2, \theta_k) \\
\vdots & \vdots & \ddots & \vdots & \vdots \\
p(\theta_{k-1}, \theta_1) & p(\theta_{k-1}, \theta_2) & & p(\theta_{k-1}, \theta_{k-1}) & p(\theta_{k-1}, \theta_k) \\
p(\theta_k, \theta_1) & p(\theta_k, \theta_2) & \cdots & p(\theta_1, \theta_{k-1}) & p(\theta_k, \theta_k)
\end{bmatrix}.
$$

The first term in $p()$, constant across rows, indicates where the chain is at the current period and the column indicates potential destinations. Each matrix element is a well-behaved probability, $p(\theta_i, \theta_j) \geq 0$, $\forall i, j \in A$. The notation here can be a little bit confusing as it looks like a *joint distribution* in the sense of Chapter 7. This is an unfortunate artifact, and one just has to remember the different context. The rows of **K** sum to one and define a conditional PMF because they are all specified for the same starting value and cover each possible destination in the state space.

We can also use this kernel to calculate state probabilities for arbitrary future times. If we multiply the transition matrix (kernel) by itself j times, the result,

K^j, gives the **j-step transition matrix** for this Markov chain. Each row is the set of transition probabilities from that row state to each of the other states in exactly j iterations of the chain. It does not say, however, what that sequence is in exact steps.

★ **Example 9.2:** **Campaign Contributions.** It is no secret that individuals who have contributed to a Congress member's campaign in the past are more likely than others to contribute in the next campaign cycle. This is why politicians keep and value donor lists, even including those who have given only small amounts in the past. Suppose that 25% of those contributing in the past to a given member are likely to do so again and only 3% of those not giving in the past are likely to do so now. The resulting transition matrix is denoted as follows:

$$
\text{last period} \begin{cases} \\ \\ \end{cases} \begin{array}{c} \\ \theta_1 \\ \theta_2 \end{array} \overbrace{\begin{bmatrix} \theta_1 & \theta_2 \\ 0.97 & 0.03 \\ 0.75 & 0.25 \end{bmatrix}}^{\text{current period}},
$$

where θ_1 is the state for no contribution and θ_2 denotes a contribution. Notice that the rows necessarily add to one because there are only two states possible in this space. This articulated kernel allows us to ask some useful questions on this candidate's behalf. If we start with a list of 100 names where 50 of them contributed last period and 50 did not, what number can we expect to have contribute from this list? In Markov chain language this is called a starting point or starting vector:

$$
S_0 = \begin{bmatrix} 50 & 50 \end{bmatrix};
$$

that is, before running the Markov chain, half of the group falls in each category. To get to the Markov chain first state, we simply multiply the initial state by the transition matrix:

$$S_1 = \begin{bmatrix} 50 & 50 \end{bmatrix} \begin{bmatrix} 0.97 & 0.03 \\ 0.75 & 0.25 \end{bmatrix} = \begin{bmatrix} 86 & 14 \end{bmatrix} = S_1.$$

So we would expect to get contributions from 14 off of this list. Since incumbent members of Congress enjoy a repeated electoral advantage for a number of reasons, let us assume that our member runs more consecutive races (and wins!). If we keep track of this particular list over time (maybe they are especially wealthy or influential constituents), what happens to our expected number of contributors? We can keep moving the Markov chain forward in time to find out:

$$\text{Second state: } S_2 = \begin{bmatrix} 86 & 14 \end{bmatrix} \begin{bmatrix} 0.97 & 0.03 \\ 0.75 & 0.25 \end{bmatrix} = \begin{bmatrix} 94 & 6 \end{bmatrix}$$

$$\text{Third state: } S_3 = \begin{bmatrix} 94 & 6 \end{bmatrix} \begin{bmatrix} 0.97 & 0.03 \\ 0.75 & 0.25 \end{bmatrix} = \begin{bmatrix} 96 & 4 \end{bmatrix}$$

$$\text{Fourth state: } S_4 = \begin{bmatrix} 96 & 4 \end{bmatrix} \begin{bmatrix} 0.97 & 0.03 \\ 0.75 & 0.25 \end{bmatrix} = \begin{bmatrix} 96 & 4 \end{bmatrix}.$$

We rounded to integer values at each step since by definition donors can only give or not give. It turns out that no matter how many times we run this chain forward from this point, the returned state will always be $[96, 4]$, indicating an overall 4% donation rate. This turns out to be a very important property of Markov chains and the subject of the next section.

In fact, for this simple example we could solve directly for the steady state $S = [s_1, s_2]$ by stipulating

$$\begin{bmatrix} s_1 & s_2 \end{bmatrix} \begin{bmatrix} 0.97 & 0.03 \\ 0.75 & 0.25 \end{bmatrix} = \begin{bmatrix} s_1 & s_2 \end{bmatrix}$$

and solving the resulting two equations for the two unknowns:

$$[0.97s_1 + 0.75s_2, 0.03s_1 + 0.25s_2] = [s_1, s_2]$$

$$0.97s_1 + 0.75s_2 = s_1 \qquad 0.03s_1 + 0.25s_2 = s_2$$

$$s_1 = \frac{7500}{78} \qquad s_2 = \frac{300}{78}$$

(using $s_1 + s_2 = 100$), where the difference from above is due to rounding.

9.2.2 The Stationary Distribution of a Markov Chain

Markov chains can have a **stationary distribution**: a distribution reached from iterating the chain until some point in the future where all movement probabilities are governed by a single probabilistic statement, regardless of time or position. This is equivalent to saying that when a Markov chain has reached its stationary distribution there is a single marginal distribution rather than the conditional distributions in the transition kernel.

To be specific, define $\pi(\theta)$ as the stationary distribution of the Markov chain for θ on the state space A. Recall that $p(\theta_i, \theta_j)$ is the probability that the chain will move from θ_i to θ_j at some arbitrary step t, and $\pi^t(\theta)$ is the corresponding marginal distribution. The stationary distribution satisfies

$$\sum_{\theta_i} \pi^t(\theta_i) p(\theta_i, \theta_j) = \pi^{t+1}(\theta_j).$$

This is very useful because we *want* the Markov chain to reach and describe a given marginal distribution; then it is only necessary to specify a transition kernel and let the chain run until the probability structures match the desired marginal.

★ **Example 9.3:** **Shuffling Cards.** We will see here if we can use a Markov chain algorithm to shuffle a deck of cards such that the marginal distribution is *uniform*: Each card is equally likely to be in any given position. So the objective (stationary distribution) is a uniformly random distribution in the deck: The probability of any one card occupying any one position is $1/52$.

The suggested algorithm is to take the top card and insert it uniformly randomly at some other point in the deck, and continue. Is this actually a Markov chain? What is the stationary distribution and is it the uniform distribution as desired? Bayer and Diaconis (1992) evaluated a number of these shuffling algorithms from a technical perspective.

To answer these questions, we simplify the problem (without loss of generality) to consideration of a deck of only three cards numbered $1, 2, 3$. The sample space for this setup is then given by

$$A = \{[1, 2, 3], [1, 3, 2], [2, 1, 3], [2, 3, 1], [3, 1, 2], [3, 2, 1]\},$$

which has $3! = 6$ elements from the counting rules given in Chapter 7. A sample chain trajectory looks like

$$[1,3,2]$$
$$[3,1,2]$$
$$[1,3,2]$$
$$[3,2,1]$$
$$\vdots$$

Looking at the second step, we took the 3 card off the top of the deck and picked the second position from among three. Knowing that the current position is currently $[3, 1, 2]$, the probabilities and potential outcomes are given by

Action	Outcome	Probability
return to top of deck	$[3, 1, 2]$	$\frac{1}{3}$
put in middle position	$[1, 3, 2]$	$\frac{1}{3}$
put in bottom position	$[1, 2, 3]$	$\frac{1}{3}$

To establish the potential outcomes we only need to know the current position of the deck and the probability structure (the kernel) here. Being aware of the position of the deck at time $t = 2$ tells us everything we need to know about the deck, and having this information means that knowing that the position of the deck at time $t = 1$ was $[1, 3, 2]$ is irrelevant to calculating the potential outcomes and their probabilities in the table above. So once the current position is established in the Markov chain, decisions about where to go are conditionally independent of the past.

It should also be clear so far that not every position of the deck is immediately reachable from every other position. For instance, we cannot move directly from $[1, 3, 2]$ to $[3, 2, 1]$ because it would require at least one additional step.

The transition kernel assigns positive (uniform) probability from each state to each reachable state in one step and zero probability to all other states:

$$K = \begin{bmatrix} 1/3 & 0 & 1/3 & 1/3 & 0 & 0 \\ 0 & 1/3 & 0 & 0 & 1/3 & 1/3 \\ 1/3 & 1/3 & 1/3 & 0 & 0 & 0 \\ 0 & 0 & 0 & 1/3 & 1/3 & 1/3 \\ 1/3 & 1/3 & 0 & 0 & 1/3 & 0 \\ 0 & 0 & 1/3 & 1/3 & 0 & 1/3 \end{bmatrix}.$$

Let us begin with a starting point at $[1, 2, 3]$ and look at the marginal distribution after each application of the transition kernel. Mechanically, we do this by pre-multiplying the transition kernel matrix by $[1, 0, 0, 0, 0, 0]$ as the starting probability (i.e., a deterministic decision to begin at the specified point. Then we record the result, multiply it by the kernel, and continue. The first 15 iterations produce the following marginal probability vectors:

Iteration	p([1,2,3])	p([1,3,2])	p([2,1,3])	p([2,3,1])	p([3,1,2])	p([3,2,1])
1	0.222222	0.111111	0.222222	0.222222	0.111111	0.111111
2	0.185185	0.148148	0.185185	0.185185	0.148148	0.148148
3	0.172839	0.160493	0.172839	0.172839	0.160493	0.160493
4	0.168724	0.164609	0.168724	0.168724	0.164609	0.164609
5	0.167352	0.165980	0.167352	0.167352	0.165980	0.165980
6	0.166895	0.166438	0.166895	0.166895	0.166438	0.166438
7	0.166742	0.166590	0.166742	0.166742	0.166590	0.166590
8	0.166692	0.166641	0.166692	0.166692	0.166641	0.166641
9	0.166675	0.166658	0.166675	0.166675	0.166658	0.166658
10	0.166669	0.166663	0.166669	0.166669	0.166663	0.166663
11	0.166667	0.166665	0.166667	0.166667	0.166665	0.166665
12	0.166667	0.166666	0.166667	0.166667	0.166666	0.166666
13	0.166666	0.166666	0.166666	0.166666	0.166666	0.166666
14	0.166666	0.166666	0.166666	0.166666	0.166666	0.166666
15	0.166666	0.166666	0.166666	0.166666	0.166666	0.166666

Clearly there is a sense that the probability structure of the marginals have converged to a uniform pattern. This is as we expected, and it means that the shuffling algorithm will *eventually* produce the desired marginal probabilities. It is important to remember that these stationary probabilities are not the probabilities that govern movement at any particular point in the chain; that is still the kernel. These are the probabilities of seeing one of the six events at any arbitrary point in time unconditional on current placement.

This difference may be a little bit subtle. Recall that there are three unavailable outcomes and three equal probability outcomes for each position of the deck. So the marginal distribution above *cannot* be functional as a state to state transition mechanism. What is the best guess as to the unconditional state of the deck in 10,000 shuffles? It is equally likely that any of the six states would be observed. But notice that this question ignores the state of the deck in 9,999 shuffles. If we do not have this information, then the marginal distribution (if known) is the best way to describe outcome probabilities because it is the long-run probability of the states once the Markov chain is in its stationary distribution.

9.3 Properties of Markov Chains

Markov chains have various properties that govern how they behave as they move around their state spaces. These properties are important because they determine whether or not the Markov chain is producing values that are useful to our more general purpose.

9.3.1 Homogeneity and Periodicity

A Markov chain is said to be homogeneous at some step t if the transition probabilities at this step do not depend on the value of t. This definition implies that Markov chains can be homogeneous for some periods and **non-homogeneous** for other periods. The homogeneity property is usually important in that Markov chains that behave according to some function of their age are usually poor theoretical tools for exploring probability statements of interest.

A related, and important, property is the **period** of a Markov chain. If a Markov chain operates on a deterministic repeating schedule of steps, then it is said to be a Markov chain of **period-n**, where n is the time (i.e., the number of steps) in the reoccurring period. It seems fairly obvious that a periodic Markov chain is not a homogeneous Markov chain because the period implies a dependency of the chain on the time t.

9.3.1.1 A Simple Illustration of Time Dependency

As an illustration of homogeneity and periodicity, consider a simple Markov chain operating on a discrete state space with only four states, $\theta:\ 1, 2, 3, 4$, illustrated by

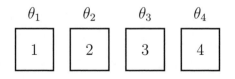

The movement of the Markov chain at time t is governed by the rule

$$p(s = 1) = \frac{1}{10} \qquad\qquad p(s = 2) = \frac{2}{10}$$

$$p(s = 3) = \frac{3}{10} \qquad\qquad p(s = 4) = \frac{4}{10},$$

where s is the number of steps that the chain moves to the right. The state space wraps around from 4 back to 1 so that $s = 4$ means that the chain returns to the same place. Does this chain actually have the Markovian property? Certainly it does, because movement is dictated only by the current location and the stipulated kernel. Is it periodic or homogeneous? Since there is no repetition or dependency on t in the kernel it is clearly both aperiodic and nonhomogeneous.

How could this Markov chain be made to be periodic? Suppose that the kernel above was replaced by the cycling rule:

$$[1, 2, 3, 4, 4, 3, 2, 1, \ 1, 2, 3, 4, 4, 3, 2, 1, \ 1, 2, 3, 4, 4, 3, 2, 1, \ldots],$$

then the period would be 8 and the chain would repeat this pattern forever. While the path of the chain depends on the time in the sense that the next deterministic step results from the current deterministic step, we usually just call this type of chain periodic rather than nonhomogeneous. This is because periodicity is more damaging to stochastic simulation with Markov chains than nonhomogeneity. To see the difference, consider the following kernel, which gives a nonhomogeneous Markov chain that is *not* periodic:

$$\theta < [t + 1] = runif[(t - 1):t] \bmod 4 + 1,$$

where the notation $runif[(t - 1):t]$ here means a random uniform choice of integer between $t - 1$ and t. So this chain does not have a repeating period, but it is clearly dependent on the current value of t. For example, now run this chain for 10 iterations from a starting point at 1:

period	0	1	2	3	4	5	6	7	8	9	10
$runif[(t-1):t]$	-	2	2	3	5	6	7	7	9	9	10
θ_t	1	2	3	3	4	2	3	4	4	2	2

There is a built-in periodicity to this chain where lower values are more likely just after t reaches a multiple of 4, and higher values are more likely just before t reaches a multiple of 4.

There is one last house-keeping detail left for this section. Markov chains are generally implemented with computers, and the underlying random numbers generated on computers have two characteristics that make them not truly random. For one thing, the generation process is fully discrete since the values are created from a finite binary process and normalized through division. This means that these are *pseudo-random* numbers and necessarily rational. Yet, truly random numbers on some defined interval are irrational with probability one because the irrationals dominate the continuous metric. In addition, while we call these values random or more accurately pseudorandom numbers, they are not random at all because the process that generates them is completely deterministic. The algorithms create a stream of values that is not random in the indeterminant sense but still *resembles a random process*. The deterministic streams varyingly lack systematic characteristics (Coveyou 1960): the time it takes to repeat the stream exactly (the period) and repeated patterns in lagged sets within the stream. So, by necessity, algorithmic implementations have to live with periodicity, and it is worth the time and energy in applied settings to use the available random number generator with the longest period possible.

9.3.2 Irreducibility

A *state* A in the state space of a Markov chain is **irreducible** if for every two substates or individual events θ_i and θ_j in A, these two substates "communicate." This means that the Markov chain is irreducible on A if every reached point or collection of points can be reached from every other reached point or collection of points. More formally,

$$p(\theta_i, \theta_j) \neq 0, \ \forall \theta_i, \theta_j \in A.$$

As an example, consider the following kernel of a **reducible** Markov chain:

$$
K = \begin{array}{c} \\ \theta_1 \\ \theta_2 \\ \theta_3 \\ \theta_4 \end{array}
\begin{array}{cccc}
\theta_1 & \theta_2 & \theta_3 & \theta_4 \\
\left(\begin{array}{cccc}
\frac{1}{2} & \frac{1}{2} & 0 & 0 \\
\frac{1}{3} & \frac{2}{3} & 0 & 0 \\
0 & 0 & \frac{3}{4} & \frac{1}{4} \\
0 & 0 & \frac{1}{4} & \frac{3}{4}
\end{array} \right)
\end{array}.
$$

The chain determined by this kernel is reducible because if is started in either θ_1 or θ_2, then it operates as if has the transition matrix:

$$
K_{1,2} = \begin{array}{c} \\ \theta_1 \\ \theta_2 \end{array}
\begin{array}{cc}
\theta_1 & \theta_2 \\
\left(\begin{array}{cc}
\frac{1}{2} & \frac{1}{2} \\
\frac{1}{3} & \frac{2}{3}
\end{array} \right)
\end{array},
$$

and if it is started in either θ_3 or θ_4, then it operates as if it has the transition matrix:

$$
K_{3,4} = \begin{array}{c} \\ \theta_3 \\ \theta_4 \end{array}
\begin{array}{cc}
\theta_3 & \theta_4 \\
\left(\begin{array}{cc}
\frac{3}{4} & \frac{1}{4} \\
\frac{1}{4} & \frac{3}{4}
\end{array} \right)
\end{array}.
$$

Thus the original Markov chain determined by K is *reducible* to one of two forms, depending on where it is started because there are in each case two permanently unavailable states. To provide a contrast, consider the Markov chain determined by the following kernel, K', which is very similar to K but is irreducible:

$$
K = \begin{array}{c c} & \begin{array}{cccc} \theta_1 & \theta_2 & \theta_3 & \theta_4 \end{array} \\ \begin{array}{c} \theta_1 \\ \theta_2 \\ \theta_3 \\ \theta_4 \end{array} & \left(\begin{array}{cccc} \frac{1}{2} & \frac{1}{2} & 0 & 0 \\ \frac{1}{3} & 0 & \frac{2}{3} & 0 \\ 0 & \frac{3}{4} & 0 & \frac{1}{4} \\ 0 & 0 & \frac{1}{4} & \frac{3}{4} \end{array} \right). \end{array}
$$

This occurs because there is now a two-way "path" between the previously separated upper and lower submatrices.

Related to this is the idea of **hitting times**. The hitting time of a state A and a Markov chain θ is the shortest time for the Markov chain to begin in A and return to A:

$$
T_A = \inf[n > 0, \theta^{[n]} \in A].
$$

Recall that the notation "inf" from Chapter 1 means the lowest (positive) value of n that satisfies $\theta^{[n]} \in A$. It is conventional to define T_A as infinity if the Markov chain never returns to A. From this definition we get the following important result:

An irreducible and aperiodic Markov chain on state space A will for each subspace of A, a_i, have a finite hitting time for a_i with probability one and a finite expected value of the hitting time:

$$
p(T_{a_i} < \infty) = 1, \qquad E[T_{a_i}] < \infty.
$$

By extension we can also say that the probability of transitioning from two substates of A, a_i and a_j, in finite time is guaranteed to be nonzero.

9.3.3 Recurrence

Some characteristics belong to *states* rather than Markov chains. Of course Markov chains operating on these states are affected by such characteristics. A state A is said to be **absorbing** if once a Markov chain enters this state it cannot leave: $p(A, A^C) = 0$. Conversely, A is **transient** if the probability of the chain not returning to this state is nonzero: $1 - p(A, A) > 0$. This is equivalent to saying that the chain will return to A for only a finite number of visits in infinite time. State A is said to be **closed** to another state B if a Markov chain on A cannot reach B: $p(A, B) = 0$. State A is clearly closed *in general* if it is absorbing since $B = A^C$ in this case (note that this is a different definition of "closed" used in a different context than that in Chapter 4).

These properties of states allow us to define an especially useful characteristic of both states and chains. If a state is closed, discrete, and irreducible, then this state and all subspaces within this subspace are called **recurrent**, and Markov chains operating on recurrent state spaces are recurrent. From this we can say something important in two different ways:

- **[Formal Definition.]** A irreducible Markov chain is called *recurrent* with regard to a given state A, which is a single point or a defined collection of points, if the probability that the chain occupies A infinitely often over unbounded time is nonzero.

- **[Colloquial Definition.]** When a chain moves into a recurrent state, it stays there forever and visits every subspace infinitely often.

There are also exactly two different, mutually exclusive, "flavors" of recurrence with regard to a state A:

- A Markov chain is **positive recurrent** if the mean time to return to A is bounded.

- Otherwise the mean time to return to A is infinite, and the Markov chain is called **null recurrent**.

With these we can also state the following properties.

Properties of Markov Chain Recurrence

$\rightarrowtail$ **Unions** If A and B are recurrent states,
then $A \cup B$ is a recurrent state

$\rightarrowtail$ **Capture** A chain that enters a closed, irreducible,
and recurrent state stays there and visits
every substate with probability one.

★ **Example 9.4: Conflict and Cooperation in Rural Andean Communities**. Robbins and Robbins (1979) extended Whyte's (1975) study of 12 Peruvian communities by extrapolating future probabilities of conflict and cooperation using a Markov chain analysis. Whyte classified these communities in 1964 and 1969 as having one of four types of relations with the other communities: high cooperation and high conflict (HcHx), high cooperation

Table 9.1. DISTRIBUTION OF COMMUNITY TYPES

Community	Type in 1964	Type in 1969
Huayopampa	HcLx	HcHx
Pacaraos	HcHx	HcHx
Aucallama	LcHx	LcLx
La Esperanza	LcLx	LcLx
Pucará	LcHx	LcLx
St. A De Caias	LcHx	LcHx
Mito	LcHx	LcLx
Virú	LcHx	LcLx
Pisaq	LcHx	LcHx
Kuyo Chico	HcLx	HcLx
Maska	HcLx	HcLx
Qotobamba	HcLx	HcLx

and low conflict (HcLx), low cooperation and high conflict (LcHx), or low

cooperation and low conflict (LcLx). The interesting questions were, what

patterns emerged as these communities changed (or not) over the five-year

period since conflict and cooperation can exist simultaneously but not eas-

ily. The states of these communities at the two points in time are given in

Table 9.1.

So if we are willing extrapolate these changes as Robbins and Robbins did

by assuming that "present trends continue," then a Markov chain transition

matrix can be constructed from the empirically observed changes between

1964 and 1969. This is given the following matrix, where the rows indicate

1964 starting points and the columns are 1969 outcomes:

	HcHx	HcLx	LcHx	LcLx
HcHx	1.00	0.00	0.00	0.00
HcLx	0.25	0.75	0.00	0.00
LcHx	0.00	0.00	0.33	0.67
LcLx	0.00	0.00	0.00	1.00

The first thing we can notice is that HcHx and LcLx are both absorbing

states as described above: Once the Markov chain reaches these states it

never leaves. Clearly this means that the Markov chain is not irreducible

because there are states that cannot "communicate." Interestingly, there are

two noncommunicating state spaces given by the 2×2 upper left and lower

right submatrices. Intuitively it seems that any community that starts out

as HcHx or HcLx ends up as HcHx (upper left), and any community that

starts out as LcHx or LcLx ends up as LcLx (lower right). We can test this

by running the Markov chain for some reasonable number of iterations and

observing the limiting behavior. It turns out that it takes about 25 iterations (i.e., 25 five-year periods under the assumptions since the 0.75 value is quite persistent) for this limiting behavior to converge to the state:

	HcHx	HcLx	LcHx	LcLx
HcHx	1.00	0.00	0.00	0.00
HcLx	1.00	0.00	0.00	0.00
LcHx	0.00	0.00	0.00	1.00
LcLx	0.00	0.00	0.00	1.00

but once it does, it never changes. This is called the stationary distribution of the Markov chain and is now formally defined.

9.3.4 Stationarity and Ergodicity

In many applications a stochastic process eventually converges to a single limiting value and stays at that value permanently. It should be clear that a Markov chain *cannot* do that because it will by definition continue to move about the parameter space. Instead we are interested in the *distribution* that the Markov chain will eventually settle into. Actually, these chains do not *have* to converge in distribution, and some Markov chains will wander endlessly without pattern or prediction. Fortunately, we know some criteria that provide for Markov chain convergence.

First, define a marginal distribution of a Markov chain. For a Markov chain operating on a discrete state space, the marginal distribution of the chain at the m step is obtained by inserting the current value of the chain, $\theta_i^{[m]}$, into the row of the transition kernel for the mth step, p^m:

$$p^m(\theta) = [p^m(\theta_1), p^m(\theta_2), \ldots, p^m(\theta_k)].$$

So the marginal distribution at the very first step of the discrete Markov chain is given by $p^1(\theta) = p^1\pi^0(\theta)$, where p^0 is the initial starting value assigned to the chain and $p^1 = p$ is a transition matrix. The marginal distribution at some (possibly distant) step for a given starting value is

$$p^n = pp^{n-1} = p(pp^{n-2}) = p^2(pp^{n-3}) = \ldots = p^n p^0.$$

Since successive products of probabilities quickly result in lower probability values, the property above shows how Markov chains eventually "forget" their starting points.

Now we are prepared to define stationarity. Recall that $p(\theta_i, \theta_j)$ is the probability that the chain will move from θ_i to θ_j at some arbitrary step t, and $\pi^t(\theta)$ is the corresponding marginal distribution. Define $\pi(\theta)$ as the stationary distribution (a well-behaved probability function in the Kolmogorov sense) of the Markov chain for θ on the state space A, if it satisfies

$$\sum_{\theta_i} \pi^t(\theta_i) p(\theta_i, \theta_j) = \pi^{t+1}(\theta_j).$$

The key point is that the marginal distribution remains fixed when the chain reaches the stationary distribution, and we might as well drop the superscript designation for iteration number and just use $\pi(\theta)$; in shorthand, $\pi = \pi p$. Once the chain reaches its stationary distribution, it stays in this distribution and moves about, or "mixes," throughout the subspace according to marginal distribution, $\pi(\theta)$, indefinitely. The key theorem is

> *An irreducible and aperiodic Markov chain will eventually converge to a stationary distribution, and this stationary distribution is unique.*

Here the recurrence gives the range restriction property whereas stationarity gives the constancy of the probability structure that dictates movement.

As you might have noticed by now in this chapter, Markov chain theory is full of new terminology. The type of chain just discussed is important enough to warrant its own name: If a chain is recurrent and aperiodic, then we call it **ergodic**, and ergodic Markov chains with transition kernel K have the property

$$\lim_{n \to \infty} K^n(\theta_i, \theta_j) = \pi(\theta_j),$$

for all θ_i and θ_j in the subspace What does this actually means? *Once an ergodic Markov chain reaches stationarity, the resulting values are all from the distribution* $\pi(\theta_i)$. The Ergodic Theorem given above is the equivalent of the strong law of large numbers but instead for Markov chains, since it states that any specified function of the posterior distribution can be estimated with samples from a Markov chain in its ergodic state because averages of sample values give strongly consistent parameter estimates.

The big deal about ergodicity and its relationship to stationarity comes from the important **ergodic theory**. This essentially states that, given the right conditions, we can collect empirical evidence from the Markov chain values in lieu of analytical calculations. Specifically

If θ_n *is a positive recurrent, irreducible Markov chain with stationary distribution given by* $\pi(\theta)$, *then*

$$\lim_{n \to \infty} \frac{1}{n} \sum f(\theta_n) = \sum_{\Theta} f(\theta)\pi(\theta).$$

Specifically, this means that empirical averages for the function $f()$ converge to probabilistic averages. This is the justification for using Markov chains to approximate difficult analytical quantities, thus replacing human effort with automated effort (at least to some degree!).

★ **Example 9.5:** **Population Migration Within Malawi.** Discrete Markov chains are enormously useful in describing movements of populations, and demographers often use them in this way. As an example Segal (1985) looked at population movements between Malawi's three administrative regions from 1976 to 1977. The Republic of Malawi is a narrow, extended south African country of 45,745 square miles wrapped around the eastern and southern parts of Lake Malawi. Segal took observed migration numbers to create a transition matrix for future movements under the assumption of stability. This is given by

Destination

$$
\text{Source} \quad \begin{array}{c} \\ \text{Northern} \\ \\ \text{Central} \\ \\ \text{Southern} \end{array} \begin{pmatrix} \overset{\text{Northern}}{0.970} & \overset{\text{Central}}{0.019} & \overset{\text{Southern}}{0.012} \\ 0.005 & 0.983 & 0.012 \\ 0.004 & 0.014 & 0.982 \end{pmatrix}.
$$

It is important to note substantively that using this transition matrix to make future predictions about migration patterns ignores the possibility of major shocks to the system such as pandemics, prolonged droughts, and political upheaval. Nonetheless, it is interesting, and sometimes important, to anticipate population changes and the subsequent national policy issues.

The obvious question is whether the transition matrix above defines an ergodic Markov chain. Since this is a discrete transition kernel, we need to assert that it is recurrent and aperiodic. This is a particularly simple example because recurrence comes from the lack of zero probability values in the matrix. Although the presence of zero probability values alone would not be proof of nonreccurence, the lack of any shows that all states communicate with nonzero probabilities and thus recurrence is obvious. Note that there is also no mechanism to impose a cycling effect through the cell values so aperiodicity is also apparent. Therefore this transition kernel defines an ergodic Markov chain that must then have a unique stationary distribution.

While there is no proof of stationarity, long periods of unchanging marginal probabilities are typically a good sign, especially with such a simple and well-behaved case. The resulting stationary distribution after multiplying the transition kernel 600 times is

Destination

Northern   Central   Southern

$$\left(\begin{array}{ccc} 0.1315539 & 0.4728313 & 0.3956149 \end{array} \right).$$

We can actually run the Markov chain much longer without any real trouble, but the resulting stationary distribution will remain unchanged from this result. This is a really interesting finding, though. Looking at the original transition matrix, there is a strong inclination to stay in the same region of Malawi for each of the three regions (the smallest has probability 0.97), yet in the limiting distribution there is a markedly different result, with migration to the Central Region being almost 50%. Perhaps more surprisingly, even though there is a 0.97 probability of remaining in the Northern Region for those starting there on any given cycle, the long-run probability of remaining in the Northern Region is only 0.13.

9.3.5 Reversibility

Some Markov chains are **reversible** in that they perform the same run backward as forward. More specifically, if $p(\theta_i, \theta_j)$ is a single probability from a transition kernel K and $\pi(\theta)$ is a marginal distribution, then the Markov chain is reversible if it meets the condition

$$p(\theta_i, \theta_j)\pi(\theta_i) = p(\theta_j, \theta_i)\pi(\theta_j).$$

This expression is called both the **reversibility condition** and the **detailed balance equation**. What this means is that the *distribution* of θ at time $t + 1$ conditioned on the *value* of θ at time t is the same as the *distribution* of θ at time t conditioned on the *value* of θ at time $t+1$. Thus, for a reversible Markov chain the direction of time is irrelevant to its probability structure.

As an example of reversibility, we modify a previous example where the probability of transitioning between adjacent states for a four-state system is determined by flipping a fair coin (states 1 and 4 are assumed adjacent to complete the system):

It should be clear that the stationary distribution of this system is uniform across the four events, and that it is guaranteed to reach it since it is recurrent and aperiodic. Suppose we modify the transition rule to be asymmetric from every point, according to

So what we have now is a chain that strongly prefers to move left at every step by the same probability. This Markov chain will also lead to a uniform stationary distribution, because it is clearly still recurrent and aperiodic. It is, however, clearly not reversible anymore because for adjacent θ values (i.e., those with nonzero transition probabilities)

$$p(\theta_i, \theta_j)\pi(\theta_i) \neq p(\theta_j, \theta_i)\pi(\theta_j), \ i < j$$
$$\frac{1}{10}\frac{1}{4} \neq \frac{9}{10}\frac{1}{4}$$

(where we say that $4 < 1$ by assumption to complete the system).

9.4 New Terminology

Exercises

9.1   Consider a lone knight on a chessboard making moves uniformly randomly from those legally available to it at each step. Show that the path of the knight (starting in a corner) is or is not a Markov chain. If so, is it irreducible and aperiodic?

9.2   For the following matrix, fill in the missing values that make it a valid transition matrix:

$$
\begin{bmatrix}
0.1 & 0.2 & 0.3 & \\
0.9 & & 0.01 & 0.01 \\
0.0 & 0.0 & & 0.0 \\
& 0.2 & 0.2 & 0.2
\end{bmatrix}.
$$

9.3   Using this matrix:

$$
\mathbf{X} =
\begin{bmatrix}
\frac{1}{4} & \frac{3}{4} \\
\frac{1}{2} & \frac{1}{2}
\end{bmatrix},
$$

find the vector of stationary probabilities.

9.4   Consider a discrete state space with only two events: 0 and 1. A stochastic process operates on this space with probability of transition one-half for moving or staying in place. Show that this is or is not a Markov chain.

9.5   There are many applications and famous problems for Markov chains that are related to gambling. For example, suppose a gambler bets $1 on successive games unless she has won three in a row. In the latter case she bets $3 but returns to $1 if this game is lost. Does this dependency on more than the last value ruin the Markovian property? Can this process be made to depend only on a previous "event"?

9.6   One urn contains 10 black marbles and another contains 5 white marbles. At each iteration of an iterative process 1 marble is picked from each urn and swapped with probability $p = 0.5$ or returned to its original urn with probability $1 - p = 0.5$. Give the transition matrix for the process and show that it is Markovian. What is the limiting distribution of marbles?

9.7   Consider the prototypical example of a Markov chain kernel:

$$\begin{bmatrix} p & 1-p \\ 1-q & q \end{bmatrix},$$

where $0 \leq p, q \leq 1$. What is the stationary distribution of this Markov chain? What happens when $p = q = 1$?

9.8   For the following transition matrix, perform the listed operations:

$$\mathbf{X} = \begin{bmatrix} 0.3 & 0.7 \\ 0.9 & 0.1 \end{bmatrix}.$$

(a) For the starting point $[0.6, 0.4]$ calculate the first 10 chain values.

(b) For the starting point $[0.1, 0.9]$ calculate the first 10 chain values.

(c) Does this transition matrix define an ergodic Markov chain?

(d) What is the limiting distribution, if it exists?

9.9   Suppose that for a Congressional race the probability that candidate B airs negative campaign advertisements in the next period, given that candidate A has in the current period, is 0.7; otherwise it is only 0.07. The same probabilities apply in the opposite direction. Answer the following questions.

(a) Provide the transition matrix.

(b) If candidate B airs negative ads in period 1, what is the probability that candidate A airs negative ads in period 3?

(c) What is the limiting distribution?

9.10   Duncan and Siverson (1975) used the example of social mobility where grandfather's occupational class affects the grandson's occupational class according to the following transition matrix:

$$
\begin{array}{c}
\begin{array}{ccc}
\phantom{\text{Upper}} & \text{Upper} \quad \text{Middle} \quad \text{Lower}
\end{array} \\
\begin{array}{c}
\text{Upper} \\
\text{Middle} \\
\text{Lower}
\end{array}
\left(
\begin{array}{ccc}
0.228 & 0.589 & 0.183 \\
0.065 & 0.639 & 0.296 \\
0.037 & 0.601 & 0.361
\end{array}
\right) ,
\end{array}
$$

where the grandfather's occupational class defines the rows and the grandson's occupational class defines the columns. What is the long-run probability of no social mobility for the three classes?

Their actual application is to Sino-Indian relations from 1959 to 1964, where nine communication states are defined by categorizing each country's weekly communication with the other as high (3 or more), medium (1 or 2), or low (zero), at some point in time:

Weekly Communication Frequency

China	India	System State
Low	Low	1
Low	Medium	2
Low	High	3
Medium	Low	4
Medium	Medium	5
Medium	High	6
High	Low	7
High	Medium	8
High	High	9

This setup nicely fits the Markovian assumption since interstate communication is inherently conditional. Their (estimated) transition matrix, expressed as percentages instead of probabilities, is

$$
P = \begin{array}{c} \\ 1 \\ 2 \\ 3 \\ 4 \\ 5 \\ 6 \\ 7 \\ 8 \\ 9 \end{array}
\begin{array}{ccccccccc}
1 & 2 & 3 & 4 & 5 & 6 & 7 & 8 & 9 \\
50 & 13 & 2 & 15 & 13 & 2 & 3 & 2 & 2 \\
15 & 26 & 2 & 15 & 28 & 4 & 4 & 6 & 0 \\
8 & 38 & 8 & 0 & 15 & 23 & 0 & 8 & 0 \\
19 & 19 & 9 & 9 & 19 & 6 & 6 & 9 & 3 \\
18 & 14 & 4 & 12 & 16 & 6 & 4 & 16 & 10 \\
8 & 8 & 8 & 6 & 19 & 19 & 6 & 17 & 8 \\
25 & 8 & 0 & 25 & 17 & 8 & 0 & 8 & 8 \\
4 & 7 & 7 & 7 & 11 & 29 & 7 & 11 & 18 \\
0 & 10 & 0 & 0 & 6 & 29 & 06 & 48 &
\end{array}
,
$$

What evidence is there for the claim that there is "a tendency for China to back down from high levels of communication and a certain lack of responsiveness for India"? What other indications of "responsiveness" are found here and what can you conclude about the long-run behavior of the Markov chain?

9.11   Given an example transition matrix that produces a *non*irreducible Markov chain, and show that it has at least two distinct limiting distributions.

9.12   For the following matrices, find the limiting distribution:

$$
\begin{bmatrix} 0.3 & 0.7 \\ 0.6 & 0.4 \end{bmatrix} \quad
\begin{bmatrix} 0.2 & 0.8 \\ 0.6 & 0.4 \end{bmatrix} \quad
\begin{bmatrix} 0.75 & 0.25 & 0.0 \\ 0.25 & 0.50 & 0.25 \\ 0.0 & 0.25 & 0.75 \end{bmatrix}.
$$

9.13   For the following transition matrix, which classes are closed?

$$
\begin{bmatrix}
0.50 & 0.50 & 0.00 & 0.00 & 0.00 \\
0.00 & 0.50 & 0.00 & 0.50 & 0.00 \\
0.00 & 0.00 & 0.50 & 0.50 & 0.00 \\
0.00 & 0.00 & 0.75 & 0.25 & 0.00 \\
0.50 & 0.00 & 0.00 & 0.00 & 0.50
\end{bmatrix}.
$$

9.14   Chung (1969) used Markov chains to analyze hierarchies of human needs in the same way that Maslow famously considered them. The key point is that needs in a specific time period are conditional on the needs in the previous period and thus are dynamic moving up and down from basic to advanced human needs. Obviously the embedded assumption is that the pattern of needs is independent of previous periods conditional on the last period. In a hypothetical example Chung constructed a proportional composition of needs for some person according to

$$
N = (N_{ph}, N_{sf}, N_{so}, N_{sr}, N_{sa}) = (0.15, 0.30, 0.20, 0.25, 0.10),
$$

which are supposed to reflect transition probabilities from one state to another where the states are from Maslow's hierarchy: physiological, safety, socialization, self-respect, and self-actualization. Furthermore, suppose that as changes in socio-economic status occur, the composition of needs changes probabilistically according to

$$
P = \begin{array}{c}
\\
N_{ph} \\
N_{sf} \\
N_{so} \\
N_{sr} \\
N_{sa}
\end{array}
\begin{array}{c}
\begin{array}{ccccc}
N_{ph} & N_{sf} & N_{so} & N_{sr} & N_{sa}
\end{array} \\
\left(\begin{array}{ccccc}
0.20 & 0.30 & 0.35 & 0.15 & 0.00 \\
0.10 & 0.40 & 0.20 & 0.20 & 0.10 \\
0.10 & 0.15 & 0.35 & 0.25 & 0.15 \\
0.05 & 0.15 & 0.20 & 0.40 & 0.20 \\
0.00 & 0.05 & 0.15 & 0.30 & 0.50
\end{array}\right)
\end{array}.
$$

Verify his claim that the system of needs reaches a stationary distribution after four periods using the starting point defined by N. How does this model change Maslow's assumption of strictly ascending needs?

9.15 Consider the following Markov chain from Atchadé and Rosenthal (2005). For the discrete state space $\Theta = \{1, 3, 4\}$, at the nth step produce the $n + 1^{st}$ value by:

- if the last move was a rejection, generate $\theta' \sim$ uniform($\theta_n - 1 : \theta_n + 1$);

- if the last move was an acceptance, generate $\theta' \sim$ uniform($\theta_n - 2 : \theta_n + 2$);

- if $\theta' \in \Theta$, accept θ' as θ_{n+1}, otherwise reject and set θ_n as θ_{n+1};

where these uniform distributions are on the inclusive positive integers and some arbitrary starting point θ_0 (with no previous acceptance) is assumed. What happens to this chain in the long run?

9.16 Markov chain analysis can be useful in game theory. Molander (1985) constructed the following matrix in his look at "tit-for-tat" strategies in international relations:

$$\begin{bmatrix} (1-p)^2 & p(1-p) & p(1-p) & p^2 \\ p(1-p) & p^2 & (1-p)^2 & p(1-p) \\ p(1-p) & (1-p)^2 & p^2 & p(1-p) \\ p^2 & p(1-p) & p(1-p) & (1-p)^2 \end{bmatrix}.$$

There are four outcomes where the rows indicate action by player C and the columns indicate a probabilistic response by player D for some stable probability p. Show that this is a valid transition matrix and find the vector of stationary probabilities. Molander modified this game to allow players the option of "generosity," which escapes the cycle of vendetta. This 4×4 transition matrix is given by

$$
\begin{bmatrix}
(1-p)(1-p-d+2pd) & (p+c-2pc)(1-p-d+2pd)\ldots \\
\ldots p(1-p) & p(p+c-2pc) \\
(1-p)(p+d-2pd) & (p+c-2pc)(p+d-2pd)\ldots \\
\ldots(1-p)^2 & (1-p)(p+c-2pc) \\
p(1-p-d+2pd) & (1-p-c+2pc)(1-p-d-2pd)\ldots \\
\ldots p^2 & p(1-p-c+2pc) \\
p(1-p+d+2pd) & (1-p-c+2pc)(p+d-2pd)\ldots \\
\ldots p(1-p) & (1-p)(1-p-c+2pc)
\end{bmatrix}
$$

where c is the probability that player C deviates from tit-for-tat and d is the probability that player D deviates from tit-for-tat. Show that this matrix defines a recurrent Markov chain and derive the stationary distribution for $p = c = d = \frac{1}{2}$.

9.17 Dobson and Meeter (1974) modeled the movement of party identification in the United States between the two major parties as a Markovian. The following transition matrix gives the probabilities of *not* moving from one status to another conditional on moving (hence the zeros on the diagonal):

	SD	WD	I	WR	SR
SD	0.000	0.873	0.054	0.000	0.073
WD	0.750	0.000	0.190	0.060	0.000
I	0.154	0.434	0.000	0.287	0.125
WR	0.039	0.205	0.346	0.000	0.410
SR	0.076	0.083	0.177	0.709	0.000

where the labels indicate SD = Strong Democrat, WD = Weak Democrat, I = Independent, WR = Weak Republican, and SR =

Strong Republican. Convert this to a transition matrix for moving from one state to another and show that it defines an ergodic Markov chain. What is the stationary distribution?

References

Aldrich, John H., and Richard D. McKelvey. (1977). A Method of Scaling with Applications to the 1968 and 1972 Presidential Elections. *American Political Science Review* 71, 111–30.

Atchadé, Yves F., and Jeffrey S. Rosenthal. (2005). On Adaptive Markov Chain Monte Carlo Algorithms. *Bernoulli* 11, 815–28

Bayer, D., and P. Diaconis. (1992). Trailing the Dovetail Shuffle to its Lair. *Annals of Applied Probability* 2, 294–313.

Bayes, Thomas. (1763). An Essay Towards Solving a Problem in the Doctrine of Chances. *Philosophical Transactions of the Royal Society of London* 53, 370–418.

Billingsley, P. (1986). *Probability and Measure.* New York: John Wiley & Sons.

Black, Duncan. (1958). *Theory of Committees and Elections.* Cambridge: Cambridge University Press.

Blackwell, David, and M. A. Gershick. (1954). *Theory of Games and Statistical Decisions.* New York: Dover Publications.

Böhm-Bawerk, Eugen von. (1959). *Capital and Interest. Volume 2, Positive Theory of Capital.* South Holland, IL: Libertarian Press.

Bonacich, Phillip. (1978). Using Boolean Algebra to Analyze Overlapping Memberships. *Sociological Methodology* 9, 101–15.

Bonacich, Phillip, and Kenneth D. Bailey. (1971). Key Variables. *Sociological Methodology* 3, 221–35.

Box-Steffensmeier, Janet M., and Bradford S. Jones. (2004). *Event History Modeling: A Guide for Social Scientists.* Cambridge: Cambridge University Press.

Brams, Steven J., and Michael K. O'Leary. (1970). An Axiomatic Model of Voting Bodies. *American Political Science Review* 64, 449–70.

Bueno de Mesquita, Bruce, and David Lalman. (1986). Reason and War. *American Political Science Review* 80, 1113–29.

Bueno de Mesquita, Bruce, David Newman, and Alvin Rabushka. (1985). *Forecasting Political Events: The Future of Hong Kong.* New Haven, CT: Yale University Press.

Casstevens, Thomas W. (1970). Linear Algebra and Legislative Voting Behavior: Rice's Indices. *Journal of Politics* 32, 769–83.

Chung, Kae H. (1969). A Markov Chain Model of Human Needs: An Extension of Maslow's Need Theory. *Academy of Management Journal* 12, 223–34.

Chung, K. L. (2000). *A Course in Probability Theory.* Second Edition. San Diego: Academic Press.

Clogg, Clifford C., Eva Petkova, and Adamantios Haritou. (1995). Statistical Methods for Comparing Regression Coefficients Between Models. *American Journal of Sociology* 100, 1261–93.

Corsi, Jerome R. (1981). Terrorism as a Desperate Game: Fear, Bargaining, and Communication in the Terrorist Event. *Journal of Conflict Resolution* 25, 47–85.

Coveyou, R. R. (1960). Serial Correlation in the Generation of Pseudo-Random Numbers. *Journal of the Association for Computing Machinery* 7, 72–4.

Dale, A. I. (1991). *A History of Inverse Probability: From Thomas Bayes to Karl Pearson.* New York: Springer-Verlag.

Dion, Douglas. (1992). The Robustness of the Structure-Induced Equilibrium.

American Journal of Political Science 36, 462–82.

DiPrete, Thomas A., and David B. Grusky. (1990).   The Multilevel Analysis of Trends with Repeated Cross-Sectional Data. *Sociological Methodology* 20, 337–68.

Dobson, Douglas, and Duane A. Meeter. (1974).   Alternative Markov Models for Describing Change in Party Identification. *American Journal of Political Science* 18, 487–500.

Doran, Charles F. (1989). Systemic Disequilibrium, Foreign Policy Role, and the Power Cycle: Challenges for Research Design. *Journal of Conflict Resolution* 33, 371–401.

Doreian, Patrick, and Norman P. Hummon. (1977).   Estimates for Differential Equation Models of Social Phenomena. *Sociological Methodology* 8, 180–208.

Downs, Anthony. (1957). An Economic Theory of Political Action in a Democracy. *Journal of Political Economy* 6, 135–50.

Duncan, George T., and Randolph M. Siverson. (1975).   Markov Chain Models for Conflict Analysis: Results from Sino-Indian Relations, 1959-1964. *International Studies Quarterly* 19, 344–74.

Duncan, O. D. (1966). Methodological Issues in the Analysis of Social Mobility. In N. J. Smelser and S. M. Lipset (eds.), *Social Structure and Mobility in Economic Development*. Chicago: Aldine.

Ebanks, Edward G. (1970). Users and Non-Users of Contraception: Tests of Stationarity Applied Members of a Family Planning Program. *Population Studies* 24, 85–91.

Fox, J. (1997). *Applied Regression Analysis, Linear Models, and Related Methods*. Thousand Oaks, CA: Sage.

Francis, Wayne L. (1982). Legislative Committee Systems, Optimal Committee Size, and The Costs of Decision Making. *Journal of Politics* 44, 822–37.

Frederick, Shane, George F. Loewenstein, and Ted O'Donoghue. (2002).   Time Discounting and Time Preference: A Critical Review. *Journal of Economic*

Literature 90, 351–401.

Frohlich, Norman, and Joe Oppenheimer. (1996). When Is Universal Contribution Best for the Group? *Journal of Conflict Resolution* 40, 502–16.

Galton, Francis. (1898). A Diagram of Heredity. *Nature* 57, 273–5.

Gill, Jeff, and Jason Gainous. (2002). Why Does Voting Get So Complicated? A Review of Theories for Analyzing Democratic Participation. *Statistical Science* 17, 383–404.

Gordon, Jerome B. (1969). *The Journal of Human Resources* 4, 343–59.

Granovetter, Mark, and Roland Soong. (1988). Threshold Models of Diversity: Chinese Restaurants, Residential Segregation, and the Spiral of Silence. *Sociological Methodology* 18, 69–104.

Grimmett, G. R., and D. R. Stirzaker. (1992). *Probability and Random Processes.* Oxford: Oxford University Press.

Gujarati, D. N. (1995). *Basic Econometrics.* New York: McGraw-Hill.

Hager, Don J. (1949). German Sociology Under Hitler, 1933-1941. *Social Forces* 28, 6–19

Hanushek, E. A., and J. E. Jackson. (1977). *Statistical Methods for Social Scientists.* San Diego: Academic Press.

Hardy, G. H., J. E. Littlewood, and G. Polya. (1988). *Inequalities.* Cambridge: Cambridge University Press.

Harvey, Charles M. (1986). Value Functions for Infinite–Period Planning. *Management Science* 32, 1123–39.

Houweling, H. W., and J. B. Kuné. (1984). Do Outbreaks of War Follow a Poisson-Process? *Journal of Conflict Resolution* 28, 51–61.

Ishizawa, Suezo. (1991). Increasing Returns, Public Inputs and Transformation Curves *Canadian Journal of Economics* 24, 144–60.

Jackman, Simon. (2001). Multidimensional Analysis of Roll Call Data via Bayesian Simulation: Identification, Estimation, Inference, and Model Checking. *Political Analysis* 9(3), 227–41.

Kail, Robert, and Marilyn A. Nippold. (1984). Unconstrained Retrieval from

Semantic Memory. *Child Development* 55, 944–51.

Katz, Lee. (1953). A New Status Index Derived from Socioeconomic Analysis. *Psychometrika* 18, 39–43.

Kendall, M. G., and A. Stuart. (1950). The Law of Cubic Proportions in Electoral Results. *British Journal of Sociology* 1, 183–97.

Kendall, M. G., and A. Stuart. (1952). La Loi de Cube dans les Elections Britanniques. *Revue Française de Science Politique* 2, 270–6.

Keynes, J. M. (1921). *A Treatise on Probability.* London: MacMillan.

Kolmogorov, A. (1933). *Grundbegriffe der Wahrscheinlichkeitsrechnung.* Berlin: Julius Springer.

Krehbiel, Keith. (2000). Party Discipline and Measures of Partisanship. *American Journal of Political Science* 44, 212–27.

Holland, Paul W., and Samuel Leinhardt. (1970). A Method for Detecting Structure in Sociometric Data. *American Journal of Sociology* 76, 492–513.

Lalman, David. (1988). Conflict Resolution and Peace. *American Journal of Political Science* 32, 590–615.

Land, Kenneth C. (1980). Modeling Macro Social Change. *Sociological Methodology* 11, 219–78.

Loewenstein, George F., and Drazen Prelec. (1992). Anomalies in Intertemporal Choice–Evidence and an Interpretation. *Quarterly Journal of Economics* 107, 573–97.

Londregan, John. (2000). Estimating Legislator's Preferred Ideal Points. *Political Analysis* 8, 35–56.

Maddala, G. S. (1977). *Econometrics.* New York: McGraw-Hill.

Manchester, Paul B. (1976). The Short-Run Supply of Nurse's Time: A Comment. *Journal of Human Resources* 11, 267–8.

Manski, Charles F. (1989). Anatomy of the Selection Problem. *Journal of Human Resources* 24, 343–60.

Marshall, Harvey, and John Stahura. (1979). Black and White Population Growth in American Suburbs: Transition or Parallel Development? *Social Forces* 58,

305–28

McFarland, David D. (1981). Spectral Decomposition as a Tool in Comparative Mobility Research. *Sociological Methodology* 12, 338–58.

McGowan, Patrick J., and Robert M. Rood. (1975). Alliance Behavior in Balance of Power Systems: Applying a Poisson Model to Nineteenth-Century Europe. *American Political Science Review* 69, 859–70.

Molander, Per. (1985). The Optimal Level of Generosity in a Selfish, Uncertain Environment. *Journal of Conflict Resolution* 29, 611–8

Moreno, Jacob L. (1934). *Who Shall Survive? A New Approach to the Problems of Human Interrlelationships* Washington, DC: Nervous and Mental Health Disease Publishing Company, No.58. Reprinted 1978, Third Edition. Beacon, NY: Beacon House.

Morrison, Rodney J. (1977). Franklin D. Roosevelt and the Supreme Court: An Example of the Use of Probability Theory in Political History. *History and Theory* 16, 137–46.

Merwe, Nikolaas J. van der. (1966). New Mathematics for Glottochronology. *Current Anthropology* 7, 485–500.

Morgenstern, Oskar and John von Neumann. (1944). *The Theory of Games and Economic Behavior.* Princeton: Princeton University Press.

Nachmius, David, and David Rosenbloom. (1973). Measuring Bureaucratic Representation and Integration. *Public Administration Review* 33, 590–7.

Neter, J., M. H. Kutner, C. Nachtsheim, and W. Wasserman. (1996). *Applied Linear Regression Models.* Chicago: Irwin.

Norton, Robert. (1983). Measuring Marital Quality: A Critical Look at the Dependent Variable. *Journal of Marriage and the Family* 45, 141–51.

Parker, Edmund M. (1909). The Law of the Constitution. *American Political Science Review* 3, 362–70.

Pearson, Jane L., Andrea G. Hunter, Margaret E. Ensminger, and Sheppard G. Kellam. (1990). Black Grandmothers in Multigenerational Households: Diversity in Family Structure and Parenting Involvement in the Woodlawn Community. *Child Development* 61, 434–42.

Petersen, Trond. (1991). Time-Aggregation Bias in Continuous-Time Hazard-Rate Models. *Sociological Methodology* 21, 263–90.

Poole, Keith T., and Howard Rosenthal. (1985). A Spatial Model for Legislative Roll Call Analysis. *American Journal of Political Science* 29, 357–84.

Poole, Keith T., and Howard Rosenthal. (1997). *Congress: A Political-Economic History of Roll Call Voting.* New York: Oxford University Press.

Powers, Denise V., and James H. Cox. (1997). Echoes from the Past: The Relationship between Satisfaction with Economic Reforms and Voting Behavior in Poland. *American Political Science Review* 91, 617–33.

Propp, J. G., and D. B. Wilson. (1996). Exact Sampling with Coupled Markov Chains and Applications to Statistical Mechanics. *Random Structures and Algorithms* 9, 223–52.

Rees, A., and G. Schultz. (1970). *Workers and Wages in an Urban Labor Market.* Chicago: University of Chicago Press.

Riker, William, and Peter Ordeshook. (1968). A Theory of the Calculus of Voting. *American Political Science Review* 62, 297–311.

Robbins, Michael C., and Linda Coffman Robbins. (1979) A Stochastic Process Model of Conflict and Cooperation in Andean Communities. *American Ethnologist* 6, 134–42.

Roby, Thornton B., and John T. Lanzetta. (1956). Work Group Structure, Communication, and Group Performance. *Sociometry* 19, 105–13.

Romano, J. P., and A. F. Siegel. (1986). *Counterexamples in Probability and Statistics.* Monterey, CA: Wadsworth and Brooks/Cole.

Salem, A. B. Z., and T. D. Mount. (1974). A Convenient Descriptive Model of Income Distribution: The Gamma Density. *Econometrica* 42, 1115–27.

Samuelson, Paul A. (1937). A Note on the Measurement of Utility. *Review of Economic Studies* 4, 155–61.

Segal, Edwin S. (1985). Projections of Internal Migration in Malawi: Implications for Development. *The Journal of Modern African Studies* 23, 315–29.

Segal, Jeffrey A. (1984). Predicting Supreme Court Cases Probabilistically: The Search and Seizure Cases, 1962-1981. *American Political Science Review* 78, 891–900.

Shannon, Claude. (1948). A Mathematical Theory of Communication. *Bell System Technology Journal* 27: 379–423, 623–56.

Singer, Burton, and Seymour Spilerman. (1973). Social Mobility Models for Heterogeneous Populations. *Sociological Methodology* 5, 356–401.

Slater, John Clarke. (1939). *Introduction to Chemical Physics.* New York: Dover.

Smirnov, Alexander D., and Emil B. Ershov. (1992). Perestroika: A Catastrophic Change of Economic Reform Policy. *Journal of Conflict Resolution* 36, 415–53.

Sørensen, A. B. (1977). The Structure of Inequality and the Process of Attainment. *American Sociological Review* 42, 965–78.

Sorenson, Richard E., and Peter E. Kenmore. (1974). Proto-Agricultural Movement in the Eastern Highlands of New Guinea. *Current Anthropology* 15, 67–73.

Sorokin, Gerald L. (1994). Arms, Alliances, and Security Tradeoffs in Enduring Rivalries. *International Studies Quarterly* 38, 421–46.

Southwood, Kenneth E. (1978). Substantive Theory and Statistical Interaction: Five Models. *American Journal of Sociology* 83, 1154–203.

Stephan, G. Edward, and Douglas R. McMullin. (1981). The Historical Distribution of County Seats in the United States: A Review, Critique, and Test of Time-Minimization Theory. *American Sociological Review* 46, 907–17.

Stevens, S. S. (1946). On the Theory of Scales of Measurement. *Science* 103, 677–80.

Stevens, S. S. (1951). Mathematics, Measurement, and Psychophysics. In S. S. Stevens (ed.), *Handbook of Experimental Psychology.* pp. 1-49. New York: John Wiley & Sons.

Stinchcombe, Arthur L., and T. Robert Harris. (1969). Interdependence and Inequality: A Specification of the Davis-Moore Theory. *Sociometry* 32, 13–

23.

Siegel, Peter E. (1990). Demographic and Architectural Retrodiction: An Ethnoarchaeological Case Study in the South American Tropical Lowlands. *Latin American Antiquity* 1, 319–46.

Stam, Allan C., III. (1996). *Win, Lose, or Draw : Domestic Politics and the Crucible of War.* Ann Arbor: University of Michigan Press.

Stigler, S. M. (1986). *The History of Statistics: The Measurement of Uncertainty before 1900.* Cambridge, MA: Harvard University Press.

Stigler, S. M. (1999). *Statistics on the Table: The History of Statistical Concepts and Methods.* Cambridge, MA: Harvard University Press.

Stimson, James A. (1976). Public Support for American Presidents: A Cyclical Model. *Public Opinion Quarterly* 40, 1–21.

Swadish, M. (1950). Salish Internal Relationships. *International Journal of American Linguistics* 16, 157–67.

Swadish, M. (1952). Lexicostatistic Dating of Prehistoric Ethnic Contacts. *Proceedings of the American Philosophical Society* 96, 452–63.

Swank, Duane, and Sven Steinmo. (2002). The New Political Economy of Taxation in Advanced Capitalist Democracies. *American Journal of Political Science* 46, 477–89.

Taagepera, Rein. (1986). Reformulating the Cube Law for Proportional Representation Elections. *American Political Science Review* 80, 489–504.

Tufte, Edward R. (1973). The Relationship between Seats and Votes in Two-Party Systems. *American Political Science Review* 67, 540–4.

Walt, S. M. (1987). *The Origins of Alliances.* Ithaca, NY: Cornell University Press.

Walt, S. M. (1988). Testing Theories of Alliance Formation: The Case of Southwest Asia. *International Organization* 42, 275–316.

Weitzman, Martin L. (2001). Gamma discounting. *American Economic Review* 91, 260–71.

Williams, Thomas H., and Charles H. Griffin. (1964). Matrix Theory and Cost Allocation. *The Accounting Review* 39, 671–8.

Whyte, W. F. (1975). Conflict and Cooperation in Andean Communities. *American Ethnologist* 2, 373–92.

Yeats, Alexander J., Edward D. Irons, and Stephen A. Rhoades. (1975). An Analysis of New Bank Growth. *Journal of Business* 48, 199–203.

Author Index

Subject Index